ANNUAL EDITIONS

World Politics 10/11

Thirty-First Edition

EDITOR

Helen E. Purkitt
United States Naval Academy

Dr. Helen E. Purkitt obtained her PhD in International Relations from the University of Southern California. She is Professor of Political Science at the U.S. Naval Academy. Her research and teaching interests include political psychology, African politics, and emerging national security issues. Currently, she is coordinating a research project designed to develop a wiki data base related to the nexus between jihadist terrorist groups and other transnational illicit networks operating in and through Africa, Latin America, and worldwide. She is the editor of a forthcoming volume entitled, *African Environmental Security* (Cambria Press, 2009). Past research findings about emerging security threats tied to dual use technology are summarized in a monograph she co-authored entitled, *Good Bugs, Bad Bugs: A Modern Approach for Detecting Offensive Biological Weapons Research* (Center for Technology and National Policy, National Defense University, September, 2008) and in an article she wrote with V. G. Wells entitled, "Evolving Bioweapon Threats Require New Counter-measures". The article, published in the October 6, 2006 edition of *The Chronicle of Higher Education,* is reprinted in this volume of *Annual Editions: World Politics 10/11.* Another well-known work is a co-authored book entitled, *South Africa's Weapons of Mass Destruction,* which is available from Indiana University Press. She has published dozens of peer-review monographs and articles, along with serving as an expert for *60 Minutes* and other media forums.

ANNUAL EDITIONS: WORLD POLITICS, THIRTY-FIRST EDITION

Published by McGraw-Hill, a business unit of The McGraw-Hill Companies, Inc., 1221 Avenue of the Americas, New York, NY 10020. Copyright © 2011 by The McGraw-Hill Companies, Inc. All rights reserved. Previous edition(s) 2007, 2008, 2009. No part of this publication may be reproduced or distributed in any form or by any means, or stored in a database or retrieval system, without the prior written consent of The McGraw-Hill Companies, Inc., including, but not limited to, in any network or other electronic storage or transmission, or broadcast for distance learning.

Some ancillaries, including electronic and print components, may not be available to customers outside the United States.

Annual Editions® is a registered trademark of The McGraw-Hill Companies, Inc.

Annual Editions is published by the **Contemporary Learning Series** group within the McGraw-Hill Higher Education division.

1 2 3 4 5 6 7 8 9 0 WDQ/WDQ 1 0 9 8 7 6 5 4 3 2 1 0

ISBN 978–0–07–805064–0
MHID 0–07–805064–2
ISSN 1098–0300

Managing Editor: *Larry Loeppke*
Developmental Editor: *Dave Welsh*
Editorial Coordinator: *Mary Foust*
Editorial Assistant: *Cindy Hedley*
Production Service Assistant: *Rita Hingtgen*
Permissions Coordinator: *DeAnna Dausener*
Senior Marketing Manager: *Julie Keck*
Senior Marketing Communications Specialist: *Mary Klein*
Marketing Coordinator: *Alice Link*
Director Specialized Production: *Faye Schilling*
Senior Project Manager: *Joyce Watters*
Production Supervisor: *Sue Culbertson*
Cover Graphics: *Kristine Jubeck*

Compositor: Laserwords Private Limited
Cover Image: © F. Schussler/PhotoLink/Getty Images (inset); CORBIS/RF (background)

Library in Congress Cataloging-in-Publication Data
Main entry under title: Annual Editions: World Politics. 2010/2011.
1. World Politics—Periodicals. I. Purkitt, Helen E., *comp*. II. Title: World Politics.
658'.05

Editors/Academic Advisory Board

Members of the Academic Advisory Board are instrumental in the final selection of articles for each edition of ANNUAL EDITIONS. Their review of articles for content, level, and appropriateness provides critical direction to the editors and staff. We think that you will find their careful consideration well reflected in this volume.

ANNUAL EDITIONS: World Politics 10/11
31st Edition

EDITOR

Helen E. Purkitt
United States Naval Academy

ACADEMIC ADVISORY BOARD MEMBERS

Preface

In publishing ANNUAL EDITIONS we recognize the enormous role played by the magazines, newspapers, and journals of the public press in providing current, first-rate educational information in a broad spectrum of interest areas. Many of these articles are appropriate for students, researchers, and professionals seeking accurate, current material to help bridge the gap between principles and theories and the real world. These articles, however, become more useful for study when those of lasting value are carefully collected, organized, indexed, and reproduced in a low-cost format, which provides easy and permanent access when the material is needed. That is the role played by ANNUAL EDITIONS.

*A*nnual Editions: World Politics 10/11 is aimed at filling a void in materials for learning about world politics and foreign policy. The articles are chosen for those who are new to the study of world politics. The goal is to help students learn more about international issues that often seem remote but may have profound consequences for a nation's well-being, security, and survival.

International relations can be viewed as a complex and dynamic system of actions and reactions by a diverse set of actors. The articles in this volume convey just how dynamic, interdependent, and complex the relations among different types of international actors are in contemporary international relations. Once, the international system was dominated by nation-states. Today's system looks more like a cobweb of nation-states, non-governmental organizations (NGOs), and a host of legal and illicit transnational networks (e.g., terrorist and criminal groups) that span continents and are highly adaptive in terms of their base of operations and modus operandi.

Increased globalization means that events in places as far away as Latin America, Asia, the Middle East, and Africa may effect the United States, just as America's actions—and inaction—have significant repercussions for other states. Interdependence also refers to the increased role of non-state actors such as multinational corporations, the United Nations, and a rich array of non-governmental actors such as the Cable News Network (CNN) and terrorist networks affiliated with or inspired by al Qaeda.

The September 11, 2001 terrorist attack on the World Trade Towers and the Pentagon tragically underscored the reality that non-state actors increasingly influence the scope, nature, and pace of events worldwide. However, the U.S.-led military interventions in Afghanistan in 2002, the U.S. military invasion of Iraq in 2003, the increased tempo of fighting between U.S. troops and insurgents in Afghanistan, the escalation of tensions between the United States and Iran, and ongoing conflicts among countries throughout the world confirm that inter-state conflicts will also continue as a key feature of international relations. At the same time, the rapid spread of a SARS epidemic since 2004, the continuing spread of new HIV/AIDS infections and the occurence of H1N1 virus worldwide, the large number of deaths and devastation caused by the South Asia Tsunami tidal wave in 2005, and the continuing threat of problems caused by global warming and other global climate trends remind us that diseases and natural disasters can also have wide ranging effects on world politics as well. A report by eleven retired senior military officials to the Center for Naval Analysis (CNA) think tank in 2007 warned that climate change will effect all aspects of the United States' national security defense readiness; yet another reminder that global warming is continuing. The CNA report was also a timely reminder that there are global security threats that may increasingly threaten the security and well-being of citizens living in nation-states in both the developing and developed world.

While leaders of nation-states attempted to wrestle with traditional security threats and newly emerging ones, the increasingly serious world recession reminds citizens worldwide of the downside of increased international interdependence. The current economic slowdown has now spread worldwide to become the worst economic slowdown since the 1930 depression. The depth of the current financial, credit, and employment crises has surprised many foreign policy and economic experts. Today, a series of intertwined economic crises are forcing leaders in developed and developing countries to devise programs to attempt to help citizens cope while also, as unemployment rises, scrambling to tap new sources of revenue, through national policies and, increasingly, through intergovernmental organizations and forums such as the G-20. The continuing adverse economic trends worldwide remind us of just how interdependent countries and citizens are in different parts of the world in a globalized system. The growing awareness of the implications of climate change and the impact of the contemporary international economic crises has also heightened awareness of just how tightly coupled national security, human security, and collective security concerns have become in the twenty-first century.

International events proceed at such a rapid pace that what is said about international affairs today may be outdated by tomorrow, therefore it is important for readers to develop a mental framework or theory of the international system. The collection of articles in this volume about international events provides up-to-date information, commentaries about the current set of issues on the world agenda, and analyses of the significance of the issues and emerging trends for the structure and functioning of the post–Cold War international system. The articles in this volume can also be used to update readers' increasingly detailed and interconnected mental models of world affairs in long-term memory as a series of loosely connected and highly adaptive subsystems and networks.

The thirty-first edition of *Annual Editions: World Politics* is divided into 11 units. While the United States remains the dominant military, political, and economic power in the post–Cold War system, indicators of an emerging multipolar system consisting of various types of subsystems and sub-national, national, and transnational networks are everywhere. Complex trends in the current structure of the international system mean that we can no longer view international relations through a prism where the United States is considered the one lone superpower across all issue areas. Instead, subnational, national, regional, and transnational issues, actors, and linkages are increasingly important aspects of international relations in a multidimensional world system.

I would like to thank Larry Loeppke, David Welsh, and their associates at McGraw-Hill Contemporary Learning Series for their help in putting this volume together. Many members of the Advisory Board and users of *Annual Editions: World Politics* took the time to contribute articles and comments on this collection of readings. I greatly appreciate these suggestions and the article evaluations. Please continue to provide feedback to guide the annual revision of this anthology by filling out the postage-paid *article rating form* on the last page of this book.

Helen Purkitt

Helen E. Purkitt
Editor

Contents

UNIT 1
The International System and Changing World Order of the Twenty-First Century

The concepts in bold italics are developed in the article. For further expansion, please refer to the Topic Guide.

UNIT 2
Managing Interstate Conflicts and the Proliferation of Weapons

The concepts in bold italics are developed in the article. For further expansion, please refer to the Topic Guide.

UNIT 3
Foreign Policy Decision Making

Unit Overview   48

The concepts in bold italics are developed in the article. For further expansion, please refer to the Topic Guide.

UNIT 4
Great Power Interstate Conflicts and Rivalries

UNIT 5
North-South Interstate Conflicts and Rivalries

The concepts in bold italics are developed in the article. For further expansion, please refer to the Topic Guide.

UNIT 6
Conflicts among Nation-States in the Global South, Sub-National Conflicts, and the Role of Non-State Actors in an Interdependent World

The concepts in bold italics are developed in the article. For further expansion, please refer to the Topic Guide.

UNIT 7
Asymmetric Conflicts: Trends in Terrorism and Counterterrorism

Unit Overview

The concepts in bold italics are developed in the article. For further expansion, please refer to the Topic Guide.

UNIT 8
Contemporary Foreign Policy Debates

UNIT 9
International Organizations, International Law, and Global Governance

The concepts in bold italics are developed in the article. For further expansion, please refer to the Topic Guide.

UNIT 10
The International Economic System

UNIT 11
Globalizing Issues

The concepts in bold italics are developed in the article. For further expansion, please refer to the Topic Guide.

The concepts in bold italics are developed in the article. For further expansion, please refer to the Topic Guide.

Correlation Guide

The *Annual Editions* series provides students with convenient, inexpensive access to current, carefully selected articles from the public press. **Annual Editions: World Politics 10/11** is an easy-to-use reader that presents articles on important topics such as *interstate conflicts and weapons proliferation, foreign policy, great power rivalries, terrorism,* and many more. For more information on *Annual Editions* and other *McGraw-Hill Contemporary Learning Series* titles, visit www.mhhe.com/cls.

This convenient guide matches the units in **Annual Editions: World Politics 10/11** with the corresponding chapters in one of our best-selling McGraw-Hill Political Science textbooks by Rourke/Boyer.

Annual Editions: World Politics 10/11	International Politics on the World Stage, Brief, 8/e by Rourke/Boyer
Unit 1: The International System and Changing World Order of the Twenty-First Century	**Chapter 2:** The Evolution of World Politics **Chapter 5:** Globalization: The Alternative Orientation **Chapter 12:** Preserving and Enhancing the Biosphere
Unit 2: Managing Interstate Conflicts and the Proliferation of Weapons	**Chapter 8:** International Law and Human Rights **Chapter 9:** Pursuing Security
Unit 3: Foreign Policy Decision Making	**Chapter 3:** Levels of Analysis and Foreign Policy **Chapter 5:** Globalization: The Alternative Orientation **Chapter 8:** International Law and Human Rights **Chapter 9:** Pursuing Security **Chapter 11:** International Economics: The Alternative Road
Unit 4: Great Power Interstate Conflicts and Rivalries	**Chapter 9:** Pursuing Security **Chapter 11:** International Economics: The Alternative Road
Unit 5: North-South Interstate Conflicts and Rivalries	**Chapter 2:** The Evolution of World Politics **Chapter 8:** International Law and Human Rights **Chapter 9:** Pursuing Security **Chapter 11:** International Economics: The Alternative Road
Unit 6: Conflicts among Nation-States in the Global South, Sub-National Conflicts, and the Role of Non-State Actors in an Interdependent World	**Chapter 2:** The Evolution of World Politics **Chapter 8:** International Law and Human Rights **Chapter 9:** Pursuing Security **Chapter 11:** International Economics: The Alternative Road
Unit 7: Asymmetric Conflicts: Trends in Terrorism and Counterterrorism	**Chapter 8:** International Law and Human Rights **Chapter 9:** Pursuing Security
Unit 8: Contemporary Foreign Policy Debates	**Chapter 1:** Thinking and Caring about World Politics **Chapter 2:** The Evolution of World Politics **Chapter 3:** Levels of Analysis and Foreign Policy
Unit 9: International Organizations, International Law, and Global Governance	**Chapter 7:** Intergovernmental Organizations: Alternative Governance **Chapter 8:** International Law and Human Rights **Chapter 11:** International Economics: The Alternative Road
Unit 10: The International Economic System	**Chapter 11:** International Economics: The Alternative Road
Unit 11: Globalizing Issues	**Chapter 5:** Globalization: The Alternative Orientation **Chapter 7:** Intergovernmental Organizations: Alternative Governance **Chapter 8:** International Law and Human Rights **Chapter 11:** International Economics: The Alternative Road **Chapter 12:** Preserving and Enhancing the Biosphere

Topic Guide

This topic guide suggests how the selections in this book relate to the subjects covered in your course. You may want to use the topics listed on these pages to search the Web more easily.

On the following pages a number of websites have been gathered specifically for this book. They are arranged to reflect the units of this Annual Editions reader. You can link to these sites by going to *http://www.mhhe.com/cls*.

All the articles that relate to each topic are listed below the bold-faced term.

Internet References

The following Internet sites have been selected to support the articles found in this reader. These sites were available at the time of publication. However, because websites often change their structure and content, the information listed may no longer be available. We invite you to visit *http://www.mhhe.com/cls* for easy access to these sites.

Annual Editions: World Politics 10/11

General Sources

Central Intelligence Agency
http://www.odci.gov

Use this official home page to learn about many facets of the CIA and to get connections to other sites and resources, such as *The CIA Factbook,* which provides extensive statistical information about every country in the world.

CIA Factbook
https://www.cia.gov/cia/publications/factbook/index.html

This site provides information on various countries.

Country Indicators for Foreign Policy
http://www.carleton.ca/cifp

Statistical data on nation-states compiled by Carlton University, Canada.

Ilike2learn.com
http://www.ilike2learn.com/ilike2learn/geography.asp

Interactive geography quizzes to help learn the locations of the countries and capitals of the world, along with important bodies of water and mountain ranges in the world.

Social Science Information Gateway
http://sosig.esrc.bris.ac.uk

A project of the Economic and Social Research Council (ESRC), this is an online catalog of thousands of Internet resources relevant to political education and research.

World Wide Web Virtual Library: International Affairs Resources
http://www.etown.edu/vl

Surf this site and its links to learn about specific countries and regions, to research think tanks and organizations, and to study such vital topics as international law, development, the international economy, human rights, and peacekeeping.

Crisisweb: The International Crisis Group (ICG)
http://www.crisisweb.org/home/index.cfm

ICG is an organization "committed to strengthening the capacity of the international community to anticipate, understand, and act to prevent and contain conflict." Go to this site to view the latest reports and research concerning conflicts around the world.

IIMCR Institute for International Mediation and Conflict Resolution
http://www.iimcr.org

Programs, including training to become international mediators, publications, online resources related to conflicts, terrorism, and counterterrorism.

UNIT 1: The International System and Changing World Order of the Twenty-First Century

The Globalization Website
http://www.emory.edu/SOC/globalization

This site discusses globalization and is a guide to available sources on globalization.

Images of the Social and Political World
http://www-personal.umich.edu/~mejn/cartograms

Cartograms showing different aspects of world nation-states on the basis of population, GNP, HIV-AIDS, greenhouse gases, and more. Created by Mark Newman, Department of Physics and the Center for the Study of Complex Systems, University of Michigan.

National Security and the Threat of Climate Change
http://www.npr.org/documents/2007/apr/security_climate.pdf

Report issued by eleven retired senior military officials in 2007 to the Center for Naval Analysis warning that climate change will affect all aspects of the United States' defense readiness.

Population Reference Bureau
http://www.prb.org

This site provides data on the world population and census information.

Women in International Politics
http://www.guide2womenleaders.com

This site contains data on women who have served as political leaders.

Avalon Project at Yale Law School
http://www.yale.edu/lawweb/avalon/terrorism/terror.htm

The Avalon Project website features documents in the fields of law, history, economics, diplomacy, politics, government, and terrorism.

UNIT 2: Managing Interstate Conflicts and the Proliferation of Weapons

U.S. Department of State
http://www.state.gov/index.cfm

The site provides information organized by categories as well as "background notes" on specific countries and regions.

Belfer Center for Science and International Affairs (BCSIA)
http://www.ksg.harvard.edu/bcsia

BCSIA is a center for research, teaching, and training in international affairs.

FACTs
http://www.ploughshares.ca

Useful site for research on inter-state conflicts.

U.S.- Russia Developments
http://www.acronym.org.uk/start

This is a site maintained by Acronym Institute for Disarmament Diplomacy which provides information on U.S. and Russian disarmament activity.

The Bulletin of the Atomic Scientists
http://www.bullatomsci.org

This site allows you to read more about the Doomsday Clock and other issues as well as topics related to nuclear weaponry, arms control, and disarmament.

Internet References

Federation of American Scientists
http://www.fas.org

This site provides useful information about, and links to, a variety of topics related to chemical and biological warfare, missiles, conventional arms, and terrorism.

UNIT 3: Foreign Policy Decision Making

Carnegie Endowment for International Peace
http://www.ceip.org

One of the goals of this organization is to stimulate discussion and learning among experts and the public on a wide range of international issues. The site provides links to the journal *Foreign Policy* and to the Moscow Center.

The Heritage Foundation
http://www.heritage.org

This page offers discussion about, and links to, many sites of the Heritage Foundation and other organizations having to do with foreign policy and foreign affairs.

UNIT 4: Great Power Interstate Conflicts and Rivalries

Archive of European Integration
http://aei.pitt.edu

The Archive of European Integration (AEI) is an electronic repository and archive for research materials on the topic of European integration and unification. The site contains official European Community/European Union documents and certain independently-produced research materials.

ISN International Relations and Security Network
http://www.isn.ethz.ch

This site, maintained by the Center for Security Studies and Conflict Research, is a clearinghouse for extensive information on international relations and security policy.

The Henry L. Stimson Center—Peace Operations and Europe
http://www.stimson.org/fopo/?SN=FP20020610372

The Future of Peace Operations has begun to address specific areas concerning Europe and operations. The site links to useful UN, NATO, and EU documents, research pieces, and news sites.

Central Europe Online
http://www.centraleurope.com

This site contains daily updated information under headings such as news on the Web today, economics, trade, and currency.

Europa: European Union
http://europa.eu.int

This server site of the European Union will lead you to the history of the EU (and its predecessors); descriptions of EU policies, institutions, and goals; and documentation of treaties and other materials.

NATO Integrated Data Service
http://www.nato.int/structur/nids/nids.htm

Check out this website to review North Atlantic Treaty Organization documentation, to read *NATO Review,* and to explore key issues in the field of European security and transatlantic cooperation.

Russia Today
http://www.russiatoday.com

This site includes headline news, resources, government, politics, election results, and pressing issues.

Russian and East European Network Information Center, University of Texas at Austin
http://reenic.utexas.edu/reenic/index.html

This is *the* website for information on the former Soviet Union.

Inside China Today
http://www.insidechina.com

Part of the European Internet Network, this site leads you to information on all of China, including recent news, government, and related sites.

Japan Ministry of Foreign Affairs
http://www.mofa.go.jp

Visit this official site for Japanese foreign policy statements and press releases, archives, and discussions of regional and global relations.

UNIT 5: North-South Interstate Conflicts and Rivalries

National Defense University Website
http://www.ndu.edu

This contains information on current studies. This site also provides a look at the school where many senior marine, and naval officers, and senior civilians attend prior to assuming top-level positions.

The North American Institute
http://www.northamericaninstitute.org

NAMI, a trinational public-affairs organization, is concerned with the emerging "regional space" of Canada, the United States, and Mexico and the development of a North American community. It provides links for study of trade, the environment, and institutional developments.

Inter-American Dialogue
http://www.iadialog.org

This is the website for IAD, a premier U.S. center for policy analysis, communication, and exchange in Western Hemisphere affairs. The 100-member organization has helped to shape the agenda of issues and choices in hemispheric relations.

African Center for Strategic Studies (ACSS)
http://www.africacenter.org

The ACSS is a U.S. Dept. of Defense Initiative and component of the National Defense University established to promote security cooperation between the United States and African states. The Africa Center includes headlines drawn from media outlets around the globe that include the most important news affecting Africa today.

Observatory of Cultural Policies in Africa (OCPA)
http://ocpa.irmo.hr/resources/index-en.html

The OCPA Secretariat web page, Maputo, Mozambique contains links to African cultural politics and other relevant documentations, such as working papers, reports, and recommendations.

United States Africa Command (AFRICOM)
http://www.africom.mil

Official site of AFRICOM, led by General William E. Ward. The site includes transcripts and documents, news articles, Africa-related links and frequently asked questions, including about employment with AFRICOM.

Internet References

UNIT 6: Conflicts among Nation-States in the Global South, Sub-National Conflicts, and the Role of Non-State Actors in an Interdependent World

Pajhwok Afghan News
http://www.pajhwak.com

This site is Afghanistan's premier news agency offering the best on-the-ground coverage of economics, politics, and security by local reporters.

EI: Electronic Intifada
http://electronicintifada.net/new.shtml

EI is a major Palestinian portal for information about the Palestinian-Israeli conflict from a Palestinian perspective.

International Security Assistance Force (ISAF)
http://www.nato.int/ISAF

This is the web page of NATO/OTAN International Security Assistance Force in Afghanistan.

Not on Our Watch: The Mission to End Genocide in Darfur and Beyond
http://notonourwatchbook.enoughproject.org

A web page created by actor Don Cheadle and human rights activist John Prendergast that includes six strategies readers can implement to help stop genocide in Sudan. Videos and online resources are also provided.

The African Executive
http://www.africanexecutive.com

The African Executive offers a wide range of opinions and analyses on Africa's socio-political and economic development. It features analytical, issue-based coverage on subjects such as finance and banking, investment opportunities in Africa, technology, agriculture, governance, travel, and entertainment among others.

IslamiCity
http://islamicity.com

This is one of the largest Islamic sites on the web, reaching 50 million people a month. Based in California, it includes public opinion polls, links to television and radio broadcasts, and religious guidance.

Palestine-Israel—American Task Force on Palestine
http://www.americantaskforce.org

The American Task Force on Palestine (ATFP) is a non-partisan organization dedicated to bringing peace to the Middle East.

Private Military Companies (Mercenaries)
http://www.bicc.de/pmc/links.php

Website developed by the Bonn International Center for Conversion (BICC) Bonn, Germany to facilitate search for the most important (online) articles dealing with PMCs classified into a few key issues. It provides a wide range of information on all sectors concerning PMCs as well as a list of PMC websites. The list is arranged by the names of the articles, not the authors, because most of the contributions were found by the title.

Kubatana.net
http://www.kubatana.net

A vitual community of Zimbabwean activities who have formed the NGO Network Alliance Project. The project aims to improve the accessibility of human rights and civic information in Zimbabwe.

African News Services

AllAfrica.com
http://allafrica.com

News 24
http://news.24.com

African Resources

Global Footprint Network
footprints@footprintnetwork.org

This website has a link to *Africa Factbook 2009,* an electronic set of some of the most up-to-date charts and recent statistics about human and environmental trends in Africa. The *Factbook* is compiled by The Global Footprint Network, the Swiss Agency for Development, and other sponsors.

Columbia University Library Africa Studies Resources
http://www.cc.columbia.edu/cu/libraries/indiv/area/Africa

Indiana University African Studies Center
http://www.indiana.edu/~afrist

Northwestern University Program of African Studies
http://nuinfo.nwu.edu/african-studies

Stanford University Guide to Internet Resoures for Africa South of the Sahara
http://www-sul.stanford.edu/depts/ssrg/africa/guide.html

University of Illinois, Urbana-Champaign, African Studies Center
http://www.afrst.uiuc.edu

University of Pennsylvania African Studies Center
http://www.sas.upenn.edu/African_Studies/AS

University of Wisconsin, Madison, African Studies Center
http://www.wisc.edu/afr

UNIT 7: Asymmetric Conflicts: Trends in Terrorism and Counterterrorism

Columbia International Affairs Online
http://www.ciaonet.org/cbr/cbr00/video/cbr_v/cbr_v.html

At this site find excerpts from al-Qaeda's 2-hour videotape used to recruit young Muslims to fight in a holy war. The tape demonstates al-Qaeda's use of the Internet and media outlets for propaganda and persuasion purposes.

Combating Terrorism Center at West Point
http://ctc.usma.edu

This site offers original analyses, translations of al-Qaeda documents, and a gateway to other terrorism research and government sites (http://ctc.usma.edu/gateway.asp).

SITE: The Search for International Terrorist Entities
http://www.siteinstitute.org/index.html

This is a site that includes background, current events, and websites about, or sponsored by, terrorist groups.

Terrorism Research Center
http://www.terrorism.com

The Terrorism Research Center features definitions and research on terrorism, counterterrorism documents, a comprehensive list of web links, and profiles of terrorist and counterterrorist groups.

Internet References

United States Government Counterinsurgency Initiative
http://www.usgcoin.org

This site describes activities and papers from recent conference on U.S. counterinsurgency activities.

UNIT 8: Contemporary Foreign Policy Debates

Iraq Web Links
http://www.usip.org/library/regions/iraq.html

This is a special web page of the United States Institute of Peace which includes general resources, NBC weapons, government agencies and international organizations, maps and guides, and other resources.

Iraq Dispatches
http://dahrjamailiraq.com

Dahr Jamail, an "unembedded journalist," offers accounts of conditions in Iraq and provides an alternative view to reports by reporters who are embedded with U.S. troops in Iraq. Jamail's dispatches are distributed through Alternet, a web-based independent media organization.

ArabNet
http://www.arab.net

This page of ArabNet, the online resource for the Arab world in the Middle East and North Africa, presents links to 22 Arab countries. Each country page classfies information using a standardized system.

UNIT 9: International Organizations, International Law, and Global Governance

The Digital Library in International Conflict Management
http://www.usip.org/library/diglib.html

This link contains peace agreements and truth commissions from around the world.

InterAction
http://www.interaction.org

InterAction encourages grassroots action, engages policy makers on advocacy issues, and uses this site to inform people on its initiatives to expand international humanitarian relief and development assistance programs.

IRIN
http://www.irinnews.org

The UN Office for the Coordination of Humanitarian Affairs provides free analytical reports, fact sheets, interviews, daily country updates, and weekly summaries through this site and e-mail distribution service. The site is a good source of news for crisis situations as they occur.

International Court of Justice (ICJ)
http://www.icj-cij.org

The International Court of Justice (commonly referred to as the World Court or ICJ) is the primary judicial organ of the United Nations. The ICJ acts to resolve matters of international law disputed by specific nations.

International Criminal Court
http://www.icc-cpi.int/home.html&l=en

The International Criminal Court is a permanent tribunal to prosecute individuals for genocide, crimes against humanity, war crimes, etc.

United Nations
http://untreaty.un.org

This site contains text on over 30,000 UN treaties.

United Nations Home Page
http://www.un.org

Here is the gateway to information about the United Nations. Also see http://www.undp.org/missions/usa/usna/htm for the U.S. Mission at the UN.

Human Rights Web
http://www.hrweb.org

This useful site offers ideas on how individuals can get involved in helping to protect human rights around the world.

United Nations Peacekeeping Home Page
http://www.un.org/Depts/dpko/dpko

This site summarizes past and current UN peacekeeping operations.

"A More Secure World: Our Shared Responsibility"
http://www.un.org/secureworld

Report delivered to Secretary General Kofi Annan in December 2004 that contains 101 recommendations regarding how to change the United Nations.

Global Policy Forum
http://www.globalpolicy.org

This site monitors several different United Nation policy initiatives and programs to evalue the effectiveness of such programs and to promote "accountability of global decisions." Visitors who know what types of material they are looking for will want to search through the headings which include such themes such as globalization, international justice, and UN reform. Each one of these sections contains a brief essay on their work, along with a smattering of reports, tables, and charts that highlight their analyses, past and present.

Amnesty International
http://www.amnesty.org

A non-governmental organization that is working to promote human rights and individual liberties worldwide.

UNIT 10: The International Economic System

The Earth Institute at Columbia University
http://www.earth.columbia.edu

The Earth Institute at Columbia University, led by Professor Jeffrey D. Sachs, is dedicated to addressing a number of complex issues related to sustainable development and the needs of the world's poor.

Graphs Comparing Countries
http://humandevelopment.bu.edu/use_existing_index/start_comp_graph.cfm

This site allows you to compare the statistics of various countries and nation-states using a visual tool.

Internet References

International Monetary Fund
http://www.imf.org

This link brings you to the homepage for the International Monetary Fund.

Kiva
http://www.kiva.org

Kiva lets indiviuals make small loans for as little as $25 to a specific entrepreneur in the developing world so they can try to lift themselves out of poverty.

Peace ParkFoundation
http://www.peaceparks.org

A private foundation to promote transfrontier conservation areas in southern Africa, including training Africans to become wildlife rangers. The organization works closely with the Southern African Development Organization (SADO) to help implement additional, or plan new, cross-border parks.

Transparency International
http://www.transparency.org

Transparency International is the global civil society organization leading the fight against corruption. TI publishes an annual International Corruption and International Bribery report that ranks nation-states in terms of the extent of corruption and bribery occurring in each country.

World Bank
http://www.worldbank.org

News (press releases, summaries of new projects, speeches) and coverage of numerous topics regarding development, countries, and regions are provided at this site. Go to the research and growth section of this site to access specific research and data regarding the world economy.

World Mapper Project
http://www.sasi.group.shef.ac.uk/worldmapper

This page offers a collection of world maps, where territories are sized to reflect basic data from as recently as 2006.

World Trade Organization
http://www.wto.org

The WTO is a place where member governments go, to try to sort out the trade problems they face with each other.

UNIT 11: Globalizing Issues

Center for Naval Analysis "National Security and the Threat of Climate Change"
http://youtube.com/watch?v=RCfRGN0YlwQ

Link to video and attachments about climate change produced by a respected Washington D.C. think tank called Center for Naval Analysis (CAN)

The UN Millennium Project
http://www.unmillenniumproject.org/

The Center for Naval Analysis (CNA) is a non-profit institution that conducts high-level, in-depth research and analysis to inform the important work of public sector decision makers.

The 11thHourAction.Com
http://www.11thhouraction.com

This is a web resource page based on the same topics as are covered in the movie. Page includes recent articles, information, blog, and action meetups based on a map, and forums focused on various environmental issues related to climate change.

CIA Report of the National Intelligence Council's 2020 Project
http://www.cia.gov/nic/NIC_globaltrend2020.html

This link contains the full text of the most recent CIA-sponsored 2020 Project Report on future global trends.

Commonwealth Forum on Globalization and Health
http://www.ukglobalhealth.org

This website is sponsored by the Commonwealth Secretariat. Launched in April 2004, the Commonwealth Forum consists of a number of articles and excerpts on various facets of globablization and health.

Commission on Global Governance
http://www.sovereignty.net/p/gov/gganalysis.htm

This site provides access to *The Report of the Commission on Global Governance,* produced by an international group of leaders who want to find ways to help the global community to better manage its affairs.

Global Footprint Network
http://footprints@footprintnetwork.org

At Global Footprint Network our programs are designed to *influence* decision makers at all levels of society and to create a critical mass of powerful institutions using the Footprint to put an end to ecological *overshoot* and get our economies back into balance.

Global Trends 2005 Project
http://www.csis.org/gt2005/sumreport.html

The Center for Strategic and International Studies explores the coming global trends and challenges of the new millenium. Read their summary report at this website. Also access Enterprises for the Environment, Global Information Infrastructure Commission, and Americas at this site.

Greenpeace International
http://www.greenpeace.org/international

"Greenpeace exists because this fragile Earth deserves a voice. It needs solutions. It needs change. It needs actions." Website details recent environmental news related to climate changes and "greenpeace victories."

HIV/AIDS
http://www.unaids.org

This is a site giving information on the rising toll of HIV/AIDS.

RealClimate
http://www.realclimate.org

This site contains reports by climate scientists on recent events related to global warming and information about recent severe climate events.

UNIT 1

The International System and Changing World Order of the Twenty-First Century

Unit Selections

Key Points to Consider

- What are some of the characteristics of a nonpolarity international system?

- What types of connections contribute to America's power in the world?

- Which countries are likely to be the most dominant in a multi-polar world?

- Are independent nation-states likely to remain the most important factor in international relations or will national sovereignty be subverted or even replaced by other actors?

- Which country, China or India, do you believe will become the dominant economic power in Asia? Why?

- Will increased pollution and environmental degradation force China to become more or less democratic in the future?

Student Website
www.mhhe.com/cls

Internet References

The Globalization Website
http://www.emory.edu/SOC/globalization
Images of the Social and Political World
http://www-personal.umich.edu/~mejn/cartograms
National Security and the Threat of Climate Change
http://www.npr.org/documents/2007/apr/security_climate.pdf
Population Reference Bureau
http://www.prb.org
Women in International Politics
http://www.guide2womenleaders.com
Avalon Project at Yale Law School
http://www.yale.edu/lawweb/avalon/terrorism/terror.htm

After the demise of the Cold War, the International System was often characterized as a unipolar system dominated by the United States. The notion of a Pax Americana meant that Americans could take their national security for granted. This assumption was quickly dashed by the September 11, 2001 terrorist attacks. The United States' retaliatory attack on Taliban forces in Afghanistan, the U.S. military invasion of Iraq, and the quick initial military victories by U.S. forces, led many observers to predict that U.S. military strength would be the determining factor in the outcome of armed conflicts for years.

However, as sectarian fighting in Iraq degenerated into civil war and the Taliban regrouped and increased their attacks against NATO forces in Afghanistan, more analysts reluctantly concluded that earlier generations of counter-insurgency writers were correct in emphasizing that guerrilla wars were brutal, nasty, and long affairs. Over time, there was an acceptance on the part of the U.S. administration that it is impossible to win a guerrilla war without simultaneously implementing programs designed to win the hearts and minds of the populous.

By mid-2007, the United States had deployed additional troops in Iraq as part of a military surge and started new civil affairs projects in Iraq. These programs succeeded in restoring more security and stability to many areas. U.S. progress resulted from successful efforts by U.S. military commanders who forged alliances with local leaders. The U.S. strategy of putting local leaders and militias on the payroll helped drive out al Qaeda cells from several communities in Iraq and allowed local authorities to assume a greater role in administering certain areas. However, at the same time that the frequency of al Qaeda attacks was declining in Iraq, there was an increase in the severity and frequency of attacks initiated by al Qaeda and Taliban forces in many parts of Afghanistan.

During 2008 the U.S. military turned over political authority to the Shi'ite-dominated national government in Iraq and gradually reduced forces in several parts of Iraq. The pace of the U.S. withdrawal of forces is scheduled to increase significantly after national elections are held in January 2010. However, a massive twin suicide bombing in downtown Baghdad during the fall of 2008 cast doubts on the credibility of the claim of the government led by Prime Minister Nouri al-Maliki to have restored security throughout most of Iraq. Uncertainty is even greater about the future security situation in Afghanistan as a new U.S. President, Barak Obama, pondered a request for an immediate increase of U.S. forces in Afghanistan to 40,000 by General McChrystal, who warned that doing any less would risk losing the battle with Taliban and al Qaeda forces.

President-elect Obama took office as the intertwined economic crises worsened at home and throughout the world. Six months into his administration, President Obama had pushed through a $787 billion economic stimulus package, had bailed out Wall Street, the major automobile companies and many large banks but had not yet devised programs that provided effective economic relief to large numbers of small businesses or distressed homeowners. The administration had, by their count, saved or created 650,000 jobs. This number was insufficient to stop the U.S. unemployment rate from reaching

© Getty Images/Photodisc

a post-World War historic high or prevent worsening economic conditions. Over the summer the new administration succeeded in defeating continuation of a high-profile fighter F-22 jet program in the Senate, but faced the prospect of having to approve another large troop increase for Afghanistan or risk continuing military setbacks in Afghanistan. The administration also failed to achieve a popular consensus on health care reform legislation at the same time that a number of ongoing international crises worsened. By fall the Obama's historic honeymoon with the public seemed to be over. The President's popularity had dropped below 50% for the first time. Polls consistently indicated that he was more popular with the public at home and abroad than were many of his policies.

Many International Relations experts now predict that the growing global financial crisis and the high costs that the United States is paying to fund financial bailouts are likely to accelerate the rise of an Asian-centered international system with China as an increasingly powerful actor. Others cite the interdependence of China with other developed economies, particularly the U.S. economy, and predict that the future world will be one of "nonpolarity," where several nation-states play key roles across certain issues. Anne-Marie Slaughter, in "America's Edge: Power in the Networked Century," takes the contrarian position that the U.S. is such a central node connecting so many key actors in the system that it will retain it's dominant edge over others in the international system for years to come. What role rising powers, such as China or India, or emerging powers such as Brazil, will play in the future is even more uncertain than before the onset of the global economic crisis. This uncertainty is due largely to the fact that no one really knows what impact the current economic crisis will have on the existing distribution of economic and political power or whether governments will be able to work together to quickly resolve the intertwined and growing global crises.

What is clear from recent trends is that major status quo powers, such as the United States, will have to undertake bold new initiatives in order to turn their countries' economies around. Current problems reflect deep-seated political conflicts and structural economic problems that will take years, if not decades, to solve. The need for major changes in such areas as energy alternatives and the environment are why some economists, businessmen, and politicians, including U.S. President Barak Obama, now call for a massive new green initiative. If successful, government-supported research and development programs might be able to serve as a stimulus for new growth and modernization much like Eisenhower's interstate highway or FDR's new deal in earlier eras.

The articles in this section reflect the diversity of viewpoints evident among experts about the relative importance of specific nation-states, the likelihood that new nation-state powers or empires will arise, and even whether traditional rules of statescraft, national security, and power politics will prevail or be overtaken by human security needs, or larger, collective security issues, such a global warming.

The Age of Nonpolarity
What Will Follow U.S. Dominance?

RICHARD N. HAASS

The principal characteristic of twenty-first-century international relations is turning out to be nonpolarity: a world dominated not by one or two or even several states but rather by dozens of actors possessing and exercising various kinds of power. This represents a tectonic shift from the past.

The twentieth century started out distinctly multipolar. But after almost 50 years, two world wars, and many smaller conflicts, a bipolar system emerged. Then, with the end of the Cold War and the demise of the Soviet Union, bipolarity gave way to unipolarity—an international system dominated by one power, in this case the United States. But today power is diffuse, and the onset of nonpolarity raises a number of important questions. How does nonpolarity differ from other forms of international order? How and why did it materialize? What are its likely consequences? And how should the United States respond?

Newer World Order

In contrast to multipolarity—which involves several distinct poles or concentrations of power—a nonpolar international system is characterized by numerous centers with meaningful power.

In a multipolar system, no power dominates, or the system will become unipolar. Nor do concentrations of power revolve around two positions, or the system will become bipolar. Multipolar systems can be cooperative, even assuming the form of a concert of powers, in which a few major powers work together on setting the rules of the game and disciplining those who violate them. They can also be more competitive, revolving around a balance of power, or conflictual, when the balance breaks down.

At first glance, the world today may appear to be multipolar. The major powers—China, the European Union (EU), India, Japan, Russia, and the United States—contain just over half the world's people and account for 75 percent of global GDP and 80 percent of global defense spending. Appearances, however, can be deceiving. Today's world differs in a fundamental way from one of classic multipolarity: there are many more power centers, and quite a few of these poles are not nation-states. Indeed, one of the cardinal features of the contemporary international system is that nation-states have lost their monopoly on power and in some domains their preeminence as well. States are being challenged from above, by regional and global organizations; from below, by militias; and from the side, by a variety of nongovernmental organizations (NGOs) and corporations. Power is now found in many hands and in many places.

In addition to the six major world powers, there are numerous regional powers: Brazil and, arguably, Argentina, Chile, Mexico, and Venezuela in Latin America; Nigeria and South Africa in Africa; Egypt, Iran, Israel, and Saudi Arabia in the Middle East; Pakistan in South Asia; Australia, Indonesia, and South Korea in East Asia and Oceania. A good many organizations would be on the list of power centers, including those that are global (the International Monetary Fund, the United Nations, the World Bank), those that are regional (the African Union, the Arab League, the Association of Southeast Asian Nations, the EU, the Organization of American States, the South Asian Association for Regional Cooperation), and those that are functional (the International Energy Agency, OPEC, the Shanghai Cooperation Organization, the World Health Organization). So, too, would states within nation-states, such as California and India's Uttar Pradesh, and cities, such as New York, São Paulo, and Shanghai. Then there are the large global companies, including those that dominate the worlds of energy, finance, and manufacturing. Other entities deserving inclusion would be global media outlets (al Jazeera, the BBC, CNN), militias (Hamas, Hezbollah, the Mahdi Army, the Taliban), political parties, religious institutions and movements, terrorist organizations (al Qaeda), drug cartels, and NGOs of a more benign sort (the Bill and Melinda Gates Foundation, Doctors Without Borders, Greenpeace). Today's world is increasingly one of distributed, rather than concentrated, power.

Today's world is increasingly one of distributed, rather than concentrated, power.

In this world, the United States is and will long remain the largest single aggregation of power. It spends more than $500 billion annually on its military—and more than $700 billion if the operations in Afghanistan and Iraq are included—and boasts land, air, and naval forces that are the world's most capable. Its economy, with a GDP of some $14 trillion, is the world's largest. The United States is also a major source of culture (through films and television), information, and innovation. But the reality of American strength should not mask the relative decline of the United States' position in the world—and with this relative decline in power an absolute decline in influence and independence. The U.S. share of global imports is already down to 15 percent. Although U.S. GDP accounts for over 25 percent of the world's total, this percentage is sure to decline over time given the actual and projected differential between the United States' growth rate and those of the Asian giants and many other countries, a large number of which are growing at more than two or three times the rate of the United States.

GDP growth is hardly the only indication of a move away from U.S. economic dominance. The rise of sovereign wealth funds—in countries such as China, Kuwait, Russia, Saudi Arabia, and the United Arab Emirates—is another. These government-controlled pools of wealth, mostly the result of oil and gas exports, now total some $3 trillion. They are growing at a projected rate of $1 trillion a year and are an increasingly important source of liquidity for U.S. firms. High energy prices, fueled mostly by the surge in Chinese and Indian demand, are here to stay for some time, meaning that the size and significance of these funds will continue to grow. Alternative stock exchanges are springing up and drawing away companies from the U.S. exchanges and even launching initial public offerings (IPOs). London, in particular, is competing with New York as the world's financial center and has already surpassed it in terms of the number of IPOs it hosts. The dollar has weakened against the euro and the British pound, and it is likely to decline in value relative to Asian currencies as well. A majority of the world's foreign exchange holdings are now in currencies other than the dollar, and a move to denominate oil in euros or a basket of currencies is possible, a step that would only leave the U.S. economy more vulnerable to inflation as well as currency crises.

U.S. primacy is also being challenged in other realms, such as military effectiveness and diplomacy. Measures of military spending are not the same as measures of military capacity. September 11 showed how a small investment by terrorists could cause extraordinary levels of human and physical damage. Many of the most costly pieces of modern weaponry are not particularly useful in modern conflicts in which traditional battlefields are replaced by urban combat zones. In such environments, large numbers of lightly armed soldiers can prove to be more than a match for smaller numbers of highly trained and better-armed U.S. troops.

Power and influence are less and less linked in an era of nonpolarity. U.S. calls for others to reform will tend to fall on deaf ears, U.S. assistance programs will buy less, and U.S.-led sanctions will accomplish less. After all, China proved to be the country best able to influence North Korea's nuclear program. Washington's ability to pressure Tehran has been strengthened by the participation of several western European countries—and weakened by the reluctance of China and Russia to sanction Iran. Both Beijing and Moscow have diluted international efforts to pressure the government in Sudan to end its war in Darfur. Pakistan, meanwhile, has repeatedly demonstrated an ability to resist U.S. entreaties, as have Iran, North Korea, Venezuela, and Zimbabwe.

The trend also extends to the worlds of culture and information. Bollywood produces more films every year than Hollywood. Alternatives to U.S.-produced and disseminated television are multiplying. websites and blogs from other countries provide further competition for U.S.-produced news and commentary. The proliferation of information is as much a cause of nonpolarity as is the proliferation of weaponry.

Farewell to Unipolarity

Charles Krauthammer was more correct than he realized when he wrote in these pages nearly two decades ago about what he termed "the unipolar moment." At the time, U.S. dominance was real. But it lasted for only 15 or 20 years. In historical terms, it was a moment. Traditional realist theory would have predicted the end of unipolarity and the dawn of a multipolar world. According to this line of reasoning, great powers, when they act as great powers are wont to do, stimulate competition from others that fear or resent them. Krauthammer, subscribing to just this theory, wrote, "No doubt, multipolarity will come in time. In perhaps another generation or so there will be great powers coequal with the United States, and the world will, in structure, resemble the pre-World War I era."

But this has not happened. Although anti-Americanism is widespread, no great-power rival or set of rivals has emerged to challenge the United States. In part, this is because the disparity between the power of the United States and that of any potential rivals is too great. Over time, countries such as China may come to possess GDPs comparable to that of the United States. But in the case of China, much of that wealth will necessarily be absorbed by providing for the country's enormous population (much of which remains poor) and will not be available to fund military development or external undertakings. Maintaining political stability during a period of such dynamic but uneven growth will be no easy feat. India faces many of the same demographic challenges and is further hampered by too much bureaucracy and too little infrastructure. The EU's GDP is now greater than that of the United States, but the EU does not act in the unified fashion of a nation-state, nor is it able or inclined to act in the assertive fashion of historic great powers. Japan, for its part, has a shrinking and aging population and lacks the political culture to play the role of a great power. Russia may be more inclined, but it still has a largely cash-crop economy and is saddled by a declining population and internal challenges to its cohesion.

The fact that classic great-power rivalry has not come to pass and is unlikely to arise anytime soon is also partly a result of the United States' behavior, which has not stimulated such a response. This is not to say that the United States under the leadership of George W. Bush has not alienated other nations; it surely has. But it has not, for the most part, acted in a manner that has led other states to conclude that the United States constitutes a threat to their vital national interests. Doubts about the wisdom and legitimacy of U.S. foreign policy are pervasive, but this has tended to lead more to denunciations (and an absence of cooperation) than outright resistance.

The transition to a nonpolar world will have mostly negative consequences for the United States.

A further constraint on the emergence of great-power rivals is that many of the other major powers are dependent on the international system for their economic welfare and political stability. They do not, accordingly, want to disrupt an order that serves their national interests. Those interests are closely tied to cross-border flows of goods, services, people, energy, investment, and technology—flows in which the United States plays a critical role. Integration into the modern world dampens great-power competition and conflict.

But even if great-power rivals have not emerged, unipolarity has ended. Three explanations for its demise stand out. The first is historical. States develop; they get better at generating and piecing together the human, financial, and technological resources that lead to productivity and prosperity. The same holds for corporations and other organizations. The rise of these new powers cannot be stopped. The result is an ever larger number of actors able to exert influence regionally or globally.

A second cause is U.S. policy. To paraphrase Walt Kelly's Pogo, the post-World War II comic hero, we have met the explanation and it is us. By both what it has done and what it has failed to do, the United States has accelerated the emergence of alternative power centers in the world and has weakened its own position relative to them. U.S. energy policy (or the lack thereof) is a driving force behind the end of unipolarity. Since the first oil shocks of the 1970s, U.S. consumption of oil has grown by approximately 20 percent, and, more important, U.S. imports of petroleum products have more than doubled in volume and nearly doubled as a percentage of consumption. This growth in demand for foreign oil has helped drive up the world price of oil from just over $20 a barrel to over $100 a barrel in less than a decade. The result is an enormous transfer of wealth and leverage to those states with energy reserves. In short, U.S. energy policy has helped bring about the emergence of oil and gas producers as major power centers.

U.S. economic policy has played a role as well. President Lyndon Johnson was widely criticized for simultaneously fighting a war in Vietnam and increasing domestic spending. President Bush has fought costly wars in Afghanistan and Iraq, allowed discretionary spending to increase by an annual rate of eight percent, and cut taxes. As a result, the United States' fiscal position declined from a surplus of over $100 billion in 2001 to an estimated deficit of approximately $250 billion in 2007. Perhaps more relevant is the ballooning current account deficit, which is now more than six percent of GDP. This places downward pressure on the dollar, stimulates inflation, and contributes to the accumulation of wealth and power elsewhere in the world. Poor regulation of the U.S. mortgage market and and the credit crisis it has spawned have exacerbated these problems.

The war in Iraq has also contributed to the dilution of the United States' position in the world. The war in Iraq has proved to be an expensive war of choice—militarily, economically, and diplomatically as well as in human terms. Years ago, the historian Paul Kennedy outlined his thesis about "imperial overstretch," which posited that the United States would eventually decline by overreaching, just as other great powers had in the past. Kennedy's theory turned out to apply most immediately to the Soviet Union, but the United States—for all its corrective mechanisms and dynamism—has not proved to be immune. It is not simply that the U.S. military will take a generation to recover from Iraq; it is also that the United States lacks sufficient military assets to continue doing what it is doing in Iraq, much less assume new burdens of any scale elsewhere.

Finally, today's nonpolar world is not simply a result of the rise of other states and organizations or of the failures and follies of U.S. policy. It is also an inevitable consequence of globalization. Globalization has increased the volume, velocity, and importance of cross-border flows of just about everything, from drugs, e-mails, greenhouse gases, manufactured goods, and people to television and radio signals, viruses (virtual and real), and weapons.

Globalization reinforces nonpolarity in two fundamental ways. First, many cross-border flows take place outside the control of governments and without their knowledge. As a result, globalization dilutes the influence of the major powers. Second, these same flows often strengthen the capacities of nonstate actors, such as energy exporters (who are experiencing a dramatic increase in wealth owing to transfers from importers), terrorists (who use the Internet to recruit and train, the international banking system to move resources, and the global transport system to move people), rogue states (who can exploit black and gray markets), and Fortune 500 firms (who quickly move personnel and investments). It is increasingly apparent that being the strongest state no longer means having a near monopoly on power. It is easier than ever before for individuals and groups to accumulate and project substantial power.

Nonpolar Disorder

The increasingly nonpolar world will have mostly negative consequences for the United States—and for much of the rest of the world as well. It will make it more difficult for Washington to lead on those occasions when it seeks to promote collective responses to regional and global challenges. One reason has to do with simple arithmetic. With so many more actors possessing meaningful power and trying to assert influence, it will be more difficult to build collective responses and make institutions work. Herding dozens is harder than herding a few. The inability to reach agreement in the Doha Round of global trade talks is a telling example.

Nonpolarity will also increase the number of threats and vulnerabilities facing a country such as the United States. These threats can take the form of rogue states, terrorist groups, energy producers that choose to reduce their output, or central banks whose action or inaction can create conditions that affect the role and strength of the U.S. dollar. The Federal Reserve might want to think twice before continuing to lower interest rates, lest it precipitate a further move away from the dollar. There can be worse things than a recession.

Iran is a case in point. Its effort to become a nuclear power is a result of nonpolarity. Thanks more than anything to the surge in oil prices, it has become another meaningful concentration of power, one able to exert influence in Iraq, Lebanon, Syria, the Palestinian territories, and beyond, as well as within OPEC. It has many sources of technology and finance and numerous markets for its energy exports. And due to nonpolarity, the United States cannot manage Iran alone. Rather, Washington is dependent on others to support political and economic sanctions or block Tehran's access to nuclear technology and materials. Nonpolarity begets nonpolarity.

Still, even if nonpolarity was inevitable, its character is not. To paraphrase the international relations theorist Hedley Bull, global politics at any point is a mixture of anarchy and society. The question is the balance and the trend. A great deal can and should be done to shape a nonpolar world. Order will not just emerge. To the contrary, left to its own devices, a nonpolar world will become messier over time. Entropy dictates that systems consisting of a large number of actors tend toward greater randomness and disorder in the absence of external intervention.

The United States can and should take steps to reduce the chances that a nonpolar world will become a cauldron of instability. This is not a call for unilateralism; it is a call for the United States to get its own house in order. Unipolarity is a thing of the past, but the United States still retains more capacity than any other actor to improve the quality of the international system. The question is whether it will continue to possess such capacity.

The United States no longer has the luxury of a "You're either with us or against us" foreign policy.

Energy is the most important issue. Current levels of U.S. consumption and imports (in addition to their adverse impact on the global climate) fuel nonpolarity by funneling vast financial resources to oil and gas producers. Reducing consumption would lessen the pressure on world prices, decrease U.S. vulnerability to market manipulation by oil suppliers, and slow the pace of climate change. The good news is that this can be done without hurting the U.S. economy.

Strengthening homeland security is also crucial. Terrorism, like disease, cannot be eradicated. There will always be people who cannot be integrated into societies and who pursue goals that cannot be realized through traditional politics. And sometimes, despite the best efforts of those entrusted with homeland security, terrorists will succeed. What is needed, then, are steps to make society more resilient, something that requires adequate funding and training of emergency responders and more flexible and durable infrastructure. The goal should be to reduce the impact of even successful attacks.

Resisting the further spread of nuclear weapons and unguarded nuclear materials, given their destructive potential, may be as important as any other set of undertakings. By establishing internationally managed enriched-uranium or spent-fuel banks that give countries access to sensitive nuclear materials, the international community could help countries use nuclear power to produce electricity rather than bombs. Security assurances and defensive systems can be provided to states that might otherwise feel compelled to develop nuclear programs of their own to counter those of their neighbors. Robust sanctions—on occasion backed by armed force—can also be introduced to influence the behavior of would-be nuclear states.

Even so, the question of using military force to destroy nuclear or biological weapons capabilities remains. Preemptive strikes—attacks that aim to stop an imminent threat—are widely accepted as a form of self-defense. Preventive strikes—attacks on capabilities when there is no indication of imminent use—are something else altogether. They should not be ruled out as a matter of principle, but nor should they be depended on. Beyond questions of feasibility, preventive strikes run the risk of making a nonpolar world less stable, both because they might actually encourage proliferation (governments could see developing or acquiring nuclear weapons as a deterrent) and because they would weaken the long-standing norm against the use of force for purposes other than self-defense.

Combating terrorism is also essential if the nonpolar era is not to turn into a modern Dark Ages. There are many ways to weaken existing terrorist organizations by using intelligence and law enforcement resources and military capabilities. But this is a loser's game unless something can be done to reduce recruitment. Parents, religious figures, and political leaders must delegitimize terrorism by shaming those who choose to embrace it. And more important, governments must find ways of integrating alienated young men and women into their societies, something that cannot occur in the absence of political and economic opportunity.

Trade can be a powerful tool of integration. It gives states a stake in avoiding conflict because instability interrupts beneficial commercial arrangements that provide greater wealth and strengthen the foundations of domestic political order. Trade also facilitates development, thereby decreasing the chance of state failure and alienation among citizens. The scope of the World Trade Organization must be extended through the negotiation of future global arrangements that further reduce subsidies and both tariff and nontariff barriers. Building domestic political support for such negotiations in developed countries will likely require the expansion of various safety nets, including portable health care and retirement accounts, education and training assistance, and wage insurance. These social policy reforms are costly and in some cases unwarranted (the cause of job loss is far more likely to be technological innovation than foreign competition), but they are worth providing nonetheless given the overall economic and political value of expanding the global trade regime.

A similar level of effort might be needed to ensure the continued flow of investment. The goal should be to create a World Investment Organization that would encourage capital flows across borders so as to minimize the chances that "investment protectionism" gets in the way of activities that, like trade, are economically beneficial and build political bulwarks against instability. A WIO could encourage transparency on the part of investors, determine when national security is a legitimate reason for prohibiting or limiting foreign investment, and establish a mechanism for resolving disputes.

Finally, the United States needs to enhance its capacity to prevent state failure and deal with its consequences. This will require building and maintaining a larger military, one with greater capacity to deal with the sort of threats faced in Afghanistan and Iraq. In addition, it will mean establishing a civilian counterpart to the military reserves that would provide a pool of human talent to assist with basic nation-building tasks. Continuing economic and military assistance will be vital in helping weak states meet their responsibilities to their citizens and their neighbors.

The Not-So-Lonely Superpower

Multilateralism will be essential in dealing with a nonpolar world. To succeed, though, it must be recast to include actors other than the great powers. The UN Security Council and the G-8 (the group of highly industrialized states) need to be reconstituted to reflect the world of today and not the post–World War II era. A recent meeting at the United Nations on how best to coordinate global responses to public health challenges provided a model. Representatives of governments, UN agencies, NGOs, pharmaceutical companies, foundations, think tanks, and universities were all in attendance. A similar range of participants attended the December 2007 Bali meeting on climate change. Multilateralism may have to be less formal and less comprehensive, at least in its initial phases. Networks will be needed alongside organizations. Getting everyone to agree on everything will be increasingly difficult; instead, the United States should consider signing accords with fewer parties and narrower goals. Trade is something of a model here, in that bilateral and regional accords are filling the vacuum created by a failure to conclude a global trade round. The same approach could work for climate change, where agreement on aspects of the problem (say, deforestation) or arrangements involving only some countries (the major carbon emitters, for example) may prove feasible, whereas an accord that involves every country and tries to resolve every issue may not. Multilateralism à la carte is likely to be the order of the day.

Nonpolarity complicates diplomacy. A nonpolar world not only involves more actors but also lacks the more predictable fixed structures and relationships that tend to define worlds of unipolarity, bipolarity, or multipolarity. Alliances, in particular, will lose much of their importance, if only because alliances require predictable threats, outlooks, and obligations, all of which are likely to be in short supply in a nonpolar world. Relationships will instead become more selective and situational. It will become harder to classify other countries as either allies or adversaries; they will cooperate on some issues and resist on others. There will be a premium on consultation and coalition building and on a diplomacy that encourages cooperation when possible and shields such cooperation from the fallout of inevitable disagreements. The United States will no longer have the luxury of a "You're either with us or against us" foreign policy.

Nonpolarity will be difficult and dangerous. But encouraging a greater degree of global integration will help promote stability. Establishing a core group of governments and others committed to cooperative multilateralism would be a great step forward. Call it "concerted nonpolarity." It would not eliminate nonpolarity, but it would help manage it and increase the odds that the international system will not deteriorate or disintegrate.

Richard N. Haass is President of the Council on Foreign Relations.

America's Edge
Power in the Networked Century

ANNE-MARIE SLAUGHTER

We live in a networked world. War is networked: the power of terrorists and the militaries that would defeat them depend on small, mobile groups of warriors connected to one another and to intelligence, communications, and support networks. Diplomacy is networked: managing international crises—from SARS to climate change—requires mobilizing international networks of public and private actors. Business is networked: every CEO advice manual published in the past decade has focused on the shift from the vertical world of hierarchy to the horizontal world of networks. Media are networked: online blogs and other forms of participatory media depend on contributions from readers to create a vast, networked conversation. Society is networked: the world of MySpace is creating a global world of "OurSpace," linking hundreds of millions of individuals across continents. Even religion is networked: as the pastor Rick Warren has argued, "The only thing big enough to solve the problems of spiritual emptiness, selfish leadership, poverty, disease, and ignorance is the network of millions of churches all around the world."

In this world, the measure of power is connectedness. Almost 30 years ago, the psychologist Carol Gilligan wrote about differences between the genders in their modes of thinking. She observed that men tend to see the world as made up of hierarchies of power and seek to get to the top, whereas women tend to see the world as containing webs of relationships and seek to move to the center. Gilligan's observations may be a function of nurture rather than nature; regardless, the two lenses she identified capture the differences between the twentieth-century and the twenty-first-century worlds.

The twentieth-century world was, at least in terms of geopolitics, a billiard-ball world, described by the political scientist Arnold Wolfers as a system of self-contained states colliding with one another. The results of these collisions were determined by military and economic power. This world still exists today: Russia invades Georgia, Iran seeks nuclear weapons, the United States strengthens its ties with India as a hedge against a rising China. This is what Fareed Zakaria, the editor of *Newsweek International,* has dubbed "the post-American world," in which the rise of new global powers inevitably means the relative decline of U.S. influence.

The emerging networked world of the twenty-first century, however, exists above the state, below the state, and through the state. In this world, the state with the most connections will be the central player, able to set the global agenda and unlock innovation and sustainable growth. Here, the United States has a clear and sustainable edge.

The Horizon of Hope

The United States' advantage is rooted in demography, geography, and culture. The United States has a relatively small population, only 20–30 percent of the size of China's or India's. Having fewer people will make it much easier for the United States to develop and profit from new energy technologies. At the same time, the heterogeneity of the U.S. population will allow Washington to extend its global reach. To this end, the United States should see its immigrants as living links back to their home countries and encourage a two-way flow of people, products, and ideas.

The United States is the anchor of the Atlantic hemisphere, a broadly defined area that includes Africa, the Americas, and Europe. The leading countries in the Atlantic hemisphere are more peaceful, stable, and economically diversified than those in the Asian hemisphere. At the same time, however, the United States is a pivotal power, able to profit simultaneously from its position in the Atlantic hemisphere and from its deep ties to the Asian hemisphere. The Atlantic and Pacific Oceans have long protected the United States from invasion and political interference. Soon, they will shield it from conflicts brought about by climate change, just as they are already reducing the amount of pollutants that head its way. The United States has a relatively horizontal social structure—albeit one that has become more hierarchical with the growth of income inequality—as well as a culture of entrepreneurship and innovation. These traits are great advantages in a global economy increasingly driven by networked clusters of the world's most creative people.

On January 20, 2009, Barack Obama will set about restoring the moral authority of the United States. The networked world provides a hopeful horizon. In this world, with the right policies, immigrants can be a source of jobs rather than a drain on resources, able to link their new home with markets and suppliers in their old homes. Businesses in the United States can orchestrate global networks of producers and suppliers. Consumers can buy locally, from revived local agricultural and customized small-business economies, and at the same time globally, from anywhere that can advertise online. The United States has the potential to be the most innovative and dynamic society anywhere in the world.

Life in a Networked World

In 2000, Procter and Gamble made a decision that reinvented how the company would do business in the twenty-first century. Instead of closely guarding its secret recipes for everything from soaps to potato chips, Procter and Gamble chose to open up its patent portfolio, making virtually all its formulas available to anyone willing to pay a licensing fee. At the same time, it asked its top managers to bring in half of their ideas for new products and services from outside the company. They now look to far-flung groups of inventors around the world and online, where innovators gather at sites such as InnoCentive, an auction website for ideas. Don Tapscott and Anthony Williams, the authors of *Wikinomics: How Mass Collaboration Changes Everything,* call businesses like InnoCentive "ideagoras," modern-day public squares that join people looking to sell their ideas with businesses seeking to buy them. In 2006, Samuel Palmisano, the head of IBM, predicted in these pages that corporations would move from being multinational, with small, self-replicated versions of themselves in every market, to being what he calls "globally integrated enterprises." Today, IBM funnels tasks to wherever they will be done best.

Consider the experience of Li and Fung, the world's largest and most successful export sourcing company. Its clients are retailers of virtually every kind of product known to man, or at least made by man. The job of Li and Fung is to identify suppliers from over 40 countries around the world and connect them in order to fill specific orders. The resulting networks must be fast, flexible, and able to work to a common high standard. According to William and Victor Fung, two of the current owners of the family business, the secret of sourcing is "orchestrating networks." It is the managerial equivalent of creating a system in which one can select a destination on a Paris metro map and see a possible route light up with a connecting web of differently colored lines—except, of course, that riders at each station might have their own ideas about how best to travel.

At first, these global webs may seem to be just the next generation of outsourcing. But something much deeper is going on. Outsourcing requires a central command that specifies precisely what and how much should be produced and then, through an established hierarchy, communicates those decisions to producers in multiple nations. In contrast, under a system of peer production, supply chains become "value webs," in which suppliers become partners and, instead of just supplying products, actually collaborate on their design. Boeing is a particularly striking example, given how it could be seen as the heart of old-style manufacturing. It has shifted from being simply an airplane manufacturer to being a "systems integrator," relying on a horizontal network of partners collaborating in real time. They share both risk and knowledge in order to achieve a higher level of performance. It is not simply a change in form but a change in culture. Hierarchy and control lose out to community, collaboration, and self-organization. At its core, a company can be quite small, often no more than a central node of leaders and manager-integrators.

But with the right networks, it can reach anywhere innovators, factories, and service providers can be found. In this world, as Tapscott and Williams write, "only the connected will survive."

Nongovernmental organizations (NGOs), too, have realized the power of connections. An early example was the International Campaign to Ban Landmines, which began in 1991 as a coalition of six NGOs from North America and Europe. It eventually grew to include over 1,100 groups in some 60 countries, and with this breadth came clout. After it won the Nobel Peace Prize in 1997, the network successfully pushed for a global treaty banning the use of land mines (although China, Russia, and the United States, among others, have refused to sign it). NGOs pursuing other causes have followed suit. In 1995, a small group of human rights organizations began calling for the creation of an international criminal court to try war criminals. They succeeded in convincing governments to establish a permanent court in 1998. Today, the Coalition for the International Criminal Court includes over 2,000 organizations from every corner of the world, which are now working to expand the court's jurisdiction. More recently, a global alliance of NGOs has been instrumental in pushing for action to stop the ongoing violence in Darfur.

In each of these cases, NGOs gained leverage over otherwise reluctant states. They formed transnational networks that multiplied their lobbying power and put their message on the agendas of international institutions. As Francis Sejersted, then chair of the Nobel Committee, noted when he recognized the land-mine campaign, "The mobilisation and focusing of broad popular involvement which we have witnessed bears promise that goes beyond the present issue. It appears to have established a pattern for how to realise political aims at the global level."

Governments have been slower to understand twenty-first-century challenges and to reform themselves accordingly, but they, too, are gradually moving toward a more networked structure. A report entitled *The Embassy of the Future,* issued by the Center for Strategic and International Studies in 2007, calls for U.S. diplomats to be "decentralized, flexible, and mobile," as well as "connected, responsive, and informed." U.S. embassy staff would have a more "distributed presence," both virtually and physically, if they worked at multiple locations and with a wide range of different groups in their host countries.

Similarly, Julie Gerberding, director of the Centers for Disease Control, realized after the anthrax scare in 2001 and the SARS crisis in 2002 that the CDC needed to create a network of public and private actors from around the world. Managing this network would, in turn, require a much more flexible and horizontal organization at the CDC's headquarters, in Atlanta. Gerberding was expected to get results but lacked the authority necessary to produce them. For Gerberding, the solution was to find partners around the world and to connect them in ways that would allow for the creation and sharing of knowledge during a crisis. Many judges and government regulators have had a similar insight. Bankruptcy judges, for example, now communicate with one another around the world, signing agreements to manage together the bankruptcies of multinational corporations. The current financial crisis could have been even worse if the world's central bankers had not already been connected and able to coordinate their actions.

Power can also flow from connections across different sectors. In his book *Superclass: The Global Power Elite and the World*

They Are Making, David Rothkopf explains how leaders connect across different power structures, from the worlds of business and finance to those of politics and the arts. "In fact," he writes, "such linkages are as distinguishing a characteristic of the superclass as wealth or individual position." In other words, it is connectivity, more than money or stature, that determines individual power. This dynamic can even extend to terrorist groups such as al Qaeda. John Robb, a former air force colonel and military strategist, has observed that Mohamed Atta was the leader of the 9/11 hijackers because, although no formal hierarchy existed in the group, "Atta had twenty-two connections to other people in the network, much more than any other, which gave him control of the operation."

The power that flows from this type of connectivity is not the power to impose outcomes. Networks are not directed and controlled as much as they are managed and orchestrated. Multiple players are integrated into a whole that is greater than the sum of its parts—an orchestra that plays differently according to the vision of its conductor and the talent of individual musicians. Obama's team-based campaign, with its relatively flat structure and emphasis on individual organizers, is a model of the twenty-first century's management style.

Most important, networked power flows from the ability to make the maximum number of valuable connections. The next requirement is to have the knowledge and skills to harness that power to achieve a common purpose. The United States is already following this model in a few specific ways. In combating terrorism, it has been able to stop planned attacks thanks to a dense global network of law enforcement officers, counterterrorism officials, and intelligence agencies. The U.S. government dramatically improved its standing in the Muslim world due to its swift and effective relief effort in Asia following the December 2004 tsunami. It coordinated an emergency-response strategy among government agencies and aid workers in Australia, India, Japan, and the United States itself. More recently, when the global financial crisis hit this past fall, the United States first reached out to central banks around the world to coordinate a monetary response and then reached out to central banks in key emerging markets to make sure their foreign currency needs were being met.

From this vantage point, predictions of an Asian century—such as those made by Kishore Mahbubani, a foreign policy scholar and dean of the Lee Kwan Yew School of Public Policy, in Singapore—seem premature. Even Zakaria's argument about "the rise of the rest" takes on a different significance. If, in a networked world, the issue is no longer relative power but centrality in an increasingly dense global web, then the explosion of innovation and entrepreneurship occurring today will provide that many more points of possible connection. The twenty-first century looks increasingly like another American century—although it will likely be a century of the Americas rather than of just America.

More People, More Problems

Demography is often cited as the chief factor behind the relative decline of the West. China and India make up over a third of the world's population, while Europe and Japan are actually shrinking and the United States is suddenly a relatively small nation of 300 million. This argument, however, rests largely on assumptions formed in the nineteenth and twentieth centuries. Throughout most of human history, territory and population translated into military and economic power. Military power depended on the number of soldiers a state could put into the field, the amount of territory an enemy had to cross to conquer it, and the economy's ability to supply the state's army. Population size mattered for economic power because without trade a state needed a domestic market large enough for manufacturers and merchants to thrive. With trade, however, small mercantile nations such as the Netherlands and Portugal were able to punch far above their weight. In the nineteenth century, to increase their power, small countries expanded their territory through colonization. But by the twentieth century, as political unrest in the colonial world grew, the advantages of trading rather than ruling became increasingly clear. Although the United States and the Soviet Union, two great continental powers, dominated the second half of the twentieth century, the countries that grew the richest were often the smallest. In 2007, the ten countries with the highest per capita GDPs all had populations smaller than that of New York City, with one notable exception: the United States.

In the twenty-first century, less is more. Domestic markets must be big enough to allow national firms to obtain a foothold so as to withstand international competition (although such markets can be obtained through free-trade areas and economic unions). But beyond this minimum, if trade barriers are low and transportation and communication are cheap, then size will be more of a burden than a benefit. When both markets and production are global, then productive members of every society will generate income across multiple societies. Business managers in one country can generate value by orchestrating a global and disparate network of researchers, designers, manufacturers, marketers, and distributors. It will remain the responsibility of government, however, to provide for the less productive members of society, namely, the elderly, the young, the disabled, and the unemployed—think of them as national overhead costs. From this perspective, the 300 million citizens in the United States look much more manageable than the more than a billion in China or India.

A shrinking population can actually act as a catalyst for innovation. In China, the answer to many problems is simply to throw people at them—both because people are the most available commodity and because the Chinese government needs to provide as many jobs as possible. In Japan, by contrast, the answer is to innovate. Nintendo, the Kyoto-based gaming giant, is bringing much of its manufacturing back to Japan from China and other parts of Asia. How can it possibly compete using high-cost Japanese labor? It will not have to—its new factories are almost entirely automated, with only a handful of highly skilled employees needed to run them. This approach uses less energy, costs less, and guarantees a higher standard of living for the Japanese population. As the priority shifts from economic growth to sustainable growth, the formula of fewer people plus better and greener technology will look increasingly attractive.

Finally, size carries its own set of political challenges. Over the past four centuries, the arrow of history has pointed in the direction of national self-determination. Empires and multiethnic countries have steadily divided and subdivided into smaller units so that nations, or dominant ethnic groups, could govern themselves. Ninety years after Woodrow Wilson laid out his vision

9

of self-determination for the Balkan states, the process continues in Kosovo. In many ways, the breakup of the Soviet Union was another round of the decolonization and self-determination movement that began in the 1940s. It continues today with the conflicts over Abkhazia and South Ossetia, as well as with the potential for conflict on the Crimean Peninsula and in eastern Ukraine. Much of China's 5,000-year history has been a saga of the country's splitting apart and being welded back together. The Chinese government, like the Indian government, legitimately fears that current pockets of instability could quickly translate into multiple secessionist movements.

The United States faces no threats to its essential unity, which has been forged by a political and cultural ideology of unity amid diversity. The principal alternative to this ideology is the solution employed by the European Union and the Association of Southeast Asian Nations (ASEAN), in which individual states come together as larger economic and, gradually, quasi-political units. The most promising dimension of recent Chinese politics has been its adoption of a version of this solution with regard to Hong Kong and Macao—and one day Beijing may apply this model to Taiwan.

The United States benefits not only from its limited population but also from who makes up that population. It has long attracted the world's most entrepreneurial, creative, and determined individuals. A vast mixing of cultures has created an atmosphere for a fruitful cross-fertilization and innovation. These arguments still hold. In San Francisco, for instance, a new municipal telephone help line advertises that it can talk with callers in over 150 languages. This diversity, and the creativity that it produces, is visible everywhere: in Hollywood movies, in American music, and at U.S. universities. At Princeton University this past fall, five of the six student award winners for the highest grade point averages had come from abroad: from China, Germany, Moldova, Slovenia, and Turkey.

In the nineteenth- and twentieth-century era of nation-states, the United States absorbed its immigrants and molded them into Americans, thereby creating the national cohesion necessary to build military and economic strength. Today, diversity in the United States means something more. Immigrant communities flourish not only in large cities but also in smaller towns and rural areas. A mosaic has replaced the melting pot, and, more than ever, immigrants connect their new communities to their countries of origin. Along the southern border of the United States, for instance, immigration experts talk about "transnational communities," about clusters of families in the United States linked with the villages of Mexico and Central America. Now, where you are from means where you can, and do, go back to—and whom you know and trust enough to network with.

Consider, for example, how valuable the overseas Chinese community has been to China. Alan Wang, a former student of mine, was born in China, moved to Australia with his family at the age of 12, and went to college and law school there. He later came to the United States to pursue a graduate degree at Harvard. For a while, he practiced law with a large British firm in London, and then moved to its Shanghai office. When I asked him how he identified himself, he replied, "overseas Chinese." Millions of people similar to Wang have spread out from China throughout Southeast Asia, Australia, the United States, and Canada, creating trading and networking opportunities for people in all those places. Similarly, the United States must learn to think of its

ethnic communities as the source of future generations of "overseas Americans." Already, young Chinese Americans and Indian Americans are heading back to their parents' homelands to seek opportunity and make their fortunes. Soon, the children of U.S. immigrants from Africa, Asia, Latin America, and the Middle East will follow a similar path and return to their ethnic homelands, at least for a time. The key to succeeding in a networked economy is being able to harvest the best ideas and innovations from the widest array of sources. In this regard, the United States is plugged into all corners of the global brain.

Beyond its immigrant communities, the United States can also depend on a new generation to forge connections around the world. John Zogby, the influential pollster, calls Americans between the ages of 18 and 29 "the First Globals," a group he describes as "more networked and globally engaged than members of any similar age cohort in American history." More than half of the respondents aged 18 to 29 in a poll conducted in the United States in June 2007 by Zogby International said that they had friends or family living outside the United States, vastly more than any other U.S. age group. Other Zogby polls have shown that this generation holds passports in roughly the same proportion as other age groups but uses them far more frequently. A quarter of this group, according to Zogby's data, believes that they will "end up living for some significant period in a country other than America."

These young people spreading out around the world will be a huge asset to the United States. Children born abroad who acquire U.S. citizenship as a result of their parents' heritage or life decisions will add to this number. A college classmate of mine was born to Hungarian immigrants in Canada and later acquired U.S. citizenship. After graduation, he moved to China and then Japan, where he gained a Japanese residency permit while also applying for Hungarian citizenship. He now lives with his Chinese wife in Beijing, where his daughter was born. Not long after her birth, he took her to Tokyo so that she could register as a U.S. citizen and reenter China on a U.S. passport. These stories are legion in any large global city—couples from two different countries who are raising their children in a third or fourth or even fifth country. For many people who orbit in this floating cloud of nationalities, a U.S. passport, particularly now that the United States has relaxed its rules on dual citizenship, has become a new kind of reserve currency. With one, even the most venturesome and peripatetic have the guarantee of the political and cultural stability of the West. The United States must devise the incentives and conditions that will allow it to both encourage this phenomenon and profit from it.

The World Is Round Again

For most of modern history, the Eurocentric view of the world has placed North and South America in a hemisphere of their own—the Western Hemisphere. Today, the world is mapped in the round, with Asia in the East and Africa, the Americas, and Europe in the West. That, at least, is how some Asians increasingly think of themselves. In his recently published book, *The New Asian Hemisphere: The Irresistible Shift of Global Power to the East,* Mahbubani argues that the era of "Western domination of world history is over" and that the world is witnessing an "Asian march to modernity."

But if half of the world is now "the East," defined as the Asian hemisphere, then the other half is the Atlantic hemisphere, made up of Africa, the Americas, and Europe. It is quite a promising neighborhood, home to a wealth of human, economic, material, and natural resources. Politically, Europe and North America constitute a spreading community of liberal democracies that accounts for one-sixth of the world's population, almost 60 percent of global GDP, and the two primary global reserve currencies. More trade and direct investment pass over the Atlantic Ocean than any other part of the world—over $2 trillion in cumulative foreign direct investment alone. The potential for further integration of the hemisphere is enormous.

Even more important is the potential for deeper economic integration within the Americas. On energy questions, Canadian oil sands and Brazilian sugar cane are more promising than depending on Russian pipelines or Sudanese oil. Markets for renewable energy—such as from biomass, wind, geothermal technology, and other sources—are growing in Latin America. Miami is already a financial center for Latin America, and the steady growth of the Latino population in the United States will only deepen intra-American investment. The rise of Brazil and, to a somewhat lesser extent, Mexico will create an emerging counterbalance to the United States south of its border. But any initiative for strengthening economic ties must come from the United States itself. It first must address its immigration policy and then, similar to the economic and political assistance it provided to the European Union, offer support for an economic union in Central and South America. The result could be an integrated market and trading bloc of 800 million people, with tremendous natural resources, enormous opportunities for development and sustainable growth, and deep ties to Africa, Asia, and Europe.

That market would still have the protection of two wide oceans, and even in a networked world, there are benefits in being disconnected. Those oceans protect the United States against massive refugee flows, against other threats to security from civil and interstate wars, and, increasingly, from the effects of climate change. Researchers at Princeton University have found that rain over the Pacific Ocean washes out of the air substantial amounts of ozone and some other gases emitted in Asia before the air can ever get to the Americas. Most climate-change projections forecast rising waters overflowing the deltas of South and Southeast Asia, potentially threatening millions of lives in countries such as Bangladesh. Increasing desertification in northern Africa will force emigrants across the Mediterranean and into Europe; a similar process in northern China could push even greater numbers into Russia. Conflict is likely to follow these displaced peoples. New democracies, such as Indonesia, and one-party states, such as China and Vietnam, will find themselves economically and politically vulnerable. Of course, the Americas will not be fully protected from rising oceans, flooding, desertification, or the other nasty consequences of climate change. Still, both geography and demography—and the absence of hundreds of millions of people on the move—will insulate the New World from the afflictions of the Old.

A Culture of Creation

A nation's economic fate depends on its being able to maintain and nurture innovation. This past year, all the U.S. presidential candidates made repeated calls for a renewal of the conditions that had long made the United States the world leader in innovative technology. In the twenty-first century, corporations, civic organizations, and government agencies will increasingly operate by collecting the best ideas from around the globe. In such an environment, it is critical not only to stimulate domestic innovation but also to foster networks that can produce collaborative innovations across the globe.

To this end, the United States needs to improve education and increase government investment in science and technology. But the most important U.S. edge in innovation is cultural. Fundamental flaws in China's political and economic systems will make it very difficult for China to move from being the world's factory to being the world's designer. The Chinese government is determined to develop innovation as if it were developing a fancy variety of soybeans, relying on industrial parks that mix equal parts technology, education, research, and recreation in self-described "talent highlands." The results can be extraordinary, as I saw last year at the Shanghai Zizhu Science-Based Industrial Park. The park, built in just five years, has enormous university campuses, research headquarters for over 20 Asian and Western firms, and a residential complex. The aim is to inspire innovation through a balance of nature, science, and ecology, or, as its planners suggest, to create the "building blocks" for a future Chinese society, just like the building blocks for a new generation of skyscrapers.

The park is awe-inspiring. "In China," our guide told us, "anything is possible." Looking at the pace, scale, and quality of the construction, it was quite possible to believe it. In the end, however, the Zizhu industrial park struck me as being similar to an aquacultural facility for manufacturing cultured pearls. But as all pearl lovers know, the richest innovations are created through unexpected and irregular irritations, not tightly controlled conditions. In 2003, the University of California alone generated more patents than either China or India. That same year, IBM generated five times as many patents as both countries combined. The problem is certainly not a lack of creativity on the part of Chinese or Indians; Silicon Valley is full of entrepreneurs from both groups. The issue is the surrounding culture, or what the urban studies theorist Richard Florida calls an "innovation ecosystem."

At the same time that China is seeking to maintain political tranquility, it depends on continued growth powered by innovation, which requires conflict—not violent conflict but positive, or constructive, conflict, the kind of conflict that produces nonzero-sum solutions. This is the kind of conflict found on American playing fields, in American courtrooms, and in the American political system. It is the conflict of structured competition, in which losers have a chance to win another day and everyone has a stake in continually improving the game. It is also the conflict of creative destruction, the process of destroying old business models to make way for new ones.

Most important, a culture of constructive conflict rewards challenging authority in every domain. Perhaps the best example is Google, a company in which hierarchy is almost nonexistent. Individuals are encouraged to go their own way, come up with their own ideas, and counter orthodoxies at every turn. In the United States, educational institutions have long emphasized critical thinking in ways that China and other countries are now trying to emulate. But a culture of innovation requires more than the ability to critique. It requires saying what you think, rather than what you believe your boss wants to hear, something many

Western managers struggle fruitlessly to encourage in China. A culture that requires a constant willingness to reimagine the world is not one that the Chinese Communist Party is likely to embrace. Indeed, a culture of innovation requires the encouragement of conflict within a larger culture of transparency and trust, placing a premium on cross-cultural competence. It is a culture for which Americans are ideally suited by both temperament and history.

The World of Wikis

Starting with Alexis de Tocqueville, nearly every observer of American culture has noted that Americans are inveterate joiners, volunteers, and debaters. Today, however, instead of sewing circles, debating societies, and charity bake sales, Americans have MySpace, blogs, and the Clinton Global Initiative. These qualities are evident in a growing number of collaborative enterprises, both online and off. In the world of wikis, perhaps best exemplified by Wikipedia, ideas are challenged, edited, and challenged again. The final product is the result of a different and gentler kind of adversarial process than that found in the U.S. legal system. But the premise is the same: multiple minds clashing and correcting one another in pursuit of the truth. The work of one contributor is open and available for others to use. Participants in this process are trusted to not take advantage of that openness but instead add their own contributions.

In a world that favors decentralization and positive conflict, the United States has an edge. Although trust and transparency are not unique to the United States, it is still one of the most open societies in the world. The Internet world, the wiki world, and the networked world all began in the United States and radiated outward. The characteristics of those worlds are the keys to innovation and problem solving in the twenty-first century.

In his book *Nonzero: The Logic of Human Destiny,* Robert Wright, a senior fellow at the New America Foundation, writes of human history as a steady process of increased exposure to complexity and the resulting ability to turn zero-sum problems into non-zero-sum solutions. The barbarian invasions that swept across Asia and Europe, for instance, were disastrous for many individual societies. Yet by adding new ideas and practices to the sum of human knowledge, the invaders spurred the process of innovation and problem solving. In other words, they brought progress. Today, the invaders are online rather than on horseback, and interaction is considerably more voluntary. The benefits will flow to those individuals and states that are most comfortable reaching across cultures. It will become increasingly necessary to appreciate and absorb contributions in any language and from any context.

Here, however, the conventional wisdom depicts Americans as woefully ignorant of foreign geography, languages, and cultures. Many Americans may still fit this description. But many others—immigrants and their children especially—negotiate cultural differences every day in their schools, in their workplaces, and on the street. From Boston to Los Angeles, recently immigrated Africans, Arabs, East Asians, Latinos, South Asians, and Southeast Asians all rub shoulders with members of more established communities, both black and white. At the elite level, the top graduate schools in the United States offer a similar education in multicultural competence; many of the cross-cultural couples

who are changing the face of global cities met at places such as Harvard and Stanford. Obama's parents may have been ahead of their time, but today far more young Americans than ever before are following their example. They are truly, as Zogby calls them, "the First Globals."

How to Get There from Here

At the moment, the United States' edge in this new world is more potential than actual. The country will face a vast amount of work in digging itself out of the many holes it has gotten itself into, both at home and abroad. In the process, the United States must adopt five policies and postures that will seize on its edge and sharpen it.

First, the United States must adopt comprehensive immigration reform that will make it easier for immigrants and guest workers to move across borders, regularize the status of the millions of illegal immigrants currently in the United States, and increase the number of visas for the world's most talented individuals. Part of changing U.S. attitudes toward immigration must include a recognition that because of their ties to their home countries, immigrants are potential engines of economic growth. New economic policies could offer subsidies or tax incentives to immigrants who create businesses based on connections they have cultivated to markets and talent in their home countries. Instead of a one-way, outgoing flow of remittances, the United States needs a two-way flow of goods, services, and people.

Second, as part of overhauling its educational system, the United States must come to see overseas study as an essential asset for all Americans. Indeed, organizations such as the Brown-Bell Foundation promote opportunities to study abroad for students at historically black colleges and universities, where such programs have traditionally been lacking. Just as important, the United States must see the children of immigrants who grow up learning Arabic, Hindi, Mandarin, Spanish, and other foreign languages as huge assets. Government programs and private initiatives should encourage them to study abroad in the countries of their parents or grandparents and, assuming they keep their U.S. passports, to gain dual citizenship.

A networked world requires a genuinely networked society, which means fostering economic and social equality. The United States has never been as egalitarian as it imagines itself to be, but this divide has worsened in the past decade, as the rich have become the superrich. Between the late 1950s and 2005, the income share of the wealthiest one percent of the U.S. population more than doubled. Even the Democratic Party is not immune: on the night that Obama accepted the nomination to be the Democratic presidential candidate, at Invesco Field in Denver, Colorado, his campaign blocked off an entire section of the stadium for big donors, stopping everyone else at the door. For a time, a culture in which money could buy status was a radically democratic and egalitarian idea. Instead of the European class system, in which breeding always trumped money, Americans could rely on education and employment for self-advancement. But this same culture becomes radically inegalitarian if only a relatively few have the chance to prosper financially. As the political scientist Larry Bartels argues, rising economic inequality is a political choice: Republican presidents have generally allowed inequality to expand, whereas Democratic presidents have not. If so, then the United States can choose to decrease inequality by making its society more horizontal, more democratic, and more integrated by class and race—and this is the third reform it should adopt. Doing so would add more potential circuits to the network.

Fourth, in foreign policy, the United States should put more effort toward engaging Latin America—not at the expense of its ties with Asia but in addition to the strong history of transpacific relations. Brazil, for example, defines its foreign policy in terms of concentric circles. It starts with Mercosur, the South American trading bloc, then continues to Latin America, the Americas, and then the rest of the world. Similarly, the United States should think in terms of the North American Free Trade Agreement and the Americas before turning to the rest of the world. The potential for growth and development in the Americas is enormous. Population links between the United States and Latin America are strong and growing stronger. Spanish is now taught in virtually every American public school from the early grades. Strengthening ties with Latin America also means cultivating links across the South Atlantic to Mediterranean countries such as Spain and Portugal, and also to France and Italy. Lastly, African blood runs in the veins of many North, Central, and South Americans. This fact is the legacy of a ghastly institution, but it means that many Americans have an African heritage that can allow them to reconnect with Africa today.

More generally, the United States must learn to see both itself and the world differently. If power is derived from connectivity, then the focus of leadership should be on making connections to solve shared problems. This approach is not only a different leadership style than that which has prevailed in the United States in recent years but also a fundamentally different concept of leadership. In contrast to the way it is in a hierarchy, in this concept of leadership a single leader cannot be directly in charge of everyone else. Different countries can mobilize diverse coalitions for specific purposes. Regional powers, for example, can address crises in their particular parts of the world: consider Australia's role in promoting stability in East Timor, ASEAN's ability to convince the Myanmar government to accept foreign aid after Cyclone Nargis, or Turkey's work in pushing for talks between Syria and Israel. The range and complexity of foreign policy challenges—and the speed with which a crisis can escalate—mean that knowing the right people to call and the right levers to pull in any corner of the world must be a key element of U.S. diplomacy.

Finally, the United States must recognize the necessity of orchestrating networks of public, private, and civic actors to address global problems. The era of government formulating and executing policy entirely on its own is over, even with a revitalized U.S. government that has a greater social and economic mandate. Outsourcing government functions to private and civic contractors is not the answer, however; government officials must instead learn to orchestrate networks of these actors and guide them toward collaborative solutions.

Sharpening the Edge

In this century, global power will increasingly be defined by connections—who is connected to whom and for what purposes. Of course, the world will still contain conflict. Networks can be as malign and deadly as they can be productive and beneficial. In addition, the gap between those who are connected to global networks and those who are excluded from them will sharply multiply existing inequities.

But on the whole, the positive effects of networks will greatly outweigh the negative. Imagine, for example, a U.S. economy powered by green technology and green infrastructure. Communities of American immigrants from Africa, Asia, Europe, Latin America, and the Middle East will share this new generation of products and services with villages and cities in their home countries. Innovation will flow in both directions. In the United States, universities will be able to offer courses in truly global classrooms, relying on their international students and faculty to connect with educational institutions abroad through travel, the Internet, and videoconferencing. Artists of all kinds will sit at the intersection of culture, learning, and creative energy. U.S. diplomats and other U.S. government officials will receive instant updates on events occurring around the world. They will be connected to their counterparts abroad, able to quickly coordinate preventive and problem-solving actions with a range of private and civic actors. The global landscape will resemble that of the Obama campaign, in which a vast network brought in millions of dollars in donations, motivated millions of volunteers, and mobilized millions of voters.

In a networked world, the United States has the potential to be the most connected country; it will also be connected to other power centers that are themselves widely connected. If it pursues the right policies, the United States has the capacity and the cultural capital to reinvent itself. It need not see itself as locked in a global struggle with other great powers; rather, it should view itself as a central player in an integrated world. In the twenty-first century, the United States' exceptional capacity for connection, rather than splendid isolation or hegemonic domination, will renew its power and restore its global purpose.

ANNE-MARIE SLAUGHTER is Dean of the Woodrow Wilson School of Public and International Affairs and Bert G. Kerstetter '66 University Professor of Politics and International Affairs at Princeton University.

The China-U.S. Relationship Goes Global

If the two sides can engage effectively . . . , Sino-U.S. relations will enter a new stage in which ties will become deeper, stronger, more stable, and more important for the international system than ever before.

KENNETH LIEBERTHAL

What should be expected in U.S.-Sino relations under the administration of President Barack Obama? During the tenure of President George W. Bush, relations developed relatively smoothly. When Bush left office the relationship could reasonably be described as mature, wide-ranging, constructive, and candid. Each of these dimensions of the relationship reflected protracted effort on both sides.

"Mature" conveys that the leaderships of the two countries had gotten to know each other well; had some understanding of each other's goals, operating styles, and major concerns; and recognized the value of maintaining effective ties even when significant problems arose. None of this was true 30 years ago, in the early days after normalization of U.S.-Sino relations. Today, major problems can arise in one part of the relationship without jeopardizing the two sides' capacity to manage other issues of mutual concern.

"Wide-ranging" reflects the reality that the two governments now deal with each other regularly across an extraordinary array of issues, including not only traditional matters of diplomacy, economics, or security, but also such concerns as public health, the environment, science and technology, and education. Accordingly, a broad array of regular meetings occurs between the two governments as a matter of course. For most ministries in each government, it would be unusual for a week to go by without direct contact with counterparts in the other country.

"Constructive" indicates that both countries value development of the relationship and therefore look for ways to reduce tensions, manage differences, and solve problems. Neither side intentionally seeks to undermine U.S.-Sino ties. On many issues, of course, differences between China and the United States are significant. Such will always be the case in relations among major powers. But in recent years each side has sought to make the relationship work more effectively.

"Candid" highlights that each side has learned how to convey its serious concerns in top-level meetings. Both sides, for example, can make clear their views on human rights. Interest in human rights will not disappear from U.S. foreign policy, and China will express its own views on this topic. Without a capacity to raise and discuss serious and sensitive issues such as this, the U.S.-China relationship inevitably would run into trouble.

The advance of global issues to a prominent role in bilateral affairs presents both opportunities and perils.

Mutually Assured Distrust

If, by themselves, the four adjectives cited above fully defined U.S.-Sino relations, prospects for the relationship's future would be very bright. But the reality is more complex than this, for two reasons. First, the U.S.-China agenda going forward will include important, relatively new issues that will increasingly shape the overall relationship. The most prominent among these today are the worldwide economic downturn and climate change. Indeed, the advance of *global* issues to a prominent role in bilateral affairs marks a significant change in the U.S.-China relationship and presents both opportunities and perils.

Second, the single biggest failure of 30 years of diplomatic ties between Washington and Beijing is that neither side, even today, trusts the long-term intentions of the other toward itself. Close observers of U.S.-China relations constantly hear evidence of this lack of trust as they listen to concerns voiced in each capital.

In Beijing, many believe that the United States is simply too zero-sum in its thinking and too wedded to maintaining its position of global hegemony ever to allow China to realize its aspirations of being wealthy and strong. This belief causes many Chinese rather readily to believe that various American actions conceal a nefarious plot to limit and complicate China's rise.

Some in China believe that the current global recession was designed by Americans to undermine China's economy.

Some in China believe, for example, that the current global recession not only started in America but was designed by Americans to undermine China's economy. Some see U.S. concerns about climate change, and U.S. pressure on China to make burdensome commitments to reduce carbon emissions, as an American scheme to slow China's economic development. To an American ear such allegations seem outrageous, but that does not make them any less credible to Chinese who distrust America's long-term intentions toward the People's Republic.

Comparable distrust of China's long-term intentions exists on the American side. Many Americans with significant influence on policy making believe that, as China becomes wealthy and strong, Beijing will seek to marginalize the United States in Asia. Because Asia is such a dynamic and important region, an attempt to marginalize America there would directly threaten key U.S. interests. Many Americans are also deeply troubled by China's annual double-digit military budget increases and the growing capabilities the Chinese military is acquiring.

This distrust on both sides is deeply rooted. Moreover, because the distrust concerns long-term (that is, 10-to-20–year) *intentions* rather than immediate goals and policies, it is very difficult to change. And it has serious consequences. It produces behavior—primarily in terms of military planning and development—that is geared toward protecting national interests if things go wrong. Each side has some understanding of the other side's long-term military investments, and each takes this information as confirmation that its distrust is warranted. This situation could, of course, amount to a self-fulfilling prophecy that over time increases the chances of U.S.-Sino relations shifting from constructive to antagonistic, at potentially great cost to both sides.

As both Washington and Beijing look to the future, therefore, they should specifically address attention to a key question: How can each side *credibly* signal that its preferred outcome over the course of the coming decades is that the United States and China maintain a normal big-power relationship, one in which the two sides cooperate when they can and try to manage and mitigate differences when their interests set them apart? This is not an easy task—conspiracy theorists in each country will always be able to develop seemingly plausible stories to "explain" how superficially good intentions in reality mask nefarious goals. But the task is critical.

Flash Points

The United States and China face a large, difficult, and significant agenda of ongoing issues. Some of these will pose tough challenges that will test the maturity of the Sino-U.S. relationship in the period ahead. North Korea's nuclear program is one important example. China took the lead in the six-party talks meant to address the issue and has played a skillful role in keeping this process going in the face of various obstacles. But the issue remains far from resolved. And now it appears that North Korea may be experiencing internal political difficulties that diminish the chances of Pyongyang's agreeing to and then implementing compromises leading to the full termination of its nuclear program. Indeed, the provocative behavior displayed by North Korea during the spring of 2009 signaled major new difficulties in keeping the nuclear talks moving forward.

The cross-strait issue, of course, also remains unresolved. The past year has witnessed serious progress toward creating a more stable, win-win situation across the Taiwan Strait. Even so, much remains to be done to relieve the concerns of both sides. In particular, both sides have addressed the military and security dimensions of the cross-strait situation in principle, but so far there has been no significant concrete progress. The capabilities of the People's Liberation Army (PLA) continue to increase with respect to Taiwan, and the United States remains committed to providing Taiwan with sufficient military capability to address the potential military threat it faces. None of the sides—Beijing, Taipei, or Washington—wants to see military force ever used across the strait, but the status quo inevitably raises periodic tensions—such as when America authorizes additional arms sales to Taiwan.

Military-to-military relations between U.S. forces and the PLA have developed to some extent but still remain far below the level necessary to develop mutual understanding and trust. The PLA's ongoing modernization and expansion of its capabilities predictably raise issues for the U.S. military, just as ongoing U.S. weapons systems development, and changes in deployments in Asia, attract serious attention in the PLA. It is thus becoming more important for the two militaries to increase the frequency, depth, and scope of their contacts and to address issues such as arms control and mutually understood operational rules, especially as the two countries' navies increasingly work in the same spaces.

The multilateral architecture in the Asia-Pacific region is undergoing rapid development and change. New multilateral forums and combinations of countries gathering for various types of consultations seem to proliferate like bamboo shoots after a spring rain. It is important for the United States and China to welcome each other into any wide-ranging Asian multilateral forum in which either one participates. This would increase mutual trust and reduce the chances of polarization in the region, but it has not always happened to date (witness the East Asia Summit and the Shanghai Cooperation Organization).

A voluminous literature treats each of the above issues, and most articles on Sino-U.S. relations deal with one or more of them. Notably, all are bilateral concerns or problems that concern China's periphery. These are the types of issues that have traditionally shaped U.S.-China relations. In the past, the United States and China have sometimes taken up more general issues or issues that concerned places farther from China's shores—such as nonproliferation and developments in the greater Middle East—but these until now have remained at the margins of the U.S.-China relationship. Given China's rapidly growing power and global engagement, some of these issues will now become more significant in Sino-U.S. relations.

For example, opportunities now exist for China and the United States to engage much more fully on problems across the Middle East—from Pakistan and Afghanistan, to Iran, to the Arab-Israeli question, to energy security in general. These challenges are all interrelated; America's approaches to this vast region are changing; and China's own interests in the area have grown to the point that systematic Sino-U.S. engagement is warranted.

But even more important, the most critical *global* issues are for the first time moving to a central place in the U.S.-China relationship. The prominence on the agenda of both the global economic downturn and the issues of clean energy and climate change is relatively new: The economic crisis only developed in the final months of the Bush administration, while the climate change issue stayed at the margins of U.S.-China relations until President Bush left office.

If the two sides can engage effectively on these issues, Sino-U.S. relations will enter a new stage in which ties will become deeper, stronger, more stable, and more important for the international system than ever before. The resulting cooperation could, in turn, reduce the mutual distrust about each country's long-term intentions.

The Dollar Trap

The global economic difficulties now at the center of international attention began with a financial crisis brought on by failures in regulation and management in the U.S. financial services system. Other countries and institutions had fully participated in that system to reap its benefits, and as a consequence when problems developed the contagion proved extremely rapid and widespread.

The resulting economic problems directly involve the United States and China on both bilateral and multilateral levels. The two countries' economies are highly interdependent in ways that go far beyond the bilateral trade relationship. China holds the vast majority of its foreign currency reserves in U.S. dollars, primarily in various debt instruments in the United States. U.S. economic recovery plans have included issuing a large amount of new sovereign debt, and it is important to the United States that China continue to purchase a portion of these new debt obligations. Beijing, in turn, views U.S. economic recovery as critical to China's own prospects for returning quickly to the growth rates to which it has grown accustomed.

The United States needs to consult closely and work cooperatively with China to address both the bilateral issues that are related to economic recovery and also multilateral issues concerning a restructuring of the global financial system's regulatory framework and substance. It is too early to ascertain how effective this effort at consultation and cooperation will be. This is in part because it is still unclear exactly how deep and long-lasting the global downturn will prove to be.

It is not too early, though, to highlight some of the difficult issues and contradictions with which the United States and China have to wrestle. President Obama adopted bold fiscal and regulatory measures to get ahead of the crisis and limit its scope and severity. But this required running a high budget deficit (exactly how high will depend on the pace of economic recovery). The president's economic calculations include an assumption that China will continue to purchase U.S. debt instruments at a significant level. Otherwise, the cost of U.S. borrowing—and therefore the size of the U.S. deficit—will grow significantly larger.

But China is nervous about how much it has already invested in U.S. debt instruments, and it fears that the U.S. government will resort to printing dollars as one way to reduce its real debt burden. A mildly cheaper dollar could be in China's interests because it would make Chinese exports somewhat more competitive, as long as China kept the value of the renminbi (RMB) roughly fixed in relation to the dollar. But a major decline in the value of the greenback would cost China many billions of dollars in the value of its foreign exchange holdings. Other countries, moreover, would object strongly to the RMB's following the dollar all the way down, thus making it difficult for China to respond to major dollar depreciation by allowing its own currency to depreciate as well. China thus wants the United States to spend enough to restore economic growth but also to manage its expenditures wisely so as to maintain the basic value of the dollar—a difficult balancing act.

Many Chinese are advising that China is already too heavily invested in dollar assets and should stop buying U.S. debt. (Indeed, some believe China should start selling off U.S. debt and move its funds into RMB or other currencies.) But China is caught in what might be called a "dollar trap." It holds so many dollars that if it tries to sell enough of them to make a serious impact on its exposure, the sale itself will weaken the dollar and increase the value of the currencies China is purchasing instead. China in that case would lose a great deal of money simply by trying to reduce its dollar exposure. If, on the other hand, China holds onto its dollars, then U.S. treasuries provide a source of debt that is deep, flexible, and secure (except for the exchange rate risk)—a very desirable set of qualities in a time of uncertainty.

Nothing will completely eliminate the contradictions and tensions in this set of monetary issues. But at a minimum, the United States and China should maintain consultations that are more in depth, frequent, and transparent than they have ever been before. This could help ensure that each side is sensitive to the requirements of the other, understands the other's strategy and concerns, and is not surprised by developments as they occur. All of this should contribute to increasing confidence and stability.

A Consuming Problem

The United States and China also need to consult closely over macroeconomic adjustments. Fundamentally, China realizes that it needs to increase personal consumption as a component of gross domestic product. Currently, China's level of personal consumption as a percentage of GDP is close to the lowest in the world. Beijing has recognized the need to change this situation for several years, but during this time personal consumption has actually declined as a percentage of GDP, despite government efforts. Now that exports have dropped off significantly, the need to increase domestic consumption demand has proportionately become even more pressing.

In terms of stimulating demand in the short run, the largest single item in the $586 billion stimulus package that China's government announced in November 2008 is infrastructure development. This spending will increase domestic demand but also production capacity, and puts China at risk of massive overcapacity if exports do not revive substantially in the next two years and domestic demand otherwise remains low. At that point, additional infrastructure investment as a way to keep stimulating the economy would be far more difficult to sustain.

The United States has the opposite problem. It permitted personal consumption to rise to such a level that the country for the past several years had no net personal savings. This high consumption model became possible because of a mistaken presumption that housing prices would continue to rise, which led banks to extend excessive credit to homeowners based on the (inflated) imputed value of their houses. The United States now needs to transition to a positive rate of personal savings—and the transition seems to be occurring extraordinarily rapidly. In the months since the initial acceleration of the economic crisis, Americans have suddenly remembered their traditional ethic of thrift, and the personal savings rate has leaped to about 5 percent.

The problem is that high American personal consumption and high Chinese personal savings are directly linked, each enabling the other. Effectively, the United States has borrowed China's savings to finance personal consumption. At the same time, China has accumulated the money to maintain high savings and make loans to the United States by producing goods that Americans buy with their consumer dollars. The complexities, moreover, do not end there.

While the United States wants to increase personal savings over the long run, it wants to foster personal consumption now in order to get out of a short-term economic crisis. And while China wants to increase personal consumption for the sake of domestic demand, it must also build institutions and capabilities to enhance its social safety net. Doing the latter involves long-term investments that do not produce the short-term stimulative effects that new infrastructure investments provide. But without social safety net enhancements, most Chinese will still want to save for unexpected expenses or bad times, and personal consumption is unlikely to rise significantly.

The necessary adjustments are thus truly society-wide in each country. At least three to five years will be required to make these changes and put them on a sustainable footing. During this time, it makes enormous sense for the United States and China to consult closely on their macroeconomic adjustment policies and plans, as each side can reduce its own problems by being more sensitive to developments in the other country. This is one of the major issues that is a focus of the new Strategic and Economic Dialogue, to which President Obama appointed Secretary of State Hillary Clinton and Treasury Secretary Timothy Geithner as special representatives.

Trade and Trouble

Another potentially serious matter is the issue of Chinese exports of goods and capital. China is now trying to increase exports in order to bolster employment. To do so, it is enhancing various forms of assistance to exporters. At a time when the U.S. unemployment rate has approached double digits, such Chinese policies could engender a very strong and negative political response from America—and this is especially true if China also increases nontariff barriers to U.S. imports.

Chinese firms at the same time may seek to purchase under-valued real manufacturing assets in the United States. If they do this, they need to be sensitive to the importance of presenting their efforts to Americans as high-quality deals—deals that seek to grow the U.S. firms, create jobs, and produce win-win situations. If Chinese merger and acquisition efforts instead appear to be "vulture" investing—that is, using takeovers to acquire brands and technology, strip assets, and undermine jobs—then such investing could become a source of major U.S.-China tensions.

Meanwhile, if America's long-term personal saving rate is at 5 to 8 percent, sufficient demand for U.S. goods and services can be created only if exports increase. But China's recovery and growth strategies depend on a revival of its own exports. The potential for trade frictions is obvious.

Multilaterally, the United States and China are critical participants in reshaping the global financial regulatory system. As recently as late 2008, it seemed unclear whether China would play a proactive role in suggesting new ideas and promoting new policies. But in the run-up to the Group of 20 meeting in April 2009, when Beijing began to take initiative on the issue of a global super-sovereign reserve currency, it became apparent that China might play a more active role in the global talks than previously expected.

The United States will, as always, be very active in putting forward ideas and working to shape revisions to the global financial system's architecture and rules. And U.S. and Chinese interests will not be identical. China wants over the long term to reduce the role of the U.S. dollar as the global reserve currency, while the United States has little interest in seeing that occur. Given the array of issues in international finance and financial regulation that China and the United States face, and given the complex connections among many of these issues, close Sino-U.S. consultation is a necessary part of reaching global consensus on how to move forward.

The issues revolving around financial uncertainties and the global recession are of core national importance to each country. Tremendous room for cooperation exists—as does tremendous room for disagreement and misunderstanding. If the latter becomes the dominant story, the chances of mutually destructive protectionism will rise, and it will be harder for everyone to emerge from the current downturn. Close consultation could lift U.S.-China relations to a new level both bilaterally and in terms of global impact. But failure to consult closely, and to find ways to reduce problems, could produce profoundly negative effects on mutual trust, expectations, and outcomes.

The Hot Topic

Alongside the global economic situation, climate change now ranks as an equally significant issue on the bilateral agenda. Climate change played a relatively minor role in U.S.-China relations until the end of the Bush administration. President Bush himself did not believe the government should play a substantial role in addressing the climate change threat. His treasury secretary, Henry Paulson, by contrast, believed deeply that global warming posed a threat to future civilization, and he sought to develop cooperation with China to address the issue. In mid-2008 the United States and China signed a 10-year framework agreement on the environment and clean energy. This pact provides one basis for future cooperation, but relatively little was accomplished under it before Bush left office.

The centrality of climate change in Sino-U.S. relations is growing rapidly for four reasons. First, President Obama's view of the issue is the opposite of President Bush's. For Obama, shifting to a low-carbon economy—both domestically and globally—must be one of America's most important goals, and the government has a serious role to play in this project. Indeed, the development of clean energy ranks with resolving the economic crisis and addressing domestic health care and education as his highest priorities.

Second, the Chinese government has greatly increased its own attention to climate change in the past two years. As reflected in the government's white paper on the issue in October 2008, China now views itself as one of the countries most vulnerable to the ravages of climate change, and this requires major efforts in China at both adaptation and mitigation.

Third, the scientific community's understanding of the speed, scope, and consequences of climate change is improving rapidly. Almost every new major scientific study of the phenomenon makes clear that previous studies underestimated the degree of global warming's danger and overestimated the amount of time available to take strong remedial action.

Fourth, a meeting is scheduled for Copenhagen in December 2009 to adopt a new climate framework agreement as a successor to the Kyoto Protocol. As a result, the international community is paying enormous attention to the issue this year, and everyone is looking particularly at the American and Chinese postures. Yet, in both the United States and China, taking strong domestic measures to reduce carbon emissions is very difficult because it affects powerful interests.

The way the United States and China handle the issue of clean energy within their own borders affects, moreover, the ability of the other country's leadership to adopt effective measures. China's leaders find it harder to take rigorous measures when the United States, a richer and more technologically advanced country that is also a major carbon emitter, does not itself take a leadership role. Similarly, China's record on carbon emissions plays into the domestic debate in the United States. Obama wants the Congress to adopt legislation that effectively puts a cap on overall carbon emissions and imposes a price on carbon. But the opponents of such "cap-and-trade" legislation point to China and argue that making carbon emissions costly in the United States will simply provide Chinese enterprises (and foreign investors in China) with a competitive advantage because China is not imposing a comparable cost on its carbon emissions. The result, they argue, would simply be an increase in American unemployment and no reduction in global emissions.

Each side, therefore, wants the other to do more—partly in order to create a better environment for advancing its own efforts

to restrain carbon emissions. This presents a natural environment in which to foster cooperation, but it also presents another arena in which failure to achieve cooperation might increase mutual suspicion and tension.

After You, Please

The Obama administration is anxious to avoid repeating Bill Clinton's experience with the Kyoto Protocol—the Clinton administration signed the document but was unable to win enough domestic support to implement it. Thus the administration hopes, before Copenhagen, to achieve real progress on domestic actions, laws, and regulations in order to instill international confidence that the United States can follow through on what it agrees to do. If Obama can honestly say to the U.S. Congress that China is very concerned about the issue of climate change; is taking strong measures to deal with it; and is willing to work with the United States and others to advance the goal of reducing emissions of greenhouse gases—the president's chances of legislative success increase considerably.

In the past, U.S. and Chinese officials, technical specialists, firms, and nongovernmental organizations have interacted quite extensively on issues related to global warming. But their interactions have lacked the momentum, direction, and support that would result from an explicit agreement between the two countries' presidents and governments to form a clean-energy partnership to promote better outcomes on carbon emissions. The United States and China in fact can identify many aspects of the climate change issue in which cooperation would provide mutual benefits. An overall partnership agreement would greatly enhance prospects for capitalizing on this.

The issue of clean energy goes to the heart of both countries' economies, and it is inherently an issue that will remain on the agenda for many decades to come. Large-scale cooperation around this issue could, therefore, greatly enhance the range of serious working relationships between the two societies, and the long-term nature of the cooperation could instill greater trust in each other's long-term intentions.

When it comes to the problem of carbon emissions, of course, serious disagreements exist over issues of principle. These center (from the Chinese perspective) on cumulative historical emissions, per capita emissions, and the two countries' stages of development—or (from the U.S. perspective) on current emissions and future trajectories, total national emissions, and legacy structures and styles of life. These differences reflect the perspectives of developing and industrialized countries.

Sea level rise will submerge Los Angeles at the same time it submerges Shanghai.

The reality, though, is that sea level rise will submerge Los Angeles at the same time it submerges Shanghai, and cooperation cannot wait until all participants agree on the "correct" perspective. China and the developing countries are raising issues that are accurate and have merit—and the same is true of the issues raised by industrialized countries. No progress is likely to be made on cooperation if each side makes the other side's capitulation on these issues a condition for moving forward.

Therefore each side, while reserving differences, needs to seek common ground, acknowledge that the perspective of the other side reflects serious realities, and achieve pragmatic cooperation on an issue that threatens both sides and will not wait. In this way U.S.-Sino cooperation on this vital global issue—involving the world's most important developed country and the world's most important developing country—could help bridge the divide between industrialized and developing nations in global negotiations over how to respond to the threat of climate change.

Two Roads

The climate change challenge highlights both the global nature of the key issues that are moving to the center of Sino-U.S. relations and the very high stakes in how these issues are handled. Finding a way to enhance serious consultation and cooperation would strengthen U.S.-China relations and move the relationship to a new stage. Cooperation on this issue would inherently be so long-term and so central to each society, moreover, that it could contribute significantly to reducing the distrust that each side currently harbors concerning the willingness of the other to maintain a cooperative relationship over the long run.

Both the United States and China want a cooperative, productive relationship, and the two countries already have extensive experience in managing the ongoing issues that have shaped their relationship to date. But the critical global issues now moving to the center of Sino-U.S. relations will significantly affect ties going forward.

How America and China deal with each other regarding these new global challenges will to a significant extent determine the relationship's prospects over the long term. Will Beijing and Washington overcome their mutual distrust over long-term intentions and create the "positive, cooperative, comprehensive" twenty-first–century relationship touted by Presidents Obama and Hu Jintao at their April meeting in London? Or will Sino-U.S. relations instead enter very troubled territory? The long-term consequences of the introduction of global issues into the bilateral agenda may be very large.

KENNETH LIEBERTHAL, professor emeritus of political science and business administration at the University of Michigan, is a senior fellow at the Brookings Institution. He served as senior director for Asia in the Clinton administration's National Security Council.

India's Path to Greatness

After decades of dormancy, India has blossomed into one of Asia's two emerging powers and an important strategic partner of the United States. How—and whether—it navigates its rise could well determine the future of the whole region.

MARTIN WALKER

When the U.S. Air Force sent its proud F-15 fighter pilots against the Indian Air Force in the Cope India war games two years ago, it received a shock. The American pilots found themselves technologically outmatched by nimbler warplanes; tactically outsmarted by the Indian mix of high, low, and converging attack waves; and outfought by the Indians, whose highly trained pilots average more than 180 flying hours a year—roughly the same as their U.S. and Israeli counterparts and slightly more than those of NATO allies such as France and Germany. U.S. General Hal Homburg said that the results of the exercise, against Indian pilots flying Russian-built Sukhoi Su-30 and French Mirage 2000 fighters, were "a wake-up call." According to testimony in a House Appropriations Defense Subcommittee hearing, the U.S. F-15s were defeated more than 90 percent of the time in direct combat exercises against the Indians.

But beyond the evidence of India's military expertise and its possession of state-of-the-art fighter aircraft, the real significance of the Cope India war games is that they demonstrated the extent of the cooperation between the Indian and U.S. militaries. Their mountain troops now train together in the Himalayas and Alaska, and their special forces mount joint exercises in jungle and underwater warfare. Their aircraft carrier task forces have conducted exercises in the Indian Ocean, and joint antipiracy and antisubmarine drills are routine. Indian and U.S. forces are working together with an intimacy once reserved for the closest NATO allies. The goal—that the militaries of the two countries be able to operate in lockstep—would have been inconceivable in the Cold War era, when India, with its Soviet-supplied military, was seen as a virtual client of Moscow.

The foundation of this new relationship was laid before George W. Bush took office in the White House. In the spring of 1999, Bush, then governor of Texas, was briefed for the first time by the team of foreign-policy advisers that became known as the Vulcans, after the Roman god of fire and iron. Bush began with the frank admission that he knew little about foreign policy. The Vulcans, led by Condoleezza Rice—later to be his national security adviser and then secretary of state—delivered a broad-brash survey of the world, its problems, and its prospects, and recommended muscular American leadership in cool-headed pursuit of American interests. When the group finished, Bush had one question: What about India? Another Vulcan team member who was present, future ambassador to India Robert Blackwill, recalled asking Bush why he was so interested in India: "He immediately responded, 'A billion people in a functioning democracy. Isn't that something? Isn't that something?'"

Bush's curiosity had been stirred by a number of Indian supporters living and prospering in Texas, including some businessmen who helped build the state's high-tech corridor, dubbed Silicon Canyon. One of those businessmen was Durga Agrawal, born in Lakhanpur, a central Indian village without water or electricity, who had earned a master's degree at the University of Houston and stayed on to found a highly successful company called Piping Technology & Products and to raise more than $100,000 for the Bush presidential campaign in the local Indian community. After Bush became president, Agrawal was invited to the White House as a guest at the banquet for visiting Indian prime minister Manmohan Singh, where Bush introduced him as "my good friend from Texas."

Bush's question to his Vulcans prompted Rice to include a highly significant paragraph in her January 2000 *Foreign Affairs* essay "Promoting the National Interest," which was widely studied as the blueprint for a Bush administration foreign policy. She contended that China should be regarded as "a strategic competitor, not the 'strategic partner' the Clinton administration once called it," and suggested that America should redirect its focus. The United States "should pay closer attention to India's role in the regional balance. There is a strong tendency conceptually to connect India with Pakistan and to think only of Kashmir or the nuclear competition between the two states. But India is an element in China's calculation, and it should be in America's, too. India is not a great power yet, but it has the potential to emerge as one."

The intervening September 11 terrorist attacks and the Iraq war perhaps explain why it took five years for the Bush administration to act formally on that calculus. But on a March 2005 visit to India, Rice told Prime Minister Singh that part of the United States' foreign policy was to "help India become a major world power in the 21st century" At a later briefing, U.S. ambassador to India David Mulford described the vision behind a broader strategic relationship with India that would foster cooperation on a number of fronts. "The U.S.-India relationship is based on our shared common values. We are multiethnic democracies committed to the rule of law and freedom of speech and religion" Mulford said, adding that "there is no fundamental conflict or disagreement between the United States and India on any important regional or global issue."

A July 2005 visit by Prime Minister Singh to Washington, and President Bush's trip this year to New Delhi, along with detailed negotiations for nuclear, military, economic, and technological cooperation, have institutionalized that relationship. But, as former deputy secretary of state Strobe Talbott said of his own earlier path-breaking negotiations with foreign minister Jaswant Singh, "What took us so long?"

The short answer is the Cold War. American officials were uncomprehending and resentful of India's determination to stay neutral as a founder and pillar of the Non-Aligned Movement. By contrast, Pakistan swiftly decided to become an American ally and to buy American weapons. In response, India bought Soviet weapons. Pakistan, with whom India has fought three wars since the two countries simultaneously became independent from Britain in 1947, was also a close ally of China, so the Sino-Soviet split gave Soviet diplomats a strong incentive to cement their ties with India, deepening American suspicions.

India's explosion of a nuclear device (not a weapon, Indira Gandhi's government insisted) in 1974 exposed India to various restrictions in obtaining nuclear supplies under the Nuclear Non-Proliferation Treaty, and to some other mildly punitive but symbolic U.S. legislation. After India's full-scale nuclear weapons tests in 1998 (swiftly followed by rather less impressive tests by Pakistan), the Clinton administration sought engagement through the Talbott-Singh talks and Bill Clinton's own highly successful visit to India. When Pakistan-backed militants crossed Kashmir's mountains into the Indian-controlled area of Kargil, Clinton's intervention prevented the incursion from escalating into a full-scale war. The Bush administration had to launch another panicked round of diplomacy in early 2002, after an attack on the Indian parliament by Kashmiri terrorists with apparent Pakistani connections. At one critical point, then-U.S. deputy secretary of state Richard Armitage asked his staff, "Who thinks they're heading for nuclear war?" and everyone except for Armitage reportedly raised a hand. One senior British official who was involved recalls it as the nearest thing to nuclear war since the 1962 Cuban Missile Crisis.

Perhaps these brushes with disaster served as an awful warning to India. Or perhaps its successful market-style economic reforms in the 1990s, along with the palpable weakness of its old friends in Moscow, gave the country's leaders the spur and the self-confidence to rethink India's foreign policy. But there was a further goad: India's nervousness at the rapid growth of its Asian neighbor, China, by whom it had been humiliated in a brief border war in 1962. In May 1998, at the time of India's nuclear tests, Indian defense minister George Fernandes claimed that China was exploiting Pakistan, Burma, and Tibet in order to "encircle" India. "China has provided Pakistan with both missile as well as nuclear know-how," Fernandes said, adding, "China has its nuclear weapons stockpiled in Tibet fight along our borders." He concluded that China was India's most severe threat, and that while India had pledged "no first use" of nuclear weapons, the Indian nuclear arsenal would be targeted appropriately.

With Pakistan to the west and China to the north and east, India has long feared encirclement. Despite soothing diplomatic statements, China has sharpened these fears with an assertive new presence in the Indian Ocean, beginning in the late 1990s with an electronic listening post in Myanmar's Coco Islands. In 2001, China agreed to help Pakistan build a new port and naval base at Gwadar, close to the Iranian border and the Persian Gulf. China has also pitched in to build a road network from the new port to the Karakoram Highway, a feat of engineering that connects China and Pakistan through the Himalayas. The Gwadar naval base planned to India's west is matched by another to the east, where Chinese engineers are building a similar facility on Myanmar's Arakan coast, connected by a new road and rail link through Myanmar to China's Yunnan Province. China is also helping Cambodia build a rail link to the sea, and in Thailand, it is proposing to help fund a $20 billion canal across the Kra Isthmus, which would allow ships to bypass the Strait of Malacca. A recent Pentagon report described these new bases as China's "string of pearls" to secure the sea routes to the vital oil fields of the Persian Gulf.

The tension between India and China, both rising powers, is underscored by their rivalry for essential energy sources.

In a number of off-the-record conversations in New Delhi on the eve of Bush's visit earlier this year, including extremely rare meetings with senior officials of the secretive Research and Analysis Wing, Indian security and military figures stressed their profound concern at these developments. The degree of alarm is evident in India's recent flurry of arms purchases, including a $3.5 billion deal to buy six Scorpene "stealth" submarines from France along with the technology to build more. The Scorpene will augment India's existing submarine fleet of 16 vessels, mainly Soviet-built Kilo and Foxtrot attack submarines. India was the world's biggest customer for arms last year, and more deals for advanced aircraft are in the works, which seem likely to include U.S.-made F-16 and F-18 warplanes, even as India builds its own family of nuclear-capable Agni missiles, the latest version of which is designed to reach Shanghai. With almost 1.4 million troops, India's armed forces are already roughly the same size as those of the United States, and they are increasingly well trained and well armed. India is so far the only Asian country with an aircraft carrier, which can deploy British-built Sea Harrier fighters, vertical-takeoff jets like those used by the U.S. Marines.

The alarm over China's rise is plain in India's military and policy debates. An article last year by the Indian Defense Ministry's Bhartendu Kumar Singh in the journal *Peace and Conflict*, published by the New Delhi-based Institute of Peace and Conflict Studies, is typical. Singh speculated that China's military buildup might be explained in part by Taiwan, but that its long-term goal could be to ensure Chinese dominance of the Asia-Pacific region. While Singh doubted that this challenge would result in an all-out war between China and India, India was bound "to feel the effects of Chinese military confidence. . . . Is India prepared? It can wage and win a war against Pakistan under every circumstance, but it is not sure about holding out against China."

The irony and the danger is that China has similar reasons to feel encircled. The United States has established new military bases in Central Asia since 9/11, adding to existing outposts in Japan and South Korea, and it is expanding its existing facilities at Guam to include a base for submarines and long-range stealth bombers. Now Beijing nervously watches the warming strategic partnership between Washington and New Delhi. Moreover, China's construction of the "string of pearls" reflects its own deep concern about the security of its oil supplies. Its tankers must pass through the Indian Ocean, and China's new pipeline from the Kazakh oil and gas fields of Central Asia will lie within easy cruise missile or air strike distance of India.

The tension between these two rising powers is underscored by their rivalry for essential energy resources. "India, panicked over future oil supply, went after international oil assets competing directly with China," *India Daily* reported last year when Subir Raha, chairman of India's Oil and Natural Gas Corporation, announced that the company was buying a fifth of Iran's giant Yadavaran oil field and was in the market to buy assets of Yukos, the Russian energy giant. The Indian company had already invested nearly $2 billion to buy a share of the Sakhalin-1 field in Siberia, run by ExxonMobil. India, which imports more than two-thirds of its oil, has since signed a $40 billion deal with Iran to import liquefied natural gas and join in developing three Iranian oil fields.

Energy geopolitics can promote harmony as well as rivalry. Pakistan and Turkmenistan have signed a memorandum of understanding on a multibillion-dollar gas pipeline through Afghanistan that could eventually end as a "Peace Pipeline" in India, in what would be a major breakthrough in Indo-Pakistani relations. Former Indian petroleum minister Mani Shankar Aiyar, a strong advocate for the pipeline, says, "Almost everywhere in the world where an Indian goes in quest of energy, chances are that he will run into a Chinese engaged in the same hunt." Aiyar proposed that India, China, Japan, and South Korea establish a system of cooperative access to energy supplies. His subsequent demotion to minister for youth and sport was widely perceived in India as reflecting U.S. pressure against the Iran oil deal.

Indian security officials already see themselves fated to play central roles in what Aaron Friedberg, a Princeton scholar now on the White House national security staff, has called "the struggle for mastery in Asia." That phrase was the title of an essay he published in the neoconservative monthly *Commentary* when Bush was first elected. Friedberg's central message was that over the next several decades the United States would likely find itself engaged in an "open and intense geopolitical rivalry" with China. "The combination of growing Chinese power, China's effort to expand its influence, and the unwillingness of the United States to entirely give way before it are the necessary preconditions of a 'struggle for mastery,'" he wrote, adding that hostilities or a military confrontation could be slow to develop or could occur as a result of a "single catalytic event, such as a showdown over Taiwan."

India is now playing tortoise to China's hare, not only in its rate of growth but also because the Indian and Chinese economies are two very different creatures.

The strategic and energy concerns of the United States, China, and India will be difficult to manage. But Pakistan, Russia, Japan, and North and South Korea all factor into the extraordinarily complex equation of Asian security. (India maintains that Pakistan's missile technology came from China and North Korea.) And through Pakistan and the terrorist attacks from militants in Kashmir, India also feels itself threatened by Islamic extremism, a matter of grave concern for a country whose population of just over one billion includes 145 million Muslims.

It is in this context that the nuclear dimension of the Bush administration's embrace of India has aroused so much controversy. The administration seeks to steer India into "compliance" with the Non-Proliferation Treaty and the International Atomic Energy Agency (IAEA) system while leaving India's nuclear weapons reactors out of the international control regime. This stance has been challenged by critics in the United States for driving a coach and horses through the Non-Proliferation Treaty just as international support for diplomatic pressure on Iran depends on strict compliance with it.

Under the deal, India will separate its civilian from its military nuclear programs, but it has until 2014 to complete this division. New Delhi will declare 14 of an expected total of 22 nuclear reactors to be for civilian use and place them under IAEA controls. But India has managed to keep its new fast-breeder reactors out of the control system, which means that there will be no nuclear fuel shortages to constrain the future manufacture and development of nuclear weapons. Moreover, because India will reserve the right to determine which parts of its nuclear program will be subject to IAEA controls and which will not, it will be able to shield its own nuclear research labs from the IAEA system. New Delhi has also reinterpreted the U.S. insistence that the deal be made "in perpetuity" by making this conditional on continued supplies of enriched uranium, of which India is desperately short, to fuel its reactors.

The main concession India made was cosmetic. It agreed not to be formally included, in the eyes of the United States and the IAEA, in the category of the five recognized nuclear weapons states (the United States, Russia, Britain, France, and China). The deal is still the subject of hard bargaining in the U.S. Congress, where it has yet to be ratified, despite intense pressure from the Bush administration. But if, as expected, the agreement succeeds, India will become a special case, with a free hand to augment its nuclear weapons systems, and to develop its nuclear power stations with full access to the fuel and technology monopolized by the 45-nation Nuclear Suppliers Group. And India will secure all this with the blessing of the IAEA, thus negating the efforts of the international community since the 1970s to constrain India's nuclear ambitions by putting sanctions on its access to nuclear fuel and technology.

In India, the agreement has come in for criticism for wedding the country to U.S. strategic interests, to the detriment of India's relations with China and Iran. The policy is also viewed by some Indians as a lever to steadily increase international control over India's nuclear assets, and to make it more dependent on the United States as the prime supplier of nuclear fuel.

India long saw itself as neutral and nonaligned, endowed by Gandhi's nonviolent legacy with a singular innocence of such geopolitical games. It has been thrust with remarkable speed into a prominent strategic role that matches its new economic robustness. But its ability to sustain military power and buy advanced weaponry will clearly depend on its economic growth, which began in earnest 15 years after China launched its own economic reforms. While India 30 years ago enjoyed a slightly higher per capita income than China, today it has an annual per capita income (at purchasing power parity) of $3,300, not quite half of China's level of $6,800, and less than one-tenth of the $41,800 level of the United States.

India is now playing the tortoise to China's hare, not only in its rate of growth but also because the Indian and Chinese economies are two very different creatures. China has become the world's low-cost manufacturing center, making and assembling components that are often designed or developed elsewhere, and relying heavily on foreign investment. India's boom, by contrast, has so far been largely based on services and software, and it has been self-financing, with about a tenth of China's level of foreign direct investment. Still, it has produced an Indian middle class—usually defined by the ability to buy a private car—of some 300 million people, a number greater than the entire population of the United States.

One central reason why India has not enjoyed a Chinese-style boom led by manufacturing is the dismal state of so much of the country's infrastructure. Its ports, railroads, highways, electricity supplies, and grid systems are aged and ramshackle, and traffic jams and power outages are routine, reinforcing each other when the traffic lights blink out. Critical segments of the economy—such as the container transport system, which allows easy shipping of freight by land, sea, and air—have been state monopolies, subject to the usual debilitating problems of the breed. Arriving foreigners receive a startling introduction to the bustle and backwardness of India before they ever reach a hotel. On my most recent trip to New Delhi and Jaipur, the maddening endemic traffic jams included bicycles, flimsy three-wheeled rickshaws, and somnolent cows, whose excrement was swiftly scooped up by hordes of small children and patted into flat, plate-shaped discs, which are dried in the sun and sold for fuel. So to the usual tourist dangers of stomach upsets from eating local foods is added the prospect of respiratory infection from breathing air suffused with fecal matter.

Yet there is no denying the furious commercial energy of a country that is currently signing up five million new mobile phone subscribers each month. Competition has come to the container industry, the airports are being privatized despite labor union opposition, and new highways are being built. The gas and electricity grids are slated for reform next. India has its high-tech centers of Bangalore and Hyderabad, as well as a few new towns such as Gurgaon, just outside Delhi, with a modern automaking plant, high-rise shopping malls, and telemarketing centers. But it can boast nothing like the jaw-dropping array of new skyscrapers that zigzag the skylines of modern Shanghai and Guangdong.

Still, some of the smart money is on the tortoise. The global consultancy firm PwC (still better known by its old name, Price Waterhouse Coopers) produced a report this year forecasting that India would have the fastest growth among all the major economies over the next 50 years, averaging 7.6 percent annually in dollar terms. In 50 years' time, the Indian and U.S. economies would be roughly equivalent in size. The report also suggested that by 2050 the existing economies of the G-7 group of advanced industrial nations (the United States, Britain, France, Germany, Italy, Japan, and Canada) would be overtaken by the E-7 emergent economies of China, India, Brazil, Russia, Indonesia, Mexico, and Turkey.

There is no denying the furious commercial energy of a country that is currently signing up five million new mobile phone subscribers each month.

The most significant difference between India and China, however, may be how their respective demographic trends and political systems shape their futures. The Chinese leadership is already coming to regret its nearly 30-year-old policy of permitting most couples to have only one child. Now China is rapidly aging and heading for a pensions crisis, as an entire generation of only children grapples with the problem of helping to support two parents and four grandparents. A recent DeutscheBank survey on China's pension challenge predicted, "China is going to get old before it gets rich." The policy has also created a serious gender disparity. The ability to predict the sex of a fetus in a country limited to one child per family has led to a situation in which 120 boys are born for every 100 girls, and President Hu Jintao last year asked a task force of scientists and officials to address the tricky problems posed by an excess of single men. India has a similar sex disparity problem in certain regions, notably those where Sikhs are numerous, but overall, with half of its population below the age of 25, it boasts a far healthier demographic profile.

The contest between the Indian tortoise and the Chinese hare has a political dimension as well. India is a democracy, without an equivalent of China's ruling Communist Party. Its elections, provincial governments, and free news media give the country great social resilience. China's breakneck economic growth and social disruption seem likely to have potent consequences as its new middle class finds a political voice.

The Chinese Communist Party is becoming less ideological and far more technocratic in its orientation, but it still can manipulate the most authoritarian levers of state power in aggressive pursuit of economic and strategic goals. Indians are stuck with their messy but comfortable democracy. Montek Singh Ahluwalia, an Oxford-educated economist who is deputy chairman of the national planning commission, says, "The biggest thing about India is that it's a very participative, very pluralistic, open democracy where even if the top 1,000 people technocratically came to the conclusion something is good, it has to be mediated into a political consensus. And I'm being realistic. I don't think it's going to be that easy to put in place everything that from a technocratic point of view everybody knows needs to be done."

In short, India's pluralism could be to China's advantage, although given the track record of bureaucratic technocrats from Moscow to Japan in wasting massive resources to pursue the wrong goals, it may not be that simple. But India has its own special asset, recognized by the American presidential candidate George W. Bush and suggested by the celebrated prediction a century ago by Otto von Bismarck that "the most important fact of the 20th century will be that the English and the Americans speak the same language." The most important factor in the 21st century may well be that Americans and Indians (and perhaps Britons and Australians and Microsoft employees and global businesspeople) all speak English. This is not simply a matter of a shared language, although that is important; it also encompasses those other aspects of the common heritage that include free speech and free press, trial by jury and an independent judiciary, private property, and individual as well as human rights. While retaining its rich and historic cultures, India is thoroughly familiar with these core values and determinants of the American civic system. And as a religiously tolerant, multi-ethnic democracy with commercial, legal, and educational systems developed during the British Raj, India is—like the English language itself—familiar and reassuring to Americans.

A decisive factor in the short term may be India's importance to the United States in the strategic and cultural campaign now being waged against Islamic extremism. This will be a struggle much deeper and longer than the mainly military effort the Bush administration calls GWOT (Global War on Terrorism), as currently being fought in Afghanistan and Iraq. India, itself a regular target, has been from the beginning a firm partner in the war on terrorism, instantly offering flyover and landing rights to U.S. aircraft engaged in the war against the Taliban. But with its 145 million Muslims, India risks becoming embroiled in the tumult now shaking so much of the Islamic world as the faithful try simultaneously to grapple with the cultural, theological, economic, and social revolutions now under way.

Facing the additional problem of militant Hindu nationalism, India has no choice but to stand in the front line against Islamic extremism. India is the great geographic obstruction to an Islamic arc that would stretch from Morocco across Africa and the Middle East all the way to Malaysia, Indonesia, and into the Philippines. Pakistan and Bangladesh are deeply uncomfortable neighbors for India, being Muslim, poor, the scenes of concerted jihadist campaigns, and worrisomely close to becoming failed states. But there is another arc, which stretches from Japan and South Korea through China and the increasingly prosperous countries of the Association of Southeast Asian Nations to India. This swath of rising prosperity and economic growth now includes three billion people—half the world's population. It is easy to foresee wretched outliers such as North Korea, Myanmar, Bangladesh, and Pakistan being swept up in the wake of this boom, should it continue, but for that to happen, Asia needs stability, peace, and a cessation of arms races.

It is an open question whether the burgeoning new strategic friendship of India and the United States will help this process or derail it. It could do both, deterring China from adventurism or bullying its neighbors, and stabilizing the strategic environment while India and China manage a joint and peaceful rise to wealth and status. But at the same time, the new U.S.-Indian accord could help spur a new nuclear arms race in Asia, where Russia, China, India, Pakistan, and probably North Korea already have the bomb, and Japan, South Korea, and Taiwan have the technological capability to build it quickly. One wild card is already being played that could bring this about: the prospect of Japan and India sharing in American antimissile technology. If India gains the ability to shoot down incoming missiles, this threatens to negate the deterrent that Pakistan and China thought they possessed against India, with potentially destabilizing results.

Even though India's prospects now look brighter than they have for a generation, the country faces some sobering challenges, including the accelerating pace of expectations among its own people and their understandable demand that the new wealth be shared quickly, that the poorest villages get schools and electricity. Almost half the population still lives in rural hamlets, and only 44 percent of these rural residents have electricity. Enemies of globalization populate the Indian Left and sit in the current coalition government. India must grapple with the familiar difficulties of Hindu nationalism, inadequate infrastructure, and a large Muslim population, as well as environmental crisis, deep rural poverty, and the caste system.

India finds itself in a delicate position. It must manage and maintain its relationship with China while accommodating American strategists who are relying on its support to keep Asia on the rails of democratic globalization. Americans also regard India as insurance against China's domination of Asia to the exclusion of the United States. India, on the other hand, wants freedom of action and does not want to serve merely as a tool of American influence.

"We want the United States to remain as the main stabilizer in Asia and the balance against China until such time as India can manage the job on its own" an influential security adviser to the Indian government said recently, very much on background. What will happen once India believes it can do this alone? I asked. "Well, then we shall see," he replied. "By then it will be a different Asia, probably a different China, and possibly a different America. It will certainly be a different world, dominated by the Indian, Chinese, and American superpowers."

MARTIN WALKER is the editor of United Press International and a senior scholar at the Wilson Center. His most recent books are *America Reborn: A Twentieth-Century Narrative in Twenty-Six Lives* (2000) and the novel *The Caves of Périgord* (2002).

UNIT 2

Managing Interstate Conflicts and the Proliferation of Weapons

Unit Selections

Key Points to Consider

- Will Russia's invasion of Georgia prevent Georgia from joining NATO?

- Do you agree with Ariel Cohen that the longer term implications of the Russian-Georgian war will be felt throughout the Middle East and beyond?

- What are some of the main reasons why Russia continues to pursue greater economic integration with the European Union at the same time that political relationships are often tense?

- Is Israel likely to launch a preemptive strike against Iran in the future? What about the United States?

- What are the steps the U.S. government is taking to implement President Obama's goals in the area of arms control?

- Do you agree with the proposal to end a NATO nuclear weapons presence in European countries that are not nuclear weapons states as part of a multipolar approach to arms control?

- What do you think of the supranational concept of having the International Atomic Energy Agency, or an alternative organization, serve as the neutral owner of fissile materials for countries who wish to pursue nuclear energy capabilities as a means to prevent additional nuclear weapons states?

- Are biological weapons a serious national security threat?

- What additional homeland defense measures should be taken to prepare for a future nuclear, biological, chemical, or radiation (NBCR) attack in the United States?

Student Website

www.mhhe.com/cls

Internet References

U.S. Department of State
http://www.state.gov/index.cfm

Belfer Center for Science and International Affairs (BCSIA)
http://www.ksg.harvard.edu/bcsia

FACTs
http://www.ploughshares.ca

U.S.- Russia Developments
http://www.acronym.org.uk/start

The Bulletin of the Atomic Scientists
http://www.bullatomsci.org

Federation of American Scientists
http://www.fas.org

As economic, political, and military power diffuses throughout the International Systems, an increased number of nation-states are using the traditional forms of statecraft to obtain their national interests. The world was reminded of the enduring nature of power politics during August of 2008. While millions worldwide watched the historic opening ceremonies of the Olympics in Beijing on televisions, millions more tuned in to news stations to view clips of Russian tanks rolling into South Ossetia, a rebel province of Georgia. The military intervention into two disputed areas inside Georgia was the former super power's first major military operation outside of Russia's national borders since the invasion of Afghanistan in 1979.

© Purestock/SuperStock

The invasion came as a surprise to many observers. However, experienced realists claimed that the incursions were part of a long-term goal of Russia that had only temporarily been suspended in the years immediately following the collapse of the Soviet Union. The immediate goal was to prevent Georgia from joining NATO but the longer-term implementations of the invasion is likely to be felt throughout Europe, Asia, and the Middle East for years to come. Other analysts stress the fact that Russia is unlikely to prevent the Baltic states, the Ukraine, and other nation-states from gaining admission into the European Community and possibly also NATO in the long-run. Despite recent political tensions between Russia and members of the EC, there is a longer trend of deepening economic integration among countries surrounding Europe, including Russia.

Russia EU states, along with the United States, China and others are currently seeking to cooperate more to stop the proliferation of nuclear capabilities and competencies. Nearly 50 nation-states may know how to make nuclear arms. As nuclear proliferation research and development continues unabated, analysts are now primarily concerned about what members of the nuclear club, especially the United States and Israel, will do as Iran moves closer to having operational nuclear weapons capabilities. An Israeli air attack on a Syrian facility believed to have been a clandestine nuclear reactor in 2007 was similar in intent to an earlier air attack in 1981 on an Iraqi facility, Osiraq. In both cases, the Israeli government decided to launch a preventive security attack. Israel's past actions are designed to provide credibility to verbal warnings that Israel will not hesitate to destroy suspected WMD facilities in neighboring countries. In "Israeli Military Calculations towards Iran," the authors describe the strategic reality that three-quarter of Israel's population is extremely vulnerable to a nuclear attack because they live "on a narrow strip of coastline from Ashkelon to Haifa." This demographic fact is one reason why Israel has relied on preemptive strikes of suspected nuclear facilities, such as the raid on an alleged covert weapons facility in Syria during the fall of 2007.

During 2009, the Obama administration released previously classified information confirming a heretofore secret nuclear reactor built inside a mountain near the holy city of Qom south of the capital in Iran. Faced with increased international pressure, Iran's President Mahmoud Ahmadinejad agreed to let International Atomic Energy Agency (IAEA) inspectors visit the recently disclosed facilities but balked at signing a UN-draft agreement to send nuclear fuel out of the country for enrichment. While many analysts predict that either Israel or the United States will launch air strikes in an attempt to dismantle Iran's nuclear facilities if diplomacy fails, most analysts also worry that such an attack will not stop the Iranians from pursuing nuclear capability. Instead, a strike at Iran's nuclear energy facilities would no doubt accelerate an ongoing race among nation-states to acquire nuclear weapons, and might even ignite a regional conflict that could have serious, disruptive rippling effects throughout the Middle East and beyond.

As a longstanding proponent of greater arms control, Barak Obama proposed, during his first year in office, deep cuts in the U.S. and Russian nuclear arsenals, support for multilateral efforts such as a ban on the production of fissile, or weapons grade, materials and efforts to establish more nuclear free zones throughout the world, and ratification of the Comprehensive Test Ban Treaty (CTBT), that was defeated in the U.S. Senate in 1999. In "The Long Road from Prague," U.S. Assistant Secretary Rose Gottemoeller outlines a series of steps the U.S. government is pursuing to implement President Obama's arms controls goals, including negotiations for a new START Treaty; the old one being set to expire at the end of 2009.

The renewed U.S. support for additional arms control measures was enthusiastically welcomed by most European states and received with only slightly less enthusiasm by other great powers, including Russia and China. Threats of rapid proliferation of nuclear capabilities seem to be spurring renewed international efforts by the major powers to achieve additional arms control agreements. In addition to concerns about Iran and North Korea, recent events in Afghanistan and Pakistan fuel worries about nuclear terrorism. There have been attacks on Pakistan's nuclear sites in the past and many now worry about the prospect that one or more individuals working in nuclear facilities in Pakistan with access to nuclear weapons might be willing to transfer nuclear weapons components or expertise to terrorists living in Pakistan.

Such threats seems plausible given the precedent of A. Q. Khan, the former head of Pakistan's nuclear weapons program, who led a covert network that sold WMD expertise and components throughout the world after he retired from government service. While the extent of proliferation damage caused by the A. Q. Kahn network remains unknown, it is clear that several nation-states, including North Korea and Libya, could not have progressed so fast towards developing sophisticated nuclear weapons without the expertise and components supplied by A. Q. Kahn's network. Such amorphous, highly adaptive, and underground transnational criminal networks may increasingly pose the greatest dangers to nation-state and the collective security of citizens in several countries

Scholars and practitioners tend to disagree whether nation-states, terrorists, or lone deviants are most likely to use chemical or biological agents as weapons of terror against civilians in the future. There is even less agreement now than in past years about whether it is possible to deter or counter the use of chemical or biological weapons. It took seven years for the FBI to announce that the former U.S. Army microbiologist Bruce Ivies was implicated in the U.S. anthrax letter attacks in 2001. The resulting skepticism that Ivies was the sole perpetrator of the attacks, even though he killed himself prior to being arrested, illustrates just how difficult it can be to determine who is the attacker in a single or series of biological incidents.

The difficulties determining the extent of sophistication of several past covert chem-bio weapons programs in such varied countries as South Africa, Iraq, and Libya further illustrate why it is probably impossible to apply the same type of control strategies to deny would-be nuclear proliferators access to nuclear energy or to control the proliferation of equipment, supplies, or expertise needed to build chemical or biological weapons. These difficulties are compounded by the fact many countries throughout the developing and developed world are attempting to develop high level biotechnology, nanotechnology, and information technologies economic sectors which can mask covert chem-bio weapons research and development, especially if the goal is mass disruption rather than mass destruction. In "Evolving Bioweapon Threats Require New Countermeasures," Helen Purkitt and Virgen Wells discuss why it is impossible to control the equipment, supplies, and knowledge needed to develop sophisticated or naturally occurring biological agents as weapons. Instead of instituting control strategies, Purkitt and Wells advocate designing public policies that will promote new transparency norms among nation-states and citizens throughout the world.

The Russian-Georgian War
Implications for the Middle East

ARIEL COHEN, PHD

- Moscow formulated far-reaching goals when it carefully prepared—over a period of at least two and a half years—for a land invasion of Georgia. These goals included: expelling Georgian troops and effectively terminating Georgian sovereignty in South Ossetia and Abkhazia; bringing down President Mikheil Saakashvili and installing a more pro-Russian leadership in Tbilisi; and preventing Georgia from joining NATO.
- Russia's long-term strategic goals include increasing its control of the Caucasus, especially over strategic energy pipelines. If a pro-Russian regime is established in Georgia, it will bring the strategic Baku-Tbilisi-Ceyhan oil pipeline and the Baku-Erzurum (*Turkey*) gas pipeline under Moscow's control.
- In recent years, Moscow granted the majority of Abkhazs and South Ossetians Russian citizenship. Use of Russian citizenship to create a "protected" population residing in a neighboring state to undermine its sovereignty is a slippery slope which is now leading to a redrawing of the former Soviet borders.
- Russian continental power is on the rise. Israel should understand it and not provoke Moscow unnecessarily, while defending its own national security interests staunchly. Small states need to treat nuclear armed great powers with respect.
- U.S. intelligence-gathering and analysis on the Russian threat to Georgia failed. So did U.S. military assistance to Georgia, worth around $2 billion over the last 15 years. This is something to remember when looking at recent American intelligence assessments of the *Iran*ian nuclear threat or the unsuccessful training of *Palestinian Authority* security forces against *Hamas*.

The long-term outcomes of the current Russian-Georgian war will be felt far and wide, from Afghanistan to Iran, and from the Caspian to the Mediterranean. The war is a mid-sized earthquake which indicates that the geopolitical tectonic plates are shifting, and nations in the Middle East, including Israel, need to take notice.

Russia's Goals

Moscow formulated far-reaching goals when it carefully prepared—over a period of at least two and a half years—for a land invasion of Georgia, as this author warned.[1] These goals included:

- **Expelling Georgian troops and effectively terminating Georgian sovereignty in South Ossetia and Abkhazia.** Russia is preparing the ground for independence and eventual annexation of these separatist territories. Thus, these goals seem to be on track to be successfully achieved.
- **"Regime change"—bringing down President Mikheil Saakashvili and installing a more pro-Russian leadership in Tbilisi.** Russia seems to have given up on the immediate toppling of Saakashvili, and is likely counting on the Georgian people to do the job once the dust settles. Russia, for its part, will pursue a criminal case against him for genocide and war crimes in South Ossetia, trying to turn him into another Slobodan Milosevic/Radovan Karadzic. This is part of psychological operations against the Georgian leader, of which more later.
- **Preventing Georgia from joining NATO and sending a strong message to Ukraine that its insistence on NATO membership may lead to war and/or its dismemberment.** Russia succeeded in attacking a state that has been regarded as a potential candidate for NATO membership since April 2008. The Russian assault undoubtedly erodes the NATO umbrella in the international community, even though Georgia is not yet formally a member, especially if it emerges that Moscow can use force against its neighbors with impunity. While it remains to be seen whether Georgia ultimately is fully accepted into NATO, some voices in Europe, especially in Germany, will see in the war a vindication of their opposition to such membership. Georgia's chances will decrease further if the next U.S. president is noncommittal on the conflict. Ukraine is standing tall in solidarity with Georgia for the time being, and has taken a strong step to limit the movements of Russia's Black Sea fleet, but has little domestic support for NATO membership.

Russia's long-term strategic goals include:

- **Increasing its control of the Caucasus, especially over strategic energy pipelines.**[2] If a pro-Russian regime is established in Georgia, it will bring the strategic Baku-Tbilisi-Ceyhan oil pipeline and the Baku-Erzurum (Turkey) gas pipeline under Moscow's control. Israel receives some of its oil from Ceyhan, and has a stake in the smooth flow of oil from the Caspian.
  Russian control over Georgia would outflank Azerbaijan, denying the U.S. any basing and intelligence options there in case of a confrontation with Iran. This kind of control would also undermine any options for pro-Western orientations in Azerbaijan and Armenia, along with any chance of resolving their conflict based on diplomacy and Western-style cooperation.

- **Recreating a nineteenth-century-style sphere of influence in the former Soviet Union and beyond, if necessary by use of force.** Here, the intended addressees included all former Soviet republics, including the Baltic States. The message may have backfired as the presidents of Poland, Ukraine, Estonia, Latvia and Lithuania came to Tbilisi and stood shoulder-to-shoulder with Saakashvili. However, without Western European and U.S. support, "New Europe" alone cannot stand up to Moscow.

Russian Proxies Inside Georgia

Russian relations with Georgia were the worst among the post-Soviet states. In addition to fanning the flames of separatism in South Ossetia since 1990, Russia militarily supported separatists in Abkhazia (1992–1993), which is also a part of Georgian territory, to undermine Georgia's independence and assert its control over the strategically important South Caucasus.[3]

Despite claims about oppressed minority status, the separatist South Ossetian leadership is mostly ethnic Russians, many of whom served in the KGB, the Soviet secret police; the Russian military; or in the Soviet communist party. Abkhazia and South Ossetia have become Russia's wholly-owned subsidiaries, their population largely militarized and subsisting on smuggling operations.

This use of small, ethnically-based proxies is similar to Iran's use of *Hizbullah* and Hamas to continuously attack Israel. Tbilisi tried for years to deal with these militias by offering a negotiated solution, including full autonomy within Georgia.

In recent years, Moscow granted the majority of Abkhazs and South Ossetians Russian citizenship and moved to establish close economic and bureaucratic ties with the two separatist republics, effectively enacting a creeping annexation of both territories. Use of Russian citizenship to create a "protected" population residing in a neighboring state to undermine its sovereignty is a slippery slope which is now leading to a redrawing of the former Soviet borders.

On August 7, after yet another Russian-backed South Ossetian military provocation, Saakashvili attacked South Ossetian targets with artillery and armor. Yet, Tbilisi was stunned by the ferocity of the Russian response. It shouldn't have been, nor should Americans be surprised. The writing was on the wall, but Washington failed to read it, despite repeated warning from allied intelligence services and a massive presence of diplomats

and military trainers on the ground. The results for Georgia are much more disastrous than for Israel in summer 2006.

"Kill the Chicken to Scare the Monkey"

Aggression against Georgia also sends a strong signal to Ukraine and to Europe. Russia is playing a chess game of offense and intimidation. Former president and current Prime Minister Vladimir Putin spoke last spring about Russia "dismembering" Ukraine, another NATO candidate, and detaching the Crimea, a peninsula which was transferred from Russia to Ukraine in 1954, when both were integral parts of the Soviet Union.

Today, up to 50 percent of Ukrainian citizens speak Russian as their first language and ethnic Russians comprise around one-fifth of Ukraine's population. With encouragement from Moscow, these people may be induced to follow South Ossetia and Abkhazia to Mother Russia's bosom. Yet, Ukraine's pro-Western leaders, such as President Victor Yushchenko and Prime Minister Yulia Timoshenko, have expressed a desire to join NATO, while the pro-Moscow Ukrainian Party of Regions effectively opposes membership. NATO opponents in Ukraine are greatly encouraged by Russia's action against Georgia.

In the near future, Russia is likely to beef up the Black Sea Fleet, which has bases in Tartus and Latakia in *Syria,* and used to have an anchorage in Libya. For over two hundred years the navy has been the principal tool of Russian power projection in the Mediterranean and the Indian Ocean.

Beyond this, Russia is demonstrating that it can sabotage American and EU declarations about integrating the Commonwealth of Independent States members into Western structures such as NATO.

By attempting to accomplish regime change in Georgia, Moscow is also trying to gain control of the energy and transportation corridor which connects Central Asia and Azerbaijan with the Black Sea and ocean routes overseas—for oil, gas and other commodities. Back in 1999, Western companies reached an agreement with Central Asian states to create the Baku-Tbilisi-Ceyhan pipeline. So far, this has allowed Azerbaijan to bypass Russia completely and transport its oil from the Caspian Sea basin straight through Georgia and Turkey, without crossing Russian territory. The growing output of the newly independent Central Asian states has been increasingly competing with Russian oil. By 2018, the Caspian basin, including Kazakhstan and Azerbaijan, is supposed to export up to 4 million barrels of oil a day, as well as a significant amount of natural gas. Russia would clearly like to restore its hegemony over hydrocarbon export routes that would considerably diminish sovereignty and diplomatic freedom of maneuver in these new independent states.

A Russian S-300 Anti-Aircraft Shield for Iran?

Russia's Georgian adventure also emboldens Iran by securing its northern tier through denial of bases, airfields, electronic facilities and other cooperation in Georgia and Azerbaijan to

Israel has been very effective in electronic warfare (EW) against Soviet- and Russian-built technologies, including anti-aircraft batteries. In 1982, Israeli Air Force F-16s smashed the Syrian anti-aircraft missiles in the Beka'a Valley and within Syria, allowing Israel full air superiority over Syria and *Lebanon.* As a result, Syria lost over 80 planes, one-third of its air force, in two days, while Israel lost one obsolete ground support A-4 Skyhawk to ground fire.

In 1981, Israeli F-15s and F-16s flew undetected over Jordan and *Saudi Arabia* on their mission to destroy *Saddam Hussein*'s Osirak reactor. More recently, the Israeli Air Force surprised the Syrians when they destroyed an alleged nuclear facility in the northeast of the country in September 2007, apparently flying undetected to and from the mission.

the U.S. and possibly Israel. At the same time, in March 2009, Russia is likely to deploy modern S-300 long-range anti-aircraft missiles in Iran. By June 2009 they will become fully operational, as Iranian teams finish training provided by their Russian instructors, according to a high-level Russian source who requested anonymity.[4]

The deployment of the anti-aircraft shield next spring, if it occurs, effectively limits the window in which Israel or the United States could conduct an effective aerial campaign aimed at destroying, delaying or crippling the Iranian nuclear program.

The Islamic Republic will use the long-range anti-aircraft system, in addition to the point-defense Tor M-1 short-range Russian-made system, to protect its nuclear infrastructure, including suspected nuclear weapons facilities, from a potential U.S. or Israeli preventive strike.

The S-300 system, which has a radius of over 90 miles and effective altitudes of about 90,000 feet, is capable of tracking up to 100 targets simultaneously. It is considered one of the best in the world and is amazingly versatile. It is capable of shooting down aircraft, cruise missiles, and ballistic missile warheads.[5] The S-300 complements the Tor-M1 air defense missile system, also supplied by Russia. In 2007 Russia delivered 29 Tor-M1s worth $700 million to Iran.

However, a mission over Iran, if and when decided upon, is very different than operations over neighboring Syria. First, if Israel waits until March 2009, there may be a president in the White House who emphasizes diplomacy over military operations. Even if the George W. Bush Administration allows Israel over-flight of *Iraq*i air space and aerial refueling, a future administration might not, opting for an "aggressive diplomacy" approach instead—especially with an emboldened and truculent Russia as a geopolitical counter-balance.

Second, Israel, military experts say, does not have long-range bomber capacity, such as the Cold War-era U.S. B-1 heavy supersonic bomber, or the B-2 stealth bomber. Israel, a Russian source estimated, can hit 20 targets simultaneously, while the Iranian nuclear program may have as many as 100. Many of the Iranian targets are fortified, and will require bunker busters.

Operational challenges abound. Israel's EW planes, needed to suppress anti-aircraft batteries, are slow and unarmed, and could become a target for Iranian anti-aircraft missiles or even fighter sorties. But the most important question analysts are asking is whether the current Israeli leadership has the knowledge and the gumption to pull it off. After all, the results of the 2006 mini-war against Hizbullah were disastrous for Israel, and the Israel Defense Forces have exposed numerous flaws in its preparedness, supply chain, and command, control, communications and intelligence.

The Need to Defang Tehran

Nevertheless, the need to preemptively defang Tehran may prove decisive in view of Tehran's hatred and intransigence.

As noted by Professor Stephen Blank of the U.S. Army War College:

> When one is dealing with a national leadership which is motivated by ethnic and religious hatred, one needs to remember that such a leadership becomes obsessed and loses its ability to calculate things. They may risk war rather than seek accommodation. This was not only the case with Nazi Germany, but also with the antebellum American South of the 1840s and 1850s, where racial hatred of the slave owners cause them to lose sight of what was at stake.

Blank goes on to conclude that the Iranian leadership believes that Russia and China will provide them with protection, of which the S-300 is an important component, and that the sanctions are not effective.

Under the circumstances, an Israel-only preventive bombing campaign—without the United States—might be too risky to pull off. If the United States sits this crisis out, Israel could possibly settle for deterring Iran by taking its cities and main oil facilities hostage.

This was known during the Cold War as Mutually Assured Destruction (MAD), brought to you courtesy of Iran's Supreme Leader Ali Khamenei and President *Ahmadinejad*. Going MAD would make the Middle East even more fragile than it already is, and would make the life of its inhabitants ever more difficult and tragic.

Clearly, with the renewal of East-West tensions as a result of Russia's moves against Georgia, it will be much more difficult to obtain Moscow's agreement to enhance sanctions and international pressures on Iran. The struggle to diplomatically halt its nuclear program will become far more difficult.

Lessons from the War

Lessons for the Middle East and Israel from the Russian-Georgian War abound, and apply both to military operations, cyber-warfare, and strategic information operations. The most important of these are:

- **Watch Out for the Bear—and Other Beasts!** Russian continental power is on the rise. Israel should understand it and not provoke Moscow unnecessarily, while defending its own national security interests staunchly.

Small states need to treat nuclear armed great powers with respect. Provoking a militarily strong adversary, such as Iran, is worthwhile only if you are confident of victory, and even then there may be bitter surprises. Just ask Saakashvili.

- **Strategic Self-Reliance.** U.S. expressions of support of the kind provided to Georgia—short of an explicit mutual defense pact—may or may not result in military assistance if/when Israel is under attack, especially when the attacker has an effective deterrent, such as nuclear arms deliverable against U.S. targets. In the future, such an attacker could be Iran or an Arab country armed with atomic weapons. Israel can and should rely on its own deterrent—a massive survivable second-strike capability.

- **Intelligence Failure.** U.S. intelligence-gathering and analysis on the Russian threat to Georgia failed. So did U.S. military assistance to Georgia, worth around $2 billion over the last 15 years. This is something to remember when looking at recent American intelligence assessments of the Iranian nuclear threat or the unsuccessful training of Palestinian Authority security forces against Hamas. Both are deeply flawed. There is no substitute for high-quality human intelligence.

- **Air Power Is Not Sufficient.** Russia used air, armor, the Black Sea Fleet, special forces, and allied militias. Clausewitzian lessons still apply: the use of overwhelming force in the war's center of gravity by implementing a combined air-land-sea operation may be twentieth century, but it does work.[6] Israel should have been taught this lesson after the last war with Hizbullah.

- **Surprise and Speed of Operations Still Matter**—as they have for the four thousand years of the recorded history of warfare. To be successful, wars have to have limited and achievable goals. Russia achieved most of its goals between Friday and Monday, while the world, including President George W. Bush, was busy watching the Olympics and parliaments were on vacation.

- **Do Not Cringe**—within reason—from taking military casualties and inflicting overwhelming military and civilian casualties at a level unacceptable to the enemy. Georgia lost some 100–200 soldiers and effectively capitulated. A tougher enemy, like the Japanese or the Germans, or even Hizbullah, could well suffer a proportionally higher rate of casualties and keep on fighting.

- **Information and Psychological Warfare Is Paramount.** So is cyber-security. It looks like the Russians conducted repeated denial of service attacks against Georgia (and in 2007 against Estonia), shutting down key websites.

Russia was ready with accusations and footage of alleged Georgian atrocities in South Ossetia, shifting the information operation playing field from "aggressor-victim" to "saving Ossetian civilians from barbaric Georgians." These operations also matter domestically, to shore up support and boost morale at home.

Conclusion

The Russian-Georgian war indicates that the balance of power in western Eurasia has shifted, and that U.S. power may be deteriorating in the face of its lengthy and open-ended commitments in Iraq, Afghanistan, and the Global War on Terror, which are leading to a global overstretch.

While the Middle East, and especially the Persian Gulf, will remain a top priority in U.S. foreign policy regardless of who wins the White House, Israel is heading towards a strategic environment in which Russia may play a more important role, especially in its southern tier, from the Black Sea to Afghanistan and western China. Twenty-first century geopolitics is presenting significant survival challenges to the Jewish state and the region.

Notes

1. Ariel Cohen, "Springtime Is for War?" The Heritage Foundation press commentary, originally published by TechCentralStation (TCSDaily), March 31, 2006, http://www.heritage.org/Press/Commentary/ed033106a.cfm, August 13, 2008.

2. Melik Kaylan, "Welcome Back to the Great Game: Failing to Stand Up to Russia Would Jeopardize Every International Gain Since the Cold War," *Wall Street Journal,* August 13, 2008.

3. Simon Sebag Montfiore, "Another Battle in the 1,000-Year Russia-Georgia Grudge Match," *The Times of London,* August 12, 2008.

4. Personal interview with the author, Washington, D.C., August 2008.

5. Dave Majumdar, "Israel's Red Line: The S-300 Missile System," Aviation.com, http://www.aviation.com/technology/080807-iran-and-s-300-missile.html, August 13, 2008.

6. Martin Sieff, "Defense Focus: Underestimating Russia. Russian Army Shocks West in Georgia Ops," United Press International 20080812-002422-8913, August 12, 2008.

ARIEL COHEN, PhD, is Senior Research Fellow in Russian and Eurasian Studies and International Energy Security at The Heritage Foundation. He is a member of the Board of Advisers of the Institute for Contemporary Affairs at the Jerusalem Center for Public Affairs.

Europe and Russia: Up from the Abyss?

Andrew C. Kuchins

The past year was the most contentious in Russia-Europe relations since the collapse of the Soviet Union. From differences over Kosovo's status, NATO enlargement, and missile defense in the spring, to the Georgia war in August, to another natural gas dispute between Russia and Ukraine that began at the end of the year, tensions and differences dominated 2008. And on many issues Europeans could not agree among themselves, or with the Bush administration, about how best to engage Vladimir Putin's recently resurgent Russia.

Yet, while political relations worsened, economic integration between Russia and the European Union continued to deepen and widen, as trade and investment volumes reached all-time highs. In the summer the Russian Ministry of Economic Development and Trade published a long report detailing Russia's economic goals through the year 2020. The most striking finding in that report is that Europeans especially, and the West more broadly, would be far and away the most important partners in helping Russia to achieve its best-case growth scenarios in the coming decade.

This combination of trends—deepening economic integration amid worsening political relations—did not seem sustainable in the summer of 2008, and now after the war in Georgia and the impact of the global economic crisis, it seems even less so. The question is: Will political relations between Europe and Russia continue to deteriorate?

Dmitri Medvedev was inaugurated as Russia's president in May 2008. Later in that month the Russian stock market hit its all-time high. And in July oil prices peaked at $147 per barrel. The Russian government had more money than it knew what to do with, as foreign currency reserves peaked at nearly $600 billion, with another $200 billion put aside in a formal "stabilization fund." The Russian GDP (in nominal dollar terms) had increased by a factor of six in less than a decade. The Ministry of Economic Development and Trade report on strategic economic goals through 2020 called for similar growth levels that would ultimately make Russia the fifth-largest economy in the world and larger than any in Europe. Kremlin officials talked about Russia possibly being a "safe haven" or "island of stability" as the impact of the U.S. mortgage crisis widened to the world economy.

But how quickly things change. Russia's economic hubris has been smashed as its economy in the past few months has been perhaps the hardest hit of large emerging markets. By January 2009 the Russian stock market had lost about 80 percent of its value, the ruble had lost more than 30 percent, and reserves had fallen by one-third, with additional tens of billions promised in various bail-out and stimulus measures. Most prognoses for economic performance have predicted zero or negative growth for 2009.

All national economies are struggling to adjust to the deepest global slump in recent times, but the change in momentum for policy makers in Moscow is especially stark and challenging. Since so many millions of Russians have benefited from the prosperity of the past decade, the impact of the current crisis affects a far greater percentage of the population than the last economic crisis, in 1998. Prime Minister Putin's approach to governance, the so-called "vertical of power," will be tested like never before as prospects for social unrest and even bankruptcy become possible, especially if the slump endures for more than 12 to 18 months.

> **Lower oil price environments correlate with a more accommodating and moderate foreign policy from Moscow.**

New Dynamics

What does this turnabout suggest for relations with Europe? Historically, since the first oil crisis in the early 1970s, there has been a powerful correlation between a high oil price environment and a more assertive and aggressive Soviet or Russian foreign policy. This dynamic corresponds to the later Brezhnev years and the Putin period, especially since 2003. Lower oil price environments, as during the Gorbachev and Yeltsin years, correlate with a more accommodating and moderate foreign policy from Moscow.

Also relevant to Europe's ties with Russia is this reality: In a world of higher oil and gas prices, Moscow, like other states that rely a great deal on hydrocarbon revenues, can make decisions about production, allocation, and distribution of energy resources on more political and less commercial terms. Not surprisingly, given the mountains of money coming into Kremlin coffers in recent years from oil and gas sales, Russians have engaged in a variety of intimidating behaviors that have particularly tended to put their neighbors in "New Europe" on edge.

At least in the short term, or however long this global recession lasts, the Russians will feel far more economically constrained than in the recent halcyon years. Even when global demand begins to recover, Russia will be competing for investment with all economies whose assets have dramatically declined in value—as opposed to 10 years ago, when Russia was more unusual as a large emerging market with undervalued assets.

A second major difference the Russians will face is that, for the near and middle term, prospects for growth in domestic production of oil and gas resources are grim. After the country's financial crash in 1998, Russian domestic oil companies, led by Yukos at the time, achieved remarkably rapid growth in production with the application of modern technologies to old Soviet wells. That feat cannot be repeated, and new production will have to come in geologically and climatically challenging conditions from greenfield projects that will be the most expensive and complicated of their kind in history.

Finally, there is another important new factor in the equation: the election of Barack Obama and the end of the George W. Bush era in the United States. While we must beware of excessive expectations regarding the new president, the Bush administration had unprecedentedly strained relations with much of Europe as well as with the Russians. Bush's deep unpopularity at home as well as abroad gave Moscow more leverage to split America's European allies, most notably over the Iraq War.

The Obama administration will bring a new dynamic to relations among the United States, Europe, and Russia. Some of the most neuralgic issues in Russia-West relations will be defused somewhat. For example, Kosovo's declaration of independence is past. Missile defense will be pursued more circumspectly. And NATO enlargement to include Ukraine and Georgia will also slow down—partly because key European allies are skeptical, and partly because a new administration in Washington will not be racing against the clock to cement its legacy.

Rebalancing Relations

The Georgia war, although it has been overshadowed by the global financial crisis, was a watershed event that confirmed, nearly 20 years after the fall of the Berlin Wall and the end of the cold war, that we have not yet succeeded in making Europe "whole, free, and secure." There is increasing evidence, however, that Europeans are ready to take more initiative, despite their cleavages regarding Russia, and rebalance responsibilities on security issues with Washington. The EU's decision to take the lead in mediating a ceasefire agreement between Georgia and Russia under the auspices of French President Nicolas Sarkozy testifies to this.

Likewise, the compromise last year on Georgia and Ukraine's requests for NATO membership action plans—essentially postponing the plans while reassuring the countries that they can eventually join the alliance—was reached by European initiative, prompted by German and other European objections to the Bush administration's approach. This too suggested a rebalancing between Europe and the United States in managing relations with Russia.

While it would be wrong to get irrationally exuberant about a new golden age in Russia-Europe relations and Russia-West relations more broadly, the coalescence of an economic downturn and a new political environment suggests that the structural environment for the relationship may be conducive to greater cooperation and less conflict than has been the case in the recent past. Hopefully we will be able to regard 2008 as the bottom of an abyss in Russia-West relations.

ANDREW C. KUCHINS is a senior fellow and director of the Russia and Eurasia Program at the Center for Strategic and International Studies.

Israeli Military Calculations towards Iran

Iran's apparent interest in a nuclear-weapons capability, which it denies, has sparked concerns in Israel mirroring those of the United States, the Gulf Cooperation Council, France, Germany and the United Kingdom. Yet there is a unique edge to Israel's worries: the concentration of three-quarters of its population on a narrow strip of coastline from Ashkelon to Haifa makes it extremely vulnerable to nuclear strikes. Israel's presumed second-strike capability might severely damage its attacker, but there would be no Israeli state left to take satisfaction.

Israelis are not the first to notice this asymmetry. Former Iranian president Ali Akbar Hashemi Rafsanjani remarked five years ago that "the use of even one nuclear bomb inside Israel will destroy everything. However, it will only harm the Islamic world. It is not irrational to contemplate such an eventuality."

Converging Concerns

Several developments have reignited Israeli concerns about the prospect of an undeterrable adversary in its vicinity. The first was alleged Iranian progress in mastering uranium enrichment against a background of deception in Tehran's dealings with the International Atomic Energy Agency (IAEA). Israel is said to have told the U.S. that Iran has not only been working on centrifuge cascades, but has also made progress toward fabricating the explosive shell essential to compressing the fissile core of a nuclear device to produce a yield. The source is a secret agent whose reporting has not been confirmed by U.S. analysts. Given the trouble previously caused by "Curveball", a German intelligence asset whose inaccurate reporting on Saddam Hussein's supposed WMD efforts buttressed the case for war against Iraq, Israel's claims have been met with scepticism by the CIA, which is reported to have concluded that Iran does not, at this point, have a weapons programme.

Secondly, Israel, like other concerned Western countries, relates Iran's putative efforts to develop a nuclear weapons capability with advances Tehran claims to have made towards an intermediate ballistic missile capability in the form of the SHAHAB III. Given the range arcs connecting hypothetical launch sites in eastern Iran to the Mediterranean coast, Israel would have no more than two or three minutes' warning of impact. Such short lead-time would inevitably limit Israel's response options and strain its command-and-control arrangements.

Thirdly, Israel perceives Iran to be on the offensive. Tehran's interventions in Israel's dispute with the Palestinians in the West Bank and Gaza strike Israelis as gratuitously provocative. Iran's ideological and rhetorical commitment to the Palestinian cause is taken for granted by most Israelis, but the extension of this commitment to financing, training and equipping Hamas and Palestine Islamic Jihad is not. To Israeli minds it suggests a willingness to take risks for a purpose that does not contribute directly to the security of the Iranian state; it seems expressive, not rational and evokes a mindset unsuited to a strategic relationship involving nuclear weapons and underpinned by deterrence. The level of Iranian support for Hizbullah before, during and after recent hostilities in Lebanon has strengthened suspicions that Iran's posture toward Israel has taken a harder, more aggressive and somewhat risk-prone turn.

Rhetorical Offensive

The context for the current tensions was set by a sequence of carefully crafted and intentionally outrageous statements by Iranian President Mahmoud Ahmadinejad. He denied the Holocaust, threatened to wipe Israel off the map, characterised the Jewish state as "artificial" and predicted that Israel would disappear shortly.

These verbal attacks serve several purposes perhaps only tangentially related to the Iranian–Israeli bilateral relationship. They are popular in the Arab world, which makes it awkward for regional regimes to side openly with the U.S. in its efforts to win support for sanctions against Iran. They also serve Ahmadinejad's determination to breathe new life into the Islamic Revolution, which had not been launched as a Shia revolt but was originally envisaged as a pan-Islamic movement. By openly challenging Israel's legitimacy, let alone viability, as a state, the Iranian President enhances the primacy of Iran even as he papers over Sunni-Shia tensions that, in Iraq, are tearing at the fabric of society. Not coincidentally, he deflects attention from the continuing poor performance of Iran's economy under his leadership.

There is thus little likelihood that Ahmadinejad will temper his rhetoric, and just as little incentive for Supreme Leader Ali Khamene'i to push him towards a more tempered presentational approach. Meanwhile, Israelis are not focusing on the collateral objectives of Ahmadinejad's words, but rather on their face value.

Israeli Adjustments

The government of Israeli Prime Minister Ehud Olmert would like this problem to go away. The nearly universal disappointment—and, in some quarters, anger—over Olmert's handling of the confrontation with Hizbullah has put the government under pressure to be resolute. This pressure has been compounded by the continued firing of Qassam rockets from Gaza, where another Israeli soldier remains captive. It is therefore imperative politically that Olmert more overtly address the issue of Iran's nuclear ambitions and the interplay between these designs and Ahmadinejad's periodic out-bursts.

A Nuclear Anti-Nuclear Option?

In early January 2006, the "Sunday Times" revealed that the Israeli military has been planning to use nuclear weapons for a possible attack against Iran's nuclear facilities, and most particularly the enrichment plant at Natanz. According to the article in the "Sunday Times," the use of nuclear weapons would be justified by the fact that the enrichment facilities at Natanz are protected by an estimated 20m of rock and concrete and are thus effectively outside reach of even the most powerful earth-penetrating bomb. However, any new use of nuclear bombs for combat purposes after Hiroshima and Nagasaki would have exceedingly heavy political and strategic implications.

Although Israeli Foreign Ministry spokesman Mark Regev formally denied the claim and restated the official stance that Israel was committed to a diplomatic solution and supported the UN Security Council resolution imposing sanctions on Iran, there are little doubts that the "tweaks" that arguably led to the newspaper's article were a deliberate move, in order to warn Iran (and the rest of the world) that Israel does have nuclear weapons and was prepared to use them. Much the same logic would seem to apply to Prime Minister Ehud Olmert's apparent "slip of the tongue" during his visit to Germany in December 2006, when he included Israel in a list of responsible nuclear powers (in contrast to Iran), and thus for the very first time indirectly acknowledged the existence of Israel's nuclear arsenal.

In addition to (re)asserting Israel deterrent vis-à-vis Iran, the calculated leaks about a conceivable Israeli pre-emptive nuclear strike might also be intended to force Washington's hand to launch a conventional attack of its own against Iran, or, at the very least, to give backing for Israel to do so.

Accordingly, Olmert has brought Avigdor Lieberman into the cabinet as part of a coalition deal that gives the newcomer the Iran portfolio. Lieberman is a right-wing politician who believes that Israel's enemies cannot be placated and must be subdued. Effie Eitam, another hardliner and former general who at one time seemed to favour the expulsion of Palestinians from the West Bank, also sits on Olmert's flank.

But the problem with being more vocal for domestic political purposes is that a prior foreign policy objective—to keep Israel out of the U.S.-UN-Iran diplomatic equation—has necessarily been compromised. The failure of the UN Security Council to agree on and enforce sanctions capable of raising the cost to Iran of pursuing its enrichment programme has reduced Olmert's room for manoeuvre. Nor is there much confidence in the willingness of third parties to deal with the problem militarily. The deputy defence minister, Ephraim Sneh, summed up Israeli sentiment by saying that the countries that would not bomb Auschwitz were not going to bomb Iran's nuclear production facilities.

American Mixed Messages

The U.S. appears to be giving Israel mixed signals regarding its own intentions to move beyond diplomacy, should this prove unavailing. Olmert met President George W. Bush in Washington on 14 November and emerged from his two-on-two meeting, at which Iran was presumed to be the main agenda item, saying that he was very happy with the discussion. Political analysts generally interpreted this to mean that Bush had given him assurances that, one way or another, Iran would not be allowed to obtain a nuclear-weapons capability. The implication drawn by some will have been that, if all else failed, the U.S. would consider facilitating an Israeli attack. But there is virtually no chance that approval would have been given by the White House at this encounter, or sought by Israel.

A crucial issue in any military calculations is the gap between the "red lines" of Israel and America. For Israel, Iranian mastery of the enrichment process represents a point of no return. For the U.S., which prudently has not specified a red line, that point would be further down the road, perhaps the moment when Iran was shown to have moved towards weaponisation. The gap between the two countries on this point could complicate diplomatic or military coordination over the next two years.

A conflicting and disconcerting message was also heard by Israelis who perceived that the defeats suffered by Republicans in the mid-term elections, which had taken place the week before Olmert's visit, ruled out the possibility of an American attack on Iran. The logic was that the White House, confounded by Iraq and under pressure from Republicans to do nothing more to damage the party's prospects in the 2008 general election, would abandon whatever plans might have been contemplated regarding military action against Iran. Donald Rumsfeld's replacement as Secretary of Defense by Robert Gates, who is on record as endorsing a dialogue with Iran, reinforced this view.

Despite the apparently encouraging substance of Bush's private remarks to Olmert, the Israeli delegation was hearing to them rather discouraging noises from others.

Military Planning

The complexities of an attack against Iran's nuclear facilities are daunting. The targets within Iran are much further from Israeli bases than was Iraq's Osirak reactor, destroyed by the Israeli Air Force in 1981. Yet Israel has reshaped its air force for deep strike missions of this kind. Its F-15s and F-16s have conformal fuel tanks that, in addition to drop tanks, increase the ability to fly long distances and reduce the need to refuel. For long-range missions such as this, however, tankers based on the C-130 and B-707 airframes are avaiiabie to support strike aircraft. The latter are big enough to loiter at refuelling stations for long periods and dispense the fuel needed to allow the raiders back to their bases after striking their targets.

Israel's air-force is sufficiently large to deploy a strike package of perhaps 50 jets—25 F-16s and 25 F-15s—which would be just enough to attack three key targets: the Natanz enrichment facility; the Arak research reactor; and the uranium conversion facility at Isfahan. The size of the attacking force would be determined by the number of aircraft needed to deliver a given amount of munitions, assuming a relatively low attrition rate. Israel has many weapons, such as 2,000-pound BLU-109 and 5,000 pound BLU-113 hardened penetration bombs, that could be used for such purposes. These can be released at standoff ranges and programmed to detonate above or below ground for maximum effect. Generating overpressures of about $0.7 kg/cm^2$, these munitions are unlikely to leave much more than rubble. To assist precise targeting, Israel could use its LITENING targeting pods in combination with GPS systems. The Israelis would probably expect all but one or two of the aircraft to hit their targets. This is an expectation shaped by historical data on similar strikes conducted against an enemy that was well aware that an attack was coming.

There is the question of how Israeli planes would get to Iran. The attackers would have to traverse Turkish air space if they chose a northern route, which would skirt the Turkish bases at Diyarbakir and Incirlik. Standing against the risk of Turkish interference would be the advantage of refuelling over international Mediterranean waters. A central route would require them to overfly Syria or Jordan and Iraq. The Syrians would certainly shoot at the intruders; the Jordanians would probably not, but King Abdullah, a tacit Israeli friend, would be gravely humiliated. If the U.S. were fully supportive and willing to be identified unambiguously with an Israeli strike, it could facilitate overflight of Iraq and provide a secure orbit in Iraqi airspace for Israeli refuelling aircraft. A southern route would require overflight of Saudi Arabia.

Main Iranian Nuclear Facilities
www.securitywatchtower.com

Since Iraq has faded as a rival to the Kingdom, and Saudi military alert levels are correspondingly lower, it is extremely improbable that the raiders would be detected, let alone successfully engaged. It seems unlikely at this juncture that the U.S. would be eager to accept the diplomatic and retaliatory costs entailed by any of these options.

Iranian retaliation does not loom large in Israel's thinking. Israelis are certainly vulnerable to Iranian reprisal in third countries, as Tehran proved when it collaborated in attacks against Jewish targets in Argentina in the early 1990s. But Hizbullah, despite its evident resilience, is no match for the Israeli Defense Force, especially if ground forces were fully unleashed, as many Israelis think they should have been recently in Lebanon. Tehran's Syrian ally would not be in a position to respond on Iran's behalf. And from an Israeli viewpoint, Iran is already pressing the Palestinian militant button as hard as it can.

For now, matters stand in delicate balance. The uncertainties regarding access are probably the ones that render the idea of attacking Iranian nuclear-related installations most unappetising to Israel. But Israel has tended to take risks in the past when it has felt most isolated and threatened. Israel's confidence in its nuclear deterrence will counterbalance the impulse to undertake the hazards of air strikes against Iran; and it is not yet clear to Israelis whether Iran would be more aggressive as a nuclear power, or more cautious and in fear of escalation. International inaction, an America with no appetite for confrontation, and an Iran whose leaders ruminate publicly on the destruction of Israel are precisely the conditions to upset this delicate balance.

From *Military Technology,* January 2007, pp. 258–260. Copyright © 2007 by Mönch Publishing Group. Reprinted by permission.

The Long Road from Prague

Rose Gottemoeller

D r. Schneider and Major General Manner, thank you so much for inviting me to speak today and for your kind introduction. I know the history of this conference and know that, over the years, it has been instrumental in bringing together people and ideas to consider how best to confront the challenges of weapons of mass destruction. I'm honored to stand here among many friends and colleagues. In many ways this is like an old homecoming gathering: I well remember speaking to this conference when it was held in Norfolk in 2001. For those I have not met, let me say that I look forward to working with you in the coming years.

Since this conference is co-sponsored by the Air Force, I want you to know that I'm aware every young Air Force officer is taught at Squadron Officer School that every briefing should have three main points. I said that I'm aware of that guidance; I didn't say I would follow it—I actually have five points to make.

First, I want to provide you some context and background on the Obama Administration's views on arms control and nuclear disarmament. Then I will brief you on the on-going negotiation of a follow-on agreement to replace the expiring START Treaty. Finally, I will make a few comments about other critical goals for this administration on nuclear security policy: the ratification of the Comprehensive Test-Ban Treaty (CTBT), the negotiation of a verifiable Fissile Material Cutoff Treaty (FMCT), and President Obama's vision for a future arms control agreement after START Follow-on.

Context and Background

President Obama and Secretary Clinton both have made clear their views on nuclear weapons reductions and have made a commitment, a commitment that I share, to making future generations safe from the horrors of nuclear war. On April 5 of this year, in Prague, President Obama made the first of four major foreign policy speeches. In Prague, the President set forth a specific agenda to address the challenges posed by the risk of the proliferation of nuclear weapons. He articulated a bold vision, to "seek the peace and security of a world free of nuclear weapons" no matter how hard it might be or how long it might take.

To achieve this goal, we must make a break from Cold War thinking and create an updated nuclear posture, the role, size, and composition of which reflects more accurately our present and future national security requirements. We must address the threats in the international environment, continue to deter our adversaries, and guarantee the defense of our allies. We recognize the realities of the world that we live in today, and the President has said that, "as long as these weapons exist, the United States will maintain a safe, secure and effective arsenal." Any changes in our nuclear posture, moreover, must result from a deliberative, diligent process. And, as you know, that process is now underway as part of the congressionally-mandated Nuclear Posture Review being led by DOD in consultation with DOE and the State Department.

We are under no illusions that we will be without challenge in aligning our nuclear posture for the 21st century in a way that simultaneously reinforces peace and security while reducing the salience of nuclear weapons worldwide. Achieving this end state requires creative transformational thinking, persistence, the assembly of a skilled workforce, and the marshalling of critical infrastructure. And you, in this room, are among the transformational thinkers and the skilled workforce upon whom we will depend to make good on our ambitions.

The United States and Russia have the largest nuclear arsenals in the world, arsenals that are legacies of the Cold War. As you know, both countries have already reduced their nuclear stockpiles significantly since the end of the Cold War. Many of those reductions were done in accordance with treaty obligations; some were done as a result of unilateral decisions made by Washington and Moscow to make further reductions. Yet ironically, now twenty years after the fall of the Berlin Wall and the end of the Cold War, and despite the implementation of arms control agreements between Russia and the United States, the chances of a nuclear detonation somewhere in the world seem greater than at points during the Cold War. Nuclear programs continue to exist elsewhere, a few countries are developing nuclear weapons, and terrorists groups seem bent on acquiring nuclear material by whatever means they can. So, while we made enormous progress reducing the number of weapons, there remains much more we must do towards fulfilling the President's increasingly broadly shared vision of "the peace and security of a world without nuclear weapons."

START Follow-On

Let me now talk about some of the steps that this Administration is taking on the long road from Prague. Our first priority is to negotiate a new START Treaty because, as you know, the current one expires on December 5, 2009. We must work with the Senate to ratify the Comprehensive Test Ban Treaty and we plan to begin work to negotiate a verifiable Fissile Material Cut-off Treaty in the UN's Conference on Disarmament in January.

As the President's START Follow-on negotiator, let me tell you where we stand on the new treaty. Of course, we are fortunate to begin our work on the foundations already established by the INF, START, and the Moscow Treaties as well as the Non-Proliferation Treaty. Our many years of experience in implementing those treaties, in both bilateral and multilateral settings, will help us as we press forward in negotiating a replacement for the START Treaty by December.

My delegation met with our Russian counterparts four times leading up to the July Moscow Summit and once after. As you've seen in the press, those talks were "businesslike and productive" and allowed us to conclude the Joint Understanding at the Summit. The Joint Understanding provides an outline of what the new treaty will look like, but a great deal of work still needs to be completed to fill in the details. With that in mind, I want to walk you through some of the main points of the new START treaty.

The first point is that it will combine the predictability of START with the flexibility of the Moscow Treaty, but at lower numbers of delivery vehicles and their associated warheads. This flexibility gives us the freedom to determine our nuclear force structure within set limits to be established by this new treaty. This flexibility is clearly stated in paragraph four of the Joint Understanding, which underscores that each party will be able to determine the structure of its strategic forces for itself. The Moscow Summit's Joint Understanding sets two separate limits—one for strategic delivery vehicles and the other for their associated warheads. The Joint Understanding stated a wide range of 500–1100 delivery vehicles and 1500–1675 warheads. These ranges will be narrowed through further negotiation—they are not the final numbers for the Treaty and this expectation is made clear in the Joint Understanding: "The specific numbers to be recorded in the treaty for these limits will be agreed through further negotiation."

The new treaty will also draw from the START verification regime; and, therefore, will provide predictability regarding the strategic forces on both sides—both for existing force structure and modernization programs.

In the Joint Understanding, Presidents Obama and Medvedev reaffirmed the long-standing common position that acknowledges the interrelationship between offensive and defensive systems, something first recognized by the Nixon Administration in 1972. The new Treaty is breaking no new ground on this issue. Both Presidents Obama and Medvedev agreed in their April 1 statement in London that the new START Treaty is about strategic offensive arms. While the United States has long agreed that there is a relationship between missile offense and defense, we believe the START Follow-on Treaty is not the appropriate vehicle for addressing missile defense. We have agreed, however, to continue to discuss the topic of missile defense with Russia in a separate venue.

The United States and Russia have agreed, in the Joint Understanding, that existing patterns of cooperation with third parties will not be affected by this treaty. This measure will appear in the new treaty exactly as it appeared in START, so there will be no treaty constraints on our longstanding strategic cooperation with the United Kingdom. The Joint Understanding also calls for a provision in the new treaty concerning the impact on strategic stability of strategic ballistic missiles in non-nuclear configurations, which are sometimes called "conventional global strike weapons." How such weapons will be addressed in the treaty is still a matter under discussion.

I want to take a minute to address some of the criticisms directed at the new START Treaty. Some say that START Follow-on will not induce other countries to give up their weapons programs. In and of itself, START Follow-on does not exist for that purpose. For the administration, the new treaty is valuable in that it will enhance our national security. It will establish a strategic balance that reflects the current security environment in a way that benefits each party and promotes peace and stability. Moreover, the ability of the United States to persuade other nations to act collectively against those states committed to developing nuclear weapons will be bolstered through reductions in the U.S. and Russian nuclear arsenals. It is a matter of moral suasion.

Critics have also said that we are agreeing on the New START Treaty ahead of the completion of the Nuclear Posture Review. That is not the case. The Obama Administration tasked the NPR working groups, as a first step, to develop a nuclear force structure and posture for use in these negotiations. While the NPR's work is still ongoing, it will continue to inform the positions taken by the United States as it negotiates the new START Treaty with Russia.

Comprehensive Nuclear Test-Ban Treaty

The second major arms control objective of the Obama Administration is the ratification of the Comprehensive Nuclear Test-Ban Treaty (CTBT). There is no step that we could take that would more effectively restore our moral leadership and improve our ability to reenergize the international nonproliferation consensus than to ratify the CTBT. We fully recognize that this will not be an easy task and we will work closely with the Senate, different parts of the administration and key stakeholders to achieve this goal. But here, too, we must construct a new paradigm from the debate over this same issue in 1999. Simply put, the world has changed. Nuclear Weapons States have adapted over the past 17 years since they undertook testing moratoria. Technology has changed. We are better able to detect nuclear tests and much more certain in our ability to certify the reliability of the U.S. stockpile without testing. But we realize there is more to do. We have embarked on a significant set of efforts that will prepare the administration to seek the advice and consent of the Senate. And even as we pursue ratification, we will work hard with others to ensure that the requirements for the CTBT's entry into force are met at the earliest possible date.

Fissile Material Cutoff Treaty

In addition, we will work to reduce the materials needed to produce nuclear weapons. Achieving a verifiable Fissile Material Cutoff Treaty (FMCT) is an essential condition for a world free of nuclear weapons. If the international community is serious about building down, we must constrain the ability to build up. We are working hard to keep the United Nations' Conference on Disarmament—the CD—focused on this goal. We firmly believe that negotiating an FMCT is both achievable and worthwhile.

Many discount the relevance of such a treaty, citing the large stockpiles of fissile materials held by nuclear weapons states. But it should be obvious that as nuclear arsenals come down, it will become increasingly important to have limitations on fissile material that could be used to produce new weapons.

Future Steps

Finally, let me close with a look to the future. When Presidents Obama and Medvedev met in London in April, they issued two Joint Statements. The first, as I've already mentioned, launched negotiation of a START Follow-on Treaty. The second statement was broader in scope and emphasized, among other items, the notion that the START Follow-on Treaty was the first step in a process of pursuing further nuclear weapons reductions. I believe a new START Treaty is an essential step on the path to deeper reductions in the future. Just as important, it begins a new narrative for our post–Cold War world, one that recognizes the need to eliminate the paralyzing threat of nuclear war by eliminating nuclear weapons.

I've titled this speech "The Long Road from Prague." And it really is a long road to a nuclear free world. There will be obstacles along the way; the journey will be difficult, and require enormous efforts to address the insecurities in many regions around the world that may lead some to seek nuclear weapons. But it is a journey that we must take. We do not have to live in a world where there is even one more nuclear-armed country. We must also confront the nightmarish possibility of terrorists getting their hands on the bomb. That's why the administration is working so hard to eliminate nuclear weapons worldwide, while simultaneously recognizing that we must proceed toward that goal in a measured, practical and mutually beneficial manner that protects and promotes our own and global security.

As I said at the beginning of this talk, this journey will require creative transformational thinking and persistence. We all must do our part and I look forward to sharing the road with you. Thank you.

ROSE GOTTEMOELLER is Assistant Secretary, Bureau of Verification, Compliance, and Implementation, Woolands Conference Center, Colonial Williamsburg, VA, August 14, 2009.

From *Speech or Remarks*, August 14, 2009. Public Domain.

The Terrorist Threat to Pakistan's Nuclear Weapons

SHAUN GREGORY

Al-Qa`ida has made numerous statements about a desire to obtain nuclear weapons for use against the United States and Western interests.[1] While many of these statements are rhetorical hyperbole, the scale of the potential destructiveness of nuclear weapons, the instability and "nuclear porosity" of the context in Pakistan, and the vulnerabilities within Pakistan's nuclear safety and security arrangements mean that the risks of terrorist groups gaining access to nuclear materials are real. Moreover, militants have recently attacked a number of Pakistan's nuclear facilities, including an August 20, 2008 incident at the Wah cantonment, widely understood to be one of Pakistan's main nuclear weapons assembly sites.

In an effort to provide insight on the scale of the threat, this article will first outline Pakistan's current nuclear safeguards, and then identify a series of weaknesses in the country's nuclear security that could result in terrorist groups such as al-Qa`ida or the Pakistani Taliban gaining access to sensitive nuclear material.

Pakistan's Nuclear Safeguards

Pakistan has established a robust set of measures to assure the security of its nuclear weapons. These have been based on copying U.S. practices, procedures and technologies, and comprise: a) physical security; b) personnel reliability programs; c) technical and procedural safeguards; and d) deception and secrecy. These measures provide the Pakistan Army's Strategic Plans Division (SPD)—which oversees nuclear weapons operations—a high degree of confidence in the safety and security of the country's nuclear weapons.[2]

In terms of physical security, Pakistan operates a layered concept of concentric tiers of armed forces personnel to guard nuclear weapons facilities, the use of physical barriers and intrusion detectors to secure nuclear weapons facilities, the physical separation of warhead cores from their detonation components, and the storage of the components in protected underground sites.

With respect to personnel reliability, the Pakistan Army conducts a tight selection process drawing almost exclusively on officers from Punjab Province who are considered to have fewer links with religious extremism or with the Pashtun areas of Pakistan from which groups such as the Pakistani Taliban mainly garner their support. Pakistan operates an analog to the U.S. Personnel Reliability Program (PRP) that screens individuals for Islamist sympathies, personality problems, drug use, inappropriate external affiliations, and sexual deviancy.[3] The army uses staff rotation and also operates a "two-person" rule under which no action, decision, or activity involving a nuclear weapon can be undertaken by fewer than two persons.[4] The purpose of this policy is to reduce the risk of collusion with terrorists and to prevent nuclear weapons technology getting transferred to the black market. In total, between 8,000 and 10,000 individuals from the SPD's security division and from Pakistan's Inter-Services Intelligence Directorate (ISI), Military Intelligence and Intelligence Bureau agencies are involved in the security clearance and monitoring of those with nuclear weapons duties.[5]

Despite formal command authority structures that cede a role to Pakistan's civilian leadership, in practice the Pakistan Army has complete control over the country's nuclear weapons. It imposes its executive authority over the weapons through the use of an authenticating code system down through the command chains that is intended to ensure that only authorized nuclear weapons activities and operations occur. It operates a tightly controlled identification system to assure the identity of those involved in the nuclear chain of command, and it also uses a rudimentary Permissive Action Link (PAL) type system to electronically lock its nuclear weapons. This system uses technology similar to the banking industry's "chip and pin" to ensure that even if weapons fall into terrorist hands they cannot be detonated.[6]

Finally, Pakistan makes extensive use of secrecy and deception. Significant elements of Pakistan's nuclear weapons infrastructure are kept a closely guarded secret. This includes the precise location of some of the storage facilities for nuclear core and detonation components, the location of preconfigured nuclear weapons crisis deployment sites, aspects of the nuclear command and control arrangements,[7] and many aspects of the arrangements for nuclear safety and security (such as the numbers of those removed under personnel reliability programs, the reasons for their removal, and how often authenticating and enabling (PAL-type) codes are changed). In addition, Pakistan uses deception—such as dummy missiles—to complicate the calculus of adversaries and is likely to have extended this practice to its nuclear weapons infrastructure.

Taken together, these measures provide confidence that the Pakistan Army can fully protect its nuclear weapons against the internal terrorist threat,[8] against its main adversary India, and against the suggestion that its nuclear weapons could be either spirited out of the country by a third party (posited to be the United States) or destroyed in the event of a deteriorating situation or a state collapse in Pakistan.[9] The fact that Pakistan has been willing to fire on U.S. soldiers during the latter's ground incursion into Pakistan's tribal areas on September 12, 2008[10] removes any debate about whether Pakistan would use force to resist attempts by the United States to secure Pakistan's nuclear assets without its consent. Similarly, the use of U.S. precision strikes to destroy the weapons would need to rely on perfect intelligence and would risk not only significant radiological hazards at strike targets, but also the ire of the Pakistan Army and the wider Islamic world.

Despite these elaborate safeguards, empirical evidence points to a clear set of weaknesses and vulnerabilities in Pakistan's nuclear safety and security arrangements.

The concern, however, is that most of Pakistan's nuclear sites are close to or even within areas dominated by Pakistani Taliban militants and home to al-Qa`ida.

Pakistan's Nuclear Security Weaknesses

When Pakistan was developing its nuclear weapons infrastructure in the 1970s and 1980s, its principal concern was the risk that India would overrun its nuclear weapons facilities in an armored offensive if the facilities were placed close to the long Pakistan-India border. As a result, Pakistan, with a few exceptions, chose to locate much of its nuclear weapons infrastructure to the north and west of the country and to the region around Islamabad and Rawalpindi—sites such as Wah, Fatehjang, Golra Sharif, Kahuta, Sihala, Isa Khel Charma, Tarwanah, and Taxila.[11] The concern, however, is that most of Pakistan's nuclear sites are close to or even within areas dominated by Pakistani Taliban militants and home to al-Qa`ida.

The Pakistani Taliban and al-Qa`ida are more than capable of launching terrorist attacks in these areas, including within Islamabad and Rawalpindi. They have also proved that they have good intelligence about the movement of security personnel, including army, ISI and police forces, all of whom have been routinely targeted. A series of attacks on nuclear weapons facilities has also occurred. These have included an attack on the nuclear missile storage facility at Sargodha on November 1, 2007,[12] an attack on Pakistan's nuclear airbase at Kamra by a suicide bomber on December 10, 2007,[13] and perhaps most

significantly the August 20, 2008 attack when Pakistani Taliban suicide bombers blew up several entry points to one of the armament complexes at the Wah cantonment, considered one of Pakistan's main nuclear weapons assembly sites.[14]

The attacks at the Wah cantonment highlight the vulnerability of nuclear weapons infrastructure sites to at least three forms of terrorist assault.

The significance of these events is difficult to overstate. Civilian nuclear weapons sites—those sites where Pakistan's nuclear weapons are manufactured, assembled or taken for refurbishment—are typically less protected than military sites where nuclear weapons are stored, deployed and operated, a problem the Pakistan Army has now moved to address.[15] The attacks at the Wah cantonment highlight the vulnerability of nuclear weapons infrastructure sites to at least three forms of terrorist assault: a) an attack to cause a fire at a nuclear weapons facility, which would create a radiological hazard; b) an attack to cause an explosion at a nuclear weapons facility involving a nuclear weapon or components, which would create a radiological hazard; or c) an attack with the objective of seizing control of nuclear weapons components or possibly a nuclear weapon. On the latter point, Pakistan's usual separation of nuclear weapons components is compromised to a degree by the need to assemble weapons at certain points in the manufacture and refurbishment cycle at civilian sites, and by the requirement for co-location of the separate components at military sites so that they can be mated quickly if necessary in crises. Furthermore, the emergence of new terrorist tactics in Pakistan (and of Pakistani terrorists in India) in which groups of armed combatants act in coordination on the ground[16]—sometimes in combination with suicide or vehicle bomb attacks at entry points to facilitate access—suggests the credibility of such an assault on a nuclear weapons facility; this is especially true because in a number of these attacks the security has been poor and disorganized, and the terrorists have been able to escape and remain at large.

The risk of the Pakistani Taliban or al-Qa`ida gaining access to nuclear weapons, components or technical knowledge takes on an even graver dimension once the possibility of collusion is introduced. It is widely accepted that there is a strong element within the Pakistan Army and within the lead intelligence agency, the ISI, that is anti-Western, particularly anti-U.S., and that there also exists an overlapping pro-Islamist strand.[17] This is attributed to the "Islamization" of the Pakistan Army, which is the result of a number of factors: General Zia-ul-Haq opening the doors of the Pakistan Army to Islamists in the late 1970s;[18] family and clan links to Islamists and extremists; the corrosive impact of what is widely seen as the Pakistan Army being asked to turn their guns on their own countrymen at Washington's behest; and the corruption of pro-Western political and military leaders.

No screening program will ever be able to weed out all Islamist sympathizers or anti-Westerners among Pakistan's military or among civilians with nuclear weapons expertise. Yet, there are at least four levels of concern about collusion.

First, those with access to nuclear weapons facilities, but not to the weapons or components themselves, could facilitate the access of terrorist groups to nuclear weapons sites, acting as a significant force multiplier for the kind of terrorist attack seen at Wah in August 2008.

Second, some individuals with nuclear weapons duties could facilitate—through intelligence, or directly—access to nuclear weapons or nuclear weapons components, circumventing two-person and other procedural obstacles.

Third, technocrats with pro-terrorist or anti-Western sympathies could transfer their knowledge to al-Qa`ida or to the Pakistani Taliban. There is already the well-known case of two senior Pakistan Atomic Energy Commission (PAEC) scientists, Sultan Bashirrudin Mahmood and Chaudhry Abdul Majeed, who traveled to Afghanistan in 2000 and again shortly before 9/11 for meetings with Osama bin Ladin himself, the content of which has never been disclosed.[19] Combined with the example of A. Q. Khan, the so-called "father" of Pakistan's nuclear bomb who was arrested in 2004 for masterminding the largest nuclear proliferation network in history, the cases of Mahmood and Majeed point to what has been termed the "porosity" of the nuclear context in Pakistan and the real risk of nuclear technology and of related technology being sold to terrorists on the black market by those involved with Khan or with Pakistan's nuclear weapons program.[20]

The final risk, and one that is usually overlooked, is that the Pakistan Army could itself decide to transfer nuclear weapons to a terrorist group. One argument for this, described in Philip Bobbitt's *Terror and Consent,*[21] is that states can become pressurized or incentivized to transfer nuclear weapons to terrorist groups because they are responding to threats from an external power but fear the consequences of being identified as the origin of a nuclear strike. In the context of severe international pressure on the Pakistan Army—particularly by India or the United States[22]—the risk exists that Pakistan might be similarly incentivized to move to such a "coercive option." This remains extremely unlikely in the present context, not least given the level of terrorist threat to the Pakistani state itself. Nevertheless, it forms a necessary strand of the calculus about the transfer of nuclear weapons to terrorist groups in Pakistan.[23]

It remains imperative that Pakistan is pressured and supported, above all by the United States, to continue to improve the safety and security of its nuclear weapons and to ensure the fidelity of those civilian and military personnel with access to, or knowledge of, nuclear weapons.

Conclusion

The risk of the transfer of nuclear weapons, weapons components or nuclear expertise to terrorists in Pakistan is genuine. Moreover, knowledge that such a transfer has occurred may not become evident until the aftermath of a nuclear 9/11 in Pakistan or elsewhere in the world. It remains imperative that Pakistan is pressured and supported, above all by the United States, to continue to improve the safety and security of its nuclear weapons and to ensure the fidelity of those civilian and military personnel with access to, or knowledge of, nuclear weapons. The challenge to Pakistan's nuclear weapons from Pakistani Taliban groups and from al-Qa`ida constitutes a real and present danger, and the recent assaults by the Pakistan Army on some of these groups in FATA and in the NWFP is a welcome development. Nevertheless, more steps must be taken before the threat is neutralized and Pakistan's nuclear weapons no longer pose an existential danger to the rest of the world.

Notes

1. "Bin Laden has Nuclear Weapons," BBC, November 10, 2001; "Al Qa'ida Threaten to Use Pakistani Nukes," *Independent,* June 22, 2009.

2. Lt. Col. Zafar Ali (SPD), *Pakistan's Nuclear Assets and Threats of Terrorism: How Grave is the Danger?* (Washington, D.C.: Henry L. Stimson Center, 2007).

3. Shaun Gregory, "Nuclear Command and Control in Pakistan," *Defense and Security Analysis* 23:3 (2007).

4. Cotta-Ramusino and Maurizio Martelline, *Nuclear Safety, Nuclear Stability and Nuclear Strategy in Pakistan* (Como, Italy: Landau Network, 2002).

5. Personal interview, General Kidwai, Director General of the SPD, Islamabad, March 2005; Personal interview, Bruno Tertrais, French Ministry of Defense, June 2007.

6. David Blair, "Code Changes 'Secure' Pakistan Warheads," *Daily Telegraph,* February 9, 2004.

7. This includes the issue of pre-delegation during crises.

8. "Zardari Says Pakistan's Nuclear Weapons are Safe," Reuters, April 27, 2009.

9. "US Has Plans to Secure Pakistan's Nuclear Weapons," *Daily Times,* May 16, 2009.

10. "Shots Fired in US-Pakistan Clash," BBC, September 25, 2008.

11. "Expansion at Pakistan's Nuclear Sites," Institute for Science and International Security, May 19, 2009.

12. Bill Roggio, "Suicide Bomber Kills Eight at Pakistani Airbase," *The Long War Journal,* November 1, 2007.

13. Bill Roggio, "Al Qaeda, Taliban Targeting Pakistani Nuclear Sites," *The Long War Journal,* December 11, 2007.

14. "Pakistan Bombers Hit Arms Factory," BBC, August 21, 2008.

15. The Pakistan Army has strengthened the security at some civilian sites by the deployment of extra troops and through the training of police and civilian nuclear security personnel. These measures, however, have not been widely implemented due to the immense pressure on Pakistan's security forces because of the operations in the Pashtun belt and to manpower problems partly due to terrorist attacks on Pakistan's security forces.

16. "Pakistan Taliban Chief Brags of Attack on Police," *Washington Post,* April 1, 2009.

17. This has many expressions, including the unwillingness of Pakistani soldiers to fight in the tribal areas, the involvement of Pakistan Army officers in protecting alleged 9/11 mastermind Khalid Shaykh Muhammad while he was on the run between September 2002 and February 2003, and the involvement of Pakistani officers in assassination attempts against Pakistan's nominally pro-Western president, General Pervez Musharraf.

18. Hassan Abbas, *Pakistan's Drift into Extremism* (Armonk, NY: M.E. Sharpe Press, 2005).

19. Douglas Frantz and Catherine Collins, *Nuclear Jihadist: The Man Who Sold the World's Most Dangerous Weapons* (New York: Twelve, 2007).

20. Adrian Levy and Katherine Scott-Clarke, *Deception: Pakistan, the United States and the Secret Trade in Nuclear Weapons* (New York: Walker and Company, 2007).

21. Philip Bobbitt, Terror and Consent (London: Allen Lane, 2008).

22. For example, in a context in which the United States was attempting to "take out" Pakistani nuclear weapons by precision airstrikes or by the insertion of special forces teams.

23. It is an interesting aside that Pakistan Army Chief of Staff Mirza Aslam Beg was instrumental in passing nuclear weapons technology to a regional and sectarian rival, Iran, in the 1980s simply for money for the Pakistan Army. The lesson is clear: under certain circumstances, senior figures in the Pakistan Army may be willing to transfer nuclear weapons technology, even when it is irrational to do so as in the case of Iran, empowering a regional and religious rival.

Professor **Shaun Gregory** is Director of the Pakistan Security Research Unit (PSRU) at the University of Bradford in the United Kingdom. He was formerly a visiting fellow at the Institute for Strategic Studies in Islamabad (ISSI) and at the Institute for Defence Studies and Analysis (IDSA) in New Delhi. He is the author of many papers and reports on Pakistani nuclear weapons, terrorism, and state stability. His latest book, *Pakistan: Securing the Insecure State,* will be published in 2010.

Evolving Bioweapon Threats Require New Countermeasures

HELEN PURKITT AND VIRGEN WELLS

To better understand possible development and uses of biological weapons by nations and terrorist groups, we have studied past covert government programs in South Africa and Iraq, and recent trends in civilian biotechnology in South Africa.

U.S. monitoring of bioweapon threats is geared primarily toward uncovering large-scale, highly sophisticated programs, like that of the former Soviet Union during the cold war. But covert bioweapon development has become more diffuse, and many potential actors have far different goals than they did then. We think the United States needs to work with other nations to build new norms of transparency and greater international cooperation in regulating the operation of civilian-biotechnology laboratories and the dispersal of relevant data that may have military applications. Only through such global cooperation can we effectively monitor trends in potential bioweapon research and look for early-warning signs of covert biowarfare-weapons development by nation-states or by terrorists and other nonstate actors.

Our research indicates that terrorists are likely to use biological weapons not to inflict mass destruction but to commit blackmail or fuel political discontent, panic, or economic disruption. That's important because the development of biological weapons of mass disruption no longer requires large capital investment, great expertise, vast infrastructure, and sophisticated delivery devices like medium- or long-range missiles. Policy analysts and some policy makers have made similar points, but many of the United States' biosecurity priorities and policies do not reflect the new realities.

In the 1960s and 70s, a common pattern for developing countries was to send the "best and brightest" of their young scientists abroad for advanced study or training. Many of those scientists went on to work in their countries' covert bioweapons programs. For instance, Rihab Rashid Taha al-Azzawi al-Tikriti, a microbiologist (nicknamed "Dr. Germ" by U.N. weapons inspectors) who headed Iraq's bacterial program at al-Hakim for several years, earned a doctorate from the University of East Anglia, in England, where she studied plant disease. Huda Salih Mahdi Ammash, who was dubbed "Mrs. Anthrax" by U.S. intelligence services for her work reconstructing Iraq's biological weapons facilities after the 1991 Persian Gulf war, studied for a master-of-science degree in microbiology at Texas Woman's University, in Denton, and later earned a doctorate in microbiology at the University of Missouri at Columbia. Also, biowarfare scientists recruited to work on covert programs in developing countries were often trained in fields other than biology. For example, South Africa's former covert bioweapons program, Project Coast, recruited many of its first researchers from among veterinarians with advanced degrees in at least two scientific fields. Some Iraqi and South African researchers participated in American or English training exercises at military and government installations, and in scientific exchanges. But the United States closed down a defensive bioweapons-research program in the 1970s, and as concerns grew about Iraqi and South African politics and development of weapons of mass destruction, it became, by the late 1980s, more difficult for scientists from those countries to travel abroad.

The United States further reduced foreign students' and scientists' access to American universities after the terrorist attacks of September 11, 2001, and the still-unsolved anthrax-letter incidents the following month. Unfortunately, the belief that students and scientists from developing countries must obtain their higher education in the West in order to acquire the skills needed to work with and weaponize biological agents is misguided and out-of-date. Today there are premier research universities throughout the world.

Visa restrictions and the rising cost of an American education have led many graduate students and scientists in the biological and physical sciences, especially from Middle Eastern countries, to study or work in countries in their own region or in Europe, Asia, or Africa. Moreover, the online availability of the information necessary to produce many biological pathogens, including step-by-step protocols, means that terrorists can obtain the requisite knowledge and even academic credentials while living almost anywhere.

If information is easy to come by, so are pathogens or potential pathogens. Before they shifted to genetic-modification techniques, both South African and Iraqi biowarfare scientists explored the feasibility of using naturally occurring pathogens. In their initial efforts, Iraqi scientists studied fungal toxins (for instance, mycotoxins and aflatoxins), anthrax spores, and a variety of other toxins, bacteria, and viruses, including those that cause botulism, cholera, polio, and influenza. Other early research involved creating deadly compounds from wheat and castor beans. Similarly, early South African experiments allegedly involved having military forces use biological agents to poison wells and putting cholera in some rivers in southern Africa. Project Coast scientists explored common viruses and bacteria and worked extensively with anthrax, which occurs naturally throughout southern Africa.

Those projects strongly suggest that covert-biowarfare scientists and terrorists are likely to use readily available, naturally occurring pathogens in initial attempts to create bioweapons. So thought the vast majority of the 43 scientists and researchers we interviewed in South Africa during 2003. Several of them noted that hundreds of different fungi found on the diverse plants and trees in rural areas throughout the world could easily be processed to form new biowarfare pathogens.

Some government officials are becoming alert to the prospect that natural pathogens could be used as a fast and easy way to acquire a seed stock for immediate use or further research on creating pathogenicity. To try to counter this emerging threat, 39 nations and the European Commission—all participants at the 2004 plenary session of the Australia Group—agreed to add five plant pathogens to its list of restricted items, the first expansion of the list since 1993. (The Australia Group is an informal network of countries that seeks to harmonize national export-licensing measures to stem the proliferation of chemical and biological weapons.)

Cloning techniques are another underestimated source of potential small-scale biological weapons. In 2003 three researchers in South Africa used an "in house" protocol for cloning that required minimal equipment and expertise to produce the first African cloned cow at a remote research station. Once scientists identify a gene that can cause disease, other scientists or terrorists can clone the gene and introduce it into common host bacteria by using a cloning kit readily available in catalogs of lab equipment.

Although cloning is a relatively common process that does not require a complex lab, safely conducting research on many viruses does demand a Biosafety Level 3 facility. Work with the most serious viruses—infectious diseases that are transmitted through the air and for which there is no known cure—require a BSL-4 laboratory. In BSL-3 labs, researchers wear protective gear to work in negative-pressure environments with transmissible infectious agents like tuberculosis. BSL-4 labs are highly secure areas for the study of the most infectious diseases, like the Ebola virus, and have multiple locked chambers, with constant monitoring of directed air flow. Scientists at those facilities wear suits with their own air supplies and work on infectious agents in special cabinets, also with their own air. The BSL-4 facilities require very careful construction, with holes for electrical, plumbing, piping, and camera outlets embedded ahead of time in their concrete walls.

Those needs have long been thought to limit the activities of scientists or terrorists working in poor countries. Recent technological advances, however, make it possible to set up a modular mobile BSL-3 lab within days, even in a remote location. As far as we know, all such facilities now are in the hands of agencies such as the U.S. Centers for Disease Control and Prevention. But recent changes in the Australia Group's export-control list reflect concern about smaller and more mobile equipment that could be used for covert biowarfare. In 2002, for instance, the group passed new export restrictions on small fermenters that could be used in the production of bacteria. But that type of equipment is already available for sale on the Internet, and if it hasn't already, it could soon fall into the wrong hands.

A great deal of public attention has focused on the use or genetic modification of extremely dangerous diseases such as Ebola or smallpox. A large portion of the money committed to date in contracts for the United States' Project BioShield ($877-million out of $5.6-billion) is for a program to buy 75 million doses of anthrax vaccine from a single company, VaxGen, even though the plan to inoculate all military personnel has run into legal, scientific, and production delays. The public concerns and large government efforts to counter those pathogens are understandable in the aftermath of the 2001 anthrax letters and public discussion of future terrorist scenarios involving Ebola, smallpox, or highly refined anthrax. However, any government or terrorist group would probably find it simpler to use common pathogens such as E. coli and salmonella, which are easier and cheaper to purchase, reproduce, and use.

Despite a flurry of recent research focused on the potential use of civilian biotechnology as a weapon, there have been remarkably few empirical studies of biotech trends in developing countries, especially African ones.

The online availability of the information necessary to produce many biological pathogens means that terrorists can obtain the requisite knowledge while living almost anywhere.

That lack of interest is unfortunate because nearly every country in the developing world is seeking to create the scientific and industrial capacity needed to compete in the biotech revolution. Even Zimbabwe, a failing state, recently passed a national biotechnology plan. Most such efforts focus on civilian biotechnology, which is widely viewed as a way to develop new high-value, high-tech products and processes for export, creating new jobs. Several countries in the developing world have also formed special-purpose transnational networks, like the Developing Country Vaccine Manufacturers Network, with a common focus like producing generic drugs for common infectious diseases. But terrorist groups interested in acquiring biotechnology expertise and products have also been reported to be forming transnational networks.

Public and private laboratories in the developing world are also gaining access to sophisticated bioinformatics-computing facilities and gene, tissue, and protein libraries. For example, the South African National Bioinformatics Institute has the long-term goal of connecting researchers at various sites in a transnational network. It will eventually permit scientists across the continent to access a common bioinformatics computer architecture, the power of the one high-speed Cray computer in South Africa, shared access to gene and protein libraries, and the computational tools necessary to conduct sophisticated bioinformatics research on shared problems.

Those trends suggest that before long the world may simultaneously face biological-weapons threats from naturally occurring pathogens and genetically modified organisms. Governments need to develop new approaches to monitor and manage this still poorly understood class of threats.

Traditional control strategies are unlikely to prevent the development of covert bioweapons by either nations or terrorists. The last major effort to ensure compliance with the 1975 Biological and Toxin Weapons Convention was in 2001–2 when a draft protocol was presented to member nations for a vote. The United States rejected it on the grounds that it was an ineffective arms-control approach, would compromise national-security and confidential business information, and would benefit would-be proliferators. But the failure to find evidence of any active WMD programs in Iraq and the suspected Iraqi mobile labs that are now believed to have been hydrogen-production units for weather balloons underscore how difficult it is to verify the existence of a covert biological-weapons program in the absence of sustained, intrusive inspections by neutral outside observers.

Many experts argue that the nature of biotech research is such that greater transparency and cooperation among nations and corporations may be the only way to monitor it. While the U.S. government worries about roughly three dozen countries that may have covert biowarfare programs, the number of possible bioterrorism threats seems limitless. One approach that might help would be to categorize possible threats emanating from different types of countries, and tailor monitoring and security efforts to each category.

Most biotechnology research and development is currently located in the United States, Europe, Japan, and Australia. However, India and China have many public and private biotech companies that are nearing the cutting edge.

A second tier of countries fosters a much smaller scale of biotech research. For example, Argentina and Brazil are significant producers of biotech agricultural crops and rank second and third, behind the United States, in the number of hectares devoted to such crops. Countries as diverse as Cuba, Egypt, Israel, South Africa, and South Korea play host to private and public biotech R&D activities. Much of that consists of civilian efforts to find a niche market in arenas dominated by large multinational businesses or to invent a unique product or process that could be sold to a multinational business. The governments of those countries share a commitment to help stimulate further biotech R&D, for which there is a modest amount of capital available from local or foreign sources. Despite their similarities, however, the countries differ in their degree of foreign collaboration, the extent of engagement in the global economy, and whether the government is a member of the biological-weapons convention.

Before long the world may simultaneously face biological-weapons threats from naturally occurring pathogens and genetically modified organisms.

A third tier consists of most other countries, which have limited civilian biotech research and little chance of closing the economic and technological gap between themselves and Tiers 1 and 2. These countries—such as Dubai, Kenya, Thailand, and the United Arab Emirates—primarily function as junior partners, labor reserves, or offshore tax shelters for multinational biotech companies.

A final tier are countries that have no functioning central government (like Somalia) or have large ungoverned and lawless spaces (like Colombia). In those nation-states the large, lawless areas can serve as attractive locations for terrorist activities.

Given that range, greater transparency seems to be a better approach than traditional control strategies. For example, Western governments should focus more attention on standardizing Good Laboratory Practice (GLP) and safety standards at public and private laboratories. GLP guidelines include inspections of active laboratories, university labs, foreign labs, and inactive labs. Those inspections are focused on standard practices and safety—for example, accountability for reagents and equipment certifications, maintenance of laboratory records, and specimen and sample tracking. The guidelines may help to control access to reagents and equipment, or to monitor illegal labs in remote areas or suburban-kitchen labs operated by terrorists or lone dissidents. But they might also, in the long term, promote greater transparency in biotechnology research and further the development of new international norms about what constitutes public and proprietary information and activities.

We need new regulations for the publication and other dissemination of peer-reviewed research that has possible biowarfare uses. Of course, creating such regulations would involve thorny, fundamental issues regarding the scientific process and the free press. On March 4, 2004, the Bush administration announced the creation of a new federal advisory board designed to help ensure that terrorists cannot make use of federally supported biological research. The new 25-member National Science Advisory Board for Biosecurity is intended to advise federal departments and agencies that conduct or support research of interest to terrorists on how best to keep it out of their hands. The creation of the board was one recommendation of a recent National Academies' National Research Council report (known as the Fink report) that focused on how to keep genetically engineered viruses and other works from being used in bioterrorism. Of course, the board's mandate does not cover research that receives no federal funds or that is conducted abroad, so there is an enormous security gap waiting to be filled.

Most of the scientists we interviewed cautioned that if handled clumsily, efforts to regulate the dissemination of federally supported biological research could damage the United States' position as a research leader. In a global world of science, American and foreign researchers working in the life sciences in America today have many options, including: opting out of research programs related to biosecurity, relying on private or foreign funds for research, or pursuing their research in other countries.

Many of the scientists also conveyed serious concerns about new restrictions on travel for graduate students. Some foreign students who left the United States to visit their home countries have had trouble returning to their American labs. The scientists were also concerned that many talented foreign graduate students who had been accepted into their programs were experiencing difficulties obtaining U.S. visas. Although entry restrictions have eased somewhat, continuing limits and bureaucratic obstacles have led many foreigners to go elsewhere for their education or advanced research. Such restrictions have been imposed in the name of security, but in the long run, they may become one of America's most serious security problems as they gradually erode our centrality in biotech innovation.

We support a significant easing of restrictions on foreigners seeking advanced scientific education or jobs in the West, but also the establishment of an enhanced monitoring system that would include more reliable procedures to ensure that all visa applicants undergo background investigations and checks. And we recommend a new reporting system that would allow the government to better track the whereabouts of foreign graduate students and scientists during their stays in the United States. We also recommend that more attention be given by relevant U.S. agencies to tracking the activities of foreign scientists and students after they have completed their work or studies and have left the United States. Perhaps if such a reporting requirement was incorporated as a condition for the initial visa it would be less controversial.

None of our suggestions would solve the host of problems created by the proliferation of biological expertise, equipment, and supplies. However, an important first step in improving security is to recognize that we face a range of biological threats from many different types of perpetrators, and that although we can monitor and reduce the dangers, we can never fully guard ourselves against attack. Enhancing our national security while also keeping American biotech research at the cutting edge are complementary goals. We can make progress toward both if we strive for greater international norms and transparency, while gauging threats in a more thoughtful and case-specific manner.

HELEN PURKITT is a professor of political science at the U.S. Naval Academy. VIRGEN WELLS, a microbiologist, is a former fellow at the American Association for the Advancement of Science. Their research cited here was supported by the Advanced Systems and Concepts Office of the Defense Threat Reduction Agency, the Institute for National Security Studies at the U.S. Air Force Academy, and the U.S. Naval Academy. However, the views expressed here are those of the authors and not those of the U.S. government.

UNIT 3

Foreign Policy Decision Making

Unit Selections

Key Points to Consider

- What are some of the ways that the foreign policies of the Obama administration are similar to and different from those of the Bush administration?

- Why does every President fail to carry out at least some of his or her campaign promises?

- What is the meaning of national security, human security, and collective security?

- What are some policy areas where two or more of these security concerns overlap?

- Should future U.S. military strategy be based on the views of the Crusaders or Conservatives among returning Iraqi War officer veterans?

- What military lessons should be drawn from the U.S. involvement in Iraq and how do these lessons relate to U.S. involvement in Vietnam?

- What are some ways that the decision making process during famous foreign policy crises, such as the Cuban Missile Crisis, differ from the process assumed by rational choice models of political decision making?

Student Website
www.mhhe.com/cls

Internet References

Carnegie Endowment for International Peace
   http://www.ceip.org
The Heritage Foundation
   http://www.heritage.org

Even before the Republican Party lost control of both the Senate and House of Representatives in 2006, Bush's policy of the preventive use of force was being revised to emphasize other instruments of foreign policy and greater reliance on multilateral diplomacy. Consequently, it is not surprising that some of Obama's foreign policies, such as the time table for the withdrawal of U.S. troops from Iraq and relations with European powers, Russia, and China, are consistent with the policies of the Bush administration. In other areas such as arms control, the Obama administration has launched significantly different proposals and positions than those of his predecessor. The deteriorating security situation in Afghanistan forced the Obama administration to consider adopting policies that are very different from his campaign promises. In "Obama's Foreign Policy: The End of the Beginning," George Friedman describes how the Obama regime has shifted "from a purely defensive posture to a mixed posture of selective offense and defense." Friedman concludes that this shift is hardly surprising because all U.S. presidents operate under in a world of constraints with limited options and "like all good Presidents, Obama is leaving behind certain campaign promises to govern."

A focus on how to maximize a nation-states' vital, important, and secondary interests have been the mainstay of a nation-state foreign policy decision makers' calculus since the formation of the nation-state system. However, as the size of the world's population and the number of people lacking the most basic needs in terms of food, water, shelter, and personal security grows exponentially in future years, there will be a greater recognition that traditional national security interests increasingly intersect with policies designed to improve human security in the developing world. The nexus between traditional and human security concerns has become more salient to U.S. foreign policy decision makers and military leaders as they have had to modify existing strategies to achieve more successful counterinsurgency operations in Iraq. A growing recognition that the two types of security are intertwined was also a core consideration on the minds of the architects who established a new unified military command, AFRICOM, for the African continent in the fall of 2008. Similar reorganization policies have occurred in the U.S. military command, SOUTHCOM that has operational responsibility for Latin America and the Caribbean and by the newly created NORTHCOM. SOUTHCOM has adopted a similar core mission to that of AFRICOM. Both commands are integrated, inter-agency organizations that are attempting to promote security while also providing help where feasible to promote economic development by working with representatives of other U.S. national agencies in countries within the region. While the increased involvement of U.S. military stationed abroad in non-traditional military missions is still controversial, most U.S. decision makers and analysts stress that these new organizational changes merely reflect budgetary realities and realities on the ground. The U.S. military often is the only agency with the operational capacity to help in emergency and non-emergency situations.

A generalized recognition that a third type of threat, collective security threats that might harm all of humankind, may be

growing, has led many policy makers and analysts to stress the future impact of collective security threats that may occur from such worldwide phenomenon as global warming and the spread of new, incurable infectious diseases. The potential threat to world civilizations in the event of a nuclear war was always present during the Cold War. However, today there is a greater possibility that national and human security issues will coincide with global collective security. Today, the United States, much like other nation-states, faces a host of novel challenges related to a longer-term, sustainable security approach.

The recognition that countries do not have an invariant set of national interests is bolstered by a great deal of research in International Relations in recent decades that have focused on how foreign policy decision makers actually make decisions. One type of factor that is important in understanding how and why leaders make their decisions is the concept of images. Understanding the shared images that foreign policy decision makers have of their own country and perceived enemies can help analysts make predictions about future foreign policy choices. Since the 1950s, research on shared images of political leaders has confirmed that leaders and their key advisers often maintain "mirror images" of their adversary. Thus, many analysts have concluded that senior U.S. decision makers underestimated the intensity of the opposition that would result from the decision to disband Saddam Hussein's old army. The U.S. decision unwittingly unleashed century-old struggles for power and control of the security forces in Iraq among Sunni, Shiite and Kurdish communities. In order to cope with the ensuring sectarian conflict and increased attacks engineered by al Qaeda terrorists and other militia groups, the U.S. military had to devise a new military strategy named after the general who formulated it, the Petraeus Doctrine. While U.S. military leaders recognize that conditions in Afghanistan will require a modified strategy, many American combat veteran officers in Iraq are now committed to using Iraq-style counterinsurgency doctrines to shape the future of U.S. ground forces. This is particularly true within the U.S. Army where extensive modernization and rebuilding are taking place after nearly a decade of armed conflict.

Andrew J. Bacevich, in "The Petraeus Doctrine," describes the contours of a great debate within the U.S. Army between two camps of Iraqi War veterans: the Crusaders and the Conservatives. A central question in this debate is how should the lessons of Iraq inform future policy? Bacevich argues that unless the next President weighs in on this and related fundamental debates, decisions by default may well devolve to soldiers. Over time such a situation could tarnish the United States' image as the leading democratic nation-state based on a few key principles, including the sanctity of civilian control of the military and the importance of political leaders in determining America's role in the world.

Prior to World War II, many realist analysts in the West assumed that foreign policy decision makers used the same maximizing logic worldwide to identify their country's important national interests. Thus, classical realists such as Hans Morgenthau talked about the vital and important interests of nation-states in universal terms. However, as recent debates over whether the United States should continue its special relationship with Israel illustrates, there is rarely a consensus on the definition of vital or important national interests within the national homeland. There are debates about what constitutes a nation-state's vital national interest, especially within democracies, because what constitutes a state's most important interests is not an objective, or universal set of values. Thus, the questions of how best to maximize a country's national interests are always a topic of political debates.

A great deal of scholarship on one of the most famous cases of foreign policy crisis decision making, the Cuban Missile Crisis, is helping to dispel notions that political decision makers and people generally, are rational choosers. Instead, scholarship based on recently released documents related to the deliberations within the U.S. and Russian government underscores the fact that the decision-making process is often characterized by misunderstandings while implementation of decisions, even high-level crisis decisions, are often not carried out in the manner intended or are not carried out at all!.

Obama's Foreign Policy: The End of the Beginning

GEORGE FRIEDMAN

A s August draws to a close, so does the first phase of the Obama presidency. The first months of any U.S. presidency are spent filling key positions and learning the levers of foreign and national security policy. There are also the first rounds of visits with foreign leaders and the first tentative forays into foreign policy. The first summer sees the leaders of the Northern Hemisphere take their annual vacations, and barring a crisis or war, little happens in the foreign policy arena. Then September comes and the world gets back in motion, and the first phase of the president's foreign policy ends. The president is no longer thinking about what sort of foreign policy he will have; he now has a foreign policy that he is carrying out.

We therefore are at a good point to stop and consider not what U.S. President Barack Obama will do in the realm of foreign policy, but what he has done and is doing. As we have mentioned before, the single most remarkable thing about Obama's foreign policy is how consistent it is with the policies of former President George W. Bush. This is not surprising. Presidents operate in the world of constraints; their options are limited. Still, it is worth pausing to note how little Obama has deviated from the Bush foreign policy.

During the 2008 U.S. presidential campaign, particularly in its early stages, Obama ran against the Iraq war. The centerpiece of his early position was that the war was a mistake, and that he would end it. Obama argued that Bush's policies—and more important, his style—alienated U.S. allies. He charged Bush with pursuing a unilateral foreign policy, alienating allies by failing to act in concert with them. In doing so, he maintained that the war in Iraq destroyed the international coalition the United States needs to execute any war successfully. Obama further argued that Iraq was a distraction and that the major effort should be in Afghanistan. He added that the United States would need its NATO allies' support in Afghanistan. He said an Obama administration would reach out to the Europeans, rebuild U.S. ties there and win greater support from them.

Though around 40 countries cooperated with the United States in Iraq, albeit many with only symbolic contributions, the major continental European powers—particularly France and Germany—refused to participate. When Obama spoke of alienating allies, he clearly meant these two countries, as well as smaller European powers that had belonged to the U.S. Cold War coalition but were unwilling to participate in Iraq and were now actively hostile to U.S. policy.

A European Rebuff

Early in his administration, Obama made two strategic decisions. First, instead of ordering an immediate withdrawal from Iraq, he adopted the Bush administration's policy of a staged withdrawal keyed to political stabilization and the development of Iraqi security forces. While he tweaked the timeline on the withdrawal, the basic strategy remained intact. Indeed, he retained Bush's defense secretary, Robert Gates, to oversee the withdrawal.

Second, he increased the number of U.S. troops in Afghanistan. The Bush administration had committed itself to Afghanistan from 9/11 onward. But it had remained in a defensive posture in the belief that given the forces available, enemy capabilities and the historic record, that was the best that could be done, especially as the Pentagon was almost immediately reoriented and refocused on the invasion and subsequent occupation of Iraq. Toward the end, the Bush administration began exploring—under the influence of Gen. David Petraeus, who designed the strategy in Iraq—the possibility of some sort of political accommodation in Afghanistan.

Obama has shifted his strategy in Afghanistan to this extent: He has moved from a purely defensive posture to a mixed posture of selective offense and defense, and has placed more forces into Afghanistan (although the United States still has nowhere near the number of troops the Soviets had when they lost their Afghan war). Therefore, the core structure of Obama's policy remains the same as Bush's except for the introduction of limited offensives. In a major shift since Obama took office, the Pakistanis have taken a more aggressive stance (or at least want to appear more aggressive) toward the Taliban and al Qaeda, at least within their own borders. But even so, Obama's basic strategy remains the same as Bush's: hold in Afghanistan until the political situation evolves to the point that a political settlement is possible.

Most interesting is how little success Obama has had with the French and the Germans. Bush had given up asking for assistance in Afghanistan, but Obama tried again. He received the same answer Bush did: no. Except for some minor, short-term assistance, the French and Germans were unwilling to commit forces to Obama's major foreign policy effort, something that stands out.

Given the degree to which the Europeans disliked Bush and were eager to have a president who would revert the U.S.-European relationship to what it once was (at least in their view), one would have thought the French and Germans would be eager to make some substantial gesture rewarding the United States for selecting a pro-European president. Certainly, it was in their interest to strengthen Obama. That they proved unwilling to make that gesture suggests that the French and German relationship with the United States is much less important to Paris and Berlin than it would appear. Obama, a pro-European president, was emphasizing a war France and Germany approved of over a war they disapproved of and asked for their help, but virtually none was forthcoming.

The Russian Non-Reset

Obama's desire to reset European relations was matched by his desire to reset U.S.-Russian relations. Ever since the Orange Revolution in the Ukraine in late 2004 and early 2005, U.S.-Russian relations had deteriorated dramatically, with Moscow charging Washington with interfering in the internal affairs of former Soviet republics with the aim of weakening Russia. This culminated in the Russo-Georgian war last August. The Obama administration has since suggested a "reset" in relations, with Secretary of State Hillary Clinton actually carrying a box labeled "reset button" to her spring meeting with the Russians.

The problem, of course, was that the last thing the Russians wanted was to reset relations with the United States. They did not want to go back to the period after the Orange Revolution, nor did they want to go back to the period between the collapse of the Soviet Union and the Orange Revolution. The Obama administration's call for a reset showed the distance between the Russians and the Americans: The Russians regard the latter period as an economic and geopolitical disaster, while the Americans regard it as quite satisfactory. Both views are completely understandable.

The Obama administration was signaling that it intends to continue the Bush administration's Russia policy. That policy was that Russia had no legitimate right to claim priority in the former Soviet Union, and that the United States had the right to develop bilateral relations with any country and expand NATO as it wished. But the Bush administration saw the Russian leadership as unwilling to follow the basic architecture of relations that had developed after 1991, and as unreasonably redefining what the Americans thought of as a stable and desirable relationship. The Russian response was that an entirely new relationship was needed between the two countries, or the Russians would pursue an independent foreign policy matching U.S. hostility with Russian hostility. Highlighting the continuity in U.S.-Russian relations, plans for the prospective ballistic missile defense installation in Poland, a symbol of antagonistic U.S.-Russian relations, remain unchanged.

The underlying problem is that the Cold War generation of U.S. Russian experts has been supplanted by the post-Cold War generation, now grown to maturity and authority. If the Cold warriors were forged in the 1960s, the post-Cold warriors are forever caught in the 1990s. They believed that the 1990s represented a stable platform from which to reform Russia, and that the grumbling of Russians plunged into poverty and international irrelevancy at that time is simply part of the post-Cold War order. They believe that without economic power, Russia cannot hope to be an important player on the international stage. That Russia has never been an economic power even at the height of its influence but has frequently been a military power doesn't register. Therefore, they are constantly expecting Russia to revert to its 1990s patterns, and believe that if Moscow doesn't, it will collapse—which explains U.S. Vice President Joe Biden's interview in *The Wall Street Journal* where he discussed Russia's decline in terms of its economic and demographic challenges. Obama's key advisers come from the Clinton administration, and their view of Russia—like that of the Bush administration—was forged in the 1990s.

Foreign Policy Continuity Elsewhere

When we look at U.S.-China policy, we see very similar patterns with the Bush administration. The United States under Obama has the same interest in maintaining economic ties and avoiding political complications as the Bush administration did. Indeed, Hillary Clinton explicitly refused to involve herself in human rights issues during her visit to China. Campaign talk of engaging China on human rights issues is gone. Given the interests of both countries, this makes sense, but it is also noteworthy given the ample opportunity to speak to China on this front (and fulfill campaign promises) that has arisen since Obama took office (such as the Uighur riots).

Of great interest, of course, were the three great openings of the early Obama administration, to Cuba, to Iran, and to the Islamic world in general through his Cairo speech. The Cubans and Iranians rebuffed his opening, whereas the net result of the speech to the Islamic world remains unclear. With Iran we see the most important continuity. Obama continues to demand an end to Tehran's nuclear program, and has promised further sanctions unless Iran agrees to enter into serious talks by late September.

On Israel, the United States has merely shifted the atmospherics. Both the Bush and Obama administrations demanded that the Israelis halt settlements, as have many other administrations. The Israelis have usually responded by agreeing to something small while ignoring the larger issue. The Obama administration seemed ready to make a major issue of this, but instead continued to maintain security collaboration with the Israelis on Iran and Lebanon (and we assume intelligence collaboration). Like the Bush administration, the Obama administration has not allowed the settlements to get in the way of fundamental strategic interests.

This is not a criticism of Obama. Presidents—all presidents—run on a platform that will win. If they are good presidents, they will leave behind these promises to govern as they must. This is what Obama has done. He ran for president as the antithesis of Bush. He has conducted his foreign policy as if he were Bush. This is because Bush's foreign policy was shaped by necessity, and Obama's foreign policy is shaped by the same necessity. Presidents who believe they can govern independent of reality are failures. Obama doesn't intend to fail.

From *Stratfor Weekly Terrorism Intelligence Report*, August 24, 2009. Copyright © 2009 by Stratfor. Reprinted by permission.

In Search of Sustainable Security
Linking National Security, Human Security, and Collective Security to Protect America and Our World

GAYLE E. SMITH

Introduction and Summary

Not long ago I conducted an informal survey during a trip to East Africa, asking everyone I met how they view America. My interlocutors were from Africa, the Middle East, and Asia. They were, in the main, educated and working in the private sector, the policy world, or government. Many of them hold dual passports.

Their answers were strikingly similar. Most of them said in one way or another that the "idea" of America has changed for the worse, and most asserted that they are less interested in traveling to, working in, or working with the United States now than in the past. But most disconcerting was the hope, expressed with striking consistency, that China would soon attain its full power so that American hegemony could be brought in check.

This was not for any love of China's ideology or even the aggressive aid and investment strategies Beijing is deploying in the developing world. It was, as a young woman attorney explained, because "America used to be the champion for all of us, and now it is the champion only for itself."

That much of the world has lost faith in America bodes ill for our national security because our role in the world is secured not simply by our military power or economic clout, but also by our ability to compel other nations to follow our lead. The next president will have the opportunity to craft a modern national security strategy that can equip the United States to lead a majority of capable, democratic states in pursuit of a global common good—a strategy that can guide a secure America that is the world's "champion for all of us."

But positioning America to lead in a 21st century world will take more than extending a hand to our allies, fixing a long list of misdirected policies, or crafting a new national security strategy that is tough but also smart. With globalization providing the immutable backdrop to our foreign policy, America is today competing on a global playing field that is more complex, dynamic, and interdependent and thus far less certain than in the past.

Leading in this new world will require a fundamental shift from our outdated notion of national security to a more modern concept of sustainable security—that is, our security as defined by the contours of a world gone global and shaped by our common humanity. Sustainable security combines three approaches:

- *National* security, or the safety of the United States
- *Human* security, or the well-being and safety of people
- *Collective* security, or the shared interests of the entire world

Sustainable security, in short, can shape our continued ability to simultaneously prevent or defend against real-time threats to America, reduce the sweeping human insecurity around the world, and manage long term threats to our collective, global security. This new approach takes into account the many (and ongoing) changes that have swept our planet since the end of the Cold War and the fall of the Soviet Union. To understand the efficacy of this new doctrine, though, requires a quick look at this new global landscape.

The New Realities of the 21st Century

During his presidency, Bill Clinton spoke often and passionately about our global interdependence and of positioning America to cross a "bridge to the 21st century." Once across, however, the Bush administration took a sharp right turn. In the wake of the September 11 terrorist attacks on the United States, the administration narrowly defined the quest for America's security, distinct from and uninformed by the interests of the larger world we inhabit.

The challenge before us, President Bush asserted, was the struggle between good and evil, our strategy was to wage his so called "war on terror," and our goal was to shape a "world without tyranny." Our primary tool was a strong military backed by the resolve to use force without seeking a "permission slip" from the international community. And our object was the "axis of evil," and the rest of the world was either "with us or against us." Anyone who suggested that it might not be quite that simple was quickly and effectively discounted as "soft on terrorism."

Despite ambitious rhetoric about the promotion of our core values—of leading "the long march to freedom" and pursuing the "non-negotiable demands of human dignity"—the Bush administration has culled its allies not from among those countries most committed to democracy, but from among those who have oil. The Bush administration had to leverage all of its diplomatic and economic clout to persuade the so-called "Coalition of the Willing" to participate at all in the invasion of Iraq. Then, the administration offered up not the shining example of an America where human and civil rights prevail, but an America where Guantanamo, Abu Gharaib, and illegal wire-tapping are justified by an elusive, greater purpose.

The United States has for the last five years defined America's role in the world with near exclusive reference to the invasion of Iraq. The deaths of 4,000[1] American soldiers, maiming of tens of thousands more, and the expenditure of well over $400 billion,[2] has failed to lay the foundations for either stability or democracy. And as defined by the Bush administration, the "War on Terror" has fared no better: Al Qaeda has not been defeated, and Osama bin Laden, its leader and the mastermind of the September 11 attacks, has yet to be captured.

Our losses, however, extend far beyond the edges of a failed Iraq policy or the shortcomings of an ill-defined "war on terror." We have also lost precious time, and are well behind the curve in our now tardy efforts to tackle the global challenges that are already shaping our future—climate change, energy insecurity, growing resource scarcity, the proliferation of illegal syndicates moving people, arms, and money—all of them global challenges that have been steadfastly ignored and in some cases denied by an ideologically driven Bush administration lodged firmly in its own distinct version of the here and now.

Perhaps most damaging, however, is this: We have lost our moral standing in the eyes of many who now believe that the United States has only its own national interests at heart, and has little understanding of or regard for either global security or our common humanity. Just as potent as the unsustainable federal budget deficit George W. Bush will leave in his wake is the unsustainable national security deficit that he will pass on to his successor. Whoever prevails in November will face a daunting list of real-time national security imperatives, among them:

- A spiraling crisis in Iraq
- Afghanistan's steady implosion
- A fragile Pakistan
- An emboldened Iran
- A raging genocide in Sudan
- The growing insecurity of our oil supplies
- A nuclear North Korea
- An increasingly dangerous Arab–Israeli conflict

Just to name a few. But the next president will also face looming and less tangible threats to our national security in a world where power has grown more diffuse and threats more potent—a world in which our security depends not only on the behavior of states, but also on a host of transnational threats that transcend national borders, such as terrorism, pandemics, money laundering, and the drug trade.

And finally, the next president will be confronted by the more subtle but potent threats and moral challenges arising from sweeping human insecurity in a world divided by sharp disparities between rich and poor, between those nations actively engaged in fast-paced globalization and those left behind, and between people who have tangible reasons to believe in a secure and prosperous world and those who daily confront the evidence that violence is a more potent tool for change than is hope.

Sustainable Security Is the Answer

The world has changed profoundly during the last 50 years, but our concept of national security has not. The concept of national security came into being after World War II, and has had as its primary focus a world dominated by the nation state. In this new era of globalization, we continue to rely upon the narrow definition offered by George Kennan, who in 1948 described our national security as "the continued ability of the country to pursue the development of its internal life without serious interference, or threat of interference, from foreign powers."[3] While Kennan's definition might have been relevant to the era of containment, it is insufficient in today's integrated and interdependent world.

A modern concept of national security demands more than an ability to protect and defend the United States. It requires that we expand our goal to include the attainment of *sustainable* security.

A modern concept of national security demands more than an ability to protect and defend the United States.

The pursuit of sustainable security requires more than a reliance on our conventional power to deflect threats to the United States, but also that we maintain the moral authority to lead a global effort to overcome threats to our common security. With its global scope, sustainable security demands that we focus not only on the security of nation states, but also of people, on *human* security. An emerging concept borne of multidisciplinary analyses of international affairs, economics, development, and conflict, human security targets the fundamental freedoms—from want and from fear—that define human dignity.

National security and human security are compatible but distinct. National security focuses on the security of the state, and governments are its primary clients, while human security is centered on the security of individuals and thus on a diverse array of stakeholders. National security aims to ensure the ability of states to protect their citizens from external aggression; human security focuses on the management of threats and challenges that affect people everywhere—inside, outside, and across state borders.

A national security strategy is commonly crafted in real time and focused on tangible, proximate threats, while a human security strategy aimed at improving the human condition assumes a longer-term horizon. Sustainable security combines the two, thus allowing for a focus on the twin challenges of protecting the United States while also championing our global humanity—not simply because it is the right thing to do, but also because our security demands it.

For a majority of the world's people, security is defined in the very personal terms of survival. The primary threats to this *human* security have far less to do with terrorism than with poverty and conflict, with governments that cannot deliver or turn on their own citizens, and with a global economy that offers differentiated access and opportunities to the powerful and the powerless. For literally billions of the world's people, weapons of mass destruction are not nuclear bombs in the hands of Iran, but the proliferation of small arms. For them, freedom is not defined simply by the demise of dictators, but also by the rise of economic opportunity.

Ensuring our security in today's world, however, also requires a focus on collective security. Among the major challenges that the United States will face over the coming decades are climate change, water scarcity, food insecurity, and environmental degradation. These are challenges that will threaten the economic well-being and security of all countries on earth, and by dint of their global nature, their effects cannot be overcome unless we adopt a global perspective and strategy.

Take the example of the world food crisis that emerged in the spring of 2008. No single cause triggered the near doubling of world food prices. Indeed, the causes included the skyrocketing price of oil, the growth of the middle class in the developing world (and thus rising demand in China and India), droughts in Australia and Ukraine, a weak dollar, and the expansion of biofuels production in the United States and Europe.

The consequent rise in food prices triggered riots or protests in Europe, Mexico, Egypt, Afghanistan, and several other countries, and plunged millions in the developing world into abject poverty. In the United States, the number of Americans seeking assistance from food banks rose 20 percent to 25 percent.

Or consider "transnational threats," such as money laundering, terrorism, and international drug and crime syndicates, all of which transcend state borders. These are threats that pose risks to the United States, but also to the well-being of our allies, to global stability, and to the world economy.

A national security approach seeks to prevent or reduce the effects of these trends and threats to the United States; a collective security approach, in contrast, assumes that the United States must act globally—in partnership with allies and in coordination with international institutions—to prevent or manage them.

Sustainable Security in Practice

Crafting a sustainable security strategy requires three fundamental steps. The first is to prioritize, integrate, and coordinate the global development policies and programs pursued by the United States. While our military power provides a critical and effective tool for managing our security, our support for the well-being of the world's people will not only provide us with a moral foundation from which to lead but will also enhance our ability to manage effectively the range of threats and trends that shape the modern world.

Second, we must modernize our foreign aid system in order to allow the United States to make strategic investments in global economic development that can help us to build capable states, open societies, and a global economy that benefits the world's majority. Third, we must re-enter the international arena, stepping up to the plate to lead the reform of international institutions that have not kept pace, and to create new institutions that are needed to manage our collective security.

In the pages that follow, this paper will present the challenges that threaten our national, human, and collective security in order to show just how important it is for the next president to embrace these sustainable security policies. As this report will demonstrate, changing course will be difficult, but changing course is imperative to secure the future prosperity of humanity— an original and time-tested American value.

Human Security under Threat

In today's world, human security is elusive. There are six billion people in the world. Nearly half of them live on less than two dollars per day, and over one billion people survive on half that amount.[4] These are not people waiting idly for a hand-out from the international community. The vast majority of them are working men and women who earn for their daily labors less than it costs to rent a DVD, and who annually take home to their families less than half of what the average American will spend on a summer vacation this year.

Women and children are the hardest hit. According to the United Nations, 70 percent of the world's poor and two-thirds of the world's illiterate are women, and though they provide the backbone for rural economies, women own only one percent of the world's titled land and control only a small percentage of rural capital.[5] Over ten million children die before their fifth birthday each year, mostly from preventable diseases,[6] while roughly a quarter of all children in the developing world do not finish primary school.[7]

More than a billion people do not have safe supplies of water,[8] and more than twice as many have no access to basic sanitation.[9] Only one-third of the world's people enjoy the kind of access to energy that we take for granted, another third have only intermittent access, and the remaining third—some two billion people— live without modern energy supplies.[10] This means that they don't have lights to read by, or refrigerators to preserve vaccines, or trucks to get their goods to market.

The antidote to economic decline is increased borrowing. Developing world debt increased to almost 3 trillion dollars early in this decade, meaning that developing countries spend on average $13 on debt repayment—to wealthy countries and private creditors in the developed world—for every one dollar they receive in grants.[11] The international debt relief supported by the current and past administrations may have staunched the bleeding, but it has not closed the wound for the poor, who remain dangerously vulnerable to external shocks because they have little or nothing to fall back on.

For this reason, shocks to already fragile societies, such as climate change, have a greater effect on the poor than on other, wealthier communities. According to the United Nations Development Program, over 250 million people were affected by climate disasters annually from 2000 to 2004, and over 98 percent of them were in the developing world. In the world's developed countries, one in 1,500 people was affected by climate disaster; in the world's poorest countries, it was one in 19.[12]

Similarly, the rising price of oil is an enormous shock to the world's poor. The fiscal gains of a majority of countries that have received debt relief through the Heavily Indebted Poor Countries Initiative, for example, had by last year been wiped out by the increase in the world price of oil. Those same countries now face a near doubling in the world market price of basic food commodities. Theirs is a losing game of catch up, and the consequences of the vicious cycle of poverty are clear—more than 50 countries are poorer today than they were in 1990.[13]

A Vicious Cycle and Downward Spiral

This stunning privation feeds on itself, in part because poverty increases the risk of war. War is development in reverse—a civil war reduces a country's growth rate by 2.3 percent, a typical seven-year war leaves a country 15 percent poorer,[14] and wars speed both the "brain drain" and the flow and volume of capital flight. The costs of conflict are also borne by citizens—largely as a consequence of war, one in every 120 people on earth is either internally displaced or a refugee.[15]

It is estimated that Africa is losing $18 billion per year to conflict, or almost twice what the continent spends on health and education.[16] Or consider Sri Lanka, where a long-running civil war has cost the country over two years of GDP. Defense expenditures average four percent to six percent of GDP while those for health and education combined run just four percent to five percent.[17] Meanwhile one quarter of Sri Lankans live in poverty.

Finally, the world's donor countries incur tremendous costs over many years. Conflict drives U.S. spending on humanitarian assistance to levels that well exceed expenditures on economic development and conflict prevention. Recent wars, most of them in the developing world, triggered the authorization of 26 new UN peacekeeping missions between 1988 and 1995.[18] Today, the UN is leading 17 peacekeeping operations, and providing support to three more.[19] Each of these missions is expensive, especially to the United States, which bears almost one quarter of the cost, and several have ended in failure.

Finally, the recovery costs are enormous. According to a study by the Center for Global Development, it takes the world's donors between 15 to 27 years to exit from a conflict country because it takes that long for post-war economies to generate sufficient internal revenues to reduce the need for the external assistance that is provided by the United Nations, the United States, and other donors.[20] As the costs of war mount, neither the victims nor the world's donors can realistically keep up.

Against this backdrop, sweeping demographic changes are altering the contours of the global socioeconomic landscape, and providing new fuel for the cycle of poverty and new triggers for instability. While the developed world is now incurring the economic burdens of an aging population, over 100 countries are grappling with an expanding youth bulge. Today, 85 percent of young people between the ages of 15 and 24 live in developing countries,[21] where educational and job opportunities are few. This means that millions of young women are denied opportunities for economic independence and that millions of young men face a future devoid of either hope or prosperity.

Urban populations have grown fourfold over the last 50 years,[22] and by 2025, 60 percent of the world's population will live in cities.[23] Many of them—Cairo, Lagos, Nairobi, and Mumbai—are ill-equipped to provide the jobs, housing, and services that this expanded urban population will require. These vast demographic convulsions will exert increased pressure on already over-stretched natural resources and exacerbate growing poverty.

As the future hurtles towards us, we will see even greater threats to human security borne of our ecological interdependence. The world is facing a threefold increase in energy use by 2050.[24]

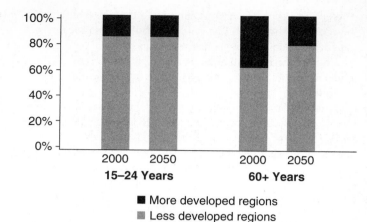

The proportions of youth and older persons in the total world population, 2000 and 2050.

Source: United Nations, *World Population Prospects: The 2002 Revisions: Volume II: Sex and Age* (Sales No. 03. XII.7).

World demand for fresh water has doubled over the last 50 years,[25] and the number of people living in water-stressed countries is expected to increase to 3 billion by 2025.[26] As global production, consumption, and population expand, so too will the competition for increasingly scarce resources. At the same time, the worst effects of climate change will reverberate in the world's poorest countries, which bear the least responsibility for global warming and have the least capacity to manage its impact.

A Different Take on "Us" and "Them"

Sweeping human insecurity also widens the gap between the world's rich and poor, a gap that might be more accurately described as a gulf. Although they constitute only 14 percent of the world's population, the world's ten wealthiest countries account for 75 percent of global GDP, and are 75 times richer than the ten poorest.[27] With the expansion of the Internet and satellite television, globalization is making this disparity more visible, including to those on the bottom.

Even with significant expansion, meanwhile, global trade has yet to yield sustainable benefits or to narrow this gap. Only two-thirds of the world's countries are engaged effectively in globalization. Low-income countries account for only three cents of every dollar generated through exports in the international trading system,[28] and the world's poorest region—sub-Saharan Africa—receives less than one percent of the total global flow of foreign direct investment.[29]

Global trade talks aimed at addressing this imbalance under the banner of the "Doha Development Round" have failed to deliver. Instead, these negotiations have all but collapsed under the weight of sharp disagreement between the world's rich and poor countries over the high subsidies paid out by the European Union and the United States to their agricultural producers.

What's worse, low- and middle-income countries bear 90 percent of the global disease burden yet they benefit least from global gains in treatment.[30] According to the Worldwatch Institute, only one percent of the over 1,200 new drugs that reached the global marketplace between 1975 and 1997 were applicable to the infectious tropical diseases that account for the most deaths around the world.[31] This is a human security problem of potentially immense proportions.

Total Youth Unemployment, 1995, 2004, and 2005

	Youth Unemployment (thousands)			
	1995	**2004**	**2005**	**% Change 1995–2005**
World	74,302	84,546	85,278	14.8
Developed Economies and European Union	10,281	8,997	8,481	−17.5
Central and Eastern Europe (non-EU) and CIS	5,962	5,724	5,900	−1.0
East Asia	13,149	11,840	12,076	−8.2
South East Asia and the Pacific	5,242	9,687	9,727	85.5
South Asia	11,765	13,561	13,662	16.1
Latin America and the Caribbean	7,722	9,263	9,495	23.0
Middle East and North Africa	7,209	8,380	8,525	18.2
Sub-Saharan Africa	12,972	17,095	17,414	34.2

Source: ILO, 2006:16.

Challenges to Our Collective Security

Democracy is making great gains, but so, too, are its opponents. Since 1974, some 90 countries have embraced democracy,[32] a positive gain to be sure, but one that is yet to be locked in. Many of the world's new democracies remain exceedingly fragile as their governments and citizens grapple simultaneously with profound political transitions, the legacies of war and repression, and the strains of poverty. Seemingly stable democracies in Kenya, Cote d'Ivoire, Georgia, and Thailand have proven to be vulnerable, while in many countries, structural poverty and corruption have precluded the delivery of a tangible democracy dividend.

In many countries, meanwhile, the failure of rulers to deliver economically or politically is speeding the rise of extremism. Across much of the Middle East, Africa, and Asia, extremism is forging a new political construct shaped by Islam, and with it the rise of a hostile, transnational political identity. In some regions, extremism takes the form of predatory movements, such as northern Uganda's Lord's Resistance Army, that prey on civilians and particularly on children.

In struggling democracies such as the Democratic Republic of the Congo, the echoes of the Rwandan genocide and the legacy of colonialism and post-colonial mis-rule reverberate in the form of militia wars, skyrocketing death rates, and rampant rape. Violence continues to threaten democratic gains in Nepal, Turkey, Sri Lanka, and the Philippines. And at the far worst and still-too-common end of the spectrum, genocide continues to rear its ugly head in places such as Darfur where, five years on, people still await a meaningful response from the international community.

The Power of Weak States

Both economic development and democracy are under further strain from the fact that a billion people live in states that do not deliver for their citizens. A recent study by the Brookings Institution notes that of the world's 193 countries, 28 qualify as weak and another 28 are critically weak or failed. Eighty-five percent of these countries have experienced conflict in the past 15 years, and the United Nations—and in some cases the United States—has had to deploy peacekeepers or observers to half of them.[33]

Governments in these countries lack the will or capacity to provide basic security or control their borders, cannot or do not meet the basic human needs of their citizens, and fail to provide either legitimate or effective governance. They are unable to adapt to the technological innovations that drive economic progress, establish the institutional foundations that are required for democratic stability, or function as reliable members of the international community.

They are equally incapable of meeting the challenges posed by environmental degradation, are more vulnerable to transnational threats than their more capable counterparts, and are unable to provide barriers to the spread of these threats across borders. Most important, they are unable (or unwilling) to offer their people economic opportunity, political freedom, or hope.

These weak and failing states include countries such as the Democratic Republic of the Congo, which by dint of the unresolved conflict in its eastern Kivu region is winning a fierce global competition for the worst humanitarian crisis on earth. They include Nigeria, where vast oil reserves have led not to prosperity but to sweeping systemic corruption, and to the rise of a pernicious insurgency in the Niger Delta. And they include Myanmar, where an authoritarian regime has not only failed to protect its citizens in the wake of a devastating cyclone, but has also prevented the world from aiding them.

These are countries often consigned to the bottom of our foreign policy priority list, but countries where unchecked instability and limited capacity risk the lives of millions. State weakness in these countries not only portends hopelessness for many of their citizens. It also poses a threat to global peace and security. Though viewed by many as of lesser import than countries in the Middle East or Asia, these African countries matter—Nigeria provides more than eight percent of our imported oil, and resource-rich Congo has, among other assets, uranium. Their security matters—to their people, and also to us.

Our Shared Interests

Americans are right to ask their government why they should add the costly charge of promoting human security and collective security to the already heavy burden of the spiraling federal budget deficit, rising gas and food prices, a home mortgage crisis, and multiple security challenges already on our national plate. The first reason is simple: It is the right thing to do. By championing the cause of the world's least powerful, the United States can build a stronger moral foundation from which to lead and a compelling example for the world to follow.

There is precedent on which to build, as both security imperatives and moral convictions have led the United States to help improve the lives of the world's poor throughout our modern history. In his inaugural address in 1961, President John F. Kennedy highlighted this commitment of the American people:

"To those peoples in the huts and villages across the globe struggling to break the bonds of mass misery, we pledge our best efforts to help them help themselves, for whatever period is required—not because the Communists may be doing it, not because we seek their votes, but because it is right. If a free society cannot help the many who are poor, it cannot save the few who are rich."[34]

Almost 50 years later, General Anthony Zinni (USMC-ret.) and Admiral Leighton Smith Jr. (USN-ret.) put it this way:

"It is time to repair our relationship with the world and begin to take it to the next level—a level defined not only by our military strength but also by the lives we save and the opportunities we create for the people of other nations . . . today our enemies are often conditions—poverty, infectious disease, political instability and corruption, global warming—which generate the biggest threats. By addressing them in meaningful ways, we can forestall crises."[35]

The second reason is more pragmatic but just as compelling. If we fail to act now, we will be forced to pay later, both financially and with our own national security. Human insecurity feeds on itself, laying the ground for conflict and the extreme vulnerability that causes people to fall over the economic edge when weather, wars, or world market prices disrupt their fragile, subsistence economies.

The United States leads the world in responding to the humanitarian crises that arise out of this acute vulnerability. Today, we spend more on emergency relief to treat the symptoms of these crises than we do to promote the development that might prevent them. The United States, for example, spends far more on food aid than it invests in agricultural development, and with food prices surging globally, we have had to increase spending on emergency food aid to forestall famine and food riots in the world's poorest countries.

Experts predict that our humanitarian and military expenditures will increase further unless the vulnerability of the world's poor to climate change is substantially reduced. A 2007 report by 11 former U.S. generals and admirals found that "Climate change can act as a threat multiplier for instability in some of the most volatile regions of the world, and it presents significant national security challenges for the United States."[36] When these new crises arise, the United States will be expected to respond.

We also pay for our failure to address our collective security. Globalization has spawned an interconnected world where capital, goods, people, and threats move freely across borders. These potent transnational threats affect the lives of ordinary Americans, whether in the form of the West Nile virus or a spike in oil prices triggered by the sabotage of oil pipelines by Nigerians desperate for fuel they cannot afford.

Moreover, threats to our collective security—the money laundering that fuels terrorist networks, crime syndicates and the drug trade, uranium smuggling and illegal weapons shipments—can be neither contained nor controlled by the United States alone. We need competent, capable partners, in all corners of the globe.

Shifting to Sustainable Security

America's power is unmatched. We account for roughly half of all global defense spending, and generate 20 percent of all global output. But in an interdependent world where power has grown more diffuse and threats more diverse, our military and economic superpower status is not enough to provide for sustainable security for us or the world we live in.

If our goal is simply to protect and defend America against external interference, then reliance on military force and a wall on the border with Mexico might suffice. But if our aim is to ensure the sustainable security of the United States in a fast-moving, rapidly-changing world driven by complex, global threats and challenges, we need to bring to bear all of the tools we can muster.

Offered up by academia and Washington's think tanks, the concepts of "soft power," "integrated power," and "smart power" bear in common the counsel that America must recalibrate its foreign policy to rely less on military power and more on other tools that can foster change and enhance our security. One of these is enhanced and robust diplomacy; the other is development.

A statement endorsed by eight former Secretaries of State, five former Secretaries of Defense, and four former National Security Advisors, put it this way: "Our increasingly interconnected world requires strong U.S. leadership to strengthen democratic governance, harness economic potential, alleviate global poverty and improve human conditions. American investments in these goals will reaffirm America's tradition of moral leadership, reduce our vulnerability to threats from destabilizing forces and improve America's image abroad."[37]

Secretary of Defense Robert Gates, meanwhile, recently called for the development of "a permanent, sizeable cadre of immediately deployable experts with disparate skills,"[38] and for beefing up our capacity to promote global development. Clearly, there is growing recognition that our sustainable security requires that we beef up our diplomatic capabilities and also strengthen our capacity to promote the development of capable, democratic states and healthy societies.

But when it comes to development, we've got it half right and upside down. Development dollars are up, but we have neither a development policy nor a development strategy. Our foreign aid system is chaotic, but instead of fixing it we are appending to it multiple new tools that, though necessary, risk complicating it further. And instead of balancing our military power with civilian-led capabilities to support development, we are giving the development lead to the Department of Defense.

When it comes to development, we've got it half right and upside down. The dollars are up, but we have neither a policy nor a strategy.

Development Earns Widespread Support

On the positive side of the ledger, we have seen during the last eight years a dramatic increase in development funding legislated with strong bipartisan support. A new milestone was set this year when 186 members of Congress—from both sides of the aisle—wrote to President Bush urging him to increase next year's (fiscal year 2009) International Affairs Budget consistent with the 2006 National Security Strategy, which states that, "Development reinforces diplomacy and defense, reducing long-term threats to our national security by helping to build stable, prosperous, and peaceful societies."[39] President Bush responded by increasing the fiscal year 2009 budget for international affairs to $39.5 billion, a 16 percent increase over the previous year.[40]

Support for two major Bush administration initiatives has also been strong. In January 2004, the United States established and pledged $4.8 billion to the Millennium Challenge Corporation (MCC), a grant-making government agency targeted to countries that are performing well against set economic and political criteria. By the end of fiscal year 2007, 14 countries had signed MCC compacts and 14 more were on the "threshold," making efforts to adhere to the social, judicial, and political reform indicators set forth under the program.[41]

The MCC has been the object of budget battles and the target of criticism for the significant gap between the Bush administration's stated ambitions and the agency's actual implementation, but it has garnered support from both Republicans and Democrats. Bipartisan support for PEPFAR—the President's Emergency Program for AIDS Relief—is even more robust, with both parties in Congress supporting both initial outlays as well as President Bush's 2008 call to double program funding.

Moreover, there is today a growing constituency for action. Driven largely by young people and faith-based communities and elevated to media visibility by celebrities, major campaigns focused on global poverty and Darfur, for example, have caught the attention of the public, Capitol Hill, and the White House. Support for development initiatives such as these was once a predominantly liberal cause, but today it stretches across the political spectrum, and is increasingly prominent among conservatives.

Among young evangelicals, for example, global poverty and human trafficking are gradually overtaking abortion and gay marriage as top priorities. The leading champions for Darfur on Capitol Hill, meanwhile, are Senator Sam Brownback (R-KS) and Representative Donald Payne (D-NJ), two men who disagree on a host of issues but are firmly united in their conviction that America has a moral obligation to end the suffering in Sudan.

Most Americans also want their leaders to do more. A 2007 Gallup poll found that 56 percent of Americans were "dissatisfied" with the current role of the United States in global affairs.[42] Another poll showed that 65 percent of Americans—and the majority of both Republicans and Democrats—support increasing global poverty reduction expenditure to 0.7 percent of GDP.[43] Doing more to improve the lives of the poor is one way in which Americans believe they can restore our global image—and a key way, they believe, for the next president to be an effective and representative global leader.

But Development Gets Short Shrift

On the negative side of the ledger, development remains the poor stepchild of defense and diplomacy. Even with substantial increases in our foreign aid budget, 95 percent of the total outlays for national security in the fiscal year 2007 federal budget were for defense, compared with 3.5 percent for development.[44] Nearly half of that development allocation goes to ten countries, including Egypt, Colombia, Pakistan and Jordan, while the world's poorest receive only six percent.[45] And where foreign aid allocations are at their highest, short-term security imperatives dominate and development comes last.

Consider the case of Pakistan, a country where the United States has used aid to enhance the security of the Pakistani state, with only brief interruptions, since the 1980s. Despite the $24 billion invested by the United States in Pakistan over the last 25 years, we now face a more dangerous mixture of political instability, entrenched poverty, and extremism than existed in the early 1980s—all in a country that possesses nuclear weapons.

According to an August 2007 report from the Center for Strategic and International Studies, the bulk of the $10.5 billion in assistance provided by the U.S. to Pakistan since 9/11 "has not been directed to Pakistan's underlying fault lines, but to specific short-term counterterrorism objectives."[46] Only 10 percent of overall funding has gone for development or for meeting humanitarian needs,[47] and in the Federally Administered Tribal Areas along the country's north-western border with Afghanistan, development assistance comprises only one percent of our total aid package.[48]

In part because development has not been a priority, our heavy financial investment in Pakistan has neither reduced the security threats that Pakistan poses nor earned us the allegiance of the Pakistani people. Our consistent disregard for human security has borne a high cost. Deaths from internal terrorist attacks have skyrocketed since 2001, from 189 in 2003 to 648 in 2005 and 3,599 in 2007.[49] But as a recent Stanley Foundation report highlighted, "most Pakistanis are much more likely to suffer a premature death as a result of poverty or non-existent medical services as they are from an Islamist attack."[50]

Thirty-five percent of Pakistanis live in abject poverty. According to the World Food Program, food insecurity is on the rise, with 60 million people unable to secure an adequate nutritional intake, and an additional 18 million affected by the recent surge in global food prices.[51] Agricultural livelihoods are further threatened by untended environmental changes as the Indus River, upon which a majority of Pakistan's rural population depends for both drinking water and irrigation, begins to go dry.

Nearly half of all Pakistanis are illiterate, literacy rates for women stand at 30 percent, and only three percent of people in Federally Administered Tribal Areas—where some believe Osama bin Laden is hiding—can read or write.[52] Of the billions of dollars in aid provided by the United States since 2001, aid allocated to education represents at most 4.2 percent of the total package—an average of less than $2 per Pakistani child per year.[53] Unable to read, with few job prospects, and angered by U.S. military action within Pakistani borders, the strong financial incentives offered by extremist groups[54] are increasingly a welcome alternative. A recent public opinion poll, meanwhile, found that 72 percent of Pakistanis have unfavorable views of the United States, and only 38 percent of Pakistanis have a favorable view of our ally, President Pervez Musharraf. The same poll showed that free elections, a free press, and an independent judiciary are the most important long-term priority for a majority of Pakistanis.[55] Each of these remains elusive and none of them is a priority in our $10 billion aid package.

Even if there was sufficient political will to elevate development alongside defense and diplomacy, it would be practically impossible because our foreign aid system is irretrievably broken. In 2007, the bipartisan HELP Commission, appointed by Congress and mandated to review U.S. foreign aid, reported that of over 100 government officials (both civilian and military), aid practitioners, foreign policy experts, academics, and private-sector representatives consulted, "not one person appeared before this Commission to defend the status quo."[56]

The System Is Broken

America's ability to invest in global development is seriously constrained. The United States has neither a global development policy nor a strategy. The legislation governing foreign aid was written in 1961, and has since been amended to include 33 goals, 247 directives, and 75 priorities,[57] rendering it so cumbersome that it provides neither coherent guidance to the executive branch nor a roadmap for oversight to the legislative branch. In the absence of a policy, strategy, or effective guiding legislation, aid programming is driven in the main by congressional earmarks, presidential directives, and reaction.

Development programming was once the purview of the U.S. Agency for International Development (USAID), an agency that had a permanent staff of 15,000 during Vietnam but just 3,000 today, and is therefore compelled to rely heavily on expensive outside contractors to manage programs in over 150 countries.[58] Presently, over half of all aid programs are administered by agencies other than USAID, and development funding is arrayed across more than 20[59] government agencies, departments, and initiatives, each with its own goals, priorities, and procedures. No single individual or agency has the authority or the responsibility to oversee or coordinate these myriad programs.

The colossal failure of reconstruction efforts in Iraq and Afghanistan, meanwhile, has rightly focused Washington's attention on crisis management, and has led to the creation of even more instruments and initiatives. In 2004, Congress authorized funds to create an Office of Reconstruction and Stabilization in the State Department, and last year the House and Senate introduced legislation calling for the creation of an expert civilian response capability to carry out our reconstruction and stabilization activities.

The Department of Defense has established a Commanders' Emergency Response Program to meet emergency and reconstruction needs in Iraq and Afghanistan, and the 2006 National Defense Authorization Act created the "1206" fund to assist countries engaged in counter-terrorism and stability operations.

The Pentagon is now seeking to make these temporary crisis management authorities permanent through the "Building Global Partnerships Act."

President Bush deserves credit for dramatic increases in U.S. aid levels and global leadership in the fight against HIV/AIDS. But the changes the U.S. foreign aid system has undergone over the last several years have exacerbated rather than repaired the flaws in the system. These changes have also set far-reaching and potentially detrimental precedents.

The State Department's 2006 "Transformational Diplomacy" plan, for example, established a new Deputy Undersecretary for Foreign Aid in the State Department as a means of achieving greater coordination and policy coherence within the Executive Branch. But the pretense of coordination is more potent than is its practice. Although "Transformational Diplomacy" consolidated some aid accounts, the new Deputy Undersecretary has no jurisdiction over the growing development aid budget managed by the military, and provides guidance to but does not have authority over either the Millennium Challenge Corporation or the anti-AIDs program PEPFAR.

The continued lack of coordination not only leads to inefficiencies in the management of taxpayer funds, but it also places an enormous burden on international development partners who are forced to deal with multiple agencies, requirements, and procedures. It also fosters policy incoherence. Research conducted by the HELP Commission, for example, found that the United States collects more in tariffs from countries eligible for funding from the Millennium Challenge Account than is provided in aid. This fact was news to senior policymakers, who missed it for the simple reason that there is no coordination between our trade agencies and our aid agencies.

Moreover, the administration has launched robust, discrete initiatives without benefit of an overarching policy or strategy, and thus allowed significant gaps to emerge. For example, although agriculture represents almost 40 percent of GDP, 35 percent of exports, and 70 percent of employment in developing countries, less than two percent of the proposed fiscal year 2009 development budget targets agricultural development.

Robust funding to fight the HIV/AIDS pandemic, meanwhile, has not been matched by parallel investments in other sectors. Clearly, global health issues like HIV/AIDS are of paramount importance, but so too are education, agricultural development, institution-building, and job creation.

Consider the case of Kenya, a country that serves as the economic anchor for east and central Africa and has for over two decades functioned—at least in the eyes of the outside world—as an island of stability in a sea of turmoil. Kenya has for years provided staging and overflight rights for U.S. military operations, is the hub for emergency relief efforts throughout the region, regularly contributes troops to U.N. peacekeeping efforts, and has been a staunch ally of the United States in our campaign against global terrorist networks since the U.S. embassy there was bombed by Al Qaeda in 1998.

Close elections late last year brought Kenya's internal contradictions to the surface, however, as the country exploded in a wave of stunning violence that led to the deaths of over 1000 people and economic losses estimated to be in the range of $3 billion.[60]

The most effective tool on hand for the United States to foster stability and functional democracy in Kenya is foreign aid, and the goal of U.S. development efforts in Kenya is in fact to build an economically prosperous country. But of the over $700 million that Kenya now receives annually, over $500 million is earmarked for HIV/ AIDS, over $120 million goes for food aid, and most of the balance is for security and counter-terrorism programs. The net result is that there is little or no funding available to counter the economic or political conditions that gave rise to Kenya's destabilizing post-electoral crisis or to consolidate the fragile peace achieved by the recent formation of a unity government.

A broken, incoherent, and understaffed foreign aid system has allowed for the emergence of some isolated successes, but has also created a vacuum. The United States has neither the policies nor the people it needs to make development an effective foreign policy tool. What may prove to be the most far-reaching of the Bush administration's efforts in the development sphere is its decision to give the lead in filling this vacuum to the Department of Defense.

The Pentagon Steps up to the Plate

Traditionally, the role of the Department of Defense (DoD) in development has been restricted to three key areas: support for humanitarian operations; engagement in small-scale community development projects linked to training missions and site visits; and, with the Department of State, "train and equip" programs for foreign militaries. But major deployments in Iraq, Afghanistan, and the Horn of Africa have taught the Pentagon three lessons.

First, from Iraq and Afghanistan it became clear that the fragile peace that can be won with military force cannot be sustained without a tangible peace dividend alongside a robust stabilization effort linked to long-term, sustainable development. The second lesson came from the deployment of U.S. forces to Djibouti under the banner of the Combined Joint Task Force-Horn of Africa, where the military has been mandated to conduct counter-terrorism operations and support the efforts of regional governments to contain and prevent the spread of terrorist networks.

It soon became clear that poor countries with weak governments cannot protect or defend their borders without also providing essential services to and securing the allegiance of the citizens who live in the vast, ungoverned spaces that are most vulnerable to terrorist infiltration. The third lesson was that with USAID's staffing eroded to bare bones levels, and with the State Department both non-operational and otherwise occupied, no government agency except the Department of Defense has the personnel or the proclivity to fill these gaps.

The Defense Department is responding, reflecting the observation of Defense Secretary Gates that "the non-military instruments of America's national power need to be rebuilt, modernized, and committed to the fight."[61] The Pentagon's development budget has soared from 5.6 percent of the executive branch total in 2002 to 21.7 percent, or $5.5 billion, in 2005,[62] and is slated to increase further. New authorities have been secured, new programs have been initiated, and with DoD Directive 3000.05, the U.S. military is now mandated to treat stability operations as a core mission on par with combat operations.[63]

But the Department's expanding role goes further than stability operations. In 2007, the Pentagon launched AFRICOM, a unified military headquarters for Africa that is focused on "war prevention," and is designed to "better enable the Department of Defense and other elements of the U.S. government to work in concert and with partners to achieve a more stable environment in which political and economic growth can take place." AFRICOM not only gives a regional military command a development mandate, it also operates with an integrated interagency staff, and thus provides the platform for the coordination of other U.S. government agencies.

The plan for AFRICOM's forward deployment in Africa, however, was poorly received by most African governments, which were not widely consulted in advance of its unveiling, and by civic groups across the continent, which opposed what they viewed as a permanent U.S. military presence in Africa. AFRICOM is thus slated to remain in Germany for the time being, but the AFRICOM model is spreading to other regional commands. SOUTHCOM's latest strategy document, for example, proposes that the command coordinate all relevant government agencies, including civilian, to address the full range of regional challenges in Latin America and the Caribbean.

There are those who believe that DoD's expanded role in development is a sign of the Department's intention to militarize foreign aid. The more plausible explanation is that the Pentagon is stepping in to fill a vacuum that has been left wanting by USAID's dire circumstances, and by the State Department's lack of intent. In much the same way that she ceded control over the Iraq war to the Pentagon during her tenure as National Security Advisor in the early years of the Bush administration, Secretary of State Condoleezza Rice has posed no visible or effective opposition to the Pentagon's expanded role in areas traditionally considered the purview of civilian agencies.

DoD's role has also grown more prominent because it is operational and capable. In contrast, the State Department is not operational, and a weakened USAID no longer has the capacity to tackle all of the development challenges the United States faces. Congress, therefore, is more inclined to allocate aid dollars to the Pentagon than to its weaker and less capable counterparts.

The greatest peril lies not in the fact that the Defense Department has stepped in to fill the development vacuum and pick up the slack on inter-agency coordination, or even that the Pentagon has no expertise or experience in the field of development. The hazard lies in the fact that the frontal face of America's support for development in the poorest corners of the world is our military, and not our civilian agencies. As the lukewarm reception to AFRICOM has made clear, this places our interest in human security squarely in the frame of our national security and, in particular, the war on terrorism—and not, as it should be, in the context of our shared commitment to the global common good.

Three Steps toward Sustainable Security

Adapting to today's world and achieving sustainable security requires that we pursue not only our national security, but also global and human security. This more modern approach can afford us the ability to deal simultaneously with short-term, nation-state based threats and with the global challenges that transcend state borders. Importantly, this sustainable security approach allows us to lead from a position of moral strength. But getting there requires three core elements:

- An organizing principle that can unite a majority of the world's people
- The elevation and strategic utilization of the full range of our foreign policy tool
- A revitalized international system that reflects not just the challenges that existed when it was created in the wake of World War II, but also the realities of today

It also requires that the next president establish the predicate for change, and speak truth to the American people. Over the course of two terms, the Bush administration has posited that the combination of its moral certitude and America's military might are sufficient to secure our national interests, and has treated threats to our global security—whether climate change or energy security—as electives rather than imperatives.

The next president instead must update and advise the American people, making clear that our ability to lead on the world stage demands not only awesome power but also moral authority, and that our interests are best served when we act in pursuit of our global security and common humanity.

The shift toward a sustainable security approach will take time, and the next president will face a daunting list of immediate challenges. But there are several steps that can be taken in 2009 to lay the ground for an increased and practical focus on the profound moral challenges of our world, to modernize our foreign aid system, and to lay the ground for the increased international cooperation that is necessary going forward. Specifically, the next president should:

- Add a third and powerful tool to our foreign policy apparatus, in addition to defense and diplomacy, by elevating, integrating, and coordinating U.S. global development policies and programs.
- Take immediate steps to modernize our foreign aid system so that a new administration can move nimbly and effectively to invest in building capable states, open societies, and a global marketplace that serves the world's majority.
- Move swiftly to re-engage on the international stage by signaling America's willingness to lead in the reform of international institutions and the creation of new mechanisms for managing our shared global interests.

The shift toward a sustainable security approach will take time, and the next president will face a daunting list of immediate challenges.

These three steps, in turn, require detailed action to ensure success. All three of these overarching policy proposals, when examined in detail, would elevate sustainable security to an active policy of global engagement within the first term of the next administration.

Prioritize, Integrate, and Coordinate Development

It will take presidential leadership to elevate development, a strong hand to integrate the concept of human security across the range of our foreign policy agencies, and high-level action to coordinate the myriad foreign aid agencies, instruments, and initiatives now spread across the executive branch. There are four key steps that the next president can take to lay the ground for progress in all three areas.

First, the president should use the administration's first National Security Strategy to lay the ground for a sustainable security approach by focusing on traditional national security, collective security, and human security. Though required by law, National Security Strategies are often boilerplate documents that provide little other than a narrative list of foreign policy priorities. The next president should use his first NSS as a tool for pivoting to sustainable security.

Second, the president should appoint a third Deputy National Security Advisor (NSA) for long-term strategic planning. In a White House facing the pressures of competing global and domestic crises, 24-hour news coverage, and a four-year election cycle, there is little time for thinking about and planning for the long term. A designated Deputy NSA mandated to think and plan ahead will not only allow the administration to make up for the time lost by the Bush administration on issues like climate change, but will also allow an administration to get out ahead of future threats like resource scarcity and new global pandemics.

Third, as the first step toward formulating a government-wide policy on development and crafting a whole-of-government development strategy, the president should issue a Presidential Directive providing initial guidance to the multiple agencies, departments, and offices that are now pursuing their own individual agendas. The guidance should neither be so vague—by pointing to, for example, "reducing global poverty"—as to be meaningless, nor so prescriptive that it undercuts the ability of professionals on the ground to make informed decisions.

Instead, it should focus on the priorities that serve our national interests and reflect a global common good, for example by building the capacity of governments and civil society; reducing the vulnerability of the poor; laying the ground for improved resource management; and enhancing the access of poor communities and low-income countries to capital and markets.

Fourth, the president should create a directorate, led jointly by the National Security Council and National Economic Council, to initiate and oversee the coordination of all foreign aid agencies, initiatives, departments, and programs. Given the growing role of non-governmental organizations, philanthropic groups, and corporations in humanitarian and development efforts overseas, the directorate should also ensure that the U.S. government is in regular consultation with these prominent partners.

Modernize Our Foreign Aid System

There is an urgent need to reform the structure, operations, and staffing of our foreign aid system, and an equally important need to coordinate a sweeping reform process with the Congress. Reform will likely require new legislation to replace the almost 50-year old Foreign Assistance Act, as well as an overhaul of critical internal procedures ranging from evaluation to procurement.

A growing number of development experts, NGOs, corporate leaders, and foreign-policy specialists are lending support to the creation of an independent, cabinet-level development agency, similar to Britain's Department for International Development, which was created by former Prime Minister Tony Blair and has been given an even more prominent role by his successor, Gordon Brown. The rationale is that because development is a field distinct from either defense or diplomacy, it warrants its own department and leadership, and a seat at the foreign policy-making table.

There is also a need, advocates argue, to bring our various foreign aid agencies under one roof. As well, there is growing recognition of the need to insulate the development portion of our foreign aid budget from the pressure of short-term security imperatives, and instead focus on long-term development objectives across the span of successive administrations.

The proposal is that military aid, including "train and equip" programs for foreign militaries, peacekeeping funds, and economic security funds, or ESF, would remain under the jurisdiction of the Departments of Defense and State. Humanitarian and development aid—including PEPFAR and the MCA—would be centralized under a new, professionally staffed department, insulated from short-term imperatives and focused on long-term goals.

Critics argue that the development portfolio should remain within State and be made a priority by the secretary. They point to the problems incurred by the creation of the Department of Homeland Security as evidence that a new independent agency will not work, and argue that an independent development agency will inevitably be sidelined. Further, there is concern that the creation of a separate development department would weaken and compete with the Department of State.

The "uber State Department" is clearly the easier option, but given the experience of USAID over the years, and the structural flaws in the State Department's "Transformational Diplomacy," it is also the least likely to bring about a fundamental change to the status quo. First of all, the State Department is not operational and is thus not equipped to manage the development portfolio. Second, the independent agency proposal entails uniting agencies and departments with common mandates, and not, as was the case with the Department of Homeland Security, creating a department that combines multiple operational agencies with distinct and varied mandates.

And third, a cabinet-level development agency reinforced by the Executive Office of the President and backed by the development budget is no more likely to be marginalized than is an office housed within the State Department. What's more, concerns about weakening the State Department overlook two salient facts.

First, development and diplomacy are two entirely different tasks that are undertaken on the basis of different time horizons, require distinct expertise and different capabilities, and entail separate and contrasting approaches. Past policy has been hindered by the assumption that development requires little expertise other than an understanding of international affairs and a concern for the plight of the poor, and that the development aspect of a given policy can thus be easily handled by either the Department of State or the Department of Defense. The dangers of this flawed assumption are now evident, however, in Iraq,

Afghanistan, Pakistan, Egypt, and countless other cases where we have failed to bring a development perspective to bear.

Second, this concern misdiagnoses the current weakness of the State Department, which has less to do with its authority over foreign aid and more to do with its failure to craft and act on a modern diplomatic agenda and its willingness to concede influence to the Department of Defense.

In the next administration, the State Department must take the foreign policy lead, including on reforming the international institutions that make up our global architecture and on crafting and implementing the policies that can enable the U.S. to manage a host of global threats and challenges. State's strength will and should derive from its leadership in formulating these and other policies that guide the use of all of our foreign policy tools—diplomacy, defense, and development.

But the next president needs to hear views forged from each of these perspectives. Just as the State and Defense Departments craft their own unique strategies, oversee their own budgets, and bring their own specific expertise and distinct perspectives to the decision-making table in the White House, so too should a department for development.

The next president, however, cannot create a new department without extensive internal deliberation or consultation with Congress. Fortunately, leading members of Congress have already taken on the cause of modernizing our foreign aid system.

The next president should immediately engage with this ongoing congressional process and appoint, during the transition, a high-level White House official to consult within and outside of government and develop options for rationalizing and modernizing our foreign aid system during his first term. Because traditional institutional imperatives may cause a new Secretary of State to oppose an independent cabinet-level agency, the president should also secure the support of the new secretary to consider the full range of options.

Re-Enter the International Arena

The next president has the opportunity to re-engage the international community and reposition America to lead. But this will take clear signals from the White House that the new administration is ready and willing to engage, and recognition that just as our own foreign policy architecture is out of date, so too is the international architecture in urgent need of reform. The next president can move on both fronts by taking four steps.

The next president has the opportunity to re-engage the international community and reposition America to lead.

First, he should work with Congress to ensure that the United States can fully cover its U.N. arrears within the first year of a new administration. As happened during the 1990s, the failure of the United States to pay its dues both hinders U.N. operations in critical areas such as peacekeeping, but also undermines our ability to make the case for, or demand, critical reforms.

Second, in an effort to begin reconciling our national interests and our global security, the next president should work with Congress, across the whole of government, and with allies from the developed and developing worlds to craft a strategy for global food security. The worldwide crisis that erupted when food prices nearly doubled exposed the need to harmonize policies in an interconnected world, and has affected consumers in every country in the world. In some cases, the crisis has triggered riots and instability, in others it has pushed millions over the edge from subsistence to hunger, and in the United States it has fostered economic hardship and a spike in demand for food stamps and other nutritional programs.

By the time the next president is sworn in, the Doha "Development Round" of trade talks will likely be dead on the mantle of disagreement between the world's rich and poor countries on agricultural policies. And barring some radical and unforeseen change, the global food market will still be volatile. Rationalizing America's agricultural policies to conform to a new global environment will take heavy political lifting, but the opportunity and indeed imperative created by collapsed trade talks and the global food crisis provide a window for starting the discussion.

Third, the next president should initiate the next phase of PEPFAR. While giving full credit to President Bush for launching and robustly funding the initiative, the next president should provide a larger share of HIV/AIDS funding through the Global Fund for AIDS, Tuberculosis, and Malaria, signaling our willingness to work collectively to address the global challenge that these diseases represent. A new and improved PEPFAR should also invest more resources in capacity-building and the ability of the world's poorest countries to manage future epidemics and health crises.

Fourth and finally, the next president should make Darfur—and indeed the issue of crimes against humanity across the globe—a top priority. There is little chance that the Darfur crisis will be resolved by next January, but there are plenty of other places where crimes against humanity are going untended by the world.

The Darfur genocide is now entering its sixth year, and cries of "never again" and pledges of "not on my watch" ring hollow. The next president needs to dedicate his time, and that of the secretary of state, to show the world that America is ready to stand up to the worst of all threats to human security, genocide, so that America's claim to global leadership will be shaped not only by the actions we take but also by those that we do not.

Conclusion

Few would envy the task of handling the long list of first priorities that awaits the next president. But while protecting and defending America's national security will be first on the list, so too should be adapting to the modern concept of sustainable security.

At the dawn of the 21st century, in a world seized by far-reaching and tumultuous change, President Bush dedicated eight years to waging a "war on terror" and reminding the rest of the world of what America is *against*. It is time for our next president to remind the rest of the world that we stand *for* the sustainable security of our shared world. To do otherwise would be to diminish our collective security and abandon our common humanity.

Notes

1. Iraq Coalition Casualty Count, available at http://www.icasualties.org/oif/ (last accessed May 2008).

2. Amy Belasco, "The Cost of Iraq, Afghanistan, and Other Global War on Terror Operations Since 9/11" (Washington: Congressional Research Service, 2008), available at http://www.fas.org/sgp/crs/natsec/RL33110.pdf (last accessed May 2008) p. 16.

3. George F. Kennan, "Comments on the General Trend of U.S. Foreign Policy" (Princeton: George F. Kennan Papers, August 20, 1948).

4. The United States Commission on Helping to Enhance the Livelihood of People around the Globe, "Beyond Assistance: The HELP Commission Report of Foreign Assistance Reform" (2007). p. 10.

5. Dr. Fareda Banda, "Project on a Mechanism to Address Laws that Discriminate Against Women" (The United Nations' Office of the High Commissioner for Human Rights, March 6 2008), available at http://www.reliefweb.int/rw/lib.nsf/db900sid/PANA-7DHGQM/$file/ohchr_mar2008.pdf?openelement (last accessed May 2008).

6. The United States Commission on Helping to Enhance the Livelihood of People around the Globe, "Beyond Assistance: The HELP Commission Report of Foreign Assistance Reform" (2007) p. 12.

7. William Easterly, *The White Man's Burden: Why the West's Efforts to Aid the Rest Have Done So Much Ill and So Little Good* (New York: Penguin Books, 2006) p. 8.

8. The Millennium Project of the World Federation of UN Associations, "Water: How Can Everyone Have Sufficient Clean Water Without Conflict?" available at http://www.millennium-project.org/millennium/Global_Challenges/chall-02.html (last accessed May 2008).

9. The World Health Organization, "Statement from WHO's Director General" (2008), available at http://www.who.int/water_sanitation_health/hygiene/iys/about/en/index.html (last accessed May 2008).

10. Energy Future Coalition, "Challenge and Opportunity: Charting a New Energy Future," available at http://www.energyfuturecoalition.org/pubs/EFCReport.pdf (last accessed May 2008) p. 36.

11. The United Nations, "Poverty Briefing," available at http://www.un.org/Pubs/CyberSchoolBus//briefing/poverty/poverty.pdf last accessed May 2008).

12. The United Nations Development Programme, "Human Development Report 2007/2008, Fighting Climate Change: Human Solidarity in a Divided World," (New York: The United Nations, 2007), available at http://hdr.undp.org/en/media/hdr_20072008_en_complete.pdf (last accessed May 2008) p. 8.

13. The United Nations Development Programme, "Human Development Report 2003: Millenium Development Goals: A Compact Among Nations to End Human Poverty," (New York: Oxford University Press, 2003), available at http://hdr.undp.org/en/media/hdr03_complete.pdf (last accessed May 2008) p. 34.

14. Paul Collier, *The Bottom Billion: Why the Poorest Countries are Failing and What Can Be Done About It,* (New York: Oxford University Press, 2007) p. 27.

15. Robert Muggah and Martin Griffiths, "Reconsidering the Tools of War: Small Arms and Humanitarian Action" (Humanitarian Practice Network, 2002) p. 13.

16. Oxfam, Saferworld, and International Action Network on Small Arms, "Africa's Missing Billions: International Arms Flows and the Costs of Conflict" (October 2007), available at http://www.oxfam.org/en/files/bp107_africas_missing_billions_0710.pdf/download (last accessed May 2008) p. 9.

17. The World Bank, "Sri Lanka: Recapturing Missed Opportunities," Report No: 20430-CE, (June 16, 2000), available at http:// siteresources.worldbank.org/SRILANKAEXTN/Resources/Missed-opportunities/full_report.pdf (last accessed June 2008).

18. Larry Minear and Ian Smillie, *The Charity of Nations: Humanitarian Action in a Calculating World,* (Connecticut: Kumarian Press, 2004) p. 10.

19. The United Nations, "United Nations Peacekeeping Operations" (March 2008), available at http://www.un.org/Depts/dpko/dpko/bnote.htm (last accessed May 2008).

20. Satish Chand and Ruth Coffman, "How Soon Can Donors Exit From Post-Conflict States?" (Center for Global Development, Working Paper Number 141, February 2008), available at http://www.cgdev.org/content/publications/detail/15464 (last accessed May 2008).

21. The United Nations, "World Youth Report 2005: Young people Today, and in 2015," (2005), available at http://www.un.org/esa/socdev/unyin/documents/wyr05book.pdf (last accessed May 2008).

22. Dapo Oyewole, "Participation of Youth As Partners in Peace and Development in Africa: An Overview of Issues and Challenge" (Paper presented at the Expert Group Meeting on Youth in Africa: Participation of Youth as Partners in Peace and Development in Post-Conflict Countries, Windhoek, Namibia, November 14–16, 2006), available at http://www.un.org/esa/socdev/unyin/documents/namibia_overview.pdf (last accessed May 2008).

23. The United Nations, "The State of World Population: Population Change and Peoples Choice" (1999), available at http://www.unfpa.org/swp/1999/chapter2d.htm (last accessed May 2008).

24. The World Business Council for Sustainable Development, "Facts and Trends to 2050: Energy and Climate Change" (2004), available at http://www.wbcsd.org/DocRoot/FjSOTYajhk3cIRxCbijT/Basic-Facts-Trends-2050.pdf (last accessed May 2008) p. 1.

25. Lester Brown, "How Water Scarcity Will Shape the New Century" (Keynote speech presented at Stockhold Water Conference, August, 14, 2000), available at http://www.earth-policy.org/Transcripts/Transcript1.htm (last accessed May 2008).

26. The United Nations Environment Programme, "Water-Two Billion People Are Dying for It" (2003), available at http://www.unep.org/wed/2003/keyfacts.htm (last accessed May 2008).

27. Oxfam International, "Rigged Rules and Double Standards: Trade, Globalization, and the Fight Against Poverty" (2002), available at http://www.oxfam.org.uk/resources/papers/downloads/trade_report.pdf (last accessed May 2008) p. 7.

28. Ibid, p. 9–10.

29. Ibid, p. 177.

30. Phillip Stevens, "Diseases of Poverty and the 10/90 Gap" (International Policy Network: London, 2004), available at http:// www.fightingdiseases.org/pdf/Diseases_of_Poverty_FINAL.pdf (last accessed May 2008) p. 3.

31. Worldwatch Institute, "Vital Signs: The Trends that are Shaping our Future" (London: W.W. Norton Company, 2001), available at http://www.worldwatch.org/system/files/EVS103.pdf (last accessed May 2008) p. 21.

32. Larry Diamond, "The Democratic Rollback" *Foreign Affairs,* March/April 2008.

33. Stewart Patrick and Susan E. Rice, "Index of State Weakness in the Developing World" (Washington: The Brookings Institution, 2008) p. 17.

34. President John F. Kennedy, "Inaugural Address" (January 20, 1961), available at http://www.bartleby.com/124/pres56.html (last accessed May 2008).

35. Leighton W. Smith Jr. and Anthony C. Zinni, "A Smarter Weapon: Why Two Retired Military Officers Believe It's Essential that the Next President Use Outreach, Good Deeds and a Strong Military to Make the United States Safer" *USA Today,* March 27, 2008, available at http://www.usatoday.com/printedition/news/20080327/oplede_wednesday.art.htm (last accessed May 2008).

36. The CNA Corporation, "National Security and the Threat of Climate Change" (2007), available at http://securityandclimate.cna.org/report/National%20Security%20and%20the%20Threat%20of%20Climate%20Change.pdf (last accessed May 2008).

37. Center for U.S. Global Engagement, "A 21st Century Vision of U.S. Global Leadership: Building a Better Safer World" (2007), available at http://www.usglobalengagement.org/SignonStatement/tabid/890/Default.asp#Signatories (last accessed May 2008).

38. Robert M. Gates, "Landon Lecture, Kansas State University" (November 26, 2007), available at http://www.defenselink.mil/speeches/speech.aspx?speechid=1199 (last access May 2008).

39. The White House, "The National Security Strategy of the United States of America" (March 2006), available at http://www.whitehouse.gov/nsc/nss/2006/nss2006.pdf (last accessed May 2008) p. 33.

40. The United States Department of State, "Summary and Highlights: International Affairs Function 150, Fiscal Year 2009 Budget Request" (2008), available at http://www.state.gov/documents/organization/100014.pdf (last accessed May 2008) p. 6.

41. The United States of America Millennium Challenge Corporation, "Changing Lives: 2007 Annual Report," available at http://www.mcc.gov/documents/mcc-2007-annualreport.pdf (last accessed May 2008) p. 6.

42. WorldPublicOpinion.org, "US Role in the World," available at http://www.americans-world.org/digest/overview/us_role/general_principles.cfm (last accessed May 2008).

43. Program on International Policy Attitudes and Knowledge Networks, "Americans on Addressing World Poverty" (June 30, 2005), available at http://www.pipa.org/OnlineReports/ForeignAid/WorldPoverty_Jun05/WorldPoverty_Jun05_rpt.pdf (last accessed May 2008).

44. Oxfam America, "Smart Development: Why US Foreign Aid Demands Major Reform" (Oxfam America Inc. 2008), available at http://www.oxfamamerica.org/newsandpublications/publications/briefing_papers/smart-development/smart-development-may2008.pdf (last accessed May 2008) p. 5–6.

45. Ibid.

46. Craig Cohen, "A Perilous Course: U.S. Strategy and Assistance to Pakistan" (Washington: Center for Strategic and International Studies, August 2007), available at http://www.csis.org/media/csis/pubs/071214_pakistan.pdf (last accessed May 2008) pg. viii.

47. Ibid, p. 26.

48. United States Government Accountability Office, "Combating Terrorism: The United States Lacks Comprehensive Plan to Destroy the Terrorist Threat to Close the Safe Haven in Pakistan's Federally Administered Tribal Areas" (April 2008), available at http://www.gao.gov/new.items/d08622.pdf (last accessed May 2008) p. 12.

49. South Asia Intelligence Review, "Casualties of Terrorist Violence in Pakistan," available at http://satp.org/satporgtp/countries/pakistan/database/casualties.htm (last accessed May 2008).

50. Owen Bennett-Jones, "US Policy Options Toward Pakistan: A Principled and Realistic Approach" (Iowa: The Stanley Foundation, February 2008) p. 4.

51. "Half of Pakistan's population is 'food insecure': WFP," *The News-International,* April 23, 2008, available at http://www.thenews. com.pk/daily_detail.asp?id=108337 (last accessed May 2008).

52. Craig Cohen, "A Perilous Course: U.S. Strategy and Assistance to Pakistan" (Washington: Center for Strategic and International Studies, August 2007), available at http://www.csis.org/media/csis/pubs/071214_pakistan.pdf (last accessed May 2008) p. 27.

53. Ibid, p. 26.

54. The United States Institute of Peace, "Islamic Extremists: How Do They Mobilize Support?" (July 2002, Special Report 89), available at http://www.usip.org/pubs/specialreports/sr89.pdf (last accessed May 2008) p. 4.

55. Terror Free Tomorrow, "Pakistanis Reject US Military Action against Al Qaeda; More Support bin Laden than President Musharraf: Results of a New Nationwide Public Opinion Survey of Pakistan" (2007) available at http://www.terrorfreetomorrow.org/upimagestft/Pakistan%20Poll%20Report.pdf (last accessed May 2008).

56. The United States Commission on Helping to Enhance the Livelihood of People around the Globe, "Beyond Assistance: The HELP Commission Report of Foreign Assistance Reform" (2007) p. 1.

57. Steven Radelet, "Foreign Assistance Reforms: Successes, Failures, and Next Steps" (Testimony for the Senate Foreign Relations Subcommittee on International Development, Foreign Assistance, Economic Affairs, and International Environmental Protection, June 12, 2007), available at http://www.senate.gov/~foreign/testimony/2007/RadeletTestimony070612.pdf (last accessed May 2008).

58. Robert M. Gates, "Landon Lecture, Kansas State University" (November 26, 2007), available at http://www.defenselink.mil/speeches/speech.aspx?speechid=1199 (last access May 2008).

59. The United States Commission on Helping to Enhance the Livelihood of People around the Globe, "Beyond Assistance: The HELP Commission Report of Foreign Assistance Reform" (2007) p. 63.

60. Cathy Majtenyi, "Economic Impact of Election Violence on Display in Western Kenyan City," *Voice of America,* March 4, 2008, available at http://www.voanews.com/english/archive/2008-03/2008-03-04-voa29.cfm (last accessed May 2008).

61. Robert M. Gates, "Address to the Marine Corps Association" (July 18, 2007), available at http://smallwarsjournal.com/blog/2007/07/secretary-gates-addresses-the/ (last accessed May 2008).

62. Kaysie Brown and Stewart Patrick, "The Pentagon and Global Development: Making Sense of the DoD's Expanding Role" (Washington: The Center for Global Development Working Paper Number 131, November 2007), available at http://www.cgdev.org/content/publications/detail/14815/ (last accessed May 2008).

63. United States Department of Defense, "Directive 3000.05" (November 28, 2005), available at http://www.dtic.mil/whs/directives/corres/pdf/300005p.pdf (last accessed May 2008) p. 2.

The Petraeus Doctrine

Iraq-style counterinsurgency is fast becoming the U.S. Army's organizing principle. Is our military preparing to fight the next war, or the last one?

ANDREW J. BACEVICH

For a military accustomed to quick, easy victories, the trials and tribulations of the Iraq War have come as a rude awakening. To its credit, the officer corps has responded not with excuses but with introspection. One result, especially evident within the U.S. Army, has been the beginning of a Great Debate of sorts.

Anyone who cares about the Army's health should take considerable encouragement from this intellectual ferment. Yet anyone who cares about future U.S. national-security strategy should view the debate with considerable concern: it threatens to encroach upon matters that civilian policy makers, not soldiers, should decide.

What makes this debate noteworthy is not only its substance, but its character—the who and the how.

The military remains a hierarchical organization in which orders come from the top down. Yet as the officer corps grapples with its experience in Iraq, fresh ideas are coming from the bottom up. In today's Army, the most creative thinkers are not generals but mid-career officers—lieutenant colonels and colonels.

Like any bureaucracy, today's military prefers to project a united front when dealing with the outside world, keeping internal dissent under wraps. Nonetheless, the Great Debate is unfolding in plain view in publications outside the Pentagon's purview, among them print magazines such as *Armed Forces Journal*, the Web-based *Small Wars Journal*, and the counterinsurgency blog Abu Muqawama.

The chief participants in this debate—all Iraq War veterans—fixate on two large questions. First, why, after its promising start, did Operation Iraqi Freedom go so badly wrong? Second, how should the hard-earned lessons of Iraq inform future policy? Hovering in the background of this Iraq-centered debate is another war that none of the debaters experienced personally—namely, Vietnam.

The protagonists fall into two camps: Crusaders and Conservatives.

The Crusaders consist of officers who see the Army's problems in Iraq as self-inflicted. According to members of this camp, things went awry because rigidly conventional senior commanders, determined "never again" to see the Army sucked into a Vietnam-like quagmire, had largely ignored unconventional warfare and were therefore prepared poorly for it. Typical of this generation is Lieutenant General Ricardo Sanchez, once the top U.S. commander in Baghdad, who in late 2003 was still describing the brewing insurgency as "strategically and operationally insignificant," when the lowliest buck sergeant knew otherwise.

Younger officers critical of Sanchez are also committed to the slogan "Never again," but with a different twist: never again should the officer corps fall prey to the willful amnesia to which the Army succumbed after Vietnam, when it turned its back on that war.

Among the Crusaders' most influential members is Lieutenant Colonel John Nagl, a West Pointer and Rhodes Scholar with a doctorate from Oxford University. In 2002, he published a book, impeccably timed, titled *Learning to Eat Soup With a Knife: Counterinsurgency Lessons From Malaya and Vietnam.* After serving in Iraq as a battalion operations officer, Nagl helped rewrite the Army's counterinsurgency manual and commanded the unit that prepares U.S. soldiers to train Iraqi security forces. (Earlier this year, he left the Army to accept a position with a Washington think tank.)

To Nagl, the lessons of the recent past are self-evident. The events of 9/11, he writes, "conclusively demonstrated that instability anywhere can be a real threat to the American people here at home." For the foreseeable future, political conditions abroad rather than specific military threats will pose the greatest danger to the United States.

Instability creates ungoverned spaces in which violent anti-American radicals thrive. Yet if instability anywhere poses a threat, then ensuring the existence of stability everywhere—denying terrorists sanctuary in rogue or failed states—becomes a national-security imperative. Define the problem in these terms, and winning battles becomes less urgent than pacifying populations and establishing effective governance.

War in this context implies not only coercion but also social engineering. As Nagl puts it, the security challenges of the 21st century will require the U.S. military "not just to dominate land operations, but to change entire societies."

Of course, back in the 1960s an earlier experiment in changing entire societies yielded unmitigated disaster—at least that's how the Army of the 1980s and 1990s chose to remember its Vietnam experience. Crusaders take another view, however. They insist that Vietnam could have been won—indeed was being won, after General Creighton Abrams succeeded General William Westmoreland in 1968 and jettisoned Westmoreland's heavy-handed search-and-destroy strategy, to concentrate instead on winning Vietnamese hearts and minds. Defeat did not result from military failure; rather, defeat came because the American people lacked patience, while American politicians lacked guts.

The Crusaders' perspective on Iraq tracks neatly with this revisionist take on Vietnam, with the hapless Sanchez (among others) standing in for Westmoreland, and General David Petraeus—whose Princeton doctoral dissertation was titled "The American Military and the Lessons of Vietnam"—as successor to General Abrams. Abrams's successful if tragically aborted campaign in Vietnam serves as a precursor to Petraeus's skillfully orchestrated "surge" in Iraq: each demonstrates that the United States can prevail in "stability operations" as long as commanders grasp the true nature of the problem and respond appropriately.

For Nagl, the imperative of the moment is to institutionalize the relevant lessons of Vietnam and Iraq, thereby enabling the Army, he writes, "to get better at building societies that can stand on their own." That means buying fewer tanks while spending more on language proficiency; curtailing the hours spent on marksmanship ranges while increasing those devoted to studying foreign cultures. It also implies changing the culture of the officer corps. An Army that since Vietnam has self-consciously cultivated a battle-oriented warrior ethos will instead emphasize, in Nagl's words, "the intellectual tools necessary to foster host-nation political and economic development."

Although the issue is by no means fully resolved, the evidence suggests that Nagl seems likely to get his way. Simply put, an officer corps that a decade ago took its intellectual cues from General Colin Powell now increasingly identifies itself with the views of General Petraeus. In the 1990s, the Powell Doctrine, with its emphasis on overwhelming force, assumed that future American wars would be brief, decisive, and infrequent. According to the emerging Petraeus Doctrine, the Army (like it or not) is entering an era in which armed conflict will be protracted, ambiguous, and continuous—with the application of force becoming a lesser part of the soldier's repertoire.

Nagl's line of argument has not gone unchallenged. Its opponents, the Conservatives, reject the revisionist interpretation of Vietnam and dispute the freshly enshrined conventional narrative on Iraq. Above all, they question whether Iraq represents a harbinger of things to come.

A leading voice in the Conservative camp is Colonel Gian Gentile, a Berkeley graduate with a doctorate in history from Stanford, who currently teaches at West Point. Gentile has two tours in Iraq under his belt. During the second, just before the Petraeus era, he commanded a battalion in Baghdad.

Writing in the journal *World Affairs,* Gentile dismisses as "a self-serving fiction" the notion that Abrams in 1968 put the United States on the road to victory in Vietnam; the war, he says, was unwinnable, given the "perseverance, cohesion, indigenous support, and sheer determination of the other side, coupled with the absence of any of those things on the American side." Furthermore, according to Gentile, the post-Vietnam officer corps did not turn its back on that war in a fit of pique; it correctly assessed that the mechanized formations of the Warsaw Pact deserved greater attention than pajama-clad guerrillas in Southeast Asia.

Gentile also takes issue with the triumphal depiction of the Petraeus era, attributing security improvements achieved during Petraeus's tenure less to new techniques than to a "cash-for-cooperation" policy that put "nearly 100,000 Sunnis, many of them former insurgents, . . . on the U.S. government payroll." According to Gentile, in Iraq as in Vietnam, tactics alone cannot explain the overall course of events.

All of this forms a backdrop to Gentile's core concern: that an infatuation with stability operations will lead the Army to reinvent itself as "a constabulary," adept perhaps at nation-building but shorn of adequate capacity for conventional war-fighting.

The concern is not idle. A recent article in *Army* magazine notes that the Army's National Training Center in Fort Irwin, California, long "renowned for its force-on-force conventional warfare maneuver training," has now "switched gears," focusing exclusively on counterinsurgency warfare. Rather than practicing how to attack the hill, its trainees now learn about "spending money instead of blood, and negotiating the cultural labyrinth through rapport and rapprochement."

The officer corps itself recognizes that conventional-warfare capabilities are already eroding. In a widely circulated white paper, three former brigade commanders declare that the Army's field-artillery branch—which plays a limited role in stability operations, but is crucial when there is serious fighting to be done—may soon be all but incapable of providing accurate and timely fire support. Field artillery, the authors write, has become a "dead branch walking."

Gentile does not doubt that counterinsurgencies will figure in the Army's future. Yet he questions Nagl's certainty that situations resembling Iraq should become an all-but-exclusive preoccupation. Historically, expectations that the next war will resemble the last one have seldom served the military well.

Embedded within this argument over military matters is a more fundamental and ideologically charged argument about basic policy. By calling for an Army configured mostly to wage stability operations, Nagl is effectively affirming the Long War as the organizing principle of post-9/11 national-security strategy, with U.S. forces called upon to bring light to those dark corners of the world where terrorists flourish. Observers differ on whether the Long War's underlying purpose is democratic transformation or imperial domination: Did the Bush administration invade Iraq to liberate that country or to control it? Yet there is no disputing that the Long War implies a vast military enterprise undertaken on a global scale and likely to last decades. In this sense, Nagl's reform agenda, if implemented, will serve to validate—and perpetuate—the course set by President Bush in the aftermath of 9/11.

Gentile understands this. Implicit in his critique of Nagl is a critique of the Bush administration, for which John Nagl serves as a proxy. Gentile's objection to what he calls Nagl's "breath-taking" assumption about "the efficacy of American military power to shape events" expresses a larger dissatisfaction with similar assumptions held by the senior officials who concocted the Iraq War in the first place. When Gentile charges Nagl with believing that there are "no limits to what American military power . . . can accomplish," his real gripe is with the likes of Dick Cheney, Donald Rumsfeld, and Paul Wolfowitz.

For officers like Nagl, the die appears to have been cast. The Long War gives the Army its marching orders. Nagl's aim is simply to prepare for the inescapable eventuality of one, two, many Iraqs to come.

Nagl's aim is simply to prepare for the inescapable eventuality of one, two, many Iraqs to come.

Gentile resists the notion that the Army's (and by extension, the nation's) fate is unalterably predetermined. Strategic choice—to include the choice of abandoning the Long War in favor of a different course—should remain a possibility. The effect of Nagl's military reforms, Gentile believes, will be to reduce or preclude that possibility, allowing questions of the second order (How should we organize our Army?) to crowd out those of the first (What should be our Army's purpose?).

The biggest question of all, Gentile writes, is "Who gets to decide this?" Absent a comparably searching Great Debate among the civilians vying to direct U.S. policy—and the prospects that either Senator McCain or Senator Obama will advocate alternatives to the Long War appear slight—the power of decision may well devolve by default upon soldiers. Gentile insists—rightly—that the choice should not be the Army's to make.

ANDREW J. BACEVICH is a professor of history and international relations at Boston University. His new book, *The Limits of Power: The End of American Exceptionalism,* was published in August.

UNIT 4

Great Power Interstate Conflicts and Rivalries

Unit Selections

Key Points to Consider

- What should the United States and European countries do to improve relations and stimulate more economic integration within the European Union?

- Why does China have excellent relations with the United States and Russia today?

- How is China creating a political and economic zone of influence throughout Southeast Asia?

Student Website
www.mhhe.com/cls

Internet References

Archive of European Integration
http://aei.pitt.edu/

ISN International Relations and Security Network
http://www.isn.ethz.ch

The Henry L. Stimson Center—Peace Operations and Europe
http://www.stimson.org/fopo/?SN=FP20020610372

Central Europe Online
http://www.centraleurope.com

Europa: European Union
http://europa.eu.int

NATO Integrated Data Service
http://www.nato.int/structur/nids/nids.htm

Russia Today
http://www.russiatoday.com

Russian and East European Network Information Center, University of Texas at Austin
http://reenic.utexas.edu/reenic/index.html

Inside China Today
http://www.insidechina.com

Japan Ministry of Foreign Affairs
http://www.mofa.go.jp

The refusal of most European countries, including France and Germany, to support the U.S. military intervention in Iraq in 2003 or answer the call of the Untied States to join the "coalition of the willing" was an unprecedented breach in the Western Alliance. Many analysts interpreted this policy breach within the context of longer term changes in the structure of the international system as the world moves from a unipolar to a multipolar world. This longer term perspective views conflicts between the United States and Europe as inevitable as the Untied States aims to assert its hegemony over Europe while France and Germany seek to create a European counter balance to U.S. dominance. Since the 2003 low point, relations between the U.S. and European states within the Atlantic alliance have steadily improved. Recent events and trends such as the Russian invasion of Georgia, Taliban advances in the war in Afghanistan against NATO forces, Iran's pursuit of sophisticated nuclear fuel capabilities, and the ad hoc cooperative maritime force that is patrolling off the coast of East Africa to prevent piracy, have stimulated efforts for greater solidarity among NATO allies. Since the election of Barak Obama, expectations for more cooperation among trans-Atlantic partners and for expanded cooperation have increased sharply among nation-states on both sides of the Atlantic.

In "The Unbalanced Triangle: What Chinese-Russian Relations Mean for the United States," Stephen Kotkin explains why China's shift from the Soviet Union to the United States is "the most important geopolitical realignment of the last several decades." He likens these relationships to an "unbalanced triangle" due to China's strategic advantage of maintaining good relationships with both the United States and Russia. However, Obama's recent overtures to Russia, along with the growing economic problems evident in the three countries are likely to result in these three partners being forced to cooperate for some time to come despite divergent interests and "significant cultural prejudices about each other. The need for the EU countries, the United States, Russia, and China to cooperate in order to maintain peace and prosperity were dramatically apparent during the fall of 2009 as the three countries sent representatives to a UN-sponsored meeting to try to dissuade Iran from pursing nuclear enrichment and storage at home.

Russia's role in the current economic crisis has less impact on relations among the major nation-state actors than the country's more aggressive foreign policies. In recent years, Russia's more assertive foreign policies have played a key role in shaping relations between Europe and the United States. Now that the Cold War is over, the relations between the Russian and Western states are expected to follow traditional norms of diplomacy. This expectation may be one reason why Russia's military invasion of Georgia caught many statesmen and observers by surprise. However, Russia's foreign policy has always contained complex and often contradictory trends. These contradictions are due in part to the fact that the current Russian political economic system and government has quickly transitioned over the past 13 years from a communist state, to a fledgling democracy and capitalist

© C. Borland/PhotoLink/Getty Images

system, to a "managed democracy" with many features of the old authoritarian regime. Worsening economic conditions facilitated a shift back to state control that has accelerated under the tutelage of former KGB leader and former President Vladimir Putin. Putin stepped down from the presidency in May of 2008 and now holds the position of Prime Minister for a second time. Most Russians supported Putin's policies of re-consolidating power in the central government, the government's hard-line approach to dealing with Chechen rebels, and the recent military intervention into Georgia. Outside observers expect the President, Dmitry Medvedev, to continue playing a supporting role to Putin who is widely thought to continue exercising power from his new position as Prime Minister. Events in the former Soviet Union are also complex because the former USSR is a region composed of 15 independent nation-states, with each state trying to define separate national interests as they experience severe economic problems. Many ex-Soviet citizens share a sense of disorientation and "pocketbook shock" as their standard of living is lower today than it was under communism. About half of the states are experiencing political instability and growing discontent.

The changing power structure of the world system means that informed observers of International Relations must pay closer attention to trends outside of the Western axis of the United States, Europe, and Russia. In "Lifting the Bamboo Curtain," Robert Kaplan helps us understand changing trends in Asia by describing how China is quietly working to create a political and economic zone of influence throughout Southeast Asia. China's foreign policies include plans for a new port, oil refinery, and hub for oil and natural gas for resources coming from East Africa and the Middle East. According to Kaplan, India is currently working to avoid being blocked from her access to ports along the coast in this region. Kaplan underscores the importance of understanding the context and dynamics of local politics in his concluding assessment that the struggle over the eastern part of the Indian Ocean may "come down to who deals more adroitly with the Burmese hill tribes."

No Time for a Time-Out in Europe

Simon Serfaty

Old Europe died in August 1914, when an unnecessary regional war was so profoundly mismanaged that it turned into a suicidal 30-year conflict that engulfed and transformed the world. When the time came at last for a new Europe to be born, the driving force was a common appreciation of shared failures, rather than a shared vision of a common future. After 1945, Europe's farewell to the past launched a process whose destination could not be imagined even by its initiators—not at least until much later when, arguably, the process could no longer be reversed.

Today Europeans can reflect with much satisfaction on the achievements of the past decades. Their continent has come a long way. But there is still a long way to go, and the path forward is not clear. A flickering public will to proceed toward Europe's institutional "finality" will not be rekindled without a renewed understanding of what "Europe" is, a credible faith in what it does, and a verifiable demonstration of its ability to provide convincingly and expeditiously for citizens' needs. At issue is leadership, and looming ahead are tests of vision, will, and efficacy. How these challenges are met not only will define Europe; they will determine whether Europe has a future as the European Union that it needs to be if it is to assert its weight in the world.

Long after the cold war, Americans also can reflect with satisfaction on the achievements of the past decades with regard to Europe. On a growing number of issues, U.S. relations with the EU matter more than do bilateral relations between the United States and any of the union's members. And bilateral relations now draw much of their relevance from EU members' ability to represent the union to which they belong. However, with such satisfaction also comes a bit of apprehension. Much remains to be done on the path to an enduring arrangement for Euro-Atlantic consultation and multilateral action, especially in a security environment transformed by the end of the cold war and the advent of the "war on terror."

High Expectations

In 2009, 20 years after the end of the cold war, expectations run high on both sides of the Atlantic for another renewal of the Atlantic alliance and a relaunching of European integration. Earlier fears that either effort might be on the brink of collapse have receded.

Still, there is no room for complacency. With citizens everywhere oblivious to the past achievements and future needs of both endeavors—and, most immediately, under demanding conditions of growing economic distress—renewing the alliance and the European project will require nothing less than a refounding of the ideas and ideals that sustained both aspirations after 1945 and throughout the cold war. This will need to be accomplished not just when it comes to facts, such as membership and capabilities, but also when it comes to feelings (which motivate members to contribute to and use those capabilities).

One can identify three core principles that were demonstrated anew during the recent Euro-Atlantic and intra-European crisis over the Iraq War, and that will need to be emphasized now on both sides of the Atlantic. First, no one country alone, however peerless or whatever its self-image, can remain for long a country without allies and privileged partners. This is equally true of the United States within the Atlantic alliance and of any European state within the union.

Second, no head of state or government, however capable, charismatic, or hyperactive, can alone provide the leadership needed to face the daunting and urgent agenda that Europeans and Americans confront. Exercises in "co-leadership" must therefore be broad and collective; otherwise, in the union as well as in the alliance, such leadership will lack the legitimacy needed to last. This is as true in 2009, for a new American president who has seduced Europe on the basis of who he is, as it was in 2008 for a new French president who reassured America with what he did.

And third, no one institution, however cohesive and powerful, can by itself manage the issues in security, economics, finance, the environment, and society that characterize an increasingly globalized world. This means that a Euro-Atlantic partnership organized around the EU and NATO can at best operate as a facilitator rather than as the executor of the policies favored by these institutions' members. The partnership must work with other, more widely representative multilateral organizations.

Still Waiting for Europe

For Europe to matter—to its members, to the United States, and in the world—it must act as a union. During the debate over the Iraq War, neither Prime Minister Tony Blair nor President Jacques Chirac was heard across the Atlantic—the former speaking in his traditional British follower's voice and the latter in the predictable voice of French discontent. For either to gain the stature that each lacked separately would have required that they act together, and in the name of the EU. Short of that, Blair could not be the counterpart that America needed and Chirac could not represent the counterweight that he aspired to be.

Now, as a multipolar normalcy gradually emerges across the globe, the success of Europe's ambition to be among the world's primary poles of power and influence still depends on the ability of EU members to agree on the mechanisms that—with decisive economic, political, and security input from the United States—will bring finality to the process that Europe started after World War II.

The time for renewed commitment is hardly premature. Thirty-five years ago, under emerging global conditions of "détente" and "normalization," the United States called for 1973 to become "the year of Europe"—a year when the allies would join the United States in "a fresh act of creation . . . equal to that undertaken by the postwar generation of leaders." That call remains unanswered: a matter of insufficient political will.

Twenty years later, in 1993, with the cold war over and the Soviet Union disintegrated, Europe formed an expectation of its own that "the hour of Europe" had come—that is, a time at which an emerging union would take care of its own security business, beginning with the Balkans. This expectation also proved to be misguided: a matter of inadequate military capabilities.

One American presidency later, the events of September 11, 2001, prompted a short-lived discourse on European unity and transatlantic solidarity. But 9/11 and its aftermath proved conducive for little else—other than self-defeating divisions between European states that were "willing" and others that were reluctant to follow American leadership: a matter of distorted vision.

Now, at long last, would the departure of George W. Bush (who in postwar Europe had been the least-liked U.S. president) and the arrival of Barack Obama (whom Europe turned into an American icon long before his inauguration) finally usher in an era of global leadership for the new Europe?

A Burst of Energy

In the context of such expectations, France's hyperactive EU presidency during the latter half of 2008 was notable. Under French leadership, the EU took a lead role in trying to end Russia's war in Georgia in late summer, and in the fall managed a constructive response to the global financial crisis, including a Group of 20 summit meeting in Washington that was convened mostly as a European initiative. Late in the year, France's presidential term ended with credible EU decisions on climate change and energy, audacious proposals on EU security strategy and nuclear disarmament, and a meritorious attempt to moderate the brutal Israeli offensive in Gaza.

All these areas were of recognized interest to the outgoing and incoming U.S. administrations, and Washington showed an unprecedented acceptance of Europe's lead role. On the other hand, Europe did come in for some occasional, predictable criticism. The French-led EU stood mildly accused of appeasement because it did not achieve the withdrawal of Russian forces from Georgian territory in August; of inflated expectations, regarding the G-20's November meeting on the economic crisis; of excessive timidity, after the December EU summit made self-defeating concessions to Poland, Germany, and others on climate change; of articulating deceptive goals, when the EU issued calls for nuclear disarmament that made no room for a global zero option; and of ineffectuality, given the meager results of an allegedly tepid attempt to establish a cease-fire in Gaza.

Whether Europe's bid for global co-leadership can be sustained in and beyond 2009 is questionable. Indeed, doubts about leadership continue to afflict the continent. The permissive consensus that conditioned the growth and enlargement of the European institutions is now long gone, and new populist pressures challenge these institutions more sharply than ever. Meanwhile, recession is spreading and deepening across the EU. Member states are increasingly divided over the most effective strategy to counter the downturn. And Germans in particular are reluctant to follow French and British leadership to which they are not accustomed and of which Chancellor Angela Merkel is openly critical.

Neither Europe nor the Atlantic alliance can afford Germany's marginalization. Without Germany's commitment, Europe can be neither a counterweight to nor a counterpart with America; it risks instead becoming counterfeit. Likewise, absent the Germans, the alliance loses its credibility as America's security institution of choice. Europe's intention to develop capabilities commensurate with its influence and renewed ambitions would fade for lack of credibility as well.

Updating the Idea of Europe

More than 50 years after the Rome Treaties laid the groundwork for the union, the postwar idea of Europe has lost much of its relevance, as fears of war have receded and affluence has spread across borders. Paradoxically, it is at a time when Europeans have never been so much alike that they seem most eager to reclaim their national particularities. As each new member state since 1973 has made the union's restrictive institutional cage more crowded, all members have longed for the sovereign space that they used to enjoy whenever they were not busy fighting to protect it. In short, there is too much policy coming out of the union to suit the politics of its members—too much leadership from the former and too much resistance from the latter.

In and beyond 2009, therefore, a relaunch of the EU's institutions will not succeed unless the European idea is updated. To help generate anew the needed public support, a touch of charisma and a bit of symbolism would help—beginning in Brussels, where European elections this year are unlikely to strengthen a European Commission that was significantly weakened by the assertive and even domineering French presidency. The current Czech presidency, restrained by one of the most Euroskeptical publics among all 27 member countries, can hardly be expected to match its predecessor's activism during its six-month term. Afterwards, the presidency will fall to Sweden, one of the few EU members that is not a member of NATO as well.

Admittedly, the reorganization of European institutions—and the rethinking of the ideas on which these institutions are based—call for more than symbolic attempts at creating a more coherent European identity. There needs to be a sense of identity and purpose around which the citizens of Europe might agree to rally without a prolonged philosophical debate. But citizens also need results, especially concerning issues that cannot effectively be tackled by national governments.

These begin with traditional economic issues that remain people's foremost concern when conditions harden, including most urgently jobs and job security. But they also include related issues of immigration, which affect Europeans' sense of identity and their perceptions of security. Unless results in these areas become more evident, the citizens of individual member states will not embrace any new vision of a more integrated union, nor will they regain their will for more solidarity within the union.

In the new Europe, prosperity is no more divisible than security, and to wait passively for U.S. recovery is not a policy.

In recent years, results from European policies have not only been poorly explained—they have in fact been missing. "Europe" has often failed to deliver the achievements that new initiatives were supposed to offer. This was true at the launch of the single market, of the single currency, and even of the European Security and Defense Policy. This problem has made it tempting for national leaders to exploit "Europe" as an excuse for their own failings.

In sum, Europe can no longer be measured just in terms of what it says regarding a never-ending series of "projects." It must also be judged on the basis of what it *does* over a narrower range of significant issues that beg for common responses.

What the EU Must Do

Four issues are especially important when it comes to the EU's dual need to say what it intends to do but also to do effectively what it says it will.

First, although it was correct to let the so-called constitutional treaty die in 2007, it is imperative to keep alive the Reform Treaty adopted in Lisbon the following year, with final ratification no later than January 1, 2010. New negotiations to address the concerns of Ireland—which is expected to hold another referendum in the fall of 2009 after that country's voters rejected the treaty last year—would raise questions of institutional credibility. A compromised treaty would raise echoes of the League of Nations, which presided over the collapse of the European security order in the twentieth century, when what is needed is a European order for the twenty-first century.

The merit of the Reform Treaty is that it salvages the key elements of the defunct constitutional treaty. This preserves the democratic legitimacy of the earlier treaty's ratification process for the sixteen countries that had already approved it when two countries—one large, one small—rejected it (and when seven countries had not yet made their decisions).

More to the point, much in the Reform Treaty is indispensable to Europe's capacity to assert itself—including a slimmed-down European Commission, new voting rules for the European

Council, a "foreign minister," and the end of the six-month rotating presidency. In all these instances, the goal is to enable the EU to carry out a dialogue with the rest of the world, including the United States, with a single voice. Lacking such reforms, too much confusion will flow from the EU's various bodies and member states.

It is understood that member states cannot speak with a single voice when they disagree. That no such voice can be heard even when agreement exists is what needs to be corrected. Only when the collective will of the EU is expressed in a common voice will the world listen to the union with an interest commensurate to Europe's power, influence, and salience.

Second, in the midst of the dramatic global financial crisis that erupted in late 2008, and amid what may be the deepest and longest recession in Europe since the union was established, a fragmented, state-by-state approach will not suffice. Admittedly, new initiatives with regard to employment, growth, economic competitiveness, and financial stability are likely to remain for the most part the responsibility of each member state (unless conditions someday permit a final shift to community-wide directives whose one-size-fits-all approaches might be equally suitable for all).

But even while each member state preserves national ownership of the reforms and initiatives that it deems economically desirable and politically possible, the European Commission can encourage and coordinate exchanges among members, formulate plans of its own, and propose selective benchmarking and best practices. The commission could, for example, promote certain EU members' approaches that seek to reconcile the need for adapting to globalization with a national predilection for retaining the state's social commitments.

Neither Europe nor the Atlantic alliance can afford Germany's marginalization.

Most urgently, the EU will need to overcome the reluctance of some of its members, including Germany, to agree to, and expeditiously enforce, a union-wide stimulus package that responds to the needs of various member states and reflects the collective size of their economies. In the new Europe, prosperity is no more divisible than security, and to wait passively for U.S. recovery is not a policy.

More profoundly, the time to engage in a long-delayed discussion on economic union is coming. Of course the very crisis conditions that call for such a discussion also make EU members reluctant to initiate it, in light of potentially insurmountable domestic objections. But the discussion must go forward nonetheless, pending the recasting of the Merkel coalition government after the German election of September 2009, and possibly the next elections in Britain as well (no later than May 2010).

Flexible Integration

Third, in the context both of institutional governance and economic union, the case for flexible integration remains compelling. European integration has always moved at various speeds, and partial communities have been created within the emerging community. In the past, however, an unwritten assumption was that every member state would ultimately share every aspect of EU life even if at first it did not, or could not, adopt each new EU initiative and all of the *acquis*.

Freer trade until it is entirely free; progressive regulatory convergence; increasing cooperation on internal security; foreign policy convergence—these are some possible benchmarks for gauging a state's ability to embrace much of the EU order while, on grounds of capability and relevance, remaining outside EU institutions or only joining institutions one piece at a time.

Extending a sense of institutional identity to neighboring countries that are not members yet, or will not be members any time soon, could be accomplished by granting observer status in the Committee of Permanent Representatives. Even ad hoc participation in the Council of Ministers could be allowed when it comes to issues regarding which certain states have particular relevance or interest. Such an arrangement might not be satisfactory to all, but to pretend that a new round of enlargement is imminent is simply not compatible with the current state of the union and the will of its members.

A fundamental belief that has prevailed ever since the launch of the European Communities is that bigger is better. This belief is now in question—not so much on grounds of desirability (that is, the geopolitical questions that arise concerning countries like Turkey but also Ukraine, Georgia, and many of the other former Soviet republics) as on grounds of feasibility (that is, sharp public resistance to the accession of members deemed not "European" enough). In such a context, the transformational power of the European Neighborhood Policy should be reinforced, and the newly formulated idea of a "layered structure" ("Europe à étages") should not be dismissed.

The latter idea especially, which proposes a regional partnership with six ex-Soviet republics, may be a credible alternative to EU membership for some countries. And it might be enough to stabilize democracy in Ukraine, end conflict in Moldova, make Georgia safer, reduce difficulties with Belarus, and overcome a prevailing sense of neglect and isolation in Armenia and Azerbaijan. Such a partnership could suffice until these states are prepared for membership and the current union members are prepared for further enlargement. A similar arrangement might ultimately be extended to Russia.

The Transatlantic Agenda

Fourth, the relationship between European integration and a stronger Atlantic alliance needs to be more explicitly defined and appreciated. That "Europe" might be a cause for ambivalence in the United States is hardly new. Although the process of European integration has never been well understood in the States, it has long been a central feature of the American vision of Europe's future and, therefore, of the future of U.S.-European relations.

In encouraging this vision, the American intention has not been to impose a model of its own. Nor has it been America's intention to secure permanent control over a weak continent (though much of that control indeed remained long after the continent ceased to be weak). Rather, the intention was to help the Europeans master their past and, literally, change the course of their history. By implication at least, Europeans would change the course of America's history as well, insofar as the United States became entangled in a Euro-Atlantic partnership from which escape has become impossible.

One can debate whether new mechanisms must be put in place to allow direct consultation between the United States and the EU. The U.S. government takes the EU seriously—often more seriously than it lets on to its own constituencies. Already, over three dozen U.S.-EU pacts, including at least 15 regulatory agreements, result in daily meetings and constant conversations involving officials from both sides of the Atlantic.

But the United States, too, deserves to be taken seriously by the EU. For all essential purposes, the United States is a nonmember member state of the EU. This status involves a level of bilateral intimacy between America and the union—itself a virtual regional state—that is currently not explicitly defined. Besides a fully integrated transatlantic market, which now carries a target date of 2015, the U.S.-EU agenda of priority goals might include advances in developing an integrated European capital market; closer and more transparent relations between the European Central Bank and the U.S. Federal Reserve; steps toward accounting equivalency; and fuller convergence of regulatory practices. In each of these areas, there is plenty for both the EU and the United States to contribute.

November of this year will mark the twentieth anniversary of the fall of the Berlin wall, a moment that serves as a symbol of the ultimate triumph of the Atlantic alliance. The anniversary will offer an historic opportunity to sign a new partnership agreement. Such an agreement should elevate the Atlantic partnership from a community willing to work together on converging concerns, compatible values, and overlapping interests into a community capable of cooperative action toward global prosperity and security.

However, any celebration of Europe's partnership with the United States must not take place at the expense of European countries that are members of NATO but not yet EU members, or vice versa. All 30 European countries that are in at least one of these two institutions should sign the partnership agreement with the United States and Canada, with the understanding that future members of either institution will also be invited to sign.

Thus would be acknowledged a community of 32 countries, including—pending further enlargement—21 European nations that belong to both the EU and NATO, all sharing close relations through a shared commitment to policy coordination that takes place within and between the two institutions.

This Defining Moment

The renewal of Europe's integration project and the Atlantic alliance, and the reformulation of the contributions America can expect from Europe, are always in fashion. More than five decades after the union's beginnings, and six decades after the Washington Treaty created NATO, each side of the Atlantic and all members of the union tend to question their partners' credibility and voice doubts over the desirability of their institutions.

As could be expected, these questions and doubts are especially audible under crisis conditions, which repeatedly create "defining moments."

This is one of those moments, when doubts about the future raise questions about past achievements and vice versa, and it leaves no time for a "time-out." Instead it calls for a commitment to action that is sensitive to the urgent issues of the security environment created by the end of the cold war in 1991 and the events of September 11, 10 years later. This is a moment that neither the United States nor the EU nor its members can face alone. It is, therefore, a moment that calls for an ever closer and stronger Europe, together with an ever more cohesive and engaged partnership across the Atlantic.

SIMON SERFATY, a professor of U.S. foreign policy at Old Dominion University, is a senior analyst at the Center for Strategic and International Studies. His most recent book is *Architects of Delusion: Europe, America, and the Iraq War* (University of Pennsylvania Press, 2008).

From *Current History*, March, 2009, pp. 99–104. Copyright © 2009 by Current History, Inc. Reprinted by permission.

The Unbalanced Triangle
What Chinese-Russian Relations Mean for the United States

Stephen Kotkin

Bobo Lo, a former Australian diplomat in Moscow and the director of the China and Russia programs at the Center for European Reform, in London, has written the best analysis yet of one of the world's more important bilateral relationships. His close examination of Chinese-Russian relations—sometimes mischaracterized by both countries as a "strategic partnership"—lays bare the full force of China's global strategy, the conundrum of Russia's place in today's world, and fundamental shortcomings in U.S. foreign policy.

China's shift in strategic orientation from the Soviet Union to the United States is the most important geopolitical realignment of the last several decades. And Beijing now enjoys not only excellent relations with Washington but also better relations with Moscow than does Washington. Lo calls the Chinese-Russian relationship a "mutually beneficial partnership" and goes so far as to deem Moscow's improved ties with Beijing "the greatest Russian foreign policy achievement of the post-Soviet period."

Precisely such hyperbole drives the alarmism of many pundits, who believe that the United States faces a challenge from a Chinese-Russian alliance built on shared illiberal values. But as Lo himself argues, the twaddle about Russia being an energy superpower was dubious even before the price of oil fell by nearly $100 in 2008. Even more important, Lo points out that the Chinese-Russian relationship is imbalanced and fraught: the two countries harbor significant cultural prejudices about each other and have divergent interests that are likely to diverge even more in the future. More accurately, the Chinese-Russian relationship is, as Lo puts it, an "axis of convenience"—that is, an inherently limited partnership conditioned on its ability to advance both parties' interests.

But even Lo does not go far enough in his debunking of the Chinese-Russian alliance: he argues that it "is, for all its faults, one of the more convincing examples of positive-sum international relations today." This is doubtful. The relationship may allow the Chinese to extract strategically important natural resources from Russia and extend their regional influence, but it affords the Russians little more than the pretense of a multipolar world in which Moscow enjoys a central role.

Strategic Mistrust

The year 2006 was the Year of Russia in China, and 2007, the Year of China in Russia, with both states hosting a slew of exhibits, cultural programs, trade talks, and state visits. At the opening ceremony in Moscow in March 2007, Chinese President Hu Jintao remarked, "The Chinese National Exhibition in Russia is the largest-ever overseas display of Chinese culture and economic development." (It is worth noting that every year could be called the Year of China in the United States and that the U.S. consumer market is essentially one endless Chinese National Exhibition.)

By showcasing in Moscow 15,000 Chinese products from 30 industries—machinery, aviation, ship building, information technology, home appliances—Beijing sent the message that regardless of the substantial role the Soviet Union played in China's post-1949 industrialization, there is now a new ascendancy, with China enjoying the dominant position. This, in fact, is a return to the historical paradigm—China has generally set the agenda for relations between the two countries. The Chinese-Russian relationship dates from the Russian conquest of Siberia in the seventeenth century. The Russian empire, then not very rich, sought to trade with China, then the world's wealthiest country. The two empires also discovered a common but often rivalrous interest in crushing the Central Asian nomads, leaving China and Russia with a 2,700-mile border, the world's longest. Since then, this shared border has shifted numerous times and served as a source of intermittent tension. As recently as 1969, the two countries clashed along the Ussuri River, which separates northeastern China from the Russian Far East, and Soviet leaders discussed retaliating with nuclear weapons if China launched a mass assault.

Now, as Lo writes, their relations are, in many ways, better than ever. In June 2005, both sides ratified a treaty settling their border disputes. Cross-border business and tourism are brisk. In 2006, two million Russian tourists went to China and nearly one million Chinese visited Russia.

Still, as Lo subtly demonstrates, the Chinese-Russian "axis of convenience" is bedeviled by "pervasive mistrust" rooted in historical grievances, geopolitical competition, and structural factors. Moreover, it is a secondary axis. China and Russia talk about being strategic partners, but neither actually is central to the other's concerns. China's indispensable partner is the United States; Russia's is Europe or, more specifically, Germany. In 2007, Chinese-Russian trade reached $48 billion, up from $5.7 billion in 1999, making China Russia's second-largest trading partner after the European Union. But current Russian-EU trade exceeds $250 billion—the lion's share of it being between Russia and Germany—and Chinese-U.S. trade exceeds $400 billion. China and Russia, Lo demonstrates, "pay far more attention to the West than they do to each other." Their relationship is opportunistic. As Lo puts it, the two giants "share neither a long-term vision of the world nor a common understanding of their respective places in it."

In addition—and this is the most important aspect of Lo's argument—whatever opportunity does exist in the relationship, China is in a better position to exploit it. China extracts considerable practical benefits in oil and weapons from Russia. In return, Beijing flatters Moscow with rhetoric about their "strategic partnership" and coddles it by promoting the illusion of a multipolar world. In many ways, the Chinese-Russian relationship today resembles that which first emerged in the seventeenth century: a rivalry for influence in Central Asia alongside attempts to expand bilateral commercial ties, with China in the catbird seat. Lo politely calls this incongruity an "asymmetry."

Giving Away the Store

The profound asymmetry in Chinese-Russian relations is most visibly illustrated by the two countries' roles in the Shanghai Cooperation Organization (SCO), a six-member security group founded in 2001, and by their energy and weapons trades.

So far, China has consistently resisted Moscow's lobbying for building the SCO—whose other members are the former Soviet states of Kazakhstan, Kyrgyzstan, Tajikistan, and Uzbekistan—into a quasi-military alliance that could counter NATO. In addition, the SCO declined to publicly endorse Russia's account of its August 2008 war with Georgia (Moscow claimed that the Georgian army attacked first, an assertion implicitly recognized even by the U.S. ambassador to Russia). China, it seems, is unwilling to impart any strategic significance to disputes in the Caucasus.

Meanwhile, using the SCO and business investments, China has been making economic inroads into Central Asia, a region that Russia has traditionally considered within its sphere of influence. Chinese companies have been on a buying spree in recent years, making investments throughout Central Asia in minerals, energy, and other industries. Beijing appears to have cracked even the difficult nut of Turkmenistan—a pipeline now under construction is slated to run from the natural gas fields in Turkmenistan to Xinjiang, in western China. To a large extent, it is Russia's single-minded focus on pushing the United States out of Central Asia—lobbying Kyrgyzstan, for example, to eject U.S. forces from a military base in Bishkek—that has allowed China's influence there to grow relatively unhindered. And whereas the United States can scarcely hope to maintain a permanent presence in Central Asia, China can be counted on to stick around.

Lo is doubtful about the prospects of a major Chinese-Russian energy deal. But in February 2009, after his book had gone to press, the two governments signed a deal under which Rosneft, the largest Russian state-owned oil company, and Transneft, the Russian state-owned oil-pipeline monopoly, would get $25 billion from the China Development Bank in exchange for supplying China with 300,000 barrels of oil a day from 2011 to 2030—or a total of about 2.2 billion barrels. Factoring in the interest payments the Russian companies will owe on the loan, the deal means that China will pay under $20 a barrel—less than half the global price at the time of the deal and less than one-third the market price for future deliveries in 2017.

This Chinese money is slated to underwrite the completion of an oil pipeline that will run from eastern Siberia to the Pacific Ocean, with an offshoot going to Daqing to serve the Chinese market. The proposed pipeline would increase roughly to eight percent Russia's share of China's oil imports, up from four percent now. Russian energy companies, laden with debt, lack the capital to build the pipeline by themselves or, for that matter, to drill for new hydrocarbons. With a projected capacity of 600,000 barrels per day, the pipeline is expected to supply Japan with Russian oil, too—provided enough is available. Still, the $20-a-barrel price borders on the shocking. Considering the perhaps more advantageous energy deals that have been on the table

with U.S. and European multinationals, Rosneft and Transneft deal with China looks like a giveaway. It appears to be a consequence of the obsession many Russian officials have with denying the United States a strategic foothold in Russia's energy sector at all costs—even if one of those costs is opening themselves up to exploitation by the Chinese.

Energy is not even the most fruitful aspect of China's relationship with Russia. According to U.S. estimates, Russia supplies China with 95 percent of its military hardware, including Kilo-class submarines and Sovremenny-class destroyers. So far, Russian officials have not viewed the buildup of the Chinese navy as a direct threat to Russia; instead, they see it as a potential problem for Japan and the United States. Also, the post-Soviet Russian military was long unable to afford weapons produced by domestic manufacturers, making arms exports a necessity. Still, whatever benefits Russia gained by keeping its defense industry alive while waiting for better times, the benefits to China have been beyond compare. After the Tiananmen Square crackdown in 1989, many of the world's largest arms merchants—France, the United Kingdom, and the United States—imposed an arms embargo on China. As Russia moved to fill this gap, China began to reverse engineer weapons systems and pressure Russia to sell it not just the finished products but also the underlying manufacturing technology. For reasons that have yet to be explained publicly, Russian arms sales to China have declined in recent years. Nonetheless, China has the money and remains an eager customer for Russia's blueprints.

According to Lo, the terms of Chinese-Russian trade "are becoming more unbalanced every year"—so much so that he compares the role of Russia for China to that of Angola, China's largest trading partner in Africa. Russia will remain important as long as the weapons and fossil fuels keep flowing (and no economically viable alternatives to hydrocarbons emerge). Lo does not say so explicitly, but in an imagined multipolar world, Russia looks like a Chinese subsidiary. China treats Russia with supreme tact, vehemently denying its own superiority—a studious humility that only helps it maintain the upper hand.

What Kind of Partner?

Lo quotes Yuri Fedorov, a Russian political analyst, who laments that Russia is "doomed to be a junior partner to everyone." In fact, it is China that has accepted the role of junior partner to the United States, and the payoff has been impressive. It is a calculated position and part of China's global strategy sometimes known as "peaceful rise," a term first introduced by the Chinese leadership soon after the Tiananmen massacre. One vital element of this strategy is for China to take advantage of its de facto strategic partnership with the United States while sometimes swallowing hard in the face of U.S. dominance. China guards its sovereignty no less than does Russia, but, as Lo writes, China, contrary to Russia, "does not deem it necessary to contest Western [i.e., American] interests and influence wherever it finds them." Nor does China view Russia as a strategic counterweight to the United States—whereas Russia hopes to use China to balance against the United States. Chinese leaders go out of their way to emphasize that China is still a developing country and that the United States will remain the sole global superpower for a long time to come. It is a concession that leaves them ample room to pursue China's interests, and so they see little point in paying the enormous costs of opposing the United States.

The second main element in China's "peaceful rise" strategy is using Russia for all it is worth—weapons, oil, or acquiescence in China's expanding influence in Central Asia. Under Vladimir Putin, Russia became more practical in its relations with China than it had been under Boris Yeltsin, in the 1990s. Moscow has made sure to trade its support for China's intransigent policies toward Taiwan, Tibet, and Xinjiang for

Beijing's endorsement of Russia's heavy-handed approach to combating domestic instability in Chechnya and the North Caucasus. But the deal remains uneven. Moscow's closer ties with Beijing, meanwhile, have not increased its leverage with Washington one iota. By rejecting the role of junior partner to the United States, Russia has, perhaps unintentionally, become China's junior partner—an arrangement, furthermore, that will last only as long as it is convenient for Beijing. Lo concludes, "China's rise as the next global superpower threatens Russia, not with the military or demographic invasion many fear, but with progressive displacement to the periphery of international decision making."

One should not forget China's many vulnerabilities, nor Russia's numerous foreign policy achievements over the last decade. After the abject humiliation of the 1990s, the sovereignty of the Russian state has been restored—no longer can foreign capitals dictate Russian policy or the appointments of government officials. Russia's annual GDP has soared from a low of $200 billion under Yeltsin to around $1.6 trillion today (a turnabout in which China's insatiable demand for global commodities and manufactures has played an enormous role). Russia enjoys strong relations with France, Germany, and Italy and cultivates these bilateral ties in Europe in order to blunt the collective power of the EU. Its European partners compete with one another for Moscow's favor. At the same time, Russia has—from its point of view at least—demonstrated anew its influence in the former Soviet republics.

But despite its revival, Russia, in contrast to China, remains unable to figure out how to benefit from the immovable fact of U.S. power and wealth. Under the Obama administration, the United States has stopped—for the time being—approaching Russia as a state to be reformed or disciplined. But a softening in tone cannot make up for the fact that the U.S.-Russian relationship lacks the kind of deep commercial basis that undergirds U.S.-Chinese ties. Although an interest in both Russia and the United States in renewed arms control negotiations may help restart bilateral relations, such gestures are no substitute for the kind of economic interdependence Washington has with Beijing.

The ultimate stumbling block between Russia and the United States—and what differentiates China from Russia from the United States' perspective—is the clash over influence in the former Soviet republics. Two factors have led to this clash. The first is that Moscow has lost its empire yet will not relinquish its assertion of "privileged interests" in Georgia, Ukraine, and the other former Soviet republics. Russia's influence in the former Soviet territories—which remained strong even during Russia's perceived weakness in the 1990s—has only grown. This reality, moreover, is an outgrowth not of military occupation or of Russia's clumsy bullying but of mutual interests forged through economic ties.

The second factor is that the United States will not cease to view these lands in terms of promoting or defending democracy, even under the Obama administration's more pragmatic foreign policy. Compare, for example, the relatively small role Tibet plays in U.S.-Chinese relations with the disproportionate hold that now-independent countries such as Georgia or Ukraine have on U.S.-Russian relations. For Washington to appear to abandon the nominal democracies living in Russia's shadow for the sake of more constructive relations with Russia is politically impossible. No matter how badly those countries misgovern themselves or provoke Russia, a withdrawal of U.S. support would be an abandonment of one of the central tenets of U.S. policy toward the region since the end of the Cold War.

The upshot is that Russia and the United States are left with something of a paradox. Although Washington can refuse to defer to Russia's claim of "privileged interests" in the former Soviet states, it cannot undo the fact that such a Russian sphere of influence does

exist, extending to property ownership, business and intelligence ties, television programming, and the Internet. Moscow, meanwhile, cannot hope to both claim its interests in its neighbors and emulate China's approach of accepting the role of junior partner to the United States for practical benefit.

This suggests that "the new geopolitics" Lo promises to illuminate are not so new, after all. As Russia pursues the chimera of a multipolar world, the United States pursues the delusion of nearly limitless NATO expansion. And in the process, both unwittingly conspire to put Russia in China's pocket.

The Triangle Tips Over

Lo's book inspires three broad observations. First, although Russia has been known as the world power that straddles Asia and Europe, today it is China that has emerged as the force to be reckoned with on both continents. Russia's Pacific coast serves not as a gateway to Asia—as San Francisco and Los Angeles do in the United States—but as a natural geographic limit. At the same time, China, as the dominant power in East Asia, denies Russia a significant say in the region.

Russia's failure to become an East Asian power over the past several centuries is amplified by emigration from Russia's Far East, where the population has shrunk from a peak of around ten million in the Soviet period to around 6.5 million today. Meanwhile, the population of China's three northeastern provinces directly across the Russian border is estimated at 108 million and growing. As Dmitry Rogozin, now Russia's ambassador to NATO, quipped on Russian radio in 2005, the Chinese are crossing the border "in small groups of five million." Actually, as Lo indicates, the number of Chinese residents in Russia—mostly laborers and petty traders—is probably only between 200,000 and 400,000. Yet Rogozin's quote reflects domestic anxieties about Russia's weak footprint in Asia, a problem for which Russia has no discernible strategy. And on Russia's western border, China's relations with Europe are at least as good as Russia's. In other words, Russia's bluff of maintaining an influential presence in Asia is becoming an ever more pronounced strategic weakness.

Second, not only has China shifted its strategic alliance from the Soviet Union to the United States; it has learned how to have its cake and eat it, too. China manages to preserve relations with its Cold War patron, Russia, while hitching its growth to the world's current hegemon, the United States. From 1949 until the Sino-Soviet split in the 1960s, China was an eager junior partner to the Soviet Union, slavishly imitating the Stalinist developmental model. In 1972, the courting of Mao Zedong by Richard Nixon and Henry Kissinger opened up a global option for China that Mao's successors would later exploit. Under Deng Xiaoping, who in 1979 became the first Chinese Communist leader to visit the United States, China began to forge its de facto strategic alliance with the United States. Then, under Jiang Zemin, a post-1991 rapprochement with Russia became a major additional instrument for Beijing. It is as if China went to the prom with one partner, Russia, went home with another, the United States, and then married the latter while wooing its jilted original date as a mistress.

Third, although the Soviet Union ultimately capitulated to the United States in the Cold War, Russia today does not feel compelled to similarly bow down to the United States. Such a proud stance may not offer many rewards for Russia, but it does confront the United States with some difficult policy questions. Simply put, if Moscow's fantasy is multipolarity, Washington's own delusion has been the near-limitless expansion of NATO. That game, however, is exhausted. For years, the cogent argument against continued NATO expansion was not that it would anger the Russians—after the Soviet collapse, the Russians were going to emerge angry regardless. Rather, the problem was that the bigger NATO became, the weaker it got. Poland agreed to install Patriot missile interceptors—a U.S. and not a NATO missile defense system—only because the United States provided Poland, a member of NATO, with a security guarantee above and beyond that offered by the NATO charter. What, then, is NATO for? Russia will never join, and for all its historic achievements, NATO is not up to solving the contemporary security dilemmas of Europe, such as those linked to energy, migration, and terrorism.

Russia has recovered from its moment of post-Soviet weakness but nonetheless remains a regional power that acts like a global superpower. China, on the other hand, has been transformed into a global superpower but still mostly acts like a regional power. Meanwhile, the United States is still busy trying to consolidate its triumph in the Cold War 18 years on. Recently, many people in Russia and the United States have begun to speak of a "new Cold War." This idea, however, is doubly wrong—wrong because Russia, a regional power, cannot hope to mount a global challenge to the United States, and wrong because the old Cold War tilting never went away, with the battleground merely having been downsized, shifting from the whole globe to Kiev and Tbilisi.

There are domestic advantages for the Russian regime in continuing to talk of a new Cold War. But what does a preoccupation with the supposed Russian menace do for the United States? And alternatively, what would the United States gain from resetting U.S.-Russian relations? At the moment, the most important U.S. policy questions are domestic, not foreign, and Russia will be of little help in solving them. Russia has no role to play in reforming the U.S. health-care system—whose cost structure is the single greatest threat to U.S. power and prosperity—nor can it help fix the crumbling U.S. retirement system. If the United States were to imitate China and indulge Russia in its fantasy about its own global relevance, it would not realize the same kind of concrete benefits the Chinese get. On the international front, although many in Washington see Moscow as Tehran's main backer—even though China has deeper commercial ties to Iran—Russia does not have the leverage over Iran to forestall the development of that country's nuclear weapons program.

The overall importance of Russia for the United States, then, is widely exaggerated. There is one crucial exception, however, an area in which Russia's power has not depreciated: in Europe, Russia remains a dominant force, and its strategic weight in the region is reason alone for the United States to pursue better bilateral relations. During the Crimean War of 1853–56, Lord Palmerston, the British prime minister, fantasized that "the best and most effectual security for the future peace of Europe would be the severance from Russia of some of the

frontier territories acquired by her in later times, Georgia, Circassia, the Crimea, Bessarabia, Poland and Finland. . . . She would still remain an enormous power, but far less advantageously posted for aggression on her neighbors." This flight of imagination has since become reality, and then some. But still, Russia remains a regional force. Indulging the claims that Russia's recent revival is solely attributable to oil—a code word for "luck"—or that Russia's demographic problems will make the country essentially vanish cannot alter the fact that enduring security in Europe cannot be had without Russia's cooperation or in opposition to Russia. An expanded NATO, meanwhile, is not providing the enduring security it once promised. It is only a matter of time before a crisis, perhaps on the territory of a former Soviet republic and now NATO member, exposes NATO's mutual defense pact as wholly inoperative.

There is another reason the United States should care about Russia: because China does. As Lo writes, "China will become steadily (if cautiously) more assertive, initially in East Asia and Central Asia, but eventually across much of Eurasia." In other words, even under a strategy of a peaceful rise, China will increasingly force the United States to accommodate Chinese power. China's development of a blue-water navy recalls the rise of the German navy in the years before World War I, a process that unnerved the United Kingdom, then the world's great power. It seems that China is already trying to recalibrate the balance of power in East Asia, as evidenced by its harassment of the *Impeccable,* a U.S. Navy surveillance ship, in the South China Sea in March 2009. In the event of a crisis, China does not want its thoroughly globalized economy to be vulnerable to a blockade by either the Japanese navy or the U.S. Navy, and it likely envisions being able to hinder U.S. access to the Taiwan Strait. Meanwhile, China is counting on the Russian navy's not rising again in East Asia and on continued strained ties between Japan and Russia over the disputed Kuril Islands, a few rocks in the Pacific Ocean.

In the end, there can be no resetting of U.S.-Russian relations without a transcending of NATO and the establishment of a new security architecture in Europe. And without such a genuine reset, China will retain the upper hand, not only in its bilateral relationship with Russia but also in the strategic triangle comprising China, Russia, and the United States.

STEPHEN KOTKIN is Professor of History and International Affairs at Princeton University. His latest book is *Uncivil Society: 1989 and the Implosion of the Communist Establishment,* which includes a contribution by Jan Gross.

Lifting the Bamboo Curtain

As China and India vie for power and influence, Burma has become a strategic battleground. Four Americans with deep ties to this fractured, resource-rich country illuminate its current troubles, and what the U.S. should do to shape its future.

ROBERT D. KAPLAN

Monsoon clouds crushed the dark, seaweed-green landscape of eastern Burma. Steep hillsides glistened with teak trees, coconut palms, black and ocher mud from the heavy rains, and tall, chaotic grasses. As night came, the buzz saw of cicadas and the pestering croaks of geckos rose through the downpour. Guided by an ethnic Karen rebel with a torchlight attached by bare copper wires to an ancient six-volt battery slung around his neck, I stumbled across three bamboo planks over a fast-moving stream from Thailand into Burma. Any danger came less from Burmese government troops than from those of its democratic neighbor, whose commercial interests have made it a close friend of Burma's military regime. Said Thai Prime Minister Samak Sundaravej recently: the ruling Burmese generals are "good Buddhists" who like to meditate, and Burma is a country that "lives in peace." The Thai military has been on the lookout for Karen soldiers, who have been fighting the Burmese government since 1948.

"It ended in Vietnam, in Cambodia. When will it end in Burma?" asked Saw Roe Key, a Karen I met shortly after I crossed the border. He had lost a leg to a Toe Popper antipersonnel mine—the kind that the regime has littered throughout the hills that are home to more than a half-dozen ethnic groups in some stage of revolt. Of the two dozen or so Karens I encountered at an outpost inside Burma, four were missing a leg from a mine. Some wore green camouflage fatigues and were armed with M-16s and AK-47s; most were in T-shirts and traditional skirts, or *longyis*. Built into a hillside under the forest canopy, the camp was a jumble of wooden-plank huts on stilts roofed with dried teak leaves, with a solar panel and an ingenious water system. Beyond the camp beckoned perfect guerrilla country.

Sawbawh Pah, 50, small and stocky with only a tuft of hair on his scalp, runs a clinic here for wounded soldiers and people uprooted from their homes, of whom there have been 1.5 million in Burma. The Burmese junta, known as the State Peace and Development Council (SPDC), has razed more than 3,000 villages in Karen state alone—one reason *The Washington Post* has called Burma a "slow-motion Darfur." With a simple,

resigned expression that some might mistake for a smile, he told me, "My father was killed by the SPDC. My uncle was killed by the SPDC. My cousin was killed by the SPDC. They shot my uncle in the head and cut off his leg while he was looking for food after the village was destroyed." Over a meal of fried noodles and eggs, I was inundated with life stories like Pah's. Their power lay in their grueling repetition.

Major Kea Htoo, the commander of the local battalion of Karen guerrillas, had reddened lips and a swollen left cheek from chewing betel nut. Like his comrades, he told me he saw no end to the war. They were fighting not for a better regime composed of more enlightened military officers, nor for a democratic government that would likely be led by ethnic Burmans like Aung San Suu Kyi, but for Karen independence. Tu Lu, missing a leg, had been in the Karen army for 20 years. Kyi Aung, the oldest at 55, had been fighting for 34 years. These guerrillas are paid no salaries. They receive only food and basic medicine. Their lives have been condensed to the seemingly unrealistic goal of independence; since Burma first fell under military misrule in 1962, nobody has ever offered them anything resembling a compromise. Although the junta has trapped the Karens, Shans, and other ethnics into small redoubts, its corrupt and desertion-plagued military lacks the strength for the final kill. So the war continues.

Endless conflict and gross, regime-inflicted poverty have kept Burma primitive enough to maintain an aura of romance. Like Tibet and Darfur, it offers its advocates in the post-industrial West a cause with both moral urgency and aesthetic appeal. In 1952, the British writer Norman Lewis published *Golden Earth,* a spare and haunting masterpiece about his travels throughout Burma. The insurrections of the Karens, Shans, and other hill tribes make the author's peregrinations dangerous, and therefore even more uncomfortable. He found that only a small region in the north, inhabited largely by the Kachin tribe, was "completely free from bandits or insurgent armies." Lewis spends a night tormented by rats, cockroaches, and a scorpion, yet wakes none the worse in the morning to the "mighty whirring of hornbills flying overhead." His bodily sufferings seem a small price to pay for the uncanny beauty of a country of broken roads and no adequate hotels, where "the condition of the soul replaces that of the stock markets as a topic for polite conversation." More than 50 years later, what shocks about this book is how contemporary it seems. A Western relief worker arriving in the wake of last spring's devastating cyclone could have followed Lewis's itinerary and had similar experiences. By contrast, think of all the places where globalization has made even a 10-year-old travel guide out of date.

But Burma is more than a place to feel sorry for. And its ethnic struggles are of more than obscurantist interest. For one thing, they precipitated the military coup that toppled the country's last civilian government almost a half century ago, when General Ne Win took power in part to forestall ethnic demands for greater autonomy. With one-third of Burma's population composed of ethnic minorities living in its fissiparous borderlands (which account for seven of Burma's 14 states and divisions), the demands of the Karens and others will return to the fore once the military regime collapses. Democracy will not deliver Burma from being a cobbled-together mini-empire of nationalities, even if it does open the door to compromise among them.

Moreover, Burma's hill tribes form part of a new and larger geopolitical canvas. Burma fronts on the Indian Ocean, by way of the Bay of Bengal. Its neighbors India and China (not to mention Thailand) covet its abundant oil, natural gas, uranium, coal, zinc, copper, precious stones, timber, and hydropower. China especially needs a cooperative, if not supine, Burma for the construction of deepwater ports, highways, and energy pipelines that can open China's landlocked south and west to the sea, enabling its ever-burgeoning middle class to receive speedier deliveries of oil from the Persian Gulf. These routes must pass north from the Indian Ocean through the very territories wracked by Burma's ethnic insurrections.

Burma is a prize to be contested, and China and India are not-so-subtly vying for it. But in a world shaped by ethnic struggles, higher fuel prices, new energy pathways, and climate-change-driven natural disasters like the recent cyclone, Burma also represents a microcosm of the strategic challenges that the United States will face. The U.S. Navy underscored these factors in its new maritime strategy, released in late 2007, which indicated that the Navy will shift its attention from the Atlantic to the Indian Ocean and the western Pacific. The Marines, too, in their new "Vision and Strategy 2025" statement, highlight the Indian Ocean as among their main theaters of activity in coming years.

But toward Burma specifically, U.S. policy seems guided more by strategic myopia. The Bush administration, like its predecessors, has loudly embraced the cause of Burmese democracy but has done too little to advance it, either by driving diplomatic initiatives in the region or by supporting any of the ethnic insurgencies. Indeed, Special Operations Command is too preoccupied with the western half of the Indian Ocean, the Arab/Persian half, to pay much attention to Burma, which lacks the energizing specter of an Islamic terror threat. Meanwhile, the administration's reliance on sanctions and its unwillingness

to engage with the ruling junta has left the field open to China, India, and other countries swayed more by commercial than moral concerns.

But some Americans are consumed by Burma, and they offer a window onto different, and perhaps more fruitful, ways of engaging with its complex realities. I saw Burma through the eyes of four such men. In most cases, I cannot identify them by name, either because of the tenuousness of their position in neighboring Thailand, whose government is not friendly to their presence, or because of the sensitivity of what they do and whom they work for. Their expertise illustrates what it takes to make headway in Burma, while their goals say a great deal about what is at stake.

The Son of the Blue-Eyed Shan

While the mess in Iraq has made the virtues of cultural expertise newly fashionable, champions of such experience often conveniently forget that many of America's greatest area experts have been Christian missionaries. American history has seen two strains of missionary area experts: the old Arab hands and the Asia, or China, hands. The Arab hands were Protestant missionaries who in the early 19th century traveled to Lebanon and ended up founding what became the American University of Beirut. From their lineage descended the State Department Arabists of the Cold War era. The Asia hands have a similarly distinguished origin, beginning, too, in the 19th century and providing the U.S. government with much of its area expertise through the early Cold War, when, during the McCarthy era, a number of them were unjustly purged. One American who counseled me on Burma is descended from several generations of Baptist missionaries from the Midwest who ministered to the hill tribes beginning in the late 19th century. His father, known as "The Blue-Eyed Shan," escaped Burma ahead of the invading Japanese and was conscripted into Britain's Indian army, in which he commanded a Shan battalion. Among my acquaintance's earliest childhood memories was the sight of Punjabi soldiers ordering work gangs of Japanese prisoners of war to pick up rubble in the Burmese capital of Rangoon. With no formal education, he speaks Shan, Burmese, Hindi, Thai, and the Yunnan and Mandarin dialects of Chinese. He has spent his life studying Burma, though the 1960s saw him elsewhere in Indochina, aiding America's effort in Vietnam.

During our conversation, he sat erect and cross-legged on a raised platform, wearing a *longyi*. Gray-haired, with a sculpted face and an authoritative, courtly Fred Thompson voice, he has the bearing of an elder statesman, tempered by a certain gentleness. "Chinese intelligence is beginning to operate with the antiregime Burmese ethnic hill tribes," he told me. "The Chinese want the dictatorship in Burma to remain, but being pragmatic, they also have alternative plans for the country. The warning that comes from senior Chinese intelligence officers to the Karens, the Shans, and other ethnics is to 'come to us for help—not the Americans—since we are next door and will never leave the area.'"

At the same time, he explained, the Chinese are reaching out to young military officers in Thailand. In recent years, the

Thai royal family and the Thai military—particularly the special forces and cavalry—have been sympathetic to the hill tribes fighting the pro-Chinese military junta; Thailand's civilian politicians, influenced by lobbies wanting to do business with resource-rich Burma, have been the junta's best allies. In sum, democracy in Thailand is momentarily the enemy of democracy in Burma.

But the Chinese, the Son of the Blue-Eyed Shan implied, are still not satisfied: they want *both* Thailand's democrats and military officers on their side, even as they work with *both* Burma's junta and its ethnic opponents. "A new bamboo curtain may be coming down on Southeast Asia," he worried. This would not be a hard-and-fast wall like the Iron Curtain; nor would it be part of some newly imagined Asian domino theory. Rather, it would create a zone of Chinese political and economic influence fostered by, among other factors, American neglect. While the Chinese operate at every level in Burma and Thailand, top Bush-administration officials have skipped summits of the Association of Southeast Asian Nations. My friend simply wanted the United States back in the game.

"To topple the regime in Burma," he says, "the ethnics need a full-time advisory capability, not in-and-out soldiers of fortune. This would include a coordination center inside Thailand. There needs to be a platform for all the disaffected officers in the Burmese military to defect to." Again, rather than a return to the early Vietnam era, he was talking about a more subtle, more clandestine version of the support the United States provided the Afghan mujahideen during the 1980s. The current Thai administration would be hostile to that, but the government in Bangkok, and its policies, routinely change. The military could yet return to power there, and even if it doesn't, if the U.S. signaled its intent to support the Burmese hill tribes against a regime hated the world over, the Thai security apparatus would find a way to assist.

"The Shans and the Kachins near the Chinese border," my friend went on, "have gotten a raw deal from the Burmese junta, but they are also nervous about a dominant China. They feel squeezed. And unity for the hill tribes of Burma is almost impossible. Somebody from the outside must provide a mechanism upon which they can all depend." Larger than England and France combined, Burma has historically been a crazy quilt of vaguely demarcated states sectioned by jungly mountain ranges and the valleys of the Irrawaddy, Chindwin, Salween, and Mekong rivers. As a result, its various peoples remain distinct: the Chins in western Burma, for example, have almost nothing in common with the Karens in eastern Burma. Nor is there any community of language or culture between the Shans and the Burmans (the ethnic group, not the nationality, which is Burmese), save their Buddhist religion. Indeed, the Shans have much more in common with the Thais across the border.

But Burma should not be confused with the Balkans, or with Iraq, where ethnic and sectarian differences simmering for decades under a carapace of authoritarianism erupted once central authority dissolved. After so many years of violence, war fatigue has set in here, and the tribes show little propensity to fight each other after the regime unravels. They are more disunited than they are at odds. Even among themselves, the Shans, as my friend told me, have been historically subdivided into states led by minor kings. As he sees it, such divisions open a quiet organizing opportunity for Americans of his ilk.

The Father of the White Monkey

Tha-U-Wa-A-Pa, or "The Father of the White Monkey" in Burmese, is also the son of Christian missionaries, originally from Texas. Except for nine years in the U.S. Army, including in Special Forces, from which he retired as a major, he has been, like his parents, a missionary in one form or another. He also speaks a number of the local languages. He is much younger than my other acquaintance and much more animated, with a ropy, muscular body in perpetual motion, as if his system were running on too many candy bars. Whereas my other contact has focused on the Shan tribes near the Chinese border, the Father of the White Monkey—the sobriquet comes from the nickname he has given his daughter, who often travels with him—works mostly with the Karen and other tribes in eastern Burma abutting Thailand, though the networks he operates have ranged as far as the Indian border.

In 1996, he met the Burmese democracy leader Aung San Suu Kyi in Rangoon, while she was briefly not under house arrest. The meeting inspired him to initiate a "day of prayer" for Burma, and to work for its ethnic unity. During the 1997 Burmese army offensive that displaced more than 100,000 people, he was deep inside the country, alone, going from one burned-out village to another, handing out medicine from his backpack. He told me about this and other army offensives that he witnessed, in which churches were torched, children disemboweled, and whole families killed. "These stories don't make me numb," he said, his eyes popping open, facial muscles stretched. "Each is like the first one. I pray always that justice will come and be done."

In 1997, after that trip inside Burma, he started the Free Burma Rangers, a relief group that has launched more than 300 humanitarian missions and has 43 small medical teams among the Karens, Karennis, Shans, Chins, Kachins, and Arakanese—across the parts of highland Burma that embrace on three sides the central Irrawaddy River valley, home to the majority of Burmans. As he told it, the Free Burma Rangers is an unusual nongovernmental organization. "We stand with the villagers; we're not above them. If they don't run from the government troops, we don't either. We have a medic, a photographer, and a reporter/intel guy in each team that marks the GPS positions of Burmese government troops, maps the camps, and takes pictures with a telephoto lens, all of which we post on our website. We deal with the Pentagon, with human-rights groups . . . There is a higher moral obligation to intervene on the side of good, since silence is a form of consent.

"NGOs," he went on in a racing voice, "like to claim that they are above politics. Not true. The very act of providing aid assists one side or another, however indirectly. NGOs take sides all the time." The Father of the White Monkey takes this hard truth several steps further. Whereas the Thais host Burmese refugee camps on their side of the border, and the ethnic insurgents run camps inside Burma for internally displaced people—even as the Karens and other ethnics have mobile clinics near Burmese army concentrations—the backpacking Free Burma Rangers operate *behind* enemy lines.

Like my other acquaintance, the Father of the White Monkey is a very evolved form of special operator. One might suspect that the Free Burma Rangers is on some government payroll in Washington. But the truth is more pathetic. "We are funded by church groups around the world. Our yearly budget is $600,000. We were down to $150 at one point; we all prayed and the next day got a grant for $70,000. We work hand to mouth." For him, Burma is not a job but a lifelong obsession.

"Burma is not Cambodia under the Khmer Rouge," he told me. "It's not genocide. It's not a car wreck. It's a slow, creeping cancer, in which the regime is working to dominate, control, and radically assimilate all the ethnic peoples of the country." I was reminded of what Jack Dunford, the executive director of the Thailand Burma Border Consortium, had told me in Bangkok. The military regime was "relentless, building dams, roads, and huge agricultural projects, taking over mines, laying pipelines," sucking in cash from neighboring powers and foreign companies, selling off natural resources at below market value—all to entrench itself in power.

Once, not long ago, the Father of the White Monkey was sitting on a hillside at night, in an exposed location between the Burmese army and a cluster of internal refugees whom the army had driven from their homes. The Karen soldiers he was with had fired rocket-propelled grenades at the Burmese army position, and in response the Burmese soldiers began firing mortar rounds at him. At that moment, he got a message on his communications gear from a friend at the Pentagon asking why the United States should be interested in Burma.

He tapped back a slew of reasons that ranged from totalitarianism to the devastation of hardwood forests, from religious persecution of Buddhist monks to the use of prisoners as mine sweepers, and much else. But, ever the missionary, the Father of the White Monkey barely touched on strategic or regional-security issues. When I asked him his denomination, he responded, "I'm a Christian." As such, he believes he is doing God's work, engaged morally first and foremost, especially with the Karens, who number many Christians, converted by people like his parents. He is the kind of special operator the U.S. security bureaucracy can barely accept, for becoming one involves taking sides and going native to a degree. And yet, operatives like him offer the level of expertise that the United States desperately needs, if it is to have influence without being overbearing in remote parts of the globe.

The Colonel

Timothy Heinemann, a retired Army colonel from Laguna Beach, California, does think strategically. He is also a veteran of Special Forces. I first met him in 2002 at the Command and General Staff College at Fort Leavenworth, Kansas, where he was the dean of academics. He now runs Worldwide Impact, an NGO that helps ethnic groups, as well as a number of cross-border projects, particularly sending media teams into Burma

to record the suffering there. Another kind of special operator, Heinemann, with his flip-flops and his engaging manner, embodies the subtle, indirect approach to managing conflict emphasized in the 2006 Quadrennial Defense Review, one of the Pentagon's primary planning documents. Heinemann says that he "privatizes condition-setting." He explains: "We are networkers on both sides of the border. We try to find opportunities for NGOs to collaborate better in supporting ethnic groups' needs. I do my small part to set conditions so that America can protect national, international, and humanitarian interests with real savvy. Our work is well known to various branches of the U.S. government. The opposition to the military dictatorship has no strategic and operational planning like Hezbollah does. Aung San Suu Kyi is little more than a symbol of the wrong issue—'Democracy first!' Ethnic rights and the balance of ethnic power are preconditions for democracy in Burma. These issues must be faced first, or little has been learned from the lessons of Afghanistan and Iraq." Heinemann, like the Father of the White Monkey, also lives hand to mouth, grabbing grants and donations from wherever he can, and is sometimes reduced to financing trips himself. He finds Burma "exotic, intoxicating."

Burma is also a potential North Korea, he says, as well as a perfect psychological operations target. He and others explained that the Russians are helping the Burmese government to mine uranium in the Kachin and Chin regions in the north and west, with the North Koreans waiting in the wings to supply nuclear technology. The Burmese junta craves some sort of weapons-of-mass-destruction capability to provide it with international leverage. "But the regime is paranoid," Heinemann points out. "It's superstitious. They're rolling chicken bones on the ground to see what to do next.

"Burma's got a 400,000-man army [the active-duty U.S. Army is 500,000] that's prone to mutiny," Heinemann went on. "Only the men at the very top are loyal. You could spread rumors, conduct information warfare. It might not take much to unravel it." (Burmese soldiers are reportedly getting only a portion of their salaries, and their weapons at major bases are locked up at night.) On the other hand, the military constitutes the country's most secure social-welfare system, and that buys a certain amount of loyalty from the troops. And yet, "there is no trust by the higher-ups of the lower ranks," according to a Karen resistance source. The junta leader, Than Shwe, a former postal clerk who has never been to the West, is known, along with his wife, to consult an astrologer. "He governs out of fear; he is not brave," notes Aung Zaw, editor of *The Irrawaddy,* a magazine run by Burmese exiles in the northwestern Thai city of Chiang Mai. "And Than Shwe rarely speaks publicly; he has even less charisma than Ne Win," the dictator from 1962 to 1988.

Heinemann and Aung Zaw each recounted to me how the regime suddenly deserted Rangoon one day in 2005 and moved the capital north, halfway to Mandalay, to Naypyidaw, "the abode of kings," which it built from scratch, with funds from Burma's natural-gas revenues. The date of the move was astrologically timed. The new capital lies deep in the forest and is fortified with underground bunkers designed to protect against an American invasion. Heinemann sees China, India, and other

Asian nations jockeying for position with one of the world's worst, weirdest, wealthiest, and most strategically placed rogue regimes, which is vulnerable to a coup or even disintegration, if only the United States adopted the kind of patient, low-key, and inexpensive approach that he and my other two acquaintances advocate.

Heinemann's last job in the military was as a planner for the occupation of Iraq, and he was an eyewitness to the mistakes of a massive military machine that disregarded local realities. He sees Burma as the inverse of Iraq, a place where the United States can do itself a lot of good, and do much good for others, if it fights smart.

The Bull That Swims

And then there is Ta Doe Tee, or "The Bull That Swims," another American, whom I met in his suite in one of Bangkok's most expensive hotels. His impeccably tailored black suit barely masked an intimidating physique—the reason for his Burmese nickname—and his business card defines him as a "compradore," an all-purpose factotum steeped in local culture, the kind of enabler who was vital to the running of the British East India Company. The Bull was a staff sergeant in Special Forces in the 1970s and now works in the security business in Southeast Asia.

He is of the Army Special Forces generation that was frustrated about having just missed service in Vietnam, with little to do overseas during the presidency of Jimmy Carter. Stationed at Fort Devens, Massachusetts, in the mid-1970s, he was mentored, commanded, and led by some of the Son Tay Raiders. "Dick Meadows, Greg McGuire, Jack Joplin, Joe Lupyak"—he recites their names with reverence—were SFs who stormed the Son Tay prison camp near Hanoi in 1970 in a failed attempt to rescue American prisoners of war. "Vietnam and Southeast Asia were all they ever talked about," he told me.

But in 1978, Jimmy Carter's head of the CIA, Admiral Stansfield Turner, fired or forced into early retirement almost 200 officers running agents stationed abroad who had been providing intelligence, and many of them were in Southeast Asia. The CIA's clandestine service was devastated. As the Bull tells the story, many of the fired officers would not simply "be turned off," and decided to maintain self-supporting networks, "picking up kids" like himself along the way, just out of Special Forces. They sent him to learn to sail and fly, and he became a certified ship's master for cargo vessels and an FAA-certified pilot. In the 1980s, he became involved in operations in Southeast Asia, such as bringing equipment to the Khmer Rouge in Cambodia. He blurred the line between such controversial and shadowy government operations and the illegal means sometimes used to sustain them: in 1988, while trying to bring 70 tons of marijuana to the West Coast of the United States with a Southeast Asian crew under his command, he was boarded by the U.S. Coast Guard. He served five years in prison in the U.S. and has been back in Southeast Asia ever since.

The Bull put on reading glasses and opened a shiny black loose-leaf notebook to a map of the Indian Ocean. A line drawn on the map went from Ethiopia and Somalia across the water past India, and then north up the Bay of Bengal, through the heart of Burma, to China's Yunnan province. "This map is just an example of how CNOC [the Chinese National Oil Company] sees the world," he explained.

He showed me another map, which zoomed in on Ethiopia and Somalia, with grid marks on the significant reserves of oil and natural gas in the Ogaden Basin on the Ethiopian-Somali border. A circle was drawn around Hobyo, a Somali port visited in the early 15th century by the Chinese admiral Zheng He, whose treasure fleets plied the same Indian Ocean sea lanes that serve as today's energy routes. "Oil and natural gas would be shipped from Hobyo direct to western Burma," the Bull said, where the Chinese are building a new port at Kyauk Phyu, in Burma's Arakan state, that will be able to handle the world's largest container ships. According to him, the map shows how easy it will be for the Chinese to operate all over the Indian Ocean, "tapping into Iran and other Persian Gulf energy suppliers." Their biggest problem, though, will be cutting through Burma. "The Chinese need to acquire Burma, and keep it stable," said the Bull.

There are other routes to energy-hungry inner China besides the one through Burma. The Chinese are also developing a deepwater port in Gwadar, in Pakistani Baluchistan, close to the Iranian border, and have plans to do the same in Chittagong in Bangladesh. Both ports would be closer than Beijing and Shanghai to cities in western China. But the Burmese route is the most direct from the Indian Ocean.

This whole development is part of the Chinese navy's "string of pearls" strategy, which—coupled with a canal that the Chinese may one day help finance across Thailand's Isthmus of Kra, linking the Bay of Bengal with the South China Sea—will give China access to the Indian Ocean. China is, in effect, expanding south, even as India, to keep from being strategically encircled by the Chinese navy, is expanding east—also into Burma.

Until 2001, India, the world's largest democracy, took the high road on Burma, condemning it for its repression and providing moral support for the cause of Aung San Suu Kyi, who had studied in New Delhi. But as senior Indian leaders told me on a recent visit, India could not just watch Chinese influence expand unchecked. Burma's jungles serve as a rear base for insurgents from eastern India's own mélange of warring ethnic groups. Furthermore, as Greg Sheridan, foreign editor of *The Australian,* has observed, India has been "aghast" to see the establishment of Chinese listening stations along Burma's border with India. So in 2001, India decided to provide Burma with military aid and training, selling it tanks, helicopters, shoulder-fired surface-to-air missiles, and rocket launchers.

India also decided to build its own energy-pipeline network through Burma. In fact, during the 2007 crackdown on the monks in Burma, India's petroleum minister signed a deal for deepwater exploration. Off the coast of Burma's western Arakan state, adjacent to Bangladesh, are the Shwe gas fields, among the largest natural reserves in the world, from which two pipeline systems will likely emerge. One will be China's at Kyauk Phyu, which will take deliveries of oil and gas from as far away as the Persian Gulf and the Horn of Africa, as well as from Shwe itself. The other pipeline system will belong to India, which is spending $100 million to develop the Arakanese port of Sittwe as a trade window for its own landlocked, insurgency-roiled northeast.

There is nothing sinister about any of this: it is the consequence of the intense need of hundreds of millions of people in India and China who will consume ever more energy as their lifestyles improve. As for China, it may not be a democracy, but little in its larger Indian Ocean strategy can be decried. China is not, and will likely never be, a truly hostile state like Iran.

But China's problems with Burma are actually just beginning, argues the Bull, and the United States must exploit them quietly. As he observed, the minutiae of tribal and ethnic differences can easily displace grand lines on a map and the plans of master strategists. Just look at Yugoslavia, at Iraq, at Israel-Palestine. Given the energy stakes, he sees the struggles of the Karens, Shans, Arakanese, and other minorities as constituting the "theater of activity" for his lifetime, something that the Turner firings had denied him. Burma is where the United States has to build a "UW [unconventional-war] capability," he said. Such would be the unofficial side of our competition with China, which should be forced over time to accept a democratic and highly federalized Burma, with strong links to the West.

Like the other three Americans, the Bull talked about the need to build and manage networks among the ethnic hill tribes, through the construction of schools, clinics, and irrigation systems. In particular, he focused on the Shan, the largest of the hill tribes, with 9 percent of Burma's population and about 20 percent of its territory. Allying with the Shans, he said, would give the United States a mechanism to curtail the flow of drugs in the area, and to create a balancing force against China right on its own border. In any Burmese democracy, the Shans would control a sizeable portion of the seats in parliament. More could be accomplished through nonmilitary aid to a specific Burmese hill tribe, he argued, than through some of the larger weapons and other defense programs the United States spends money on. The same strategy could be applied to the Chins in western Burma, with the help of India. Not just in Iraq, but in Burma, too, American policy in the coming years should be all about the tribes.

Winning the Endgame

But while the former Special Forces and other Asia hands I interviewed see Burma as central to American strategy, the active-duty Special Operations community does not, because it is under orders to focus on al-Qaeda. This, my acquaintances say, shows how America's obsession with al-Qaeda has warped its strategic vision, which should be dominated by the whole Indian Ocean, from Africa to the Pacific.

Larger U.S. policy toward the Burmese regime, meanwhile, has remained unchanged over several administrations. George H. W. Bush, Bill Clinton, and George W. Bush have all declared their support for Burmese democracy, even as they have demonstrated little appetite for supporting the ethnic insurgencies,

however covertly. In that respect, American policy toward Burma can seem more moralistic than moral, and President Bush in particular, despite Laura Bush's intense interest in Burma, may seem prone to the same ineffectual preachiness of which former President Jimmy Carter has often been accused. Bush, by some accounts, should either open talks with the junta, rather than risk having the U.S. ejected from the whole Bay of Bengal region; or he should support the ethnics in an effective but quiet manner. "Right now, we get peanuts from the U.S.," Lian Sakhong, general secretary of the Burmese Ethnic Nationalities Council, told me.

American officials respond that they have in fact backed their affirmations of democracy with actions. The United States has banned investment in Burma since 1997 (though the ban is not retroactive, thereby leaving Chevron, which took over its concession from Unocal, free to operate a pipeline from southern Burma into Thailand). The United States added new sanctions in 2003 and 2007 and provides humanitarian aid through NGOs operating from Thailand. As for cross-border support for the Karen and Shan armies, officials note that the moment the word of such a policy got out, America's embassy presence in Burma would be gutted. Of course, it's unclear what good the U.S. diplomatic presence in Burma is doing.

Nevertheless, according to a top member of the nongovernmental-aid community, the United States is the only major power that sends the junta a "tough, moral message, which usefully prevents the International Monetary Fund and World Bank from dealing with Burma." As a result, Burma has less money to build dams and roads to further despoil the landscape and displace more people. U.S. policy, this source went on, "also rallies Western and international pressure that has led to cracks in the Burmese military." The regime will collapse one day, maybe sooner than later; when it does, America would presumably be in excellent stead with the Burmese people.

Though the prospect of another mass uprising excites the Western imagination, what's more likely is another military coup, or something more nuanced—a simple change in leadership, with Than Shwe, 75 years old and in poor health, allowed to step aside. Then, new generals would open up talks with Aung San Suu Kyi and release her from house arrest. Even with elections, this would not solve Burma's fundamental problems. Aung San Suu Kyi, as a Nobel Peace Prize laureate and global media star, could provide a moral rallying point that even the hill tribes would accept. But the country would still be left with no public infrastructure, no institutions, no civil society, and with various ethnic armies that fundamentally distrust the dominant Burmans. As one international negotiator told me, "There will be no choice but to keep the military in a leading role for a while, because without the military, there is nothing in Burma." In power for so long, however badly it has ruled, the military has made itself indispensable to any solution. "It's much more complicated than the beauty-and-the-beast scenario put forth by some in the West—Aung San Suu Kyi versus the generals," says Lian Sakhong. "After all, we must end 60 years of civil war."

Burma must somehow find a way to return to the spirit of the Panglong Agreement of February 1947, the pact that the

MacEwan Library
Express Check Out Receipt
City Centre

Borrower ID: *********3611

Rich and poor : disparities, percept
Barcode: 1004646558
DUE: Apr 14, 2011

Ethics codes, corporations, and the
Barcode: 1004338362
DUE: Apr 14, 2011

Annual editions : world politics.
Barcode: 1006755530
DUE: Apr 14, 2011

Total items: 3
Mar 31, 2011

View your MacEwan Library account at
http://webpac.lrc.macewan.ca

nationalist leader, General Aung San, negotiated among the country's tribes shortly before independence from Great Britain. It was based on three principles: a state with a decentralized federal structure, recognition of the ethnic chieftaincies in the hills, and their right of secession after a number of years. Failure to implement that agreement, which collapsed after Aung San's assassination that summer, has been the cause of all the problems since.

Meanwhile, the war continues. When I asked Karen military leaders in the Thai border town of Mae Sot what they needed most, they told me: assault rifles, C-4 plastic explosives to make Claymore mines, and .50-caliber sniper systems with optics to knock out the microwave relay stations and bull-dozers that the Burmese army uses to communicate and to build roads through Karen areas.

In his bunker in the jungle capital of Naypyidaw, Than Shwe sits atop an unsteady and restless cadre of mid-level officers and lower ranks. He may represent the last truly centralized regime in Burma's postcolonial history. Whether through a peaceful, well-managed transition or through a tumultuous or even anarchic one, the Karens and Shans in the east and the Chins and Arakanese in the west will likely see their power increased in a post-junta Burma. The various natural-gas pipeline agreements will have to be negotiated or renegotiated with the ethnic peoples living in the territories through which the pipelines would pass. The struggle over the Indian Ocean, or at least the eastern part of it, may, alas, come down to who deals more adroitly with the Burmese hill tribes. It is the kind of situation that the American Christian missionaries of yore knew how to handle.

From *The Atlantic*, September 2008. Copyright © 2008 by Robert D. Kaplan. Reprinted by permission of the author.

UNIT 5

North-South Interstate Conflicts and Rivalries

Unit Selections

Key Points to Consider

- In what ways is U.S. involvement in Afghanistan similar to U.S. involvement in Vietnam?

- What additional measures need to be taken to supplement the naval Combined Task Force 150 (CTF150) currently attempting to minimize piracy in the Indian Ocean?

- According to Senator Jim Webb, why can't we afford to ignore Myanmar?

- How do other, large Latin American countries run their economies and deal with their citizens as compared to Venezuela?

Student Website
www.mhhe.com/cls

Internet References

National Defense University Website
   http://www.ndu.edu
The North American Institute
   http://www.northamericaninstitute.org
Inter-American Dialogue
   http://www.iadialog.org
African Center for Strategic Studies (ACSS)
   http://www.africacenter.org
Observatory of Cultural Policies in Africa (OCPA)
   http://ocpa.irmo.hr/resources/index-en.html
United States Africa Command (AFRICOM)
   http://www.africom.mil/

Mao made famous the phrase the "Third World," in referring to the large number of countries that were united by their economic status and historical experiences. Mao and many others urged the countries in the "Third World" to remain apart from the Western "First World" or the former communist "Second World" during the Cold War and unite instead, in a new coalition. Since the 1960s, there has been a growing recognition that most of the developing countries of the "Third World" are located south of the equator and thus, share a number of common problems related to climate, geography, and transportation that make economic development difficult.

The "North-South" label has increasingly been adopted to designate both an informal and formal grouping of nation-states based on their economic level of development, shared history, and common continuing problems. Negotiations over many issues between Northern and Southern countries take place in the United Nations General Assembly, and in more specialized U.N. organizations such as the United Nations Conference on Trade and Agricultural Development or UNCTAD. UNCTAD has continued to operate as a forum for dialogue between the poor and wealthy states. However, by the 1980s, the unity of the South's Group of 77 (G77) had largely collapsed. Most analysts cite the rise of OPEC and the newly industrialized countries in Asia as important trends that helped shatter the facade of a united developing world. Throughout the 1990s and continuing today many of the most important multinational economic negotiations have occurred between developing country members of the G-20 and members of the G-8, i.e. France, the United States, the UK, Russia, Germany, Japan, Italy, and Canada.

Most observers believe that such labels as the "North-South conflict" are too simplistic to capture the diverse range of issues among countries at different levels of development. However, the term continues to be used as a convenient short-hand label. The label is useful for referencing the fact that there are frequent conflicts between developed and developing countries over a host of non-traditional security issues (i.e., economic and environmental) that result in very different interests and experiences among large numbers of countries in the developed and developing world. Another simplifying device often used to understand complex political conflicts are analogies often framed as "lessons of history." In "Obama's Vietnam," John Barry and Evan Thomas acknowledge that "the analogy isn't exact but the war in Afghanistan is starting to look disturbingly familiar . . . The Taliban has one resource that the Viet Cong never enjoyed: a steady stream of income from Afghanistan's massive heroin trade."

One region where the "North-South," and even the "Third World" label still resonates with many leftist politicians and intellectuals is Latin America. For nearly two centuries, the United States viewed Latin America as being within its exclusive sphere of influence. Over the past three decades, most countries in the region shifted from military dictatorships, to democracies, to civilian-led governments that adopted neo-liberal economic reforms. Political changes and economic growth occurred, but few economic benefits trickled down to most citizens. The result was a wave of leftist leaders elected in several Latin American

countries who have promised to bring more tangible results to the people.

After two decades of privatization and trade liberalization across the hemisphere, leftist leaders were elected, first in Venezuela with the election of Hugo Chávez and next in Brazil. Evo Morales was elected in Bolivia and all were promising to exert more state control over their nations' economies to promote wealth distribution. The return of leftists even extends to Nicaragua where a nemesis of the Reagan administration, Daniel Ortega, was elected in 2006. While some analysts warn that recent leftist-populist alliances threaten U.S. interests in the region, others are not so alarmed. Chávez and other leftist leaders were losing support even before the financial crisis of 2008. Regardless of how one interprets the varying support for more radical leaders in key Latin American countries, a basic reality facing the current generation of leaders is that they must find ways to produce tangible results to everyday problems for increased numbers of middle class and poor citizens.

Many of the same economic and political problems facing leaders and citizens in Latin America are also found throughout Africa. For example, most Somali pirates when captured, explain that they have been forced to become pirates because they have lost their traditional livelihoods as fishermen. While this may be a convenient excuse, it is true that decades of overfishing by foreign commercial vessels has been an important contributor to the collapse of commercial fishing off the coast of Somalia. From the perspective of most commercial vessels transiting off the coast of Somalia and their home nation-states, such pirates are outlaws rather than victims. In "Somali Piracy: A Nasty Problem, a Web of Responses," James Kraska and Brian Wilson describe the recent reaction of the international community to the recent upsurge of illegal ship seizures in the Indian Ocean. To try to deter pirates many states located in the "North" now participate in an international naval presence in the region to try to prevent maritime security from deteriorating. This initially ad hoc response has been formalized as the cooperative naval Combined Task Force 150 (CTF150). The main mission of the group is to combat piracy. According to Kraska and Wilson, what is still needed is more bilateral efforts and more emphasis on "disposition," such as investigation, trial, and punishment and political commitments to repress piracy and safeguard the region's water from coastal and affected states. "Lasting solutions require a political commitment to repressing piracy and safeguarding a region's waters must, for lasting effectiveness, emanate from coastal and affected states."

In Asia, much like many regimes in Latin America, Africa, and the Middle East, many of the problems and conflicts are tied to corrupt and undemocratic regimes. Senator Jim Webb in "We Can't Afford to Ignore Myanmar," outlines why the United States and Europe need to change their policies toward the military regime in Myanmar. Senator Webb describes how, for more than ten years, the United States and Europe have tried but failed to influence the behavior of the military government ruling Myanmar, formerly called Burma, with economic sanctions in response to the government's failure to recognize the results of the 1990 election won by Aung San Suu Kyi's party. Senator Webb concludes that the results have been counterproductive and that it's time to try another strategy.

In the last article, "Not Your Father's Latin America," Duncan Currie explains how many other Latin American countries have veered away from the controversial policies instituted under Hugo Chávez.

Obama's Vietnam

The analogy isn't exact. But the war in Afghanistan is starting to look disturbingly familiar.

JOHN BARRY AND EVAN THOMAS

About a year ago, Charlie Rose, the nighttime talk-show host, was interviewing Lt. Gen. Douglas Lute, the military adviser at the White House coordinating efforts in Afghanistan and Iraq. "We have never been beaten tactically in a fire fight in Afghanistan," Lute said. To even casual students of the Vietnam War, his statement has an eerie echo. One of the iconic exchanges of Vietnam came, some years after the war, between Col. Harry Summers, a military historian, and a counterpart in the North Vietnamese Army. As Summers recalled it, he said, "You never defeated us in the field." To which the NVA officer replied: "That may be true. It is also irrelevant."

Vietnam analogies can be tiresome. To critics, especially those on the left, all American interventions after Vietnam have been potential "quagmires." But sometimes clichés come true, and, especially lately, it seems that the war in Afghanistan is shaping up in all-too-familiar ways. The parallels are disturbing: the president, eager to show his toughness, vows to do what it takes to "win." The nation that we are supposedly rescuing is no nation at all but rather a deeply divided, semi-failed state with an incompetent, corrupt government held to be illegitimate by a large portion of its population. The enemy is well accustomed to resisting foreign invaders and can escape into convenient refuges across the border. There are constraints on America striking those sanctuaries. Meanwhile, neighboring countries may see a chance to bog America down in a costly war. Last, there is no easy way out.

True, there are important differences between Afghanistan and Vietnam. The Taliban is not as powerful or unified a foe as the Viet Cong. On the other hand, Vietnam did not pose a direct national-security threat; even believers in the "domino theory" did not expect to see the Viet Cong fighting in San Francisco. By contrast, while not Taliban themselves, terrorists who trained in Afghanistan did attack New York and Washington in 2001. Afghanistan has always been seen as the right and necessary war to fight—unlike, for many, Iraq. Conceivably, Gen. David Petraeus, the architect of the successful surge in Iraq and now, as the head of Central Command in charge of the fight in Afghanistan, could pull off another miraculous transformation.

Privately, Petraeus is said to reject comparisons with Vietnam; he distrusts "history by analogy" as an excuse not to come to grips with the intricacies of Afghanistan itself. But there is this stark similarity: in Afghanistan, as in Vietnam, we may now be facing a situation where we can win every battle and still not win the war—at least not within a time frame and at a cost that is acceptable to the American people.

A wave of reports, official and unofficial, from American and foreign (including Afghan) diplomats and soldiers, present and former, all seem to agree: the situation in Afghanistan is bad and getting worse. Some four decades ago, American presidents became accustomed to hearing gloomy reports like that from Vietnam, although the public pronouncements were usually rosier. John F. Kennedy worried to his dying day about getting stuck in a land war in Asia; LBJ was haunted by nightmares about "Uncle Ho." In the military, now as then, there are a growing number of doubters. But the default switch for senior officers in the U.S. military is "can do, sir!" and that seems to be the light blinking now. In Afghanistan, as in Vietnam, when in doubt, escalate. There are now about 30,000 U.S. troops in Afghanistan. The outgoing Bush administration and the incoming Obama administration appear to agree that the number should be twice that a year or so from now.

To be sure, even 60,000 troops is a long way from the half million American soldiers sent to Vietnam at the war's peak; the 642 U.S. deaths sustained so far pale in comparison to the 58,000 lost in Vietnam. Still, consider this: that's a higher death toll than after the first *nine* years of U.S. involvement in Vietnam. And what is troubling is that no one in the outgoing or incoming administration has been able to say what the additional troops are for, except as a kind of tourniquet to staunch the bleeding while someone comes up with a strategy that has a chance of working. The most uncomfortable question is whether any strategy will work at this point.

It's still too early to say exactly what President Obama will do in Afghanistan. But there are some signs—difficult to read with certainty, yet nonetheless suggestive—that reality is sinking in, at least in some important corners of the new administration. Defense Secretary Robert Gates, the one Bush cabinet holdover, worries that increasing the size of the U.S. military's footprint in Afghanistan will merely fan the locals' antipathy toward foreigners. "We need to be very careful about the nature of the goals we set for ourselves in Afghanistan," he told a congressional committee last week. "My worry is that the Afghans come to see us as part of the problem, rather than as part of the solution. And then we are lost."

Vietnam, half a world away, seemed alien to many Americans and to Westerners generally. Afghanistan might as well be the moon. At least Vietnam had been a French colony, albeit a troubled one. Afghanistan resisted colonization, dispatching 19th-century British and 20th-century Russian soldiers with equal efficiency. "Afghanistan is not a nation, it is a collection of tribes," according to a Saudi diplomat who did not wish to publicly disparage a Muslim neighbor. In Vietnam, the Ngo Dinh Diem government was seen as illegitimate because Diem was a Roman Catholic in a mostly Buddhist country and because it was propped up by the United States. In Afghanistan, Hamid Karzai's government was essentially created by the United States after local warlords, backed by American airpower, ousted the Taliban in 2001. (Karzai was elected in his own right in 2004, but at a time when he was clearly favored by America and faced no serious rivals.)

As in Diem's Vietnam, government corruption is epic; even Karzai says so. "The banks of the world are full of the money of our statesmen," he said last November. His former finance minister, Ashraf Ghani, rates his old government as "one of the five most corrupt in the world" and warns that Afghanistan is becoming a "failed, narco-mafia state." In a country where seven out of 10 citizens live on about a dollar a day, the average family each year must pay about $100 in baksheesh, or bribes (in Vietnam, this was known as "tea" or "coffee" money). Foreign aid is, after narcotics, the readiest source of income in Afghanistan. But it has been widely estimated that because of stealing and mismanagement in Kabul, the capital, less than half of the money actually finds its way into projects, and only a quarter of that makes it to the countryside, where 70 percent of the people live.

To Afghans now, as to Vietnamese then, the government is more often an arbitrary force to be feared than a benevolent protector. Ordinary Vietnamese lived with the fear of crossing someone more powerful, who could always turn them over to the Americans as an enemy sympathizer; a similar fear pervades Afghanistan now. When U.S. forces quickly crushed the Taliban after 9/11, many Afghans welcomed them, thinking the all-powerful Americans would transform their streets and schools and the economy. Now bitterness has set in. "What have the people of Afghanistan received from the Coalition?" asks Zamir Kabulov, the Russian ambassador to Afghanistan. "They lived very poorly before, and they still live poorly—but sometimes they also get bombed by mistake."

Nation-building in Afghanistan may be a hopeless cause. Periods of peace under centralized rule have been few and far between. Violence has been the norm: in the 18th century

a Persian king, Nadir Shah, suppressed a revolt and beheaded 6,500 tribesmen (chosen by lot). He stacked their heads in a pyramid—with one of the instigators of the revolt entombed inside. And the Saudi diplomat is right in this sense: especially across the Pashtun belt in southern Afghanistan, local leaders have traditionally held more sway than whoever's in power in Kabul. The Taliban may not be fighting in a nationalist cause per se, as the Viet Cong were. But they certainly are more local, better rooted than the U.S.-led coalition.

The basic mantra of counterinsurgency is "clear, hold and build." Clear the area of insurgents. Hold it so the insurgents cannot return. Build the civic works and government structures so that the community decides to back the government. That's a coherent approach. But while foreign troops can clear better than the Taliban, they simply can't hold as well. In fact, the Taliban are getting pretty good at counterinsurgency themselves—"clear, hold and build" is what they're doing across southern Afghanistan. Their strict brand of justice is appealing to some Afghans, who crave order and security. In some areas Taliban commanders have even relaxed some of their more unpopular dictates, allowing girls to go to school, for instance. Last month, the sober and respected International Council on Security and Development reported that the Taliban "now holds a permanent presence in 72 percent of Afghanistan, up from 54 percent a year ago." They are moving in on Kabul; according to the ICOS report, "three of the four main highways in Kabul are now compromised by Taliban activity."

The Taliban also has one resource that the Viet Cong never enjoyed: a steady stream of income from Afghanistan's massive heroin trade. Afghan poppies produce roughly 93 percent of the world's opium. Although, nominally, eradication has been a high priority since 2004, poppy cultivation has more than doubled. Farmers can't be persuaded to switch to other crops unless they feel confident that the Taliban won't return to kill them as punishment. And besides, they'd need passable roads to move more legitimate crops to functioning markets. The Americans don't have anywhere near enough troops—their own or those of increasingly disillusioned NATO allies—to secure the roads and the farm areas. That's not only because of Afghanistan's size (similar to Texas), but also because of a failure of strategy reminiscent of Vietnam.

America has been trying to pacify Afghanistan essentially through a counterterrorist campaign. The consequence has been that some of the military's most valuable warriors—its Special Forces—have been largely misused. Most people think of Special Forces as jumping out of helicopters on secret and dangerous missions. Actually, until George W. Bush launched his Global War on Terror—and Defense Secretary Donald Rumsfeld gave the Special Operations Command the lead role—their normal (and arguably more useful) mission was to train up the armies of developing countries. In Vietnam, the Green Berets were initially (and successfully) sent into the highlands to train indigenous tribesmen as guerrilla fighters.

After 1962, however, they were diverted to fruitless efforts to seal Vietnam's frontiers. Similarly, the Special Forces in Afghanistan have been used mostly as strike teams to go after Al Qaeda and Taliban leaders—or deployed along the 1,400-mile border in an effort to stop insurgents from Pakistan—rather than to train Afghanistan's own forces. "The development of Afghan security forces has been a badly managed, grossly understaffed and poorly funded mess," concluded Center for Strategic and International Studies analyst Anthony Cordesman in a briefing to Democratic congressional leaders in January. The United States didn't even seriously fund the development of Afghanistan's own forces until 2007.

To Afghans now, the government is more often an arbitrary force to be feared than a benevolent protector.

Even now, America and its NATO allies have provided fewer than half the trainers the Afghans need; and many of those are unskilled. As a result, the Afghan Army is too small and too poorly trained to take over the counterinsurgency missions that constitute the real battle in Afghanistan. The Afghan Army is getting better, but slowly. U.S. commanders privately think it may be five years before most units are able to operate on their own. The Afghan police remain a disaster—leaving U.S. forces to fill the vacuum.

As in Vietnam, efforts to seal the frontier have failed. The Taliban, like the North Vietnamese, has depended crucially on supply routes and sanctuaries just over the border. Just as NVA units were able to slip up and down the Ho Chi Minh trail running through Laos, the Taliban can fade away into the mountains and over the border into the lawless regions of Pakistan. These safe havens give them an invaluable space in which to train and resupply. Taliban fighters are much more willing to return to the fight knowing that their families are parked safely in Pakistan, and that they themselves can retreat there if wounded. One Taliban commander based in Pakistan even gave his men five cell-phone numbers to call for help if they got shot fighting U.S. troops across the border, promising they'd be evacuated and treated quickly.

The Americans have to be careful about chasing after the Taliban into their sanctuaries. In Vietnam, American strategists worried about bringing Russia or China into the war if they bombed too freely in and around Hanoi (by, say, sinking a Russian freighter in Haiphong Harbor). In Pakistan, the Americans worry that a heavy-handed intervention could destabilize the government, a risky move in a country with nuclear weapons. The Pakistanis have shared intelligence on Qaeda targets—and have from time to time launched offensives against Pakistani Taliban fighters along the border—but meanwhile, members of the Pakistani intelligence service, the ISI, have formed covert alliances with some Afghan Taliban factions. The Pakistanis have a strategic interest in keeping Afghanistan—which has developed close ties to archenemy India—weak. Since many Pakistani leaders are convinced that America will eventually leave, they're covering their bets for the future.

In Vietnam, America worried about covert Russian and Chinese backing for the North Vietnamese (some would say too much). Here, Pakistan may not be the only country playing a double game. While neighboring Iran is predominantly Shiite, and has traditionally backed the Sunni Taliban's foes in the Northern Alliance, Tehran may also be the source of some of the more sophisticated IEDs turning up on the battlefield in Afghanistan. Certainly Iran has some interest in seeing the American forces on its border bleed a little. At times, though, the United States can seem like its own worst enemy in Afghanistan. Lacking enough troops, forced to cover vast areas, U.S. forces depend far too heavily on strikes by A-10s, F-15s, even B-1 bombers. In 2004, the U.S. Air Force flew 86 strike sorties against targets in Afghanistan. By 2007, the number was up to 2,926—and that doesn't count rocket or cannon fire from helicopters. U.S. commanders have become much more careful about collateral damage since Vietnam. There are no more "free fire zones" or Marines using Zippo lighters to torch villages. But innocents die in the most carefully planned raids, especially when the enemy cynically uses civilians as cover—as the Viet Cong did, and the Taliban does. Already, civilian casualties have climbed from 929 in 2006 to close to 2,000 in 2008, according to the United Nations. "When we kill innocents, especially women and children, you lose that village forever," says Thomas Johnson of the Naval Postgraduate School in Monterey, Calif. In the dominant Pashtun tribe, revenge is a duty. Kill one Pashtun tribesman, sadly observes a U.S. Special Forces colonel who spoke anonymously to be more frank, and you make three more your sworn enemy.

This, then, is the mess that faces General Petraeus. He was a near-miracle worker in Iraq, and it may be that just as Lincoln eventually found Grant, Obama will have been lucky to inherit Petraeus. So far, Petraeus is not signaling a new grand strategy, instead letting various policy reviews go forward. A shrewd politician, he may be seeking to quietly educate the new president on the high cost and many years required to "win" in Afghanistan—if such a thing is even possible.

It is a sure bet that Petraeus will want to unify the different commands now muddling the situation in Afghanistan. (Divided command was a chronic problem in Vietnam, too.) Some soldiers report to the Special Operations Command, some to the regular military; some to the U.S. Central Command and some to NATO; and, within NATO, to their own national governments. There are some 37,000 NATO troops in Afghanistan but many are more concerned with "force protection"—not sustaining casualties—than seeking out and engaging the enemy.

Petraeus will work closely with Richard Holbrooke, a veteran diplomat who helped broker peace in the Balkans. Holbrooke is being sent by the State Department to coordinate the scattered and easily corrupted foreign-aid programs and to knock heads to make sure the diplomats, politicians and soldiers are on the same page. Holbrooke is a force of nature; still, he could wind up like Robert (Blowtorch Bob) Komer in Vietnam in the late 1960s—brilliant, capable and too late.

In some ways, there is no mystery to what must be done to fight a successful counterinsurgency. As Petraeus himself has said, the United States cannot kill its way to success. Foreign troops cannot defeat insurgents. Only local forces with popular support can do that. (A RAND study of 90 insurgencies since World War II showed that "governments defeated less than a third of the insurgencies when their competence was medium or low.") It is a good bet that Petraeus will want American soldiers to train local village militias to fight the Taliban. The catch is that the Soviets already tried this (nothing is really new in counterinsurgency) and failed. In Afghanistan, local warlords quickly turn to fighting each other. The local saying is that they can be rented, not bought. And who wants to kill a Taliban fighter if the result is a blood feud?

For the dominant Pashtun tribes, revenge is a duty. Kill one, and you make three more your sworn enemy.

Americans are appropriately skeptical about the chances of success in Afghanistan. A recent *Newsweek* poll shows that while 71 percent of the people believe that Obama can turn around the cratering economy, only 48 percent think he can make progress in Afghanistan. Deploying a U.S. force of 60,000 will cost about $70 billion a year. Training and supporting the 130,000 to 200,000 troops required for a proper Afghan Army would take another decade and could cost at least $20 billion. Petraeus has consistently warned that Afghanistan will be "the longest campaign in the long war" against Islamic extremism. But it's far from clear that Americans have the appetite for such a commitment: after the economy, their top priority is health care (36 percent). Only 10 percent put Afghanistan at the top of their list, even fewer than nominate Iraq. If there is no real improvement on the ground, by the 2010 midterm elections, candidates for office may be decrying "Obama's war."

So why not just get out? As always, it's not so simple. If the Americans pull their troops out, the already shaky Afghan Army could collapse. (Once they lost U.S. air support, South Vietnamese troops sometimes refused to take the field and fight.) Afghanistan could well plunge into civil war, just as it did after the Soviets left in 1989. Already, the Pashtuns in the south regard the American-backed Tajiks who dominate Karzai's administration as the enemy. The winning side would likely be the one backed by Pakistan, which may end up being the Taliban—just as it was in the last civil war.

Some argue this wouldn't be such a bad outcome, if the Taliban could be bribed or persuaded to not let Al Qaeda set up terrorist training bases on Afghan territory. According to one senior Taliban leader, a former deputy minister in Mullah Mohammed Omar's government who would only speak anonymously, some Pakistani officials are urging the insurgents to do something like this now—in return for talks with the Americans. On the other hand, Islamabad could be playing with fire. Given the longstanding ties between the Pakistani and Afghan Taliban, a jihadist state on its border is a threat to Pakistan, too. And here, U.S. national-security interests definitely do come into play.

Some problems do not have a solution, or any good solution. Two studies of the Afghanistan mess cochaired by retired Marine Gen. Jim Jones, now President Obama's national-security adviser, asserted last year that America cannot afford to lose in Afghanistan. Who wants to be the American president who allows jihadists to claim that they defeated and drove out American forces? Daniel Ellsberg, the government contractor who leaked the Pentagon papers, used to say about Vietnam, "It was always a bad year to get out of Vietnam." The same is all too true for Afghanistan.

With Ron Moreau and Sami Yousafzai.

Somali Piracy: A Nasty Problem, a Web of Responses

JAMES KRASKA AND BRIAN WILSON

On April 12, U.S. Navy Seals staged a dramatic rescue of an American cargo ship captain who had been held hostage during a five-day standoff in the Indian Ocean. The episode highlighted a problem that has drawn increasing international attention over the past year: piracy off the Somali coast. Approximately 125 ships carrying cargo that included oil, weapons, and chemicals were attacked in 2008. In the first two months of 2009, another 30 ships were attacked near Somalia.

To be sure, armed gangs demanding ransom have successfully boarded only a small fraction of the 33,000 vessels that annually ply the region's strategically important waters—waters that include the Gulf of Aden, the key gateway to trade between the East and West. Still, several seamen have been killed or injured, and the global merchant shipping supply chain has been adversely affected (for instance through increased insurance premiums). Some vessels, especially slower ships with low free-boards, have opted to avoid the area altogether.

In response to the crisis, an unprecedented combination of national commitment, naval force, and international action has emerged. Impressive diplomatic collaboration is unfolding in various venues, including the United Nations Security Council and the International Maritime Organization. Collectively, these developments represent a unity of effort that presages yet more partnering; utilization of the rule of law to address regional instability at sea; "out-of-area" employment of naval forces; and integration of international organizations to facilitate repression of maritime piracy. Capitalizing on this transformational synergy is key to effectively battling maritime crime throughout the world.

Fire Hoses and Razor Wire

The Somalia piracy problem has been simmering for years. The country has lacked a functioning government since the early 1990s. Adversity and hardship permeate the area. Somalia's security and political environment has long been volatile, in part because of endemic poverty and an unemployment rate greater than 50 percent. These problems have been compounded by foreign poaching of Somali fisheries and a drought that has obliterated the country's agriculture.

Because piracy is a phenomenon that tends to surge when poverty, lack of economic growth, and crime are not addressed at the national and regional level, the result has been a proliferation of piracy in the Horn of Africa. Somali pirates are not terrorists pursuing a political cause—they are armed robbers at sea. As the leader of one pirate gang remarked, "What we need is money."

Toward that end, pirates successfully boarded more than 40 ships in 2008 and took nearly 900 seafarers and vessel passengers hostage. Currently, more than 120 people are being held prisoner in the vicinity of Harardhere, Somalia, the headquarters of most of the region's maritime piracy. The pirates last year secured from ship, cargo, and insurance companies $150 million in ransom payments for crews and vessels.

Last November, for example, Somali pirates seized the Sirius Star, a Saudi-owned supertanker with a cargo of crude oil valued at $100 million. The 25-member crew was held hostage, the pirates demanded a ransom, and a two-month standoff ensued. Finally on January 9, 2009, a package said to contain $3.2 million was photographed floating in a parachute down to the tanker. Later that day, five of the pirates drowned with their share of the ransom when their small boat capsized as they sped toward the Somali shore.

The situation has grown so dire that, after the seizure of the Sirius Star, the leading Norwegian shipping group Odfjell suspended transits through the area. And Danish shipper Maersk, one of the world's largest, is considering forgoing the Suez Canal and routing ships around southern Africa in order to avoid piracy-prone Somalia. Such decisions increase the cost of shipping: The route around the Cape of Good Hope entails an additional 10 to 14 days of transit time.

Private industry naturally is engaged in the fight against piracy. Firms offer vessel security services for crew protection and have developed new technologies to repel boarders. Ships have ramped up their defensive capabilities by employing a variety of passive and nonlethal methods, which include ringing lifelines with razor concertina wire, employing evasive rudder handling tactics, and repelling boarders with fire hoses.

But more importantly, remarkable coordination has recently unfolded in the fight against piracy. This includes partnering among countries to expand communication, intelligence, legal capabilities, and maritime security. Over the past few years, a spontaneous and loosely linked armada of warships from China, Iran, Russia, Britain, France, India, the United States, and other countries has deployed to the Horn of Africa to protect sea lines of communication.

This coordinated effort already is producing results. In the first two months of 2009, while approximately 30 ships were attacked off the Somali coast, only 4 were boarded and hijacked—a significantly reduced success rate for the pirates. Internationally deployed warships have successfully disrupted piracy attacks in the region, destroyed pirate skiffs, and captured dozens of Somali pirates.

The campaign has been backed, moreover, by impressive diplomacy. In 2008 the UN Security Council adopted four resolutions to repress piracy. These resolutions are unprecedented in the scope and authority that they provide the international community to counter threats in the maritime domain. The resolutions prevent pirates from using the territorial waters of Somalia to avoid capture, increase the number of states deploying naval forces to the area, strengthen legal authorities' ability to prosecute pirates, and improve international cooperation, particularly with regard to the disposition of captured pirates. The resolutions, furthermore, are legally binding on all states.

In addition to making breakthroughs in multilateral diplomacy, nations are also working bilaterally and regionally. The United Kingdom and Kenya in late 2008 signed an agreement that enables Britain to transfer piracy suspects to Kenya for prosecution. The United States and Kenya finalized a similar accord in January 2009. Washington also was instrumental in establishing a UN "contact group" to help states in the region and international maritime powers better coordinate efforts.

These collaborative and innovative endeavors, which have required overcoming logistical, military, legal, and diplomatic challenges, will likely turn out to be the enduring legacy of the Somali piracy crisis. So, in a surprising way, piracy provides an opportunity to harness the collective strength of states in securing the maritime domain.

The Long Arm

As a matter of law, piracy is considered an illegal act of violence committed for private (rather than political) ends by the crew or passengers of a ship against another ship outside of a state's territorial waters. Inside territorial waters, such crimes constitute "armed robbery at sea," and they are the responsibility of the coastal state. But if armed robbery at sea occurs just a few meters seaward from the 12–nautical mile limit of the territorial waters that all coastal states have, it may be considered "maritime piracy."

This definition of piracy is codified in the UN Convention on the Law of the Sea. Yet, despite the convention's detailed provisions regarding many matters, issues of legal jurisdiction at sea are a complex affair, and this complicates international efforts to combat piracy. For example, the convention assigns primary jurisdiction for law enforcement at sea to the flag state—a vessel's nation of registry—and lays out specific circumstances

under which a vessel suspected of piracy may be boarded. Yet, because the seas are a combination of flag, port, and coastal-state juridical authorities, determining which state will assume jurisdiction is not always clear.

Moreover, criminal offenses on the oceans frequently involve suspects, victims, and witnesses who are nationals of various countries. Ensuring criminal accountability is further complicated if a state does not have domestic criminal codes proscribing the conduct in question, because that state will most likely not have jurisdiction to initiate a prosecution, nor have an interest in detaining the suspects. What all this means is that international cooperation is particularly vital with regard to piracy—no single nation in any case has the naval capability to patrol the vast areas affected by these maritime crimes.

The definition of piracy codified in the Law of the Sea developed from centuries of customary international law, but in recent years other definitions of piracy have emerged that cover armed robbery at sea and other maritime crimes such as murder at sea. So far, such supplementary definitions are mainly used for shipping industry statistics. Still, it has been suggested that the political and legal focus on protecting ocean shipping would be sharpened if piracy were combined with marine cargo theft, maritime drug smuggling and human trafficking, and maritime terrorism under the single category of maritime crime.

Historically, piracy has been considered a subset of violent maritime predation that is not part of a widely recognized or declared war. In the West, maritime piracy was a feature of life in the Mediterranean from the ancient world to the age of steam. Throughout two millennia the threat of piracy was brought under control only by powerful navies, such as the imperial Roman fleet during the reign of Augustus Caesar. With the rise of nation states, piracy was kept in check by powerful Dutch and English fleets composed of fast sailing ships and, eventually, steam-powered vessels. During the cold war, large and active super-power navies, making routine port visits throughout the world, helped to contain piracy.

No Eye Patches, Many Vessels

Since the end of the cold war, however, problems of failed states and ungoverned areas, of weak governments and tribalism—problems that affect stability and prosperity on land—have also promoted piracy at sea. After an upswing in piracy in the Straits of Malacca and Singapore earlier this decade, the littoral states of Indonesia, Malaysia, and Singapore began cooperating closely to suppress piracy. Their efforts have led to a dramatic reduction in the number of piracy attacks in Southeast Asia. Yet, just as piracy in Asia was declining, regional instability and a declining naval presence in the Horn of Africa fueled a rapid increase in piracy off the coast of Somalia.

Today warships from various countries are on station in the Horn of Africa conducting piracy repression missions. But this arena is a vast swath of water, as long as the U.S. Atlantic seaboard—the operating area comprises more than 2 million square miles. Preventing an attack in an area this big is made even more difficult when the criminals plying the waters disguise their purpose by appearing to engage in legitimate activities, such as fishing. As chief NATO spokesman James Appathurai has said, pirates do not typically identify themselves "with eye patches and hook hands," so it is not immediately obvious that they are pirates. And in some instances, pirates feign distress at sea, attracting mariners who are bound by international law to render assistance.

Further compounding the piracy problem is a lack of capacity within Somalia and neighboring states to patrol the regional seas. Indeed, pirates routinely seize ships or hostages in international waters and then flee into Somalia's territorial waters to avoid capture. As a result, even with the large number of warships currently deployed to the area, maritime piracy continues to be a daily occurrence off the coast of East Africa.

Still, the international naval presence in the region has prevented maritime security from deteriorating even further. For example, a current European Union mission against piracy off the coast of East Africa, Operation Atalanta, represents the EU's first deployment as a maritime security force. The undertaking has benefited shipping immediately: A German frigate thwarted an attack on an Egyptian ship in December 2008. In January 2009, EU naval forces successfully intervened to stop hijackings of the Panamanian-flagged S. Venus and the Greek-flagged tanker Kriti Episkopi. A French warship, a Corvette-class naval patrol vessel, responded to the S. Venus and captured eight pirates, who were turned over to Somali authorities for prosecution.

> **Somali pirates are not terrorists pursuing a political cause. As the leader of one gang remarked, "What we need is money."**

A cooperative naval operation known as Combined Task Force 150 (CTF 150) is also at work in the region conducting operations against piracy. Membership in CTF 150 has varied, with warships being provided by Pakistan, Britain, Canada, France, and Germany, among others. In 2008, CTF 150 operations thwarted more than two dozen pirate attacks.

In January 2009, the U.S. Fifth Fleet created a task force dedicated solely to confronting maritime piracy—Combined Task Force 151 (CTF 151). The new task force was created because some navies in CTF 150 were operating under counterterrorism authority, and did not have the authority to conduct counter-piracy missions within that framework. CTF 151 accommodates such legal concerns by establishing a staff that is focused on maritime constabulary issues such as maritime piracy, drug smuggling, and weapons trafficking. Australia is considering sending a warship to CTF 151; Turkey, Denmark, and the United Kingdom have already done so. The U.S. Navy has contributed approximately 1,000 sailors, along with surface warship and naval aviation assets, to CTF 151.

The infusion of naval assets has materially altered the operational landscape. However, given that attacks are still occurring with disturbing frequency, albeit with a reduced success rate, a maritime presence alone is not a long-term solution. Furthermore, it is unlikely that many of the nations that have sent naval forces to the region can sustain their deployments indefinitely. Perhaps additional means of addressing the problem may be borrowed from diplomatic precedents in regions outside the Horn of Africa.

Strength in Numbers

In Southeast Asia and West Africa, in particular, states have invested considerable effort in securing sea lines of communication, protecting navigational freedoms, and reducing both crime and regional instability. This international focus has been elevated in recent years—but some such initiatives have existed for decades.

In Southeast Asia, approximately 50,000 ships annually transit the Malacca straits, carrying one-third of the globe's trade. Pirates in the area sometimes wear military uniforms to imitate legitimate maritime security forces. After they strip fishing vessels of their equipment, typically pirates demand "protection money" that varies from $3,000 to more than $12,000. These criminal acts are occurring in one of the world's busiest waterways, making effective patrolling especially challenging.

Yet piracy in the area has declined significantly over the past five years because of decisive state action, collaboration, and multiple regional initiatives. In 2004 Asia produced a "Regional Agreement on Combating Piracy and Armed Robbery Against Ships in Asia," or ReCAAP, the first treaty dedicated solely to combating piracy. This Japan-led accord has 16 state parties and operates a state-of-the-art information sharing center in Singapore that fuses and disseminates among member states time-critical piracy-related information.

One year after the introduction of ReCAAP, more than 30 nations and international and nongovernmental organizations met in Jakarta, Indonesia, to develop a framework to improve maritime safety, security, and environmental protection in the Straits of Malacca and Singapore. The discussions continued in Kuala Lumpur in 2006 and Singapore in 2007. The meetings resulted in adoption of a "Cooperative Mechanism" that is proving effective at increasing the number of maritime patrols by the straits states, and in attracting donors from outside the littoral region to build maritime security capacity in Indonesia, Singapore, and Malaysia. The Cooperative Mechanism is an example of unprecedented partnering among littoral states to provide for the safety and security of an international strait.

In 2008, at the Asia-Pacific Economic Cooperation forum, Malaysia's foreign affairs minister called on members of that body to confront piracy more aggressively. The Royal Malaysian Navy is expected to place a greater emphasis on maritime security in the straits, and Indonesia has enhanced its maritime ship patrols and airborne surveillance. Such a focus could prove beneficial for counter-piracy efforts in the straits in 2009, as piracy may intensify because of the global economic crisis.

Africa has its own substantial history of multilateral anti-piracy efforts. In 1975 the Maritime Organization of West and Central Africa (MOWCA) was formed—though only recently has the organization realized its potential to create a regional maritime security network. Headquartered in Abidjan, Ivory Coast, MOWCA exercises an influential role in port security and shipping coordination. The forum supports member states in cooperatively managing all maritime issues—vessel security and littoral security, maritime constabulary functions, safety of navigation, and environmental protection. Several programs have been launched under the network to enhance collaboration in the international shipping transport sector, including an effort to establish a regional coast guard network. Of the 25 MOWCA states, five are landlocked, a fact that underscores the widespread support for regional maritime stability.

In the Red Sea area, cooperation is not nearly as developed or structured as in the regions covered by MOWCA and ReCAAP. Nevertheless, associations are emerging that, although they are relatively informal, could prove a vitally important component in piracy repression and regional stability. Red Sea states are of course affected by piracy near Somalia, in the Gulf of Aden. The problem is particularly pernicious for Egypt, since the Suez Canal generates more than 1 percent of Egypt's gross domestic product and some vessels are already avoiding it because of the threat in the neighboring Gulf.

In November 2008, Egypt hosted a meeting in Cairo for the Red Sea states to discuss the problem of maritime piracy. Representatives from Yemen, Jordan, Saudi Arabia, and Sudan, as well as Somalia, participated in the closed-door sessions. During a later UN Security Council debate, Egypt's representative discussed the deliberations at the Cairo meeting. He noted that there had been no recent pirate attacks in the Red Sea because of the capacity of coastal countries to secure their shores—and because of coordination among the Arab countries bordering the Red Sea.

Multilateral efforts are crucial for combating piracy off the Somali coast, but bilateral efforts are important as well. A 2006 agreement between India and the United States might underpin one such bilateral effort—but the agreement has been underutilized. Washington and Delhi developed the pact to promote maritime security cooperation and coordination. The accord calls for the two states to conduct bilateral maritime exercises, cooperate in search and rescue operations at sea, exchange information, and enhance cooperative capabilities.

In October 2008, 8,500 naval personnel from India and the United States participated in "Malabar," a week-long naval exercise in the Arabian Gulf. The exercise was designed to help both countries' naval forces better understand the tactics, techniques, and procedures employed by the other force, thereby promoting interoperability. The Indian navy chief of staff credited such confidence-building partnership activities between the United States and India with improving coordination and making naval forces more effective in fighting piracy off the Somali coast. This sentiment takes on added significance when one considers the Indian navy's prominent role in Gulf of Aden repression operations—Indian warships escort many vessels through the Gulf of Aden and have thwarted several piracy attacks.

Unfortunately, years after the presidential-level maritime accord was reached between India and the United States, the agreement has not yet been fully implemented. The two nations still have to define and structure protocols for staff-level meetings and informal discussions, as well as increase training, exchanges, and combined maritime exercises.

Dispose of Properly

Another area in which greater international cooperation is needed is "disposition," or the component of piracy repression efforts that deals with investigation, trial, and punishment. Disposition poses enormous legal and political challenges for the states involved. The U.S. and UK prosecution agreements with Kenya are exactly the sort of thing that is required to ensure that pirates are held accountable. Previously, maritime powers such as Denmark and France had in several instances released captured pirates because of the evidentiary and logistical difficulties in conducting trials originating in the Horn of Africa.

Kenya has been a regional leader for disposition and legal action, having prosecuted pirates in 2006 after a U.S. ship disrupted a vessel hijacking. Kenya has since held piracy trials, with trial judges denying defense motions to dismiss on jurisdictional grounds.

No single nation has the naval capability to patrol the vast areas affected by maritime crimes.

In the short term, it is critical to ensure that those caught hijacking a vessel be brought to criminal trial. But to meaningfully reduce piracy in the long term, the crushing, sustained poverty and lack of governance in Somalia must be addressed. In the meantime, as piracy continues off the Somali coast, effectively repressing this threat to national security interests, shipping, and global commerce requires collaboration. We have seen how, in Asia, ReCAAP has had a remarkable impact in reducing piracy. In West Africa, MOWCA has been reenergized and is now a force for regional stability. Also in West Africa, a pioneering new coast guard network is promising.

What this tells us is that—although warships, UN Security Council resolutions, and legal authority are all part of the solution to piracy—any political commitment to repressing piracy and safeguarding a region's waters must, for lasting effectiveness, emanate from coastal and affected states.

JAMES KRASKA is on the faculty of the international law department at the U.S. Naval War College. **BRIAN WILSON** is a senior Navy lawyer.

We Can't Afford to Ignore Myanmar

JIM WEBB

Eight years ago I visited Myanmar as a private citizen, traveling freely in the capital city of Yangon and around the countryside. This lush, breathtakingly beautiful nation was even then showing the strain of its severance from the outside world. I was a guest of an American businessman, and I understood the frustration and disappointment that he and others felt, knowing even then that tighter sanctions would soon drive them out of the country.

This month I became the first American political leader to visit Myanmar in 10 years, and the first-ever to meet with its reclusive leader, Senior Gen. Than Shwe, in the haunting, empty new capital of Naypyidaw. From there I flew to an even more patched-and-peeled Yangon, where I met with Daw Aung San Suu Kyi, the opposition leader and Nobel laureate who remains confined to her home. Among other requests, I asked Than Shwe to free her and allow her to participate in politics.

Leaving the country on a military plane with John Yettaw—an American who had been sentenced to seven years of hard labor for immigration offenses, and whose release I had also requested of Than Shwe—I was struck again by how badly the Burmese people need outside help. They are so hardened after decades of civil war and political stalemate that only an even-handed interlocutor can lift them out of the calcified intransigence that has damaged their lives and threatened the stability of Southeast Asia.

For more than 10 years, the United States and the European Union have employed a policy of ever-tightening economic sanctions against Myanmar, in part fueled by the military government's failure to recognize the results of a 1990 election won by Aung San Suu Kyi's party. While the political motivations behind this approach are laudable, the result has been overwhelmingly counterproductive. The ruling regime has become more entrenched and at the same time more isolated. The Burmese people have lost access to the outside world.

Sanctions by Western governments have not been matched by other countries, particularly Russia and China. Indeed, they have allowed China to dramatically increase its economic and political influence in Myanmar, furthering a dangerous strategic imbalance in the region.

According to the nonprofit group EarthRights International, at least 26 Chinese multinational corporations are now involved in more than 62 hydropower, oil, gas and mining projects in Myanmar. This is only the tip of the iceberg. In March, China and Myanmar signed a $2.9-billion agreement for the construction of fuel pipelines that will transport Middle Eastern and African crude oil from Myanmar to China. When completed, Chinese oil tankers will no longer be required to pass through the Straits of Malacca, a time-consuming, strategically vital route where 80 percent of China's imported oil now passes.

If Chinese commercial influence in Myanmar continues to grow, a military presence could easily follow. Russia is assisting the Myanmar government on a nuclear research project. None of these projects have improved the daily life of the average citizen of Myanmar, who has almost no contact with the outside world and whose per capita income is among the lowest in Asia.

It would be wrong for the United States to lift sanctions on Myanmar purely on the basis of economic self-interest, or if such a decision were seen as a capitulation of our long-held position that Myanmar should abandon its repressive military system in favor of democratic rule. But it would be just as bad for us to fold our arms, turn our heads, and pretend that by failing to do anything about the situation in Myanmar we are somehow helping to solve it.

So what can and should be done?

First, we must focus on what is possible. The military government in Myanmar has committed itself to elections in 2010, as part of its announced "seven steps toward democracy." Many point out that the Constitution approved last year in a plebiscite is flawed, since it would allow the military to largely continue its domination of the government, and that the approval process itself was questionable. The legislation to put the Constitution into force has yet to be drafted. The National League for Democracy, Aung San Suu Kyi's political party, has not agreed to participate in next year's elections.

But there is room for engagement. Many Asian countries—China among them—do not even allow opposition parties. The National League for Democracy might consider the advantages of participation as part of a longer-term political strategy. And the United States could invigorate the debate with an offer to help assist the electoral process. The Myanmar government's answer to such an offer would be revealing.

Second, the United States needs to develop clearly articulated standards for its relations with the nondemocratic world. Our distinct policies toward different countries amount to a form of situational ethics that does not translate well into clear-headed diplomacy. We must talk to Myanmar's leaders. This does not

Re: We Can't Afford to Ignore Myanmar by Senator Jim Webb

Posted by Thunderbolts–2009/08/27 06:49

Dear Myanmar Myo Chits, Patriots,

When I ask, "Who do you think you are kidding, Mr Webb." You might like to know why. Well read on, you will know why.

I have a lot of things to talk about. I have talked a lot. I still have a lot of things to talk about.

A few days or a week ago when Ko Myanmar praised Mr J. Webb, in New Light of Myanmar, I went as far as attacking Ko Myanmar for over doing. Now I have read what Mr Webb wrote in New York times. I still stand by for what I said to Ko Myanmar. Now, Ko Myanmar know, what I was talking about by. Snake will always be a snake.

For good relation, a better one, and friendly relations, compromise, settlement, for peace, are always desirable. In this give and take business, who is going to give what to who and who is taken what form who is a big question.

Union of Myanmar never unfriendly to anybody, especially to US. United States of America is the only one making everybody its enemies, especially weaker nations like Union of Myanmar. For some United States may be their great hero. But for me the ways things are United States of America is a coward, it is chicken, it is yellow belly.

It not only pick weaker small nations, but also ganged up with other countries which can not say "No" to US, for their own reasons.

Mr Webb tone is nothing new, nothing wonderful, he said what he had to say. Mr Webb is not special. As an US citizen or as a Senator, he may be speaking in his own rights, but as expected he is also repeating what the US wants from Myanmar. What US wants Myanmar to be. But glad to know his intention for reducing sanctions, but still under conditions.

What I am seeing here is, US is not changing. Still wants to give pressures, US is inviting, Russia, especially China to join them and put pressures on Myanmar.

Mr Webb should know that Union of Myanmar, the size or the area is small than State of Taxes.

Mr Webb, after his visits he realised the realities of Myanmar. He also realised how much business opportunities, US is loosing, and how much China is gaining.

It is obvious, that Mr Webb does not have pleasure that Myanmar is help by China in many areas and fields of Myanmar's infrastructures for mutual benefits. That is all business. These are for Union of Myanmar, these are for all people Union of Myanmar.

Among many things, I just want to say to Mr Webb that, to change Myanmar, US must change. I would say, "Myanmar is a lamb Mr Webb, US is the wolf".

There is a television series titled, "The Dad's Army". A comedy, based on WWII, about the home guards in England. The opening song says like this, " who do you think you are kidding Mr Hitler ?".

I want to put that question to Mr Webb like this, " who do you think you are kidding Mr Webb?"

Because among other things, what Mr Webb said finally was, " We might also seek cooperation on our long-held desire to recover the remains of World War II airmen at crash sites in the country's north."

United States seems to have specially and very much interest in the North of our nation Union of Myanmar.

US supported KMT forces (White Chinese) of Cheng Kai Shek in Nothern Myanmar. They had to be driven out of North of Union of Myanmar. Many of our Myanmar Tatmadaw lives were lost.

In 1987, US approached Myanmar Government to search the missing USAF aircraft d Myanmar provided all the assistance and found the wreckage. The discovery of USAF C47 in the Northern Myanmar within Kachin State. In 1991, crashed aircrasft was found. Three dog tags belonged to James B. Heise, Bob D. Torbert and F.P Reybold Jr. and items were found and informed US. But US did not show any interest to collect them for five years Only in 1996. US accepted the items.

United States even tried to negotiate with the late Drug War Lord Khunza, to have a strong foot hole in Union of Myanmar in President Carter's time.

In 1994 April, Mr Peter Bourne who was an advisor on narcotic affairs to President Jimmy Carterwent to Khunza's MTA head quarter in Ho Mong and tried to make a deal including US Cruise missile site with Khunza.

The so called some Wa and former MTA are, according to the opposition sources still active in the ares. I wonder who is supporting them supply arms.

Not to forget that the late KNU leader Saw Bo Mya was benefiting funds through Khunza. Not to forget that MTA representatives went to England met members of British Parliament.

With these backgrounds. I am again asking, " who do you think you are kidding Mr Webb?"

I am not saying anything or telling anything to US or Mr Webb what to do. But I am giving the facts to the audience and to Mr Webb, if he had missed out, so that they can see the whole picture clearly.

But I want to say only one thing, please, please come clean Mr Webb, it is time for you and US to come clean. Haven't you had enough?

Regards,
Thunderbolts.

mean that we should abandon our aspirations for a free and open Burmese society, but that our goal will be achieved only through a different course of action.

The United States refused to talk to the Chinese until 1971, more than 20 years after the Communist takeover, and did not resume full diplomatic relations until 1979. And yet China, with

whom we seem inextricably tied both as a business partner and a strategic competitor, has no democracy and has never held a national election.

The Hanoi government agreed to internationally supervised elections for Vietnam in 1973, as a result of the Paris peace talks; Washington did not raise this as a precondition to furthering relations. As someone who has worked hard to build a bridge between Hanoi and America's strongly anticommunist Vietnamese community, I believe the greatest factor in creating a more open society inside Vietnam was the removal of America's trade embargo in 1994.

Third, our government leaders should call on China to end its silence about the situation in Myanmar, and to act responsibly, in keeping with its role as an ascending world power. Americans should not hold their collective breaths that China will give up the huge strategic advantage it has gained as a result of our current policies. But such a gesture from our government would hold far more sway in world opinion than has the repeated but predictable condemnation of Myanmar's military government.

Finally, with respect to reducing sanctions, we should proceed carefully but immediately. If there is reciprocation from the government of Myanmar in terms of removing the obstacles that now confront us, there would be several ways for our two governments to move forward. We could begin with humanitarian projects. We might also seek cooperation on our long-held desire to recover the remains of World War II airmen at crash sites in the country's north.

Our ultimate goal, as it always has been, should be to encourage Myanmar to become a responsible member of the world community, and to end the isolation of its people so that they can live in economic prosperity, under an open political system.

Jim Webb is a Democratic senator from Virginia.

Not Your Father's Latin America

Its troubles continue, but the region has made real progress.

DUNCAN CURRIE

Hugo Chávez likes to boast that history is on his side. During a recent broadcast of his talk show, *Aló Presidente,* the Venezuelan leader informed Barack Obama that "the process of change in Latin America is not going to stop," even if the U.S. deploys naval fleets and fighter planes. It's easy to dismiss such rhetoric as typical Chávez bluster. But is there a nugget of truth in it? Is Venezuela's illiberal "Bolivarian revolution" really sweeping Latin America?

The short answer is no. The longer answer is that, while various small countries have embraced Chávez-style populism, most of the region's large economic powers have not. In general, Latin American officials have greatly improved their fiscal and monetary policies, making their economies less sensitive to external shocks. Though Latin America has not escaped the global recession and is still plagued by many of its perennial troubles—such as widespread corruption, high levels of violent crime, ethnic fissures, and yawning inequality—its recent progress offers grounds for optimism.

We must appreciate just how far Latin America has come. From the late 1970s through the early 2000s, the region went through a seemingly endless series of economic and financial implosions. Meanwhile, frequent military coups and prolonged civil wars stifled its movement toward liberal democracy.

Even after free elections and constitutional government became the norm, inflation remained a scourge, and currency meltdowns continued to wreak havoc. The 2001–02 Argentine financial crisis sparked a full-blown economic collapse and a massive debt default, which fueled severe turmoil in neighboring countries. In mid-2002, the Bush administration endorsed a $30 billion International Monetary Fund bailout for Brazil (which was suffering from its own domestic woes) and dispatched a $1.5 billion Treasury loan to Uruguay. The U.S. took a sterner line on Argentina but eventually supported a new IMF loan package after Argentine economy minister Roberto Lavagna implemented some prudent reforms that mitigated the crisis.

As the global economy recovered, so did Latin America's. Between 2002 and 2008, the region enjoyed its most robust expansion in decades. Unlike the growth spurt during the 1990s, this one led to substantial poverty reduction. According to World Bank estimates, the poverty rate in Latin America and the Caribbean—that is, the share of the population living on less than $4 a day (in purchasing-power-parity terms)—fell from 45.4 percent in 2002 to 32.5 percent in 2008. Over that same period, the rate of extreme poverty (the portion living on less than $2 a day) dropped from 21.5 percent to 13.1 percent.

Had Latin America just gotten lucky? After all, its anti-poverty gains occurred during an era of abundant liquidity, high commodity prices, and booming global trade. But that wasn't the whole story: Latin America also strengthened its fundamentals, taming inflation

and accumulating foreign-exchange reserves while slashing its external debt. An April 2008 Inter-American Development Bank study pointed to lingering vulnerabilities but affirmed that economic management in the region had "noticeably improved." More recently, a May 2009 IMF survey said that many Latin American countries "have made strides in strengthening fiscal positions and public debt structures, solidifying financial systems and their regulation, anchoring inflation expectations, and building more credible policy frameworks."

Latin America's experience during the current global slump has underscored these achievements. The downturn has been painful (in some countries, deeply painful) but not cataclysmic. Previous recessions in Latin America triggered banking and currency disasters. Not this one. The region has demonstrated that it is much more resilient now than it was in the past. Alberto Ramos, senior Latin America economist at Goldman Sachs, says the difference is "night and day."

Perhaps the most pleasant surprise of recent Latin American history has been the performance of Brazilian president Luiz Inácio Lula da Silva, a former union boss whose 2002 election spooked the investment community. Lula's predecessor, Fernando Henrique Cardoso, was a more conservative social democrat who had helped devise and manage the anti-inflationary "Plano Real" during his tenures as Brazilian finance minister (1993–94) and president (1995–2003). As former Federal Reserve chairman Alan Greenspan writes in *The Age of Turbulence,* the Plano Real "successfully brought the nation's roaring inflation to a halt after it had surged more than 5,000 percent during the twelve months between mid-1993 and mid-1994."

Lula, a member of the left-wing Workers' Party and a longtime friend of Cuban dictator Fidel Castro, had fiercely opposed the Plano Real. He had also spent years attacking free-market economics and calling for major social changes. How would he govern as president? "To the surprise of most, myself included," writes Greenspan, "he has largely followed the sensible policies embodied in the Plano Real." Indeed, there has been a great deal of continuity between the Cardoso and Lula administrations. Despite being dogged by assorted scandals, Lula has acquired enormous popularity and international stature.

He is part of a bigger trend: Throughout Latin America, there is a growing center-left political class that broadly agrees with conservatives about the basic tenets of good economic stewardship. "This is a very positive development for the region," says economist Luis Oganes, head of Latin America research at J. P. Morgan. In a 2007 *New Republic* article, foreign-affairs scholar Walter Russell Mead wrote that "Latin America is now beginning to acquire something it has sorely lacked: a left-of-center political leadership able to combine its mission of serving the poor with a firm commitment to currency stability, the rule of law, and the development of a favorable business climate."

This can be seen in countries such as Chile, Uruguay, and Peru. The Chilean economy remains the most dynamic in Latin America. Since 1990, it has been piloted by the center-left Concertación coalition, which inherited a slew of free-market reforms from the Pinochet dictatorship. Successive Concertación governments "kept the broad thrust of the dictatorship's economic policies, deepened some of them and reformed others," writes journalist Michael Reid in *Forgotten Continent*. "That bestowed democratic legitimacy on the 'Chilean model.'" During the recent commodity boom, Chile saved a hefty chunk of its copper windfall. As the *Wall Street Journal* reports, this enabled it to craft "one of the largest stimulus packages in the world relative to the size of its economy."

In Uruguay, the center-left administration of Pres. Tabaré Vázquez has promoted a solid economic agenda and completed a "trade and investment framework agreement" with the United States. In Peru, Pres. Alan García has effectively repudiated his earlier stint as chief executive in the late 1980s, when he espoused economic populism and unleashed hyperinflation. Since returning to the presidency in 2006, García has governed as a born-again neoliberal.

His 2006 election campaign reflected a larger ideological struggle. García defeated Ollanta Humala, a radical populist favored by Chávez, after telling voters to choose "between Hugo Chávez and Peru." That same year, conservative Felipe Calderón won a razor-thin victory over leftist Andrés Manuel López Obrador to capture the Mexican presidency. Just as García did in Peru, Calderón linked his opponent to Chávez. It proved a smart strategy, as Calderón came from behind to triumph.

All of these countries—Brazil, Chile, Uruguay, Peru, and Mexico—have rejected *Chavismo*. All five have inflation-targeting central banks. So does Colombia, which has made greater progress over the past half-decade than any other country in the hemisphere. Pres. Álvaro Uribe took office in 2002 amid a horrendous guerrilla war that threatened to turn Colombia into a failed state. Since then, the government has reclaimed Bogotá, Medellín, and other cities from left-wing rebels; demobilized thousands of right-wing paramilitaries; dramatically reduced violence; and fostered a more attractive business environment. Prior to the recession, Colombia's GDP was growing at its fastest rate since the 1970s. National police data show that in 2008, the country had 44 percent fewer homicides and 75 percent fewer massacres than it did in 2002.

Yet the number of massacres increased slightly from 2007 to 2008, and new scandals have emerged concerning extrajudicial killings by the army. Uribe helped expose paramilitary infiltration of the political system, but the subsequent discoveries have implicated many of his supporters. As for the drug war, an October 2008 Government Accountability Office report said that Plan Colombia, the vast U.S. aid package begun under President Clinton, had "not fully achieved" its drug-reduction goals but had nonetheless contributed to "major security advances." Uribe is still immensely popular, though he has raised eyebrows by musing about a third term in office. (His current term expires in 2010.) Colombian lawmakers already amended their constitution to let him run for a second term in 2006.

It would be the height of moral confusion to associate Uribe, a staunch democrat, with Latin America's populist rabble. But revising constitutions to extend or abolish term limits is the preferred strategy of Chávez and his ilk. That's what ousted Honduran president Manuel Zelaya was trying to do, via an illegal "referendum," before the supreme court and the military intervened.

His removal trimmed the ranks of Chávez allies. In 2008, Honduras had joined the "Bolivarian Alternative for the Americas," a Chávez-led trade group whose members now include Venezuela, Cuba, Bolivia, Nicaragua, Ecuador, and a few tiny Caribbean nations. Heavily dependent on tourism, the impoverished Caribbean islands are especially susceptible to Chávez's petro-diplomacy. The governments of Bolivia, Nicaragua, and Ecuador feel an ideological attachment to Venezuela. All of them have, to varying degrees, embraced illiberal populism. So has Argentina, where Pres. Cristina Kirchner nationalized the private-pension system late last year.

Though Venezuela, Argentina, and Ecuador posted impressive growth rates when commodity prices were booming, they are now dealing with the consequences of reckless policy decisions. The Kirchner government suffered a crushing setback in Argentina's June 28 congressional elections. "There was definitely a shift to the right in Argentina," says Oganes. In Venezuela, unfortunately, Chávez won a referendum on scrapping term limits this past February, and he has intensified his attacks on independent media outlets and opposition politicians. Chávez is also lending full-throated support to Zelaya as the deposed Honduran leader seeks to reclaim his former office.

Beyond the unrest in Honduras, Central America faces a raft of economic and security challenges. Costa Rica and Panama remain its most stable and prosperous countries. The latter is now led by a conservative supermarket baron named Ricardo Martinelli. El Salvador also has a new president, Mauricio Funes, who represents the FMLN, a former leftist guerrilla outfit turned political party. Funes cites Lula as his model and "has filled the cabinet mostly with moderates," says Michael Shifter, a vice president at the Inter-American Dialogue. But it is unclear whether Funes can genuinely transform the FMLN and curb soaring crime. In neighboring Guatemala, Pres. Álvaro Colom has been hobbled by a sensational murder scandal at a time when his country is being overwhelmed by drug violence.

Meanwhile, such violence continues to generate grisly headlines in Mexico. It has exacerbated a nasty recession (the worst in Latin America), as has the swine-flu panic. President Calderón deserves credit for tackling the narco-gangs with military force. Though his anti-crime campaign is still widely popular, his party got thrashed in Mexico's July 5 congressional elections. That makes it even less likely that Calderón will be able to undertake the tax, energy, and labor-market reforms necessary to boost his country's long-term economic performance.

"To change Mexico, you really need an extraordinary leader," says economist Rafael Amiel, regional managing director for Latin America at IHS Global Insight. "I'm more hopeful about Brazil than Mexico." Like other Latin American countries, both Brazil and Mexico require deep structural changes in order to realize their full growth potential. "The Latin American experience has laid bare the fact that private ownership and fiscal prudence yield only limited benefits in a regime of overbearing taxation and regulation," writes Harvard economist Andrei Shleifer.

While the ongoing recession has aggravated social tensions and reversed some of the region's anti-poverty gains, Latin America's recent record is one of significant progress. "Many countries are on the right track," says Amiel. But a smaller cluster—the Chávez bloc—is clearly on the wrong track. As Shifter puts it, "We have different Latin Americas, and they're moving in very different directions."

From *The National Review*, August 10, 2009. Copyright © 2009 by National Review, Inc, 215 Lexington Avenue, New York, NY 10016. Reprinted by permission.

UNIT 6

Conflicts among Nation-States in the Global South, Sub-National Conflicts, and the Role of Non-State Actors in an Interdependent World

Unit Selections

Key Points to Consider

- What are some factors that threaten stability in Iraq and the wider region today?

- What makes Somalia such a dangerous place?

- Why aren't more outside actors coming to the aid of Somalis suffering through Africa's worst humanitarian crisis?

- Do you agree with the assessment that new modes of communication, such as twitter, have the potential to help weaken repressive regimes and blur further the lines between domestic and foreign policy? Why or why not?

Student Website
www.mhhe.com/cls

Internet References

Pajhwok Afghan News
  http://www.pajhwak.com
EI: Electronic Intifada
  http://electronicintifada.net/new.shtml
International Security Assistance Force (ISAF)
  http://www.nato.int/ISAF
Not on Our Watch: The Mission to End Genocide in Darfur and Beyond
  http://notonourwatchbook.enoughproject.org
The African Executive
  http://www.africanexecutive.com
IslamiCity
  http://islamicity.com

Palestine-Israel—American Task Force on Palestine
  http://www.americantaskforce.org
Private Military Companies (Mercenaries)
  http://www.bicc.de/pmc/links.php
Kubatana.net
  http://www.kubatana.net
AllAfrica.com
  http://allafrica.com
News 24
  http://news.24.com

Civil wars are now the most common form of warfare in International Relations. Civil conflicts are extremely costly in terms of the number of lives lost, the damage to the local economy and environment, and the violence and disruption that spills over into neighboring countries. One dramatic example of these destructive trends is recent and ongoing violence in the Congo, now called the Democratic Republic of the Congo. The second civil war in the Democratic Republic of the Congo (DRC) escalated to become Africa's first continental war. More lives were lost during the conflict than during World War II.

A similar spillover effect of civil conflict into neighboring countries is a continuing feature of the conflict between the Palestinians and the Israelis. This intractable conflict acquired a dangerous new dimension in 2007 after Hamas seized control from Fatah forces in Gaza while Fatah remains in control in the West Bank. Since Hamas's victory, Gaza residents have had to cope with a continuing border closure between Israel and Gaza and international sanctions, implemented after Hamas seized power. During 2009 there were periodic riots in East Jerusalem that escalated from Palestinian protests over Israel's controls in the international zone of the Temple Mount, including around the Al-Aqsa Mosque.

In a speech in Cairo that was supposed to be a bold overture to the Islamic world in Egypt during June of 2009, President Barak Obama expressed sympathy for the Palestinians for what he called the "daily humiliations, large and small, that come with occupation." Obama noted that while America's bond with Israel was "unbreakable," the "intolerable" plight of the Palestinian people after 60 years of statelessness needed to change. Obama called on Hamas to abandon violence and recognize Israel's right to exist. The speech received a variety of responses. While many Palestinians were jubilant, Israel and American backers of Israel were furious at the President for elevating the Palestinians to an equal status. To date, the lofty rhetoric has failed to trigger progress in efforts to normalize relations between Israel and the Palestinians. Instead, new waves of riots occurred around the Al-Aqsa Mosque during October 2009 shortly before U.S. Secretary of State Clinton arrived in the region in an attempt to revive peace negotiations. However, many observers are expressing the view that the new wave of unrest is symptomatic of an ongoing condition and that it may be too late to create a state of Palestinian territories characterized by factional politics and the continued growth of Israeli settlements.

In a separate effort to restore normality, U.S. combat forces exited Iraqi cities in June 2009 as part of the two withdrawal deadlines for the Status of Forces Agreement signed in December 2008. Renewed attacks, widely thought to be the work of al Qaeda, punctured a recent trend of decreasing violence since the highs of 2006 and 2007. Ramzy Mardini in "Factors Affecting Stability in Northern Iraq," describes the current state of Iraq as a very fragile state riddled with poor institutions, intense subgroup identities, and threats in several provinces from al Qaeda supporters.

Equally complex, ongoing civil conflicts threaten to escalate to regional inter-state wars in Somalia and Sudan in the Horn of Africa. In both countries, millions of civilians are at risk.

© Photodisc/Getty Images

Although the government of Sudan finally agreed during 2007 to accept 26,000 international peacemakers under the auspices of the United Nations and the African Union (AU) after extensive international pressures and publicity of ongoing atrocities in Darfur, Sudan, outside peacekeepers were unable to prevent continuing attacks in Darfur or rebel operations in neighboring Chad. The situation for many in Darfur worsened in 2009 as the Khartoum government expelled foreign relief workers in response to the International Criminal Court's indictments against President Bashir. Tensions between Arabs and Africans have also been increasing in other parts of Sudan since 2008. The world ignored a major violation of the Comprehensive Peace Accords (CPA) when Sudanese government troops violently took control of a disputed town on the border with Southern Sudan. Most observers are now predicting that a planned referendum to be held in 2011 to let the people of Southern Sudan decide whether or not to secede will probably not be held even if elections proceed peacefully in 2010 since both sides are now preparing for resumption of armed conflict in Africa's longest running civil war.

One of the few reporters who still periodically reports from inside Somalia is U.S. journalist, Jeffrey Gettleman. In "The Most Dangerous Place in the World," Gettleman describes how the first thing he does before leaving the Mogadishu airport is hire his own militia. Gettleman describes how ongoing conflicts among rival factions, including tensions between former allies within the Islamic Courts coalition, and how the Al Shabab (Youth) militia, along with their al Qaeda allies, succeeded in quickly retaking control of large parts of central and southern Somalia after the Ethiopian troops withdrew. Gettleman warns that the endless chaos in Somalia "threatens to engulf an entire region" while the world once again simply watches. The hands-off approach of all major powers continues even though most analysts agree that the root causes of the growing piracy problem throughout Indian Ocean coastal areas will not be solved until the conflict in Somalia is resolved.

Another ongoing domestic conflict that threatens to expand to a regional or even global conflict given the regime's apparent goal of developing domestic uranium enrichment capabilities and presumably developing nuclear weapons is Iran. The world watched in June, 2009 as police blocked downtown streets in Tehran and used tear gas and water cannons to disrupt a planned march by protesters demanding the nullification of President Mahmoud Ahmadinejad's reelection. The real loser in these confrontations is widely thought to be the Ayatollah Ali Khomeini, Iran's supreme leader. Khomeini attempted to use his full authority to back the reelection of Ahmadinejad, despite protests tied to allegations of widespread fraud. Khomeini denied these allegations of vote fraud and declared that foreign "enemies," including the United States, were behind a week of massive street demonstrations. Khomeini's actions failed to stop the protesters and served as a catalyst for even more fractionalization among the ruling mullahs. Despite the regime's warnings, protesters continued with a planned demonstration at Revolution Square in Tehran where thousands chanted "Death to the dictator" and Allahu Akbar (God is Great) before police cracked down and violently broke up the demonstrations. The world was able to watch these dramatic and often violent clashes in real or near-real time until the regime cut off television broadcasting. As John Palfrey, Bruce Etling, and Robert Faris report in "Reading Twitter in Tehran? Why the Real Revolution Is on the Streets—and Offline," the government successfully exerted control over Internet use and text-messaging, but failed to stop the use of Twitter. The new communication medium was such a vital link for the protesters to the outside world that the U.S. State Department asked Twitter to delay a scheduled maintenance so this line of communication could remain open between Iran and the world. The Iranian protesters' use of Twitter is now cited as a dramatic example of how online chatter can be a powerful medium of communication in repressive societies that is helping to blur further the distinction between foreign and domestic policies.

Factors Affecting Stability in Northern Iraq

Ramzy Mardini

Iraq entered a new security environment after June 30, 2009, when U.S. combat forces exited Iraqi cities in accordance with the first of two withdrawal deadlines stipulated in the Status of Forces Agreement (SOFA). Signed in December 2008 by President George W. Bush and Iraqi Prime Minister Nuri al-Maliki, the SOFA concedes that December 31, 2011 will be the deadline for the complete withdrawal of U.S. forces from Iraq. President Barack Obama, however, has signaled his intention to withdraw U.S. combat forces by August 2010.

Iraqi Security Force (ISF)-capability has improved remarkably since the 2007 implementation of the U.S. counterinsurgency strategy. Nevertheless, successfully pacifying Iraq without the ground presence of U.S. forces is contingent on a number of factors, not all related to ISF-readiness. This article highlights an array of critical factors that are likely to shape the new security challenges facing Iraq: the current unstable political and security environment in Mosul, rising Arab-Kurdish tensions over disputed territories and the possible politicization of the upcoming January 2010 parliamentary elections.[1]

Continued Violence in Mosul

The withdrawal and relocation of U.S. combat forces outside of Iraq's cities represents a major change in the country's security environment. With a less proficient ISF patrolling Iraq's streets, "deterrence by denial" is less of an effective strategy; dissuading insurgents from challenging the government by demonstrating that they hold a grim likelihood for success is less credible absent U.S. forces. For this reason, insurgents are testing the ISF on its capability, resolve, and credibility as a fair and non-sectarian institution.

This litmus test is most likely to occur in Mosul, the capital of Ninawa Province. In its current political and security context, the city is best situated for insurgents to make early gains in propagating momentum. Geographically located 250 miles north of Baghdad along the Tigris River, Mosul is Iraq's second largest city with a population of 1.8 million.[2] Described as an ethnic tinderbox, the city is approximately 70% Sunni Arab and 25% Kurd. The remaining population is composed of Shi'a, Turcoman, Yezidis, and Christians.[3] The city's large Sunni Arab population makes it an attractive base for recruiting Sunni insurgents. Before Operation Iraqi Freedom in 2003, for example, Mosul was home to a sizeable Ba`athist presence, with some estimates suggesting that as many as 300,000 inhabitants were willing to contribute to military, security, and intelligence efforts under Saddam Hussein.[4]

In 2008, as much of Iraq reached an improved level of stability, Mosul continued to witness a high level of violence. On January 23, 2008, for example, a massive 20,000-pound bomb killed and wounded more than 300 people.[5] The next day, during inspections of the bombing site, a suicide bomber killed Ninawa's police chief.[6] As a result, al-Maliki sent additional Iraqi forces to the city in January 2008 to engage in a "decisive" battle against the remnants of al-Qa`ida's in Iraq (AQI).[7] Al-Maliki's "decisive" battle, however, achieved questionable success against AQI and other terrorist elements. In March 2008, the chief of special operations and intelligence information for Multi-National Force-Iraq called the city the "strategic center of gravity" for AQI.[8] Months later, in a new Mosul offensive directly commanded by al-Maliki called "Lion's Roar," the lack of resistance among insurgents disappointed some commanders who were expecting a decisive Alamo-style battle.[9]

Today, AQI and affiliated terrorist groups, such as the Islamic State of Iraq, still possess a strategic and operational capacity to wage daily attacks in Mosul.[10] Although the daily frequency of attacks in Mosul dropped slightly from 2.43 attacks in June 2009 to 2.35 attacks in July 2009, the corresponding monthly death tolls have increased from 58 to 79.[11] This can be attributed to AQI's motive of executing more high-profile attacks since June 30.[12] On August 7, for example, a suicide bomber in a vehicle killed 38 people in front of a Shi`a mosque just outside the city.[13] A second attack near Mosul in Khazna village brought the total number of killed and injured to 400 in the Mosul-area in a 10-day period.[14] Speaking to Pentagon reporters via satellite at the time, Army Major General Robert Caslen suggested that the increased violence in Mosul was a sign that AQI had reconstituted its capability in the city:

> What has increased, however, is the capability (of al-Qaeda and its allies) to conduct the high-profile attacks . . . So you see an increase in the numbers of casualties post-30 June.[15]

It is likely that insurgents have altered their methods and adapted to the U.S. counterinsurgency posture. Open urban warfare has become less of an advantage for insurgents because the switch toward population-protection has motivated local Iraqis to collaborate and share information with the U.S. military. In response, political assassinations might become a more attractive tool for insurgents in undermining opponents, instead of battlefield engagements with the goal of taking and holding territory.[16] Suicide attacks have also increased since the United States withdrew from Iraq's cities.[17]

Only by demonstrating quick and decisive victories and denying the enemy success in Mosul can the ISF deter the sprout of insurgents elsewhere. If the ISF does not quickly establish itself as a capable and non-sectarian institution, perceptions about its weakness could solidify and gain momentum in the minds of insurgents throughout Iraq.

Rising Ethnic Tensions in the North

A second major factor affecting stability in Iraq is continued ethnic tensions between Arabs and Kurds. In late July 2009, the commander of U.S. forces in Iraq, General Ray Odierno, told reporters that tensions between Arabs and Kurds is the "No. 1 driver of instability" in Iraq.[18] The conflict is concentrated over the issue of "disputed territories," which UN Representative to Iraq Staffan de Mistura claimed had "infected almost every aspect of the political scene."[19] The Kurds demand the political execution of Article 140, a constitutional provision seeking the reversal of past Ba`athist "Arabization" campaigns committed in northern Iraq.[20]

Through a legal procedure of normalization, census and referendum, residents will determine whether the area under dispute will be under the Kurdistan Regional Government (KRG) in Arbil or remain under the authority of the federal government in Baghdad. The oil-rich city of Kirkuk is at the heart of the dispute. Yet al-Maliki has purposefully delayed the implementation of Article 140 while maneuvering to escape his political dependency on the Kurds by courting Sunni Arab nationalists and southern Shi`a tribes.[21]

A power-sharing agreement between Kurds and Arabs in Mosul and in the Ninawa provincial government is crucial to the stability of northern Iraq.

Today, Kurdish leverage over al-Maliki is waning. They fear that U.S. withdrawal will permit al-Maliki to behave more assertively in marginalizing them, even by violent means. As Dr. Fuad Hussein, chief of staff to KRG President Massoud Barzani, asserted: "If the problems which exist now cannot be resolved in one or two years, the withdrawal of the American army will lead to unrest in Baghdad and perhaps a return of sectarian fighting."[22] After a January 22, 2009 military move by al-Maliki to send the army's 12th division north toward Kirkuk, many Kurds viewed it as an operation to militarily encircle and cut off the city from being influenced by the surrounding Kurdish provinces.[23] By February 2009, fearful rhetoric suggested the possibility of an Arab-Kurdish civil war.[24] The debate over Article 140 would not be as problematic if the disputes were over an issue other than territory. According to one report, the Kurds claim somewhere between 30–40 disputed territories inside Iraq.[25] To date, not one has been resolved.

Growing tensions in Mosul between Kurds and Sunni Arabs is another major concern.[26] As Philip Zelikow, former counselor of the State Department, stated in February 2009:

As important as Anbar is in the "Sunni story," Mosul may turn out to be much more significant for the future. The United States could find itself caught in the middle between Kurdish friends, local Sunni nationalists, and a central government in Baghdad that might be tempted to win Sunni friends by "dealing" forcefully with the Kurds.[27]

Violence in Mosul has increased since the provincial elections of January 31, 2009. The results of the elections in Ninawa Province shifted the balance of power away from the Kurdish parties toward the majority Sunni Arabs, the latter of whom had largely boycotted the previous provincial elections in January 2005. The winning Arab nationalist coalition, al-Hadba, has refused to appoint Kurds to any

cabinet positions even though the Kurdish party carried one-third of the vote.[28] In response, Kurdish officials, including Ninawa mayors, have withdrawn from their posts in boycott.[29] The Kurds have refused to recognize the authority of the newly-elected Sunni governor Atheel al-Nujaifi over all of Ninawa.[30] They are concerned about his connections to powerful Arab tribes, members of the Ba`ath Party, and allegedly insurgents.[31] Some areas within the province are under the control of *peshmerga* (Kurdish militia) forces because Kurds have labeled them "disputed" territories under Article 140. Yet al-Nujaifi has denied them the right to administer those areas, claiming in a February 2009 interview:

The existence of disputed areas in the province does not imply that the Kurdish Region can put them under its control until a resolution is reached. These areas should be under one authority, that of Ninawa Province, which is controlled by the central authority in the capital city of Baghdad.[32]

In May 2009, Kurdish forces prevented the governor from entering Bashiqa, a town northeast of Mosul that was administered by Kurds. Al-Nujaifi claimed the Kurds had issued a "shoot to kill" order on him if he were to enter the area.[33] A similar episode occurred when Kurdish forces stopped the Ninawa police chief from crossing a bridge into a disputed territory.[34] A statement released by the KRG blamed the al-Hadba leadership for the recent deaths of 2,000 Kurds in Ninawa, claiming that they were "adopting a policy of national, sectarian and religious cleansing in Ninawa."[35] According to *Azzaman,* an Iraqi news source, Arab parties in Ninawa have decided to form a joint anti-Kurdish front to "deny Iraqi Kurds a say in the forthcoming parliamentary elections."[36]

In attempting to lower the heightened tensions in northern Iraq, on August 17 General Odierno proposed a tripartite deployment of U.S., ISF, and *peshmerga* forces to disputed areas in Ninawa.[37] Holding insurgents accountable for the upsurge in violence, Odierno blamed AQI for exploiting the discord between Arabs and Kurds. The deployment was described to be short-lived and directed toward protecting the local population and serving as a trust and "confidence-building measure" between the ISF and *peshmerga.*[38] The proposal, later to be discussed in high level meetings in September, comes at the backdrop of a January 2010 national referendum to be held on the continued U.S. presence stipulated in the SOFA, essentially making the redeployment of U.S. forces in Ninawa a complicated balancing act.[39]

The Unstable Shadow of Elections

Another source of instability is the current period leading to the parliamentary elections in January 2010. The domestic challenge presented by this circumstance is two-fold: 1) the risk that securitization might be politicized by al-Maliki's government; and 2) the possibility that violence is used among political factions in hopes of undermining the other's electoral prospects. Unfortunately, both have occurred in the past.[40]

Today, al-Maliki has staked his 2010 electoral prospects on two performance goals in the eyes of the Iraqi public: 1) stabilizing and providing security to facilitate reconstruction and economic growth; and 2) solidifying his status as the national leader by ending the U.S. occupation. Iraq's former precarious environment, however, had placed these two goals in zero-sum terms: security was only maintained when U.S. forces remained engaged in Iraqi neighborhoods while patrolling the streets. The current decrease in violence inside Iraq has allowed al-Maliki to rapidly consolidate and centralize his power at the expense of parties advocating federalism, such as the two main Kurdish parties—the Patriotic Union of Kurdistan and the Kurdistan Democratic Party—and the Shi`a Islamic Supreme Council of Iraq (ISCI) headed by Abdul Aziz al-Hakim.[41] Al-Maliki's first place finish in nine out of the 14 provinces that took part in the January 2009 provincial elections have instilled deep concern among Kurds and some Sunni and Shi`a parties over their waning ability to check al-Maliki's growing strength.[42]

One concern amidst increasing violence in Mosul and elsewhere is that al-Maliki may be hesitant to call for the assistance of U.S. troops stationed outside Iraqi cities. Hoping to stay consistent with his campaign message of achieving both security and sovereignty, such a situation forces the prime minister to make an unattractive trade-off: security versus credibility. As suggested by one U.S. military officer, "The last thing we want is to see this area fail because of some question of Arab pride in not being able to ask for our help."[43]

Reports already indicate that al-Maliki will leave his political bloc—the Shi`a United Iraqi Alliance, which is dominated by the federalism-advocate ISCI—in hopes of establishing a national coalition with Sunni Arab tribes and Shi`a parties devoted to a strong central government.[44] A broad-based alliance in the new 2010 parliament will decrease the chance of the Council of Representatives removing al-Maliki from power if he seeks further centralization.

Parties from all major ethnic groupings may come to believe that with the exiting of all U.S. combat forces in August 2010, elections earlier that year may become the last credible chance at balancing al-Maliki. The consequences that may result from the elections offer an enormous incentive for challengers threatened by Baghdad's drift to a strong central government to undermine the prime minister. Without the U.S. active in patrolling Iraqi cities, electoral politics may revert back to Iraq's violent politics when politicians engaged one another via militias on the urban battlefield.

Conclusion

Although violence has decreased significantly since the 2006–2007 highs, Iraq remains a fragile state riddled with poor institutions and intense subgroup identities. The security environment is no longer characterized by the constant presence of the "American pacifier." Today, the prospect for stability in Mosul and elsewhere are determined by an array of volatile factors.

The critical factor, however, toward satiating the power gap inherited in the new security environment is not only the capability and readiness of the ISF, but their integrity as a national and unitary institution dedicated toward the protection of all Iraqis. The local population's collaboration and trust in the ISF is critical for continuing a successful counterinsurgency campaign. Yet political developments in Mosul, rising Arab-Kurdish tensions, and conflicting interests—both foreign and domestic—toward the upcoming parliamentary elections risk politicizing ISF missions by suggesting them as a means for achieving political ends. Such prospects will permeate mistrust between the different ethnic segments of the population and the government. This could cause a security dilemma leading back to sectarian violence.

To alleviate the influence such factors could have, the United States must play the central mediating role. In particular, a power-sharing agreement between Kurds and Arabs in Mosul and in the Ninawa provincial government is crucial to the stability of northern Iraq. Even if a provincial power-sharing agreement is accomplished, however, northern Iraq is unlikely to remain stable if the problems surrounding Article 140 remain unresolved. In general, bringing about reconciliation between the contentious parties is the only guarantee of long-term stability absent the presence of U.S. forces.

Notes

1. Iraq has other major problems, including power shortages, unemployment, corruption, crime, and the many political disagreements, such as on a national oil law. The factors stated here, however, are considered most critical for affecting Iraq's new security environment because of their influence in potentially contributing toward nationwide destabilization and Iraqi death rates. One major security factor not discussed in this article is the slow government integration of the Sons of Iraq into the Iraqi security and civil sectors. For recent reporting on the latter issue, see "Slow Sunni Integration a Risk to Iraq Security—US," Reuters, July 31, 2009.

2. Eric Hamilton, "The Fight For Mosul," Institute for the Study of War, April 2008.

3. Ibid.

4. Eric Hamilton, "The Fight for Mosul," Institute for the Study of War, June 2008.

5. Ibid.

6. Sam Dagher, "Al Qaeda Goes North: Police Chief Killed in Mosul," *Christian Science Monitor,* January 25, 2008.

7. Joshua Partlow, "Maliki Sending Troops to Mosul," *Washington Post,* January 26, 2008.

8. William Selby, "Coalition Focuses on Clearing Mosul Terrorist Networks," American Forces Press Service, March 4, 2008.

9. As one report indicated, "the lack of significant resistance among the hardened fighters who had been operating in Mosul suggested the insurgency was offering Maliki and his American backers a message of their own: we fight on our terms, not yours." See Mark Kukis, "Maliki's Mosul Offensive," *Time Magazine,* May 16, 2008.

10. Jane Arraf, "Stabilizing Iraq: Why Mosul is a Special Case," *Christian Science Monitor,* June 24, 2009.

11. For statistics, see "Mosul Remains As Violent As Ever," *Ground Truth,* August 11, 2009.

12. This was the reasoning offered by U.S. Major General Robert Caslen. See "Al Qaeda Shows Resilience in N.Iraq-US Commander," Reuters, August 11, 2009.

13. Qassim Khidhir, "Talks Between Kurds and Hadba End Unsuccessfully," *Kurdish Globe,* August 14, 2009.

14. Ibid.

15. Ibid.

16. See the story on the recent political assassination of Harith al-Ubaydi, head of the Sunni parliamentary bloc, the Iraqi Accord Front: Rod Nordland and Abeer Mohammed, "Sunni Lawmaker Assassinated in Iraq," *New York Times,* June 12, 2009. For information on the rise of assassinations in Iraq, see Arraf. Also see Fatih Abdulsalam, "Assassinations Become Trademark of Iraq's New Political Epoch," *Azzaman,* June 14, 2009.

17. Omar al-Mansouri, "Suicide Bombers' Comeback Unnerves Iraqi Government," *Azzaman,* August 14, 2009.

18. Anne Gearan, "Gates: Kurd-Arab Friction Top Problem in Iraq," Associated Press, July 29, 2009.

19. Staffan de Mistura, "Challenges on Iraq's Election Day," *Washington Post,* January 31, 2009.

20. The Ba`athist Arabization campaigns were policies adopted by the Baghdad government to reduce the number of Kurdish

inhabitants in areas deemed of strategic and economic value. Beginning in 1963 and commencing again in 1974 and 1984, hundreds of thousands of Kurds were systematically deported or killed and replaced with outside Arab families. The Kurdish language and other forms of Kurdish culture were outlawed and replaced with Arabic.

21. In August 2007, al-Maliki's government was saved from political paralysis by the formation of a Quartet Alliance, which involved along with al-Maliki's Dawa Party the two main Kurdish parties and the Shi`a Islamic Supreme Council of Iraq. For al-Maliki's political maneuvering to escape his dependency on the Quartet Alliance, see Anthony Shadid, "New Alliances in Iraq Cross Sectarian Lines," *Washington Post,* March 20, 2009; Scott Weiner, "Maliki Makes a Play for the Southern Tribes," Institute for the Study of War, November 6, 2008; Jeremy Domergue and Marisa Cochrane, "Balancing Maliki: Shifting Coalitions in Iraqi Politics and the Rise of the Iraqi Parliament," Institute for the Study of War, June 2009.

22. Eli Lake, "Kurds Anxious Over U.S. Withdrawal," *Washington Times,* April 17, 2009.

23. Ramzy Mardini, "Rising Arab-Kurdish Tensions Over Kirkuk Will Complicate U.S. Withdrawal From Iraq," *Terrorism Focus,* 6:6 (2009).

24. Rahmat al-Salaam, "Kurdish Officials Warn of Potential Kurd-Arab War," *Asharq Alawsat,* February 19, 2009.

25. "Article 140 Must be Adhered To, Say Kurdish Officials," *Kurdish Globe,* December 4, 2008.

26. "Kurdish-Sunni Tensions In Nineveh," *Entrepreneur,* May 25, 2009.

27. Philip Zelikow, "The New Strategic Situation in Iraq," *Foreign Policy,* February 9, 2009.

28. Quil Lawrence, "Arab-Kurd Conflict Deepens in Mosul," National Public Radio, July 2, 2009.

29. Ibid.

30. Sam Dagher, "Tensions Stoked Between Iraqi Kurds and Sunnis," *New York Times,* May 18, 2009.

31. Ibid.

32. Adel Kamal, "New Ninawa Governor Rejects Kurdish Alliance," *Niqash,* February 24, 2009.

33. Dagher.

34. Ibid.

35. "KRG Blames Hadba for Murder of Kurds, Displacement of Christians in Mosul," *Aswat al-Iraq,* August 14, 2009.

36. Jareer Mohammed, "Arabs Form Anti-Kurdish Bloc in Iraq's Mosul," *Azzaman,* August 10, 2009.

37. According to an Associated Press report, Odierno "said the deployment of the U.S.-Iraqi-Kurdish protection forces would start in Ninevah province, which includes the volatile city of Mosul, and then extend to Kirkuk and to Diyala province north of the capital." See Kim Gamel, "U.S. Iraq Boss Wants Troops in Disputed Land," Associated Press, August 18, 2009.

38. Liz Sly, "U.S. Troops May be Sent to Iraq's Arab-Kurdish 'Trigger Line,'" *Los Angeles Times,* August 18, 2009.

39. Odierno has not stipulated the number of U.S. soldiers to be deployed in the new proposal. If the Iraqi people do not approve the SOFA in a referendum held on the same day as the January 2010 parliamentary elections, U.S. soldiers will be forced to leave a year earlier than the December 31, 2011 deadline agreed to in the SOFA. For recent reporting on the referendum, see Ernesto Londoño, "Iraq May Hold Vote On U.S. Withdrawal," *Washington Post,* August 18, 2009.

40. The use of the Iraqi Army has been suspected of serving al-Maliki's political goals in the past. In August 2008, al-Maliki gave direct orders for the Iraqi Army to enter the disputed city of Khanaqin, forcing out *peshmerga* forces from the area and raiding offices belonging to Kurdish political parties. Kurdish observers viewed the maneuver as an attempt to marginalize Kurdish influence in Diyala Province ahead of the 2009 provincial elections. For al-Maliki's suspicious and political use of the army, in particular before the 2009 provincial elections, see "Kirkuk and Khanaqin on Alert," *Kurdish Globe,* January 22, 2009. For more information on the standoff between the government and the Kurds in Khanaqin, see Ramzy Mardini, "Iraqi Military Operation in Diyala Province Risks Renewal of Kurdish-Arab Conflict," *Terrorism Focus,* 5:33 (2008).

41. Al-Hakim's interest in federalism is based on the desire to form a semi-autonomous Shi`a region, similar to that of the Kurdish region, consisting of nine southern Shi`a provinces.

42. Iraq has a total of 18 provinces, but only 14 participated in the January 2009 provincial elections. The three provinces belonging to the semi-autonomous Kurdish region conducted their own provincial elections on July 25, 2009. Because of the political sensitivities surrounding the disputed city of Kirkuk, its province had not commenced provincial elections. The national parliament has yet to come to agreement on an election law for Kirkuk.

43. Arthur MacMillan, "US Army Commanders Say Pull-out From Mosul Mired in Confusion," Agence France-Presse, June 18, 2009.

44. For recent reporting, see Ammar Karim, "Iraq PM Set to Break with Shiite Coalition in January Polls," Agence France-Presse, August 13, 2009. For further reading about al-Maliki's strategy for a national coalition, see Shadid; Weiner; Domergue and Cochrane.

RAMZY MARDINI is an analyst on international security affairs. He currently writes on Iraq affairs at The Jamestown Foundation, a foreign policy think tank in Washington, D.C. Mr. Mardini has served at the State Department's Bureau of Near Eastern Affairs, the Executive Office of the President, and the Center for Strategic Studies in Amman, Jordan. He holds an M.A. in international relations from the University of Chicago.

The Most Dangerous Place in the World

Somalia is a state governed only by anarchy. A graveyard of foreign-policy failures, it has known just six months of peace in the past two decades. Now, as the country's endless chaos threatens to engulf an entire region, the world again simply watches it burn.

JEFFREY GETTLEMAN

When you land at Mogadishu's international airport, the first form you fill out asks for name, address, and caliber of weapon. Believe it or not, this disaster of a city, the capital of Somalia, still gets a few commercial flights. Some haven't fared so well. The wreckage of a Russian cargo plane shot down in 2007 still lies crumpled at the end of the runway.

Beyond the airport is one of the world's most stunning monuments to conflict: block after block, mile after mile, of scorched, gutted-out buildings. Mogadishu's Italianate architecture, once a gem along the Indian Ocean, has been reduced to a pile of machine-gun-chewed bricks. Somalia has been ripped apart by violence since the central government imploded in 1991. Eighteen years and 14 failed attempts at a government later, the killing goes on and on and on—suicide bombs, white phosphorus bombs, beheadings, medieval-style stonings, teenage troops high on the local drug called *khat* blasting away at each other and anything in between. Even U.S. cruise missiles occasionally slam down from the sky. It's the same violent free-for-all on the seas. Somalia's pirates are threatening to choke off one of the most strategic waterways in the world, the Gulf of Aden, which 20,000 ships pass through every year. These heavily armed buccaneers hijacked more than 40 vessels in 2008, netting as much as $100 million in ransom. It's the greatest piracy epidemic of modern times.

In more than a dozen trips to Somalia over the past two and a half years, I've come to rewrite my own definition of chaos. I've felt the incandescent fury of the Iraqi insurgency raging in Fallujah. I've spent freezing-cold, eerily quiet nights in an Afghan cave. But nowhere was I more afraid than in today's Somalia, where you can get kidnapped or shot in the head faster than you can wipe the sweat off your brow. From the thick, ambush-perfect swamps around Kismayo in the south to the lethal labyrinth of Mogadishu to the pirate den of Boosaaso on the Gulf of Aden, Somalia is quite simply the most dangerous place in the world.

> **I've felt the incandescent fury of the Iraqi insurgency. I've spent freezing-cold nights in an Afghan cave. But nowhere was I more afraid than in today's Somalia.**

The whole country has become a breeding ground for warlords, pirates, kidnappers, bomb makers, fanatical Islamist insurgents, freelance gunmen, and idle, angry youth with no education and way too many bullets. There is no Green Zone here, by the way—no fortified place of last resort to run to if, God forbid, you get hurt or in trouble. In Somalia, you're on your own. The local hospitals barely have enough gauze to treat all the wounds.

The mayhem is now spilling across Somalia's borders, stirring up tensions and violence in Kenya, Ethiopia, and Eritrea, not to mention Somalia's pirateinfested seas. The export of trouble may just be beginning. Islamist insurgents with al Qaeda connections are sweeping across the country, turning Somalia into an Afghanistan-like magnet for militant Islam and drawing in hard-core fighters from around the world. These men will eventually go home (if they survive) and spread the killer ethos. Somalia's transitional government, a U.N.-santioned creation that was deathly ill from the moment it was born four years ago, is about to flatline, perhaps spawning yet another doomed international rescue mission. Abdullahi Yusuf Ahmed, the old war horse of a president backed by the United States, finally resigned in December after a long, bitter dispute with the prime minister, Nur Hassan Hussein. Ostensibly, their conflict was about a peace deal with the Islamists and a few cabinet posts. In truth, it may be purely academic. By early this year, the government's zone of control was down to a couple of city blocks. The country is nearly as big as Texas.

Just when things seem as though they can't get any worse in Somalia, they do. Beyond the political crisis, all the elements for a full-blown famine—war, displacement, drought, skyrocketing food prices, and an exodus of aid workers—are lining up again, just as they did in the early 1990s when hundreds of thousands of Somalis starved to death. Last May, I stood in the doorway of a hut in the bone-dry central part of the country watching a sick little boy curl up next to his dying mother. Her clothes were damp. Her breaths were shallow. She hadn't eaten for days. "She will most likely die," an elder told me and walked away.

Just when things seem they can't get any worse in Somalia, they do. Beyond the political crisis, all the elements for a full-blown famine are lining up again.

It's crunch time for Somalia, but the world is like me, standing in the doorway, looking in at two decades of unbridled anarchy, unsure what to do. Past interventions have been so cursed that no one wants to get burned again. The United States has been among the worst of the meddlers: U.S. forces fought predacious warlords at the wrong time, backed some of the same predacious warlords at the wrong time, and consistently failed to appreciate the twin pulls of clan and religion. As a result, Somalia has become a graveyard of foreign-policy blunders that have radicalized the population, deepened insecurity, and pushed millions to the brink of starvation.

Somalia is a political paradox—unified on the surface, poisonously divided beneath. It is one of the world's most homogeneous nation-states, with nearly all of its estimated 9 to 10 million people sharing the same language (Somali), the same religion (Sunni Islam), the same culture, and the same ethnicity. But in Somalia, it's all about clan. Somalis divide themselves into a dizzying number of clans, subclans, sub-subclans, and so on, with shifting allegiances and knotty backstories that have bedeviled outsiders for years.

At the end of the 19th century, the Italians and the British divvied up most of Somalia, but their efforts to impose Western laws never really worked. Disputes tended to be resolved by clan elders. Deterrence was key: "Kill me and you will suffer the wrath of my entire clan." The places where the local ways were disturbed the least, such as British-ruled Somaliland, seem to have done better in the long run than those where the Italian colonial administration supplanted the role of clan elders, as in Mogadishu.

Somalia won independence in 1960, but it quickly became a Cold War pawn, prized for its strategic location in the Horn of Africa, where Africa and Asia nearly touch. First it was the Soviets who pumped in weapons, then the United States.

A poor, mostly illiterate, mainly nomadic country became a towering ammunition dump primed to explode. The central government was hardly able to hold the place together. Even in the 1980s, Maj. Gen. Mohamed Siad Barre, the capricious dictator who ruled from 1969 to 1991, was derisively referred to as "the mayor of Mogadishu" because so much of the country had already spun out of his control.

When clan warlords finally ousted him in 1991, it wasn't much of a surprise what happened next. The warlords unleashed all that military-grade weaponry on each other, and every port, airstrip, fishing pier, telephone pole—anything that could turn a profit—was fought over. People were killed for a few pennies. Women were raped with impunity. The chaos gave rise to a new class of parasitic war profiteers—gunrunners, drug smugglers, importers of expired (and often sickening) baby formula—people with a vested interest in the chaos continuing. Somalia became the modern world's closest approximation of Hobbes's state of nature, where life was indeed nasty, brutish, and short. To call it even a failed state was generous. The Democratic Republic of the Congo is a failed state. So is Zimbabwe. But those places at least have national armies and national bureaucracies, however corrupt. Since 1991, Somalia has not been a state so much as a lawless, ungoverned space on the map between its neighbors and the sea.

In 1992, U.S. President George H.W. Bush tried to help, sending in thousands of Marines to protect shipments of food. It was the beginning of the post-Cold War "new world order," when many believed that the United States, without a rival superpower, could steer world events in a new and morally righteous way. Somalia proved to be a very bad start. President Bush and his advisors misread the clan landscape and didn't understand how fiercely loyal Somalis could be to their clan leaders. Somali society often divides and subdivides when faced with internal disputes, but it quickly bands together when confronted by an external enemy. The United States learned this the hard way when its forces tried to apprehend the warlord of the day, Mohammed Farah Aidid. The result was the infamous "Black Hawk Down" episode in October 1993. Thousands of Somali militiamen poured into the streets, carrying rocket-propelled grenades and wearing flip-flops. They shot down two American Black Hawk helicopters, killing 18 U.S. soldiers and dragging the corpses triumphantly through the streets. This would be Strike One for the United States in Somalia.

Humiliated, the Americans pulled out and Somalia was left to its own dystopian devices. For the next decade, the Western world mostly stayed away. But Arab organizations, many from Saudi Arabia and followers of the strict Wahhabi branch of Sunni Islam, quietly stepped in. They built mosques, Koranic schools, and social service organizations, encouraging an Islamic revival. By the early 2000s, Mogadishu's clan elders set up a loose network of neighborhood-based courts to deliver a modicum of order in a city desperate for it. They rounded up thieves and killers, put them in iron cages, and held trials. Islamic law, or *sharia*, was the one set of principles that different clans could agree on; the Somali elders called their network the Islamic Courts Union.

Mogadishu's business community spotted an opportunity. In Mogadishu, there are warlords and moneylords. While the warlords were ripping the country apart, the moneylords, Somalia's big-business owners, were holding the place together, delivering many of the same services—for a tidy profit, of course—that a government usually provides, such as healthcare, schools, power plants, and even privatized mail. The moneylords went as far as helping to regulate Somalia's monetary policy, and the Somali shilling was more stable in the 1990s—without a functioning central bank—than in the 1980s when there was a government. But with their profits came very high risks, such as chronic insecurity and extortion. The Islamists were a solution. They provided security without taxes, administration without a government. The moneylords began buying them guns.

By 2005, the CIA saw what was happening, and again misread the cues. This ended up being Strike Two.

In a post-September 11 world, Somalia had become a major terrorism worry. The fear was that Somalia could blossom into a jihad factory like Afghanistan, where al Qaeda in the 1990s plotted its global war on the West. It didn't seem to matter that at this point there was scant evidence to justify this fear. Some Western military analysts told policymakers that Somalia was too chaotic for even al Qaeda, because it was impossible for anyone—including terrorists—to know whom to trust. Nonetheless, the administration of George W. Bush devised a strategy to stamp out the Islamists on the cheap. CIA agents deputized the warlords, the same thugs who had been preying upon Somalia's population for years, to fight the Islamists. According to one Somali warlord I spoke with in March 2008, an American agent named James and another one named David showed up in Mogadishu with briefcases stuffed with cash. Use this to buy guns, the agents said. Drop us an e-mail if you have any questions. The warlord showed me the address: no_email_today@yahoo.com.

The plan backfired. Somalis like to talk; the country, ironically, has some of the best and cheapest cellular phone service in Africa. Word quickly spread that the same warlords no one liked anymore were now doing the Americans' bidding, which just made the Islamists even more popular. By June 2006, the Islamists had run the last warlords out of Mogadishu. Then something unbelievable happened: The Islamists seemed to tame the place.

I saw it with my own eyes. I flew into Mogadishu in September 2006 and saw work crews picking up trash and kids swimming at the beach. For the first time in years, no gunshots rang out at night. Under the banner of Islam, the Islamists had united rival clans and disarmed much of the populace, with clan support of course. They even cracked down on piracy by using their clan connections to dissuade coastal towns from supporting the pirates. When that didn't work, the Islamists stormed hijacked ships. According to the International Maritime Bureau in London, there were 10 pirate attacks off Somalia's coast in 2006, which is tied for the lowest number of attacks this decade.

The Islamists' brief reign of peace was to be the only six months of calm Somalia has tasted since 1991. But it was one thing to rally together to overthrow the warlords and another to decide what to do next. A rift quickly opened between the moderate Islamists and the extremists, who were bent on waging jihad. One of the most radical factions has been the Shabab, a multiclan military wing with a strict Wahhabi interpretation of Islam. The Shabab drove around Mogadishu in big, black pickup trucks and beat women whose ankles were showing. Even the other Islamist gunmen were scared of them. By December 2006, some of the population began to chafe against the Shabab for taking away their beloved khat, the mildly stimulating leaf that Somalis chew like bubble gum. Shabab leaders were widely rumored to be working with foreign jihadists, including wanted al Qaeda terrorists, and the U.S. State Department later designated the Shabab a terrorist organization. American officials have said that the Shabab are sheltering men who masterminded the bombings of the U.S. embassies in Kenya and Tanzania in 1998.

Somalia may indeed have sheltered a few unsavory characters, but the country was far from the terrorist hotbed many worry it has now become. In 2006, there was a narrow window of opportunity to peel off the moderate Islamists from the likes of the Shabab, and some U.S. officials, such as Democratic Rep. Donald M. Payne, the chairman of the House subcommittee on Africa, were trying to do exactly that. Payne and others met with the moderate Islamists and encouraged them to negotiate a powersharing deal with the transitional government.

But the Bush administration again reached for the gunpowder. The United States would not do much of the fighting itself, since sending large numbers of ground troops into Somalia with Iraq and Afghanistan raging would have been deemed insane. Instead, the United States anointed a proxy: the Ethiopian Army. This move would be Strike Three.

Ethiopia is one of the United States' best friends in Africa, its government having carefully cultivated an image as a Christian bulwark in a region seething with Islamist extremism. The Ethiopian leadership savvily told the Bush administration what it wanted to hear: The Islamists were terrorists and, unchecked, they would threaten the entire region and maybe even attack American safarigoers in Kenya next door.

Of course, the Ethiopians had their own agenda. Ethiopia is a country with a mostly Christian leadership but a population that is nearly half Muslim. It seems only a matter of time before there is an Islamic awakening in Ethiopia. On top of that, the Ethiopian government is fighting several rebel groups, including a powerful one that is ethnically Somali. The government feared that an Islamist Somalia could become a rebel beachhead next door. The Ethiopians were also scared that Somalia's Islamists would team up with Eritrea, Ethiopia's archenemy, which is exactly what ended up happening.

Not everyone in Washington swallowed the Ethiopian line. The country has a horrendous human rights record, and the Ethiopian military (which receives aid for human rights training from the United States) is widely accused of brutalizing its own people. But in December 2006, the Bush administration shared prized intelligence with the Ethiopians and gave them the green light to invade Somalia. Thousands of Ethiopian troops rolled across the border (many had secretly been in the country for months), and they routed the Islamist troops within a week. There were even some U.S. Special Forces with the Ethiopian units. The United States also launched several airstrikes in an attempt to take out Islamist leaders, and it continued with intermittent cruise missiles targeting suspected terrorists. Most have failed, killing civilians and adding to the boiling anti-American sentiment.

The Islamists went underground, and the transitional government arrived in Mogadishu. There was some cheering, a lot of jeering, and the insurgency revved up within days. The transitional government was widely reviled as a coterie of ex-warlords, which it mostly was. It was the 14th attempt since 1991 to stand up a central government. None of the previous attempts had worked. True, some detractors have simply been war profiteers hell-bent on derailing any government. But a lot of blame falls on what this transitional government has done—or not done. From the start, leaders seemed much more interested in who got what post than living up to the corresponding job descriptions. The government quickly lost the support of key clans in Mogadishu by its harsh (and unsuccessful) tactics in trying to wipe out the insurgents, and by its reliance on Ethiopian troops. Ethiopia and Somalia have fought several wars against each other over the contested Ogaden region that Ethiopia now claims. That region is mostly ethnically Somali, so teaming up with Ethiopia was seen as tantamount to treason.

The Islamists tapped into this sentiment, positioning themselves as the true Somali nationalists, and gaining widespread support again. The results were intense street battles between Islamist insurgents and Ethiopian troops in which thousands of civilians have been killed. Ethiopian forces have indiscriminately shelled entire neighborhoods (which precipitated a European Union investigation into war crimes), and have even used white phosphorous bombs that literally melt people, according to the United Nations. Hundreds of thousands of people have emptied out of Mogadishu and settled in camps that have become breeding grounds for disease and resentment. Death comes more frequently and randomly than ever before. I met one man in Mogadishu who was chatting with his wife on her cellphone when she was cut in half by a stray mortar shell. Another man I spoke to went out for a walk, got shot in the leg during a crossfire, and had to spend seven days eating grass before the fighting ended and he could crawl away.

> **Death comes more frequently and randomly than ever before. I met one man in Mogadishu who was chatting with his wife on her cellphone when she was cut in half by a stray mortar shell.**

It's incredibly dangerous for us journalists, too. Few foreign journalists travel to Somalia anymore. Kidnapping is the threat du jour. Friends of mine who work for the United Nations in Kenya told me I had about a 100 percent chance of being stuffed into the back of a Toyota or shot (or both) if I didn't hire a private militia. Nowadays, as soon as I land, I take 10 gunmen under my employ.

By late January, the only territory the transitional government controlled was a shrinking federal enclave in Mogadishu guarded by a small contingent of African Union peacekeepers. As soon as the Ethiopians pulled out of the capital vicious fighting broke out between the various Islamist factions scrambling to fill the power gap. It took only days for the Islamists to recapture the third-largest town, Baidoa, from the government and install sharia law. The Shabab are not wildly popular, but they are formidable; for the time being they have a motivated, disciplined militia with hundreds of hard-core fighters and probably thousands of gunmen allied with them. The violence has shown no signs of halting, even with the election of a new, moderate Islamist president—one who had, ironically, been a leader of the Islamic Courts Union in 2006.

If the Shabab do seize control of the country, they might not stop there. They could send their battle-hardened fighters in battered four-wheel-drive pickup trucks into Ethiopia, Kenya, and maybe even Djibouti to try to snatch back the Somali-speaking parts of those countries. This scenario has long been part of an ethereal pan-Somali dream. Pursuit of that goal would internationalize the conflict and surely drag in neighboring countries and their allies.

The Shabab could also wage an asymmetric war, unleashing terrorists on Somalia's secular neighbors and their secular backers—most prominently, the United States. This would upend an already combustible dynamic in the Horn of Africa, catalyzing other conflicts. For instance, Ethiopia and Eritrea fought a nasty border war in the late 1990s, which killed as many as 100,000 people, and both countries are still heavily militarized along the border. If the Shabab, which boasts Eritrean support, took over Somalia, we might indeed see round two of Ethiopia versus Eritrea. The worst-case scenario could mean millions of people displaced across the entire region, crippled food production, and violence-induced breaches in the aid pipeline. In short, a famine in one of the most perennially needy parts of the world—again.

The hardest challenge of all might be simply preventing the worst-case scenario. Among the best suggestions I've heard is to play to Somalia's strengths as a fluid, decentralized society with local mechanisms to resolve conflicts. The foundation of order would be clan-based governments in villages, towns, and neighborhoods. These tiny fiefdoms could stack together to form district and regional governments. The last step would be uniting the regional governments in a loose national federation that coordinated, say, currency issues or antipiracy efforts, but did not sideline local leaders.

Western powers should do whatever they can to bring moderate Islamists into the transitional government while the transitional government still exists. Whether people like it or not, many Somalis see Islamic law as the answer. Maybe they're not fond of the harsh form imposed by the Shabab, who have, on at least one occasion, stoned to death a teenage girl who had been raped (an Islamic court found her guilty of adultery). Still, there is an appetite for a certain degree of Islamic governance. That desire should not be confused with support for terrorism.

A more radical idea is to have the United Nations take over the government and administer Somalia with an East Timor-style mandate. Because Somalia has already been an independent country, this option might be too much for Somalis to stomach. To make it work, the United Nations would need to delegate authority to clan leaders who have measurable clout on the ground. Either way, the diplomats should be working with the moneylords more and the warlords less.

But the problem with Somalia is that after 18 years of chaos, with so many people killed, with so many guntoting men rising up and then getting cut down, it is exceedingly difficult to identify who the country's real leaders are, if they exist at all. It's not just Mogadishu's wasteland of blown-up buildings that must be reconstructed; it's the entire national psyche. The whole country is suffering from an acute case of post-traumatic stress disorder. Somalis will have to move beyond the narrow interests of clans, where they have withdrawn for protection, and embrace the idea of a Somali nation.

If that happens, the work will just be beginning. Nearly an entire generation of Somalis has absolutely no idea what a government is or how it functions. I've seen this glassy-eyed generation all across the country, lounging on bullet-pocked street corners and spaced out in the back of pickup trucks, Kalashnikovs in their hands and nowhere to go. To them, law and order are thoroughly abstract concepts. To them, the only law in the land is the business end of a machine gun.

JEFFREY GETTLEMAN is East Africa bureau chief for the *New York Times*.

Reading Twitter in Tehran?
Why the Real Revolution Is on the Streets—and Offline

JOHN PALFREY, BRUCE ETLING, AND ROBERT FARIS

P ray that today at 4 P.M. Toopkhane Sq. will turn into a sea of green, biggest march in 30 years, Mousavi WILL be there #iranelection.

This message, posted on Twitter Thursday morning, is one of countless tweets emerging from the Iranian Revolution Version 2009, in which a love affair between elite young Iranians and the latest Web technologies has become the feel-good story to the otherwise frightening standoff in the streets of Tehran.

Yes, this revolution is being tweeted, blogged and Facebooked—and not just in Tehran. Blogger Andrew Sullivan helped kick off the cyber hype with his June 13 post "The Revolution Will be Twittered?" in which he argued that the use of this platform means that "you cannot stop people any longer. You cannot control them any longer." And after the State Department asked Twitter to delay a scheduled maintenance last week so that this line of communication between Iran and the rest of the world could remain open, the company's co-founder Biz Stone offered a somewhat self-congratulatory aw-shucks post on his blog: "It's humbling to think that our two-year old company could be playing such a globally meaningful role that state officials find their way toward highlighting our significance."

Certainly, a powerful new force is developing here. Citizens who once had little public voice are using cheap Web tools to tell the world about the drama that has unfolded since President Mahmoud Ahmadinejad was declared the winner of Iran's disputed election. The government succeeded last week in exerting control over Internet use and text-messaging, but Twitter has proven nearly impossible to block. The most common search topic on Twitter for days has been "#iranelection"—the "hashtag" for discussions on Iran—and global media outlets are relying on information and images disseminated via Twitter feeds.

Yet for all their promise, there are sharp limits on what Twitter and other Web tools such as Facebook and blogs can do for citizens in authoritarian societies. The 140 characters allowed in a tweet are not the end of politics as we know it—and at times can even play into the hands of hard-line regimes. No amount of Twittering will force Iran's leaders to change course, as supreme leader Ayatollah Ali Khamenei made clear Friday with his rebuke of the protesters, reportedly followed

by the security forces' use of tear gas, batons, water cannons and gunfire to break up demonstrations yesterday. In Iran, as elsewhere, if true revolution is coming, it must happen offline.

First, Twitter's own internal architecture puts limits on political activism. There are so many messages streaming through at any moment that any single entry is unlikely to break through the din, and the limit of 140 characters—part of the service's charm and the secret of its success—militates against sustained argument and nuance. (Yes, "Give me liberty or give me death" totals just 32 characters, but Patrick Henry's full speech exceeded 1,200 words.) What's most exciting is the aggregate effect of all this speech and what it reveals about the zeitgeist of the moment, but it still reflects a worldwide user population that skews wealthy, English-speaking and well-educated. The same is true of the blogosphere and social networks such as Facebook.

Second, governments that are jealous of their power can push back on cyberspace when they feel threatened. The Iranian state runs one of the world's most formidable online censorship regimes. In the past week alone, officials have blocked access to YouTube, Facebook and the majority of websites most often cited by reformist segments of the Persian blogosphere. They supplement this censorship with surveillance and the threat of imprisonment for those who speak out. Even if they fail to block political speech or organizing activities, the possibility of future retaliation can chill the most devoted activists and critics.

Paradoxically, the "freedom to scream" online may actually assist authoritarian regimes by serving as a political release valve of sorts. If dissent is channeled into cyberspace, it can keep protesters off the streets and help state security forces track political activism and new online voices. As Egyptian democracy activist Saad Ibrahim said last week during a discussion at the U.S. Institute of Peace in Washington, this appears to be part of a long tradition for governments in the Middle East, especially in Egypt, where dissent is channeled into universities and allowed to thrive there, as long as it does not escape the university walls.

Third, the blogosphere is not limited to young, liberal, anti-regime activists; state sympathizers are increasingly active in the battle for online supremacy. Our research into the Iranian blogosphere shows that political and religious conservatives are no less prominent than regime critics. While the Iranian blogosphere is indeed a place where women speak out for their rights, young people criticize the morality police, journalists fight censorship, reformists press for change, and dissidents call for revolution, it is also a place where the supreme leader is praised, the Holocaust denied, the Islamic Revolution defended and Hezbollah celebrated. It is also a place where Islamist student groups mobilize and pro-establishment leaders, including President Ahmadinejad, reach out to their constituents within the Iranian public. Our most recent research suggests that the number and popularity of politically conservative and Islamic bloggers has grown over the past year, relative to the number of secular reformists, possibly due to the events leading up to the presidential election.

Online chatter has enormous value when it offers a window into an otherwise closed society, but much of the cyber conversation in Iran has absolutely nothing to do with politics or revolution. Religion is a major topic for bloggers—and not necessarily the politics of religion, but rather its historical, theological and personal aspects. And the most frequently discussed topic on Iranian blogs? Poetry.

Authoritarian regimes are also eager to employ the Web for their own brand of political activism. In Iran, for example, the Basij, a volunteer paramilitary force under the authority of the Revolutionary Guard, pledged to create 10,000 blogs to combat what it described as foreign elements that are trying to foment revolution online. (The effort ultimately failed.) Government supporters have also carried out increasingly sophisticated attacks against popular Persian websites deemed not sufficiently supportive of the government or critical of Israel's actions in Gaza last winter.

In Russia, those sympathetic to Russia's renewed geopolitical assertiveness have launched online attacks against critics of the government. During the Orange Revolution in Ukraine in 2004 and 2005, protesters' websites were hacked and temporarily shut down. The same thing happened to official government and banking websites in Estonia in 2007 after the government there decided to move a Cold War-era monument that honored Soviet soldiers. And in the run-up to last year's conflict between Russia and Georgia, so-called DDOS (distributed denial of service) attacks were carried out against Georgian government websites. It is nearly impossible to tell who is responsible for these attacks, but in Estonia, the pro-Kremlin youth movement Nashi claimed responsibility for the attacks.

In China, the government has helped train and finance a group that infiltrates Chinese chat rooms and Web forums to combat anti-party discussions. Dubbed the "50-cent party" for the payments they reportedly receive for each pro-government post, these Internet thought cops seek out popular bulletin boards and try to turn around discussions that might be critical of the Communist Party or government policy.

And yet the Twittering goes on. As states such as Iran crack down on online speech and organizing, clever netizens find ways around the controls. In Iran as well as in China, Burma and parts of the former Soviet Union, there's an on-again, off-again process of citizens speaking out and states pushing back.

Of course, governments always have the nuclear option when it comes to the Internet: They can shut it down and keep it down. It's what Burma did when monks took to the streets in 2007. It's the policy of North Korea and Cuba, where only very few people can access the Internet, usually for very narrow purposes.

But most hard-line governments appear more ambivalent. They fear the political repercussions of widespread Internet use, but they may fear the economic and political consequences of banning it even more.

Consider the repeated blocking and unblocking of Facebook over the past year in Iran. When the site is up, citizens use it as an effective organizing tool for an opposition candidate—in this case, presidential candidate Mir Hossein Mousavi's 65,000-plus Facebook group. The state then gets nervous about the force of this collective action and blocks access to Facebook. After a while, enough people complain that the ban is lifted, only to be reimposed.

The same thing happens in China, where in each of the past four years, Wikipedia has been blocked and unblocked, and where Twitter and YouTube were shut down recently during the 20th anniversary of the Tiananmen Square crackdown.

So who will prevail? Are authoritarian regimes willing to grant their people the autonomy that comes with unfettered access to the Internet? Or will these regimes bend the network to their will through censorship, surveillance and propaganda?

With so many individuals overcoming government efforts to block online communication, particularly via Twitter, it is notable that the Iranian government has not shut down Internet access completely. Similarly, as we discovered in our recent study of the Arabic blogosphere, the Egyptian government tolerates extensive blogging by the Muslim Brotherhood while outlawing its other activities. The Chinese often ease the harshest of their Internet regulations over time. And the military junta in Burma didn't keep the Net down for long. Ultimately, almost all such regimes choose to leave the Internet more open than closed, then move to regulate specific activities that they deem worrisome.

After all, it appears that people living under authoritarian regimes such as the one in Iran are as addicted to the Internet as the rest of us are. Even though states push back, they can't keep the Internet down for long without serious blowback from their citizens. Iranian officials have the power to shutter the Internet just as they once clamped down on reformist newspapers, but they may be more concerned now about any move that pushes those watching—or blogging or tweeting—from the sidelines into the throngs of protesters already in the streets.

The authors are researchers at Harvard University's Berkman Center for Internet & Society. cyber@law.harvard.edu

UNIT 7

Asymmetric Conflicts: Trends in Terrorism and Counterterrorism

Unit Selections

Key Points to Consider

- What actions would you recommend the U.S. government take in order to counter al-Qaeda activities in the Middle East, Central Asia, and Europe, but most notably in Pakistan?

- What are the three integrated pillars of a successful counterinsurgency campaign?

Student Website

www.mhhe.com/cls

Internet References

Columbia International Affairs Online
http://www.ciaonet.org/cbr/cbr00/video/cbr_v/cbr_v.html

Combating Terrorism Center at West Point
http://ctc.usma.edu/

SITE: The Search for International Terrorist Entities
http://www.siteinstitute.org/index.html

Terrorism Research Center
http://www.terrorism.com

United States Government Counterinsurgency Initiative
http://www.usgcoin.org/

The terrorist attacks against the World Trade Center and the Pentagon on September 11, 2001, and the anthrax letter attacks the following month highlighted the vulnerabilities of economically developed societies to attacks by disaffected radicals who can now pursue their political goals by killing large numbers of civilians. The United States' decision to pursue the al-Qaeda terrorists using the military as the lead agency in the Global War on Terrorism (GWOT) resulted in a comprehensive offensive that has mobilized large amounts of the resources and time of the U.S. and allied governments. Although Osama bin Laden and Ayman al-Zawahiri remain at large, much of the leadership and organizational structure of al-Qaeda has been destroyed or disrupted.

For many observers, al-Qaeda's decision to take the fight directly to America was a strategic mistake since it prompted an unprecedented and largely effective response from a previously distracted giant, the United States. During the early years of the war many analysts believed that the United States had succeeded in its struggle against terrorism. However, many analysts and U.S. voters concluded that the United States was also wrong to attack Iraq rather than finish the hunt for Osama bin Laden and eliminate the residual Taliban threat in Afghanistan. During 2008, many well-known western terrorist analysts pronounced al-Qaeda's military and strategic campaign against the United States and 'near enemies' as having failed even though legacy residual groups would continue to operate worldwide. The resurgence of the Taliban attacks and success at controlling large parts of Afghanistan, and growing evidence that al-Qaeda leaders were living comfortably in houses, not caves, in several urban areas within the Tribal Trust areas of Pakistan, led many of the same analysts to reassess the security situation in Afgahnistan and Pakistan.

Don Rassler in "Al-Qa´ida's Pakistan Strategy," discusses al-Qa´ida's recent shift in strategy to a more confrontational approach with Pakistan. Rassler outlines the reasons he believes this shift in tactics has occurred. According to Rassler,

al-Qa'ida's current strategy reflects an effort on the part of the organization's leader to work towards implementing it's highest priorities today: to destabilize the Pakistani government, divert U.S. attention from the fight in Afghanistan, and undermine Islamabad's alliance with the United States. The increased frequency of high profile suicide attacks widely attributed to al-Qaeda in several civilian locations in different urban areas of Pakistan is only one of several signs of a shift in al-Qaeda's strategy.

Many Pakistanis blame the United States for the increased violence within their borders. During a visit to the country in October of 2008, U.S Secretary of State Hillary Clinton, in response to charges by Pakistani citizens that they are forced to endure small 9/11 attacks due to U.S. actions, asked these citizens why their government had not yet moved to crush al-Qaeda leaders living inside Pakistan. Although the Pakistani military launched several high profile campaigns into the Frontier territories during 2009 with the ostensive goal of dismantling al-Qaeda sanctuaries and made some progress retaking ground, Secretary Clinton's query remains an important unanswered question that is causing tensions between the United States and Pakistan.

Peter Bergen, in "Al-Qaeda at 20 Dead or Alive?," explains why he believes Al-Qaeda's military and strategic campaigns against the United States and other Western democracies have failed. He goes on to warn that the links between radicals in places such as the United Kingdom and bin Ladin remain a serious threat. He states that the "legacy will endure, even after Al-Qaeda is defeated."

To counter the Tigers, the government implemented a policy of very accurate targeted assassinations which eventually succeeded in wiping out the leadership of this long-running guerrilla movement. Unfortunately, the Sri Lanka government's counterinsurgency campaign plan may not be an effective recipe worldwide because large numbers of young people in many developing countries are likely to continue providing recruits for terrorist cells for jihadist extremists inspired by, or trained by, al-Qaeda. In fact, some analysts stress that we are at the start of an asymmetric battle that may take 50 years to win. This more pessimistic view is based on several trends. Al-Qaeda has proven to be a highly adaptive movement in the face of a successful Global War on Terrorism (GWOT) launched and led by the United States. Although al-Qaeda Central may be highly constrained and remain in hiding until Osama bin Laden is found or dies, the al-Qaeda movement has transformed itself into a looser, global collection of decentralized cells and groups. Some of these networks span the globe and are only loosely linked, or linked only by shared political beliefs, to al-Qaeda central run by Osama bin Laden and Ayman al-Zawahiri. Nearly all of the local cells fund their low-cost operations through criminal scams that are difficult to detect and thwart.

Several recently thwarted attacks were small cells that were largely self-financed and thus difficult for authorities to detect by monitoring cash flows or bank transfers—the basis of many of the anti-terrorism financing laws in place today. Another reason why most western security analysts characterize the War on Terrorism, or the preferred Obama administration term of "complex overseas operations," as being far from over is because there is a growing recognition that successful counterinsurgency campaigns are complicated affairs to implement effectively and often take a long time. David J. Kilcullen emphasizes in "Three Pillars of Counterinsurgency" that the last time the United States attempted to implement an inter-agency counterinsurgency doctrine was in 1962 and it didn't work very well. Kilcullen warns that the conflict environment today is even more complicated and that the U.S. government must mobilize all of its agencies, along with host nations, multiple foreign allies and coalition partners, non-government organizations, media, community groups, and business in order to win the war. In his article, Kilcullen proposes an inter-agency counterinsurgency framework based on three integrated pillars—economic, political, and security activities.

Al-Qa`ida's Pakistan Strategy

Don Rassler

Al-Qa`ida's strategy in Pakistan remains intentionally opaque, but has demonstrably shifted in recent years to promote increased confrontation with the Pakistani state. Al-Qa`ida's fighters originally used Pakistan as a key logistics base and facilitation point for the Afghan and Arab mujahidin during the 1980s, but since 2001 Pakistan has served primarily as an operational safe haven where al-Qa`ida and its affiliates can plan local, regional and international terrorist attacks. Pakistan's Federally Administered Tribal Areas (FATA) and smaller parts of Baluchistan and the North-West Frontier Province (NWFP) comprise al-Qa`ida's physical center of gravity. Increasingly, however, al-Qa`ida has utilized its media prowess and ideological authority to discredit the Pakistani state and promote cooperation among a variety of Pakistani militants to challenge the state's authority and undermine its support for U.S. efforts in Afghanistan.

A review of al-Qa`ida's statements pertaining to Pakistan, militant activity in the country, and the alliances al-Qa`ida has fostered among Pakistani factions reveals that the group is acting to shape Pakistan's militant environment and foster jihad against the Pakistani while taking a secondary role in the organization and operationalization of violence. Al-Qa`ida accomplishes this in three primary ways: 1) by providing religious "justification" and rallying support for anti-government militancy; acting as a force multiplier for violent activities by providing specific expertise; and 3) serving as a mediator and coalition builder for militant groups within Pakistan to further al-Qa`ida's aims.

Western counterterrorism analysts assessing al-Qa`ida's operations in Pakistan typically focus their attention on al-Qa`ida's "external" activities, primarily its support for terrorist attacks and plots in Europe, Africa, the Middle East, and the United States. Although this perspective is important, the focus on al-Qa`ida's direct role in the conduct of violence has obscured the critical, but largely behind-the-scenes, role that al-Qa`ida is playing to foster militancy in Pakistan. The Pakistan example is important not only because it threatens a critical U.S. ally, but because it illustrates the dangerous role that al-Qa`ida can play even when it is not primarily responsible for violent operations.

Calls for Action: Justifying and Rallying Support for the Pakistan Jihad

Since 9/11, al-Qa`ida's attention in South Asia has mainly focused on facilitating and supporting the jihad in Afghanistan.[1] Similarly, al-Qa`ida's messages directed at Pakistani audiences focused on Pakistan's role in supporting U.S. efforts in Afghanistan. Al-Qa`ida devoted significant energy attempting to portray former Pakistani President Pervez Musharraf as an apostate, the Pakistani government as an un-Islamic regime, and the Pakistani Army as a servant of the United States' campaign in Afghanistan.[2] A review of statements made by senior al-Qa`ida leaders from 2001 to September 2008 reveals that the group's calls for Musharraf's ouster were fairly consistent and continued with great regularity from 2003 until his departure from office in 2008.

Al-Qa`ida has targeted these messages to a variety of Pakistani audiences depending on current events and has pressed three basic themes: the need to target Pakistan, the Pakistani government's "un-Islamic" character, and the need for unified opposition to the state. As part of that campaign, al-Qa`ida's communications have attempted to divide state resources by urging soldiers of the Pakistani Army to revolt against the entity they committed to protect.[3] Al-Qa`ida's calls for violent action against the Pakistani government were limited in scope until the *Lal Masjid* (Red Mosque) conflict erupted in July 2007. Recognizing an opportunity to broaden its support, al-Qa`ida seized upon the event and used it to renew calls for jihad in Pakistan. In a statement issued in response to the *Lal Masjid* event, Usama bin Ladin publicly acknowledged al-Qa`ida's failure to prioritize the jihad in Pakistan, noting: "the obligation on us [al-Qa`ida] remains, and we have been extremely late in carrying it [jihad] out, six years having passed, so we should make up for lost time."[4] Appeals urging jihad against the Pakistani government have become more frequent and direct since the *Lal Masjid* incident.[5]

Al-Qa`ida's post-*Lal Masjid* statements have been more religiously focused than those made beforehand. One important statement made in September 2007 attempted to nullify targeting distinctions between "near" and "far" enemies, which in the past have served as a point of disagreement among jihadist groups in Pakistan. As notable al-Qa`ida figure Abu Yahya al-Libi argued:

> There is no doubt that the original, confirmed ruling laid down by the nobles and attested by the biography of the Prophet, peace and prayers be upon Him . . . is that we begin fighting the nearest [enemy], then the next nearest [enemy]. But this is when the situation is uniform and regular.[6]

Further contextualizing his distinction, al-Libi added that

> the question of special nearness and farness in our modern age does not have the same significance it once had . . . The relations which tie the major infidel states to the statelets [sic] and their apostate governments are close, overlapping relations.

Therefore, he concluded, "they [the United States, Pakistan, Afghanistan] are a single entity, a single enemy, and a single army."[7] Al-Qa`ida's conflation of the near and far enemy target sets is an attempt to re-frame the jihad in Pakistan as one that is both local and global. In doing so, al-Qa`ida is trying to obviate the differences among Pakistani militant groups that vary widely in their commitment to global jihad, the war in Afghanistan, sectarianism, and the fight against India in Kashmir. This reflects an important ideational shift within al-Qa`ida that has significant implications for its strategic goals and tactical objectives.

Al-Qa`ida aims to destabilize the Pakistani government, divert U.S. attention from the fight in Afghanistan, and undermine Islamabad's alliance with the United States.

Force Multiplier: Facilitating Attacks Against Pakistan

Many observers expect al-Qa`ida to take a leadership role in regions where it develops a major presence, but the Pakistani example belies that expectation. Perhaps counterintuitively, al-Qa`ida has chosen to remain in the background in Pakistan while fostering support for attacks against the Pakistani state and supporting Pakistani militants by providing technical expertise and capabilities.[8] Since its return to the tribal areas of Pakistan in late 2001, al-Qa`ida has been "lying low" within Pakistan and deferring leadership roles to local militant leaders. Given the U.S. focus on al-Qa`ida in Pakistan, the group might not have any other choice. Working in the background not only protects al-Qa`ida's leadership, but it also helps to protect its safe haven in the Pakistani tribal areas by not offending the multitude of jihadist and Taliban

groups sheltering al-Qa`ida's activities. A less overt presence in Pakistan also makes it easier for al-Qa`ida to manage local perceptions and deny involvement in controversial terrorist attacks within the country.

Although al-Qa`ida has only claimed responsibility for a small number of attacks in Pakistan, it is suspected of working with and through local groups to actively fight the Pakistani government. Al-Qa`ida has a deep history with many local Pakistan-based groups, including its primary partner in the fight, Tehrik-i-Taliban Pakistan (TTP) and its associated elements. While the precise nature of al-Qa`ida's operational relationships with groups such as Lashkar-i-Jhangvi or elements of the TTP are less than clear, these groups share a similar cause.[9] In 2003, for example, al-Qa`ida operative Abu Faraj al-Libi allegedly ordered an assassination attempt (one of two attempted during December 2003) against Pervez Musharraf, the Pakistani president at the time.[10] The double suicide attack that was executed on December 25, 2003 was reportedly planned by al-Qa`ida but executed by the Kashmiri group Jayshi-Muhammad.[11] More recently, in June 2009 a "major terrorist cell" with plans to target Pakistani President Asif Ali Zardari and a number of provincial chief ministers was disrupted in Karachi.[12] According to analyst Bruce Riedel, the group was led by a troika comprised of "one member of the Pakistani Taliban, one member of Lashkar-e-Taiba, and one member of al Qaeda."[13] Other attacks, such as the September 2008 Marriott Hotel bombing in Islamabad, went unclaimed by al-Qa`ida, but have hallmarks of an al-Qa`ida attack.[14] These instances suggest that al-Qa`ida is operating under a model distinct from that expected by most analysts, who seem to assume that al-Qa`ida will attempt to seize operational and political control of a militant environment, as its franchise did in Iraq. Such an assumption is misguided. Al-Qa`ida does not need to conduct bombings itself in order to be dangerous; in fact, al-Qa`ida is more likely to produce successful revolutionary movements when it defers to local groups to do the bulk of the fighting.

Al-Qa`ida as Mediator and Coalition Builder

To further its strategic aims, al-Qa`ida has assumed a role as mediator and coalition builder among various Pakistani militant group factions by promoting the unification of entities that have opposed one another or had conflicting ideas about whether to target the Pakistani state. For example, from December 2007 to mid-2008 Pakistani Taliban groups led by Mullah Nazir Ahmed and Hafiz Gul Bahadur were in violent conflict with Baitullah Mehsud's anti-government TTP.[15] The hostilities between the two rival factions threatened to distract them from conducting attacks in both Afghanistan and Pakistan, collectively hindering the efforts of al-Qa`ida, the Afghan Taliban and the Pakistani Taliban.[16] In an effort to protect his own interests, Mullah Omar reportedly urged both factions to reconcile their differences; he also fostered the creation of the Shura Ittihad-i-Mujahidin, an umbrella group led by Baitullah Mehsud with Gul Bahadur serving as deputy *amir*.[17] Al-Qa`ida served a critical role certifying the new relationship. In early April 2009, al-Qa`ida's media production arm al-Sahab released a 56-minute video interview with Mullah Nazir, in which he was specifically asked about his cooperation with other Taliban groups in Waziristan.[18] The question was an indirect reference to his conflict with Baitullah Mehsud. Nazir's response is telling: "We [the Pakistani Taliban] have forgotten all of our differences and merged this alliance as one. There shall be no more disputes in the future."[19]

As a mediator, al-Qa`ida is able to exert additional influence upon other groups, foster militant coalitions, and shape Pakistan's militant environment in ways that benefit its strategic vision and goals. Mullah Nazir's own view of the jihad waged by the Pakistani Taliban reflects the depth of al-Qa`ida's influence. "Our jihad is not limited to Pakistan or Afghanistan," Nazir explained. "Our jihad is a global jihad."[20] A "united" Pakistani Taliban waging a three-front global war against Pakistan, the Afghan government, and the United States and its allies in Afghanistan is undoubtedly in al-Qa`ida's interests.

Al-Qa`ida does not need to conduct bombings itself in order to be dangerous; in fact, al-Qa`ida is more likely to produce successful revolutionary movements when it defers to local groups to do the bulk of the fighting.

Conclusion

Al-Qa`ida recognizes the critical role Pakistan plays for the United States in its efforts to stabilize Afghanistan and the broader region. As Abu Yahya al-Libi noted this past April, "the United States, despite its strength and its developed equipment, cannot go forward or backward without the support of Pakistan in the war against Muslims in Afghanistan and Pakistan."[21] With that in mind, al-Qa`ida has redirected substantial energy toward promoting the cooperation and effectiveness of local Pakistani groups opposed to the Pakistani state. Al-Qa`ida has recognized that by promoting violence against this "near" enemy, it can inflict severe pain on U.S. efforts in Afghanistan. Al-Qa`ida aims to destabilize the Pakistani government, divert U.S. attention from the fight in Afghanistan, and undermine Islamabad's alliance with the United States. By rallying support for jihad in Pakistan, helping to facilitate attacks against the Pakistani state, and serving as a mediator, al-Qa`ida has positioned itself to play an important role within Pakistan in the future. The U.S. and

international community's focus on al-Qa`ida's "external" posture must therefore be accompanied by an increased focus on the group's "internal" posture and the implications of al-Qa`ida's willingness to take a supporting rather than primary role in the anti-government insurgency in Pakistan. Such techniques are more subtle and sophisticated than the activities generally expected of al-Qa`ida, and thus the U.S. policy response will have to be similarly nuanced.

Notes

1. The jihad in Afghanistan has primarily been led by Mullah Omar and the now Baluchistan-based Quetta *shura* council. There are, however, multiple actors involved in the insurgency, each responsible for different areas.

2. See, for example, OSC, "Second Round of 'Open Interview' with al-Zawahiri Released," April 22, 2008; "Al-Zawahiri Attacks Pakistani President, Urges Army to Topple Him," al-Jazira, March 25, 2004.

3. "Al-Zawahiri Praises Iraq's Al-Qa`ida, Urges Pakistani Soldiers to Disobey Orders," al-Sahab, April 29, 2006.

4. Usama bin Ladin, "Remove the Apostate," posted on the al-Buraq Islamic Network website, September 20, 2007.

5. The author identifies at least four such statements released since the *Lal Masjid* event.

6. OSC, "Abu Yahya al-Libi, 'No Room' for International Legitimacy," September 10, 2007.

7. Ibid.

8. Dr. Bruce Hoffman, discussion at the Combating Terrorism Center, U.S. Military Academy, March 4, 2009.

9. Christine Fair, "Militant Recruitment in Pakistan: Implications for Al-Qaeda and Other Organizations," *Studies in Conflict and Terrorism* 27:6 (2004): pp. 489–504.

10. "Attack on Musharraf; 5 Get Capital Punishment," *Pakistan Times*, August 28, 2005; "Arrests Follow Musharraf Attack," BBC, December 27, 2003.

11. B. Raman, "Jihadis Strike at Pak Army and ISI Again," South Asia Analysis Group, November 25, 2007.

12. "Seven Qaida Commanders Enter Pakistan," *Daily Times*, June 4, 2009; "ISI is Not a Rogue Agency: Riedel," *Dawn*, June 6, 2009. *The Long War Journal* claims that Prime Minister Gilani and General Kiyani were also targets. For more, see Bill Roggio, "Al Qaeda Operatives Targeting Pakistani Leaders," *The Long War Journal*, June 4, 2009.

13. Ibid. It should also be noted that significant disagreements exist among academics and counterterrorism professionals about the strength of the links between al-Qa`ida and Lashkar-i-Tayyiba.

14. An unknown Pakistani group, Fidayin-i-Islam, claimed responsibility for the attack. See "'Fedayeen' Claims Responsibility," *Dawn*, September 23, 2008.

15. The author thanks Vahid Brown for this point. Syed Saleem Shahzad, "Plot To Divide the Taliban Foiled," *Asia Times Online*, July 22, 2008.

16. Ibid.

17. Carlotta Gal, "Afghan and Pakistan Taliban Close Ranks," *New York Times*, March 26, 2009.

18. "Interview with the Amir of Mujihadeen in South Waziristan/ Mullah Nazir Ahmed," Jamia Hafsa Forum, April 7, 2009.

19. Ibid.

20. Ibid.

21. Abu Yahya al-Libi, "Sharpening the Blades of Battle Against the Government and Army of Pakistan," al-Fajr Media Center, April 30, 2009.

DON RASSLER is an Associate at the Combating Terrorism Center (CTC) at West Point, where he manages the Harmony Program and is developing the CTC's South Asian research program. Prior to joining the CTC, Mr. Rassler worked on intelligence, defense reform and NATO transformation projects for the Department of Defense as a Senior Consultant at Detica. He holds an M.A. in International Affairs from Columbia University's School of International and Public Affairs.

Al-Qaeda at 20 Dead or Alive?

PETER BERGEN

Two decades after al-Qaeda was founded in the Pakistani border city of Peshawar by Osama bin Laden and a handful of veterans of the war against the Soviets in Afghanistan, the group is more famous and feared than ever. But its grand project—to transform the Muslim world into a militant Islamist caliphate—has been, by any measure, a resounding failure.

In large part, that's because Osama bin Laden's strategy for arriving at this Promised Land is a fantasy. Al-Qaeda's leader prides himself on being a big-think strategist, but for all his brains, leadership skills and charisma, he has fastened on an overall strategy that is self-defeating.

Bin Laden's main goal is to bring about regime change in the Middle East and to replace the governments in Cairo and Riyadh with Taliban-style theocracies. He believes that the way to accomplish this is to attack the "far enemy" (the United States), then watch as the supposedly impious, U.S.-backed Muslim regimes he calls the "near enemy" crumble.

This might have worked if the United States had turned out to be a paper tiger that could sustain only a few blows from al-Qaeda. But it didn't. Bin Laden's analysis showed no understanding of the vital interests—oil, Israel and regional stability—that undergird U.S. engagement in the Middle East, let alone the intensity of American outrage that would follow the first direct attack on the continental United States since the British burned the White House in 1814.

In fact, bin Laden's plan resulted in the direct opposite of a U.S. withdrawal from the Middle East. The United States now occupies Iraq, and NATO soldiers patrol the streets of Kandahar, the old de facto capital of bin Laden's Taliban allies. Relations between the United States and most authoritarian Arab regimes, meanwhile, are stronger than ever, based on their shared goal of defeating violent Islamists out for American blood and the regimes' power.

For most leaders, such a complete strategic failure would require a rethinking. Not for bin Laden. He could have formulated a new policy after U.S. forces toppled the Taliban in the winter of 2001, having al-Qaeda and its allies directly attack the sclerotic near-enemy regimes; he could have told his followers that, in strictly practical terms, provoking the world's only superpower would clearly interfere with al-Qaeda's goal of establishing Taliban-style rule from Indonesia to Morocco.

Instead, bin Laden continues to conceive of the United States as his main foe, as he has explained in audio- and videotapes that he has released since 2001. At the same time, al-Qaeda has

fatally undermined its claim to be the true representative of all Muslims by killing thousands of them since Sept. 11, 2001. These two strategic blunders are the key reasons why bin Laden and his group will ultimately lose. But don't expect that defeat anytime soon. For now, al-Qaeda continues to gather strength, both as a terrorist/insurgent organization based along the Afghan-Pakistani border and as an ongoing model for violent Islamists around the globe.

So how strong—or weak—is al-Qaeda at 20? Earlier this year, a furious debate erupted in Washington between two influential counterterrorism analysts. On one side is a former CIA case officer, Marc Sageman, who says that the threat from al-Qaeda's core organization is largely over and warns that future attacks will come from the foot soldiers of a "leaderless jihad"—self-starting, homegrown radicals with no formal connection to bin Laden's cadre. On the other side of the debate stands Georgetown University professor Bruce Hoffman, who warns that al-Qaeda is on the march, not on the run.

This debate is hardly academic. If the global jihad has in fact become a leaderless one, terrorism will cease to be a top-tier U.S. national security problem and become a manageable, second-order threat, as it was for most of the 20th century. Leaderless organizations can't mount spectacular operations such as 9/11, which required years of planning and training. On the other hand, if al-Qaeda Central is as strong as Hoffman thinks it is, the United States will have to organize its policies in the Middle East, South Asia and at home around that threat for decades.

Sageman's view of the jihadist threat as local and leaderless is largely shared by key counterterrorism officials in Europe, who told me that they can't find any evidence of al-Qaeda operations in their countries. Baltasar Garzon, a judge who has investigated terrorist groups in Spain for the past decade, says that while bin Laden remains "a fundamental reference point for the al-Qaeda movement," he doesn't see any of the organization's fingerprints in his recent inquiries.

But this view is not shared by top counterterrorism officials in the United Kingdom and the United States. A 2007 U.S. National Intelligence Estimate concluded that al-Qaeda was growing more dangerous, not less.

Why the starkly differing views? Largely because U.S. and British officials are contending with an alarming new phenomenon, the deadly nexus developing between some militant British Muslims and al-Qaeda's new headquarters in Pakistan's lawless borderlands. The lesson of the July 2005 London subway bombings, the foiled 2006 scheme to bring down transatlantic jetliners and several other unnerving plots uncovered in the United Kingdom is that the bottom-up radicalization described by Sageman becomes really lethal only when the homegrown wannabes manage to make contact with the group that so worries Hoffman, al-Qaeda Central in Pakistan.

"Hotheads in a coffeehouse are a dime a dozen," said Michael Sheehan, who until 2006 was the deputy New York police commissioner responsible for counterterrorism. "Al-Qaeda Central is often the critical element in turning the hotheads into an actual capable cell." Which is why it's so worrisome that counterterrorism officials have noticed dozens of Europeans making their way to the tribal areas of Pakistan in the past couple of years.

That's a major shift. Until 2006, hardcore European jihadists would have traveled to Iraq. But the numbers doing so now have dwindled to almost zero, according to several European counterterrorism officials. That's because al-Qaeda's affiliate in Iraq has committed something tantamount to suicide.

Al-Qaeda in Iraq once held vast swaths of Sunni-dominated turf and helped spark a civil war by targeting Iraqi Shiites. But when the group imposed Taliban-style measures, such as banning smoking and shaving, on Iraq's Sunni population and started killing other insurgents who didn't share its ultra-fundamentalist views, other Sunnis turned against it. Today al-Qaeda in Iraq is dead, at least as an insurgent organization capable of imposing its will on the wider population. It can still perpetrate large-scale atrocities, of course, and could yet spoil Iraq's fragile truce by again attacking Iraqi Shiites. But for the moment, al-Qaeda in Iraq is on the run, demoralized and surrounded by enemies.

While that's good news for Iraq, there are alarming signs elsewhere. The border region of Pakistan and Afghanistan, an area where jihadists operate with something close to impunity, has become a magnet for foreign fighters. One particularly unwelcome development here: Al-Qaeda Central now exerts a great deal of ideological sway over Baitullah Mehsud, the new leader of the Taliban movement inside Pakistan, who has vowed to attack New York and London.

Next door in Afghanistan, the Taliban have also increasingly adopted bin Laden's worldview and tactics, which has helped them launch a dangerously effective insurgency based on sustained suicide attacks and the deft use of IEDs. And bin Laden's influence extends well beyond the Afghanistan-Pakistan theater. The same mainland European counterterrorism officials who are relieved not to be finding al-Qaeda Central cells in their own countries now worry that bin Laden's North African ally, al-Qaeda in the Islamic Maghreb, may be finding recruits among poorly integrated North African immigrants living in France, Belgium, Spain and Italy.

Al-Qaeda's war for hearts and minds goes on, too. Bin Laden once observed that 90 percent of his battle is waged in the media—and here, above all, he remains both relevant and cutting-edge. The most reliable guide to what al-Qaeda and the wider jihadist movement will do have long been bin Laden's public statements.

Since 9/11, bin Laden has issued more than two dozen video- and audiotapes, according to IntelCenter, a government contractor that tracks al-Qaeda's propaganda activities. Those messages have reached untold millions worldwide via TV, the Internet and newspapers. The tapes exhort al-Qaeda's followers to continue to kill Westerners and Jews, and some have also carried specific instructions for militant cells. In the past year, for instance, bin Laden has called for attacks on the Pakistani state—one of the reasons Pakistan saw more suicide attacks in 2007 than at any other time in its history.

Despite al-Qaeda's recent resurgence, I think it highly unlikely that the group will be able to attack inside the United States in the next five years. In the past, al-Qaeda terrorists trying to strike the U.S. homeland have had to slip inside from elsewhere, as the 9/11 hijackers did. No successful past plot has relied on al-Qaeda "sleeper cells" here, and there is little evidence that such cells exist today. Moreover, the United States is a much harder target than it was before 9/11. The U.S. government is on alert, as are ordinary citizens. (Just ask the would-be shoe-bomber, Richard Reid.)

Of course, homegrown terrorists inspired by al-Qaeda might carry out a small-bore attack inside the United States, although the U.S. Muslim community, which is far better integrated than its European counterparts, has produced few violent radicals. And al-Qaeda itself remains quite capable of attacking a wide range of U.S. interests overseas, killing U.S. soldiers in Iraq and Afghanistan and targeting U.S. embassies. But on balance, we have less to fear from al-Qaeda now than we did in 2001.

We would also be far better off if we managed to kill or capture al-Qaeda's innovative chief. So what is the U.S.-led hunt for bin Laden turning up? The short answer is nothing. Washington hasn't had a solid lead on him since radio intercepts placed him at the battle of Tora Bora in eastern Afghanistan in December 2001. U.S. intelligence officials widely assume that he is now in or near Pakistan's tribal areas—a particularly shrewd hiding place, according to Arthur Keller, a former CIA officer who ran a spy network there in 2006.

Keller told me that al-Qaeda's leaders have excellent operational security. "They have had a Darwinian education in what can give them away, and their tradecraft has improved as we have eliminated some of the less careful members of their organization," he noted. "They're hiding in a sea of people who are very xenophobic of outsiders, so it's a very, very tough nut to crack."

No matter what bin Laden's fate, Muslims around the world are increasingly taking a dim view of his group and its suicide operations. In the late 1990s, bin Laden was a folk hero to many Muslims. But since 2003, as al-Qaeda and its affiliates have killed Muslim civilians by the thousands from Casablanca to Kabul, support for bin Laden has nose-dived, according to Pew polls taken in key Muslim countries such as Indonesia and Pakistan.

At 20, al-Qaeda is losing its war, but its influence will live on. As Michael Scheuer, who founded the CIA's bin Laden unit in 1996, points out, "Their mission is accomplished: worldwide instigation and inspiration." To our grief, that legacy will endure, even after al-Qaeda is defeated.

PETER BERGEN is a fellow at both the New America Foundation and New York University's Center on Law and Security. He is the author of *The Osama bin Laden I Know*.

Three Pillars of Counterinsurgency

DR DAVID J. KILCULLEN[*]

Introduction

We meet today in the shadow of continuing counterinsurgencies that have cost thousands of lives and a fortune in financial, moral and political capital. And we meet under the threat of similar insurgencies to come. Any smart future enemy will likely sidestep our unprecedented superiority in traditional, force-on-force, state-on-state warfare. And so insurgency, including terrorism, will be our enemies' weapon of choice until we prove we can master it.[1] Like Bill Murray in *Groundhog Day,* we are going to live this day over, and over, and over again—until we get it right.

So we seek a common doctrine to integrate national power against the threat. This has happened before, it turns out.

The United States produced an inter-agency counterinsurgency doctrine in 1962. Called the *Overseas Internal Defense Policy* (OIDP),[2] it was "prepared by an Interdepartmental Committee consisting of representatives of State (Chair), DOD, JCS, USIA, CIA and AID."[3] It was approved under *National Security Action Memorandum 182* of 24 August 1962, signed by McGeorge Bundy[4] and overseen by a Special Group (Counter-Insurgency), comprising "the Chairman of the Joint Chiefs of Staff, the Deputy Secretary of Defense, the Director of Central Intelligence, the heads of AID and USIA, a staff member of the National Security Council, and . . . the Attorney General of the United States".[5] OIDP lays out a framework for whole-of-government counterinsurgency, assigns responsibilities and resources, and explains what each agency brings to the fight.

Why the history lesson? Because last time we tried this, it did not work very well. OIDP was classified, and while it informed senior leaders it filtered only fitfully down to the field. It was applied in only the minor campaigns of the day. And it lasted only until 1966. As Vietnam escalated, OIDP (used during the advisory phase of the war) was dropped and the campaign was handed off to the conventional military and the State Department's "A" Team of Europeanists and Cold Warriors.[6] And so, as many have observed, our problem is not that we lack doctrine but that we continually forget, relearn, discard our corporate knowledge, and treat as exceptional one of the most common forms of warfare.[7]

Today, things are even more complicated than in 1962. To be effective, we must marshal not only all agencies of the USG (and there are more than 17 agencies in the foreign policy arena alone[8]), but also all agencies of a host nation, multiple foreign allies and coalition partners, international institutions, non-government organizations of many national and political flavors, international and local media, religious and community groups, charities and businesses. Some have counterinsurgency doctrine that is more or less compatible with ours. Some have different doctrines, or none. Some reject the very notion of counterinsurgency—but all must collaborate if the conflict is to be resolved.

This means we need a way to generate purposeful collaboration between a host of actors we do not control. No doctrinal handbook will ever be flexible enough for such a fluid environment (though, something tells me, we will develop one anyway). Rather, we need an easily grasped mental model that helps individuals and agencies cooperate, creates platforms for collaboration, and forms a basis for improvisation. In conventional war we might call this an "operational design", or "commander's intent". I will call it a "model".

There are two parts to this model. The first is a description of the "conflict ecosystem" that forms the environment for 21st century counterinsurgency operations. The second is a tentative framework for whole-of-government counterinsurgency in that environment.

The Conflict Environment

An insurgency is a struggle for control over a contested political space, between a state (or group of states or occupying powers), and one or more popularly based, non-state challengers.[9] Insurgencies are popular uprisings that grow from, and are conducted through pre-existing social networks (village, tribe, family, neighborhood, political or religious party) and exist in a complex social, informational and physical environment.[10]

Think of this environment as a sort of "conflict ecosystem".

It includes many independent but interlinked actors, each seeking to maximize their own survivability and advantage in a

---

* Chief Strategist, Office of the Coordinator for Counterterrorism, U.S. Department of State. Correspondence address: 2201 C St NW Washington D.C. 20520 e-mail kilcullendj@state.gov This presentation represents the author's personal opinions only.

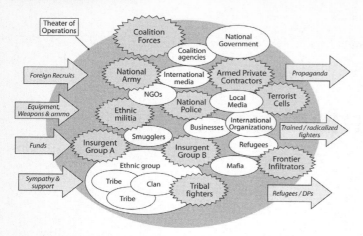

Figure 1 The Conflict Ecosystem.

chaotic, combative environment. Pursuing the ecological metaphor, these actors are constantly evolving and adapting, some seeking a secure niche while others seek to become "top predator" or scavenge on the environment. Some actors existed in the environment before the conflict. They include government, ethnic, tribal, clan or community groups, social classes, urban and rural populations, and economic and political institutions. In normal times, these actors behave in a collaborative or competitive way: but now, due to the internal power struggle, they are combative and destructive. The relatively healthy competition and creative tension that sustains normal society has spun out of control, and the conflict threatens to destroy the society.

This new state of the environment also produces new actors. These include local armed organizations, and foreign armed groups drawn into the conflict from outside. Often, that includes intervening counterinsurgent forces such as ourselves. Foreign terrorists are also increasingly "swarming" from one conflict to another in pursuit of their global agenda. In addition, the conflict produces refugees, displaced persons and sometimes mass migration. It creates economic dislocation, leading to unemployment and crime, and creating armed groups such as bandits, narcotics traffickers, smugglers, couriers and black marketeers.

This might be illustrated graphically as in Figure 1.

It is critically important to realize that we, the intervening counterinsurgent, are not outside this ecosystem, looking in at a Petrie dish of unsavory microbes. Rather, we are inside the system. The theater of operations is not a supine, inert medium on which we practise our operational art. Rather it is a dynamic, living system that changes in response to our actions and requires continuous balancing between competing requirements.

Where the counterinsurgent differs from other actors is largely a matter of intent. Like other players, we seek to maximize our survivability and influence, and extend the space which we control. But unlike some other players (the insurgents, for example) our intent is to reduce the system's destructive, combative elements and return it to its "normal" state of competitive interaction. This has sometimes been expressed as "bringing democracy" but, of course, democratic processes without the foundation of a robust civil society may simply create instability

and perpetuate conflict. Thus, whatever our political objective, our functional objective is to impose a measure of control on the overall environment. But in such a complex, multi-actor environment, "control" does not mean imposing order through unquestioned dominance, so much as achieving collaboration towards a set of shared objectives.

If this sounds soft, non-lethal and non-confrontational, it is not: this is a life-and-death competition in which the loser is marginalized, starved of support and ultimately destroyed. The actors mount a lethal struggle to control the population. There is no known way of doing counterinsurgency without inflicting casualties on the enemy: there is always a lot of killing, one way or another. But killing the enemy is not the sole objective—and in a counterinsurgency environment, operating amongst the people, force is always attended by collateral damage, alienated populations, feuds and other unintended consequences. Politically, the more force you have to use, the worse the campaign is going. Marginalizing and out-competing a range of challengers, to achieve control over the overall socio-political space in which the conflict occurs, is the true aim.

Remembering that this is simply a theoretical model, and thus a brutal oversimplification of an infinitely complex reality, how might we seek to operate in this environment?

A Framework for Inter-Agency Counterinsurgency

Obviously enough, you cannot command what you do not control. Therefore, "unity of command" (between agencies or among government and non-government actors) means little in this environment. Instead, we need to create "unity of effort" at best, and collaboration or deconfliction at least. This depends less on a shared command and control hierarchy, and more on a shared diagnosis of the problem, platforms for collaboration, information sharing and deconfliction. Each player must understand the others' strengths, weaknesses, capabilities and objectives, and inter-agency teams must be structured for versatility (the ability to perform a wide variety of tasks) and agility (the ability to transition rapidly and smoothly between tasks).

A possible framework for inter-agency counterinsurgency operations, as a means to creating such a shared diagnosis, is the "three pillars" model depicted at Figure 2.

This is a framework, not a template. It helps people see where their efforts fit into a campaign, rather than telling them what to do in a given situation. It provides a basis for measuring progress and is an aid to collaboration rather than an operational plan. And clearly, it applies not only to counterinsurgency but also to peace operations, Stabilization and Reconstruction, and complex humanitarian emergencies. The model is structured as a base (Information), three pillars (Security, Political and Economic) and a roof (Control). This approach builds on "classical" counterinsurgency theory, but also incorporates best practices that have emerged through experience in peacekeeping, development, fragile states and complex emergencies in the past several decades.

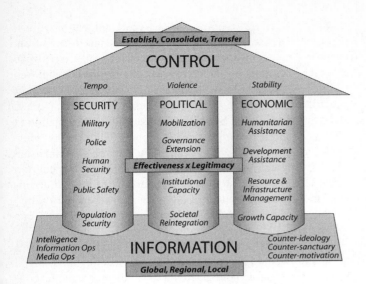

Figure 2 Inter-agency counterinsurgency framework.

Within this "three pillars" model, information is the basis for all other activities. This is because perception is crucial in developing control and influence over population groups. Substantive security, political and economic measures are critical but to be effective they must rest upon, and integrate with a broader information strategy. Every action in counterinsurgency sends a message; the purpose of the information campaign is to consolidate and unify this message. It includes intelligence collection, analysis and distribution, information operations,[11] media operations (including public diplomacy) and measures to counter insurgent motivation, sanctuary and ideology. It also includes efforts to understand the environment through census data, public opinion polling, collection of cultural and "human terrain" information in denied areas. And it involves understanding the effects of our operations on the population, adversaries and the environment. Clearly, not all actors will collaborate in these efforts; but until an information base is developed, the other pillars of counterinsurgency cannot be effective. Importantly, the information campaign has to be conducted at a global, regional and local level—because modern insurgents draw upon global networks of sympathy, support, funding and recruitment.

Resting on this base are three pillars of equal importance. Indeed, as Figure 2 illustrates, unless they are developed in parallel, the campaign becomes unbalanced: too much economic assistance with inadequate security, for example, simply creates an array of soft targets for the insurgents. Similarly, too much security assistance without political consensus or governance simply creates more capable armed groups. In developing each pillar, we measure progress by gauging effectiveness (capability and capacity) and legitimacy (the degree to which the population accepts that government actions are in its interest). This approach is familiar to anyone who has participated in a USAID conflict assessment, or worked on fragile states or complex humanitarian emergencies. It has a solid basis in empirical field experience in the aid and development community.[12]

The security pillar comprises military security (securing the population from attack or intimidation by guerrillas, bandits, terrorists or other armed groups) and police security (community policing, police intelligence or "Special Branch" activities, and paramilitary police field forces). It also incorporates human security, building a framework of human rights, civil institutions and individual protections, public safety (fire, ambulance, sanitation, civil defense) and population security. This "pillar" most engages military commanders' attention, but of course military means are applied across the model, not just in the security domain, while civilian activity is critically important in the security pillar also. Clearly, also, security is *not* the basis for economic and political progress (as some commanders and political leaders argue). Nor does security depend on political and economic progress (as others assert). Rather, all three pillars must develop in parallel and stay in balance, while being firmly based in an effective information campaign.

The political pillar focuses on mobilizing support. As for the other pillars, legitimacy and effectiveness are the principal dimensions in which it is developed. It comprises efforts to mobilize stakeholders in support of the government, marginalize insurgents and other groups, extend governance and further the rule of law. A key element is the building of institutional capacity in all agencies of government and non-government civil institutions, and social re-integration efforts such as the disarming, demobilization and reintegration (DDR)[13] of combatants. Like the security pillar for military forces, the political pillar is the principal arena for diplomatic and civil governance assistance efforts—although, again, civil agencies play a significant role in the security and economic pillars also.

The economic pillar includes a near-term component of immediate humanitarian relief, as well as longer-term programs for development assistance across a range of agricultural, industrial and commercial activities. Assistance in effective resource and infrastructure management, including construction of key infrastructure systems, is critically important. And tailoring efforts to the society's capacity to absorb spending, as well as efforts to increase absorptive capacity, underpin other development activities.

These three pillars support the overarching objective of control, which—as we have seen—is the counterinsurgent's fundamental aim. The aim is not (as some have argued) simply to create stability. Stability may actually not be our objective, as the President emphasized in his recent speech to the United Nations General Assembly, when he observed that "on 9/11, we realized that years of pursuing stability to promote peace left us with neither. Instead, the lack of freedom made the Middle East an incubator for terrorism. The pre-9/11 status quo was dangerous and unacceptable."[14] Moreover, even if we do seek stability, we seek it as a means to an end, a step on the way to regaining control over an out-of-control environment, rather than as an end in itself.

In achieving control, we typically seek to manage the tempo of activity, the level of violence, and the degree of stability in the environment. The intent is not to reduce violence to zero or to kill every insurgent, but rather to return the overall system to normality—noting that "normality" in one society may look different from normality in another. In each case, we seek not only to establish control, but also to consolidate that control and then transfer it to permanent, effective and legitimate institutions.

Operationalizing the "Three Pillars"

If this model represents a possible framework for inter-agency counterinsurgency, how might we apply it in practice? Arguably, the basis for doing so exists already, in National Security Presidential Directive 44 (NSPD 44) which authorizes the creation of civilian capabilities for stabilization and reconstruction. True enough, the words "insurgency", "insurgent" or "counterinsurgency" do not appear in NSPD 44, but it clearly envisages the need to deploy integrated whole-of-government capabilities in hostile environments.

Personnel policies to develop human capital also require effort, but might be less of a burden than we currently envisage. Rather than sweeping policy changes, we simply need relatively minor modifications such as the ability to identify and record civilian officials with appropriate skills for conflict environments, track them throughout their careers, provide financial and legal cover for deployments, give them the necessary individual and team training to operate in hostile areas, and create career structures (perhaps in the form of "additional skills identifiers") that recognize time in conflict zones as equivalent, for career purposes, to time in standard postings.

Organizations, again, perhaps need less modification than we might imagine. We already have a near-perfect instrument for inter-agency counterinsurgency in the form of the Country Team, a 1950s innovation that has proven highly effective in adapting to complex environments. It remains the only standing inter-agency organization in the USG that can deliver integrated whole-of-government effects. It is thus an extremely valuable tool that we should be working to improve even further. Other organizational approaches, such as the Provincial Reconstruction Team (PRT), provide a basis for adaptation. PRTs were invented in 2003 in Afghanistan and have often been treated as a panacea for civilian counterinsurgency. They are not. But careful analysis of why PRTs succeed in some areas and do less well in others can help tailor approaches for specific situations. In this context, the efforts of private firms like Aegis Defence Services, whose Reconstruction Operations Centres and Regional Liaison Teams are flexible inter-agency organizations that have worked extremely well in Iraq, are worth emulating. Similarly, while NSPD 44 envisions a civilian reserve corps deploying field personnel and middle-management into conflict environments, we could also use it to establish a smaller expert cadre of advisors who could assist Ambassadors, Country Teams or force commanders.

Systems capabilities (electronic and otherwise) require significant work. These might include skills registers, personnel databases, and field capabilities such as communications, transportation and protection equipment. We could also benefit from electronic platforms to enable sharing of information between agencies, including non-government organizations. ReliefWeb is a good example of this, allowing multiple agencies to post and share information, identify opportunities to collaborate, and deconflict efforts. Security protocols allow information to be shared only with authorized participants, while public information can be widely disseminated. ReliefWeb's Afghanistan page (http://www.reliefweb.int/rw/dbc.nsf/doc104?OpenForm&rc=3&cc=afg) covers many components of the "three pillars" model, in the context of a complex emergency. Building on this would be less difficult, and less expensive, than one might think.

Training and education (for civil, military, and non-government personnel) would also create shared understanding, and spread best practices throughout a "counterinsurgency community"—again helping us achieve collaboration across a wide variety of players whom we cannot control. Besides specific educational outcomes, these programs develop personal relationships and erode institutional paranoia. Specific training needs include the development of civilian teams capable of "early entry" into environments not yet secured by military or police forces, with the movement, communications and self-protection skills and equipment to operate in these areas. Other needs are a capability for "denied area ethnography" to collect human terrain and population data for effective planning, and education for military leaders in the significant body of expertise that aid, humanitarian assistance and development communities have built up over time.

Finally, doctrine—a common USG handbook, common funding and legal authorities, and common operating standards—might be useful. And so we come full circle, to the OIDP of 1962. But it should now be clear that, without a common mental model for the environment and the pillars of a counterinsurgency effort, and without the personnel, organizations, systems, training and education elements of capability in place, merely producing a doctrinal handbook is likely to be as little use in 2006 as it was in 1962.

Conclusion

These thoughts are tentative; they need a large amount of work. The "three pillars" model is clearly incorrect—all models are, in that they are systematic oversimplifications of reality. But this, or something like it, might be a basis for further development.

And time is of the essence: regardless of the outcome of current campaigns, our enemies will keep applying these methods until we show we can defeat them. Thus, this is one of the most important efforts that our generation of national security professionals is likely to attempt. Our friends and colleagues' lives, the security of our nation and its allies, and our long-term prospect of victory in the War on Terrorism may, in part, depend on it.

Notes

1. United States Department of Defense, *Quadrennial Defense Review Report 2006,* U.S. Government Printing Office, Washington D.C. 2006, Chapter 1 for a detailed exposition of this argument.

2. See State Department, Office of the Historian, *Foreign Relations of the United States, 1961–63,* Volume VIII, Document 106, U.S. Government Printing Office, Washington D.C., 1990, pp. 382–383

3. *Ibid.* p. 3

4. *Ibid,* Document 105.

5. Charles Maechling, "Camelot, Robert Kennedy, and Counter-Insurgency: A Memoir", in *The Virginia Quarterly Review,* at http://www.vqronline.org/printmedia.php/prmMediaID/7976 accessed Sep 06.

6. *Ibid.*

7. See Robert R. Tomes, "Relearning Counterinsurgency Warfare" in *Parameters,* Spring 2004, pp.16–28. See also John A. Nagl, *Learning to East Soup with a Knife: Counterinsurgency Lessons from Malaya and Vietnam,* 2nd Edition, University of Chicago Press, Chicago, 2005; Robert M. Cassidy, "Back to the Street Without Joy: Counterinsurgency Lessons from Vietnam and Other Small Wars" in *Parameters,* Summer 2004 pp. 73–83; and N. Aylwin-Foster, "Changing the Army for Counterinsurgency Operations" in *Military Review,* November–December 2005, pp. 2–15.

8. Including, but not limited to, the Department of State, Agency for International Development, Department of Homeland Security, Department of Justice, Federal Bureau of Investigation, Department of Treasury, Central Intelligence Agency, Department of Commerce (International Trade Administration), Department of Defense, Department of Energy (National Nuclear Security Administration), Department of Labor (Bureau of International Labor Affairs), International Trade Commission, National Security Agency, National Security Council, United States Trade Representative, etc.

9. This definition follows that put forward by Gordon H. McCormick, who suggests that "an insurgency is a struggle for power (over a political space) between a state (or occupying power) and one or more organized, popularly based internal challengers". (McCormick, "Things Fall Apart: The 'Endgame Dynamics' of Internal Wars," RAND, draft paper, forthcoming, p. 2). But, to take into account the trans-national nature of several contemporary insurgencies, I have replaced McCormick's notion of a single state entity facing an internal challenger with the broader concept of a state *or group of states* confronting one or more (internal or external) *non-state* challengers.

10. I am indebted to Dr. Gordon McCormick of the Naval Postgraduate School, Monterrey, and to Colonel Derek Harvey for insights into the "small world, scale-free" aspects of insurgent social networks and the enduring influence of the pre-war Iraqi oligarchy on the current Iraqi insurgency.

11. Including psychological operations, electronic warfare, computer network operations, military deception and operations security. See U.S. Department of Defense, *Joint Publication 3–13 Information Operations,* 13 February 2006.

12. For a description of this approach, see United States Agency for International Development, *Fragile States Strategy,* January 2005, PD-ACA-999, USAID, Washington D.C. 2005, p. 3 ff.

13. See United Nations, Department of Peacekeeping Operations, *Disarmament, Demobilization and Reintegration of ex-Combatants: Principles and Guidelines,* United Nations, New York, 1999, available online at http://www.un.org/Depts/dpko/lessons/DD&R.pdf

14. See The White House, "President Bush Addresses United Nations General Assembly" at http://www.whitehouse.gov/infocus/mideast/ accessed September 2006.

From *U.S. Government Counterinsurgency Conference,* September 2006. Public domain.

UNIT 8

Contemporary Foreign Policy Debates

Unit Selections

Key Points to Consider

- According to Tom H. Johnson and M. Chris Mason, what has to change for U.S. engagement in Afghanistan to be successful?

- Why do you agree or disagree with Johnson and Mason's assessment that such an approach would not require more military troops?

- Do you agree or disagree with Stephen Biddle's claim that there is now a bipartisan consensus about U.S. policy for Iraq and Afghanistan and only partisan disagreements about the pace of withdrawals from Iraq or when and how to negotiate with elements of the Taliban in Afghanistan?

Student Website

www.mhhe.com/cls

Internet References

Iraq Web Links
http://www.usip.org/library/regions/iraq.html

Iraq Dispatches
http://dahrjamailiraq.com

ArabNet
http://www.arab.net

The United States' military progress in Iraq during 2007 occurred at the same time that attacks on U.S. and NATO military personnel increased dramatically in Afghanistan. By the spring of 2008, more international troops had died in Afghanistan than in Iraq. The 40-nation international coalition is much broader in Afghanistan. Half of the U.S. forces operate under NATO command and all are struggling to cope with a resurgence of Taliban attacks that are becoming increasingly complex, and deadly. In early November of 2008, a Taliban attack on a NATO supply convoy on the Pakistani side temporarily closed traffic through Torkharm and caused NATO forces to seek a safer, alternate route through the European Caucasus and Central Europe. The increased Taliban attacks in Afghanistan in recent years have shown a remarkable similarity to the same suicide and IED bomb attacks as were used against U.S. troops in Iraq. An important difference between Iraq and Afghanistan today is that the Taliban insurgency operates in every province and controls many districts, including areas surrounding the capital. The Taliban have also formed a parallel government that includes websites with 24-hour propaganda that rivals many Western organizations.

While Barak Obama campaigned on a pledge to bring most U.S. troops home from Iraq, his position in Afghanistan was less clear during the campaign. After winning the election, in March, 2009, U.S. President Obama approved additional troop increases to Afghanistan and declared that the U.S. strategy was to defeat the Taliban. However, by summer his newly appointed head general in Afghanistan, Army General Stanley McChrystal, after completing a strategic review, warned the President and Congress that the security situation was deteriorating so fast that he needed 40,000 more troops or else there was a risk that the Taliban might take control of the country. McChrystal also recommended more resources for training more Afghan military and police and that a thousand more civilian experts should be hired to help with development projects designed to win the hearts and minds of rural Afghans. President Obama and his national security team engaged in extensive examination of alternative options after receiving McChrystal's recommendations.

By the fall of 2009 the situation on the ground had become much more complicated in the region as the deeply entrenched nature of al-Qaeda presence in Pakistan had come to light with the fierce resistance that Pakistani military troops faced as they tried to penetrate certain parts of the Tribal Trust areas where al-Qaeda had operated without any constraints for years. What to do about Taliban and al-Qaeda controlled areas in Pakistan became intertwined with the requested massive troop build up in Afghanistan. The political context also became more complicated after a UN-led review commission declared the first round of voting for a new Afghanistan President was so corrupt that a second round of Presidential elections was required. President Karzai, who received less than 50 percent of the vote during the first round despite the massive cheating, only agreed to a run-off election after extensive outside pressure. As the November 7th presidential election runoff approached, the Taliban increased the number and location of attacks. October of 2009 was the deadliest month for U.S. forces since the war began in late 2001

© The McGraw-Hill Companies, Inc./John Flournoy, photographer

as 56 American military lost their lives. Allied forces, notably the British and German forces, also experienced heightened casualties and mounting pressures at home to withdraw during 2009. Opposition to U.S. air strikes in Afghanistan and Pakistan that killed civilians was another complicating factor, especially in Pakistan given it's key role in the U.S. military efforts in the region. In response to local tribal leaders' complaints and growing international opposition, General McChrystal's new military strategy gives priority to avoiding civilian casualties in U.S. air strikes in Afghanistan, places more attention on winning the hearts and minds of villages in areas dominated by the Taliban, and emphasizing more development projects designed to wean many Afghan farmers from growing and selling heroin.

As violence increased, additional ideas about U.S. policy options were debated more widely in the United States. In September, after General McChrystal's recommendations became public, Vice President Biden declared that military victory was tied to the legitimacy of the Kabul government and that it was premature to greatly increase the U.S. troop presence in the country. He recommended a scaled down military strategy that focused on defeating al-Qaeda rather than the Taliban. Still other analysts and policy makers recommended trying to split the Taliban in order to negotiate an agreement with Taliban leaders who were not necessarily supporters of al-Qaeda. By the end of 2009 a few former military personnel, with extensive experience in Afghanistan and/or Iraq, were publically advocating declaring victory in both countries and bringing U.S. military troops home before these conflicts became Obama's "Vietnam."

The split between Obama's military advisers, who all backed the counterinsurgency plan and massive troop increase recommended by General McChrystal and the more modest troop increase associated with the counterterrorism proposals backed by Vice President Biden and others among Obama's civilian advisers seemed to encourage the President to search for a compromise option. One compromise option is to blend the two approaches by emphasizing counterterrorism in the north and some parts of western Afghanistan and an expanded counterinsurgency effort in the south and east. Prior to making his decision, Obama asked for a province-by-province review of the country to determine which areas can be managed effectively by local levels. By early November the president appeared committed to adding at least 10,000 to 15,000 troops in Afghanistan in order to increase the U.S. ability to train Afghan army and police. The current plan calls for the United States to double the size of the Afghan army and police forces to about 400,000 as quickly as possible so they can take over security responsibilities.

Many of the policy debates and options being considered by national policy makers during the summer and fall of 2009 are discussed in the two articles contained in this section. In "All Counterinsurgency Is Local," Thomas H. Johnson and M. Chris Mason argue that the U.S. engagement in Afghanistan is foundering because of the endemic failure to engage and protect rural villages, and to immunize them against insurgency. They argue that the best way to reverse the U.S. fortunes in Afghanistan is for the United States to reconfigure its operations, creating small development and security teams posted at new compounds in every district in the south and east of the country. Johnson and Mason outline why they believe this approach would not necessarily require adding troops but rather 200 district-based teams of 100 people or 20,000 personnel. Their contention is that such teams would be able replace many U.S. troops deployed today.

Stephen Biddle argues that there is already the outlines of a bipartisan consensus of U.S. policy for Iraq and Afghanistan and that much of the debate today are partisan disagreements over details such as the pace of withdrawals from Iraq and when and how to negotiate with elements of the Taliban.

Since the late summer of 2009, U.S. military planners have accepted estimates that a successful counterinsurgency campaign in Afghanistan will require 40,000 more U.S. troops, an extensive civilian component, similar to the one outlined by Johnson and Mason, and a protracted strategy designed to separate civilians from fighters in areas currently controlled by the Taliban. One problem is that the United States does not have enough troops to deploy immediately. It will take nearly a year to deploy 40,000 U.S. troops to Afghanistan even if Obama approved the request. In a similar vein, it has proven difficult to recruit enough experienced civilian personnel to fill the positions outlined by the new counterinsurgency strategy. While U.S. and Afghan troops are now training together at a new Counterinsurgency University in Kabul, experts agree that it will take several years for the new Afghan military and police to take the lead in fighting the Taliban and maintaining stability in areas the Taliban may have only made a tactical withdrawal from until national government forces or foreign military personnel leave the area. It also remains uncertain whether the American public will support a protracted U.S. presence in Afghanistan.

All Counterinsurgency Is Local

Prosecuting the war in Afghanistan from provincial capitals has been disastrous; we need to turn our military strategy inside out.

THOMAS H. JOHNSON AND M. CHRIS MASON

June was the deadliest month for the U.S. military in Afghanistan since the invasion in October 2001. July became the second straight month in which casualties exceeded those in Iraq, where four times as many U.S. troops are on the ground. More Americans have been killed in Afghanistan since the invasion began than in the first nine years of the Vietnam War, from 1956 to 1964.

As in Vietnam, the U.S. has never lost a tactical engagement in Afghanistan, and this tactical success is still often conflated with strategic progress. Yet the Taliban insurgency grows more intense and gains more popular traction each year. More and more, the American effort in Afghanistan resembles the Vietnam War—with its emphasis on body counts and air strikes, its cross-border sanctuaries, and its daily tactical victories that never affected the slow and eventually decisive erosion of rural support for the counterinsurgency.

As the Russian ambassador to Afghanistan, Zamir Kabulov, noted in a blunt interview with the BBC in May, the current military engagement is also beginning to look like the Soviets' decade-long Afghan adventure, which ended ignominiously in 1989. That intervention, like the current one, was based on a strategy of administering and securing Afghanistan from urban centers such as Kabul and the provincial capitals. The Soviets held all the provincial capitals, just as we do, and sought to exert influence from there. The mujahideen stoked insurgency in the rural areas of the Pashtun south and east, just as the Taliban do now.

The backbone of the international effort since 2003—extending the reach of the central government—is precisely the wrong strategy.

The U.S. engagement in Afghanistan is foundering because of the endemic failure to engage and protect rural villages, and to immunize them against insurgency. Many analysts have called for more troops inside the country, and for more effort to eliminate Taliban sanctuaries outside it, in neighboring Pakistan. Both developments would be welcome. Yet neither would solve the central problem of our involvement: the paradigm that has formed the backbone of the international effort since 2003—extending the reach of the central government—is in fact precisely the wrong strategy.

National government has never much mattered in Afghanistan. Only once in its troubled history has the country had something like the system of strong central government that's mandated by the current constitution. That was under the "Iron Emir," Abdur Rehman, in the late 19th century, and Rehman famously maintained control by building towers of skulls from the heads of all who opposed him, a tactic unavailable to the current president, Hamid Karzai.

Politically and strategically, the most important level of governance in Afghanistan is neither national nor regional nor provincial. Afghan identity is rooted in the *woleswali:* the districts within each province that are typically home to a single clan or tribe. Historically, unrest has always bubbled up from this stratum—whether against Alexander, the Victorian British, or the Soviet Union. Yet the *woleswali* are last, not first, in U.S. military and political strategy.

Large numbers of U.S. and NATO troops are now heavily concentrated in Kabul, Kandahar, and other major cities. Thousands of U.S. personnel are stationed at Bagram Air Force Base, for instance, which is complete with Burger King, Dairy Queen, and a shopping center, but is hundreds of miles from the heart of the insurgency. Meanwhile, the military's contact with villagers in remote areas where the Taliban operate is rare, typically brief, and almost always limited to daylight hours.

The Taliban are well aware that the center of gravity in Afghanistan is the rural Pashtun district and village, and that Afghan army and coalition forces are seldom seen there. With one hand, the Taliban threaten tribal elders who do not welcome them. With the other, they offer assistance. (As one U.S. officer recently noted, they're "taking a page from the Hezbollah organizations in Lebanon, with their own public works to assist the tribes in villages that are deep in the inaccessible regions of the country. This helps support their cause with the population, making it hard to turn the population in support of the Afghan government and the coalition.")

The rural Pashtun south has its own systems of tribal governance and law, and its people don't want Western styles of either. But nor are they predisposed to support the Taliban, which espouses an alien and intolerant form of Islam, and goes against the grain of traditional respect for elders and decision by consensus. Re-empowering the village councils of elders and restoring their community leadership is the only way to recreate the traditional check against the powerful political network of rural mullahs, who have been radicalized by the Taliban. But the elders won't commit to opposing the Taliban if they and their families are vulnerable to Taliban torture and murder, and they can hardly be blamed for that.

To reverse its fortunes in Afghanistan, the U.S. needs to fundamentally reconfigure its operations, creating small development and security teams posted at new compounds in every district in the south and east of the country. This approach would not necessarily require adding troops, although that would help—200 district-based teams of 100 people each would require 20,000 personnel, one-third of the 60,000 foreign troops currently in the country.

Each new compound would become home to roughly 60 to 70 NATO security personnel, 30 to 40 support staff to manage logistics and supervise local development efforts, and an additional 30 to 40 Afghan National Army soldiers. The troops would provide a steady security presence, strengthen the position of tribal elders, and bolster the district police. Today, Afghan police often run away from the superior firepower of attacking Taliban forces. It's hard to fault them—more than 900 police were killed in such attacks last year alone. But with better daily training and help only minutes away, local police would be far more likely to put up a good fight, and win. Indirectly, the daily presence of embedded police trainers would also prevent much of the police corruption that fuels resentment against the government. And regular contact at the district and village levels would greatly improve the collection and analysis of intelligence.

Perhaps most important, district-based teams would serve as the primary organization for Afghan rural development. Currently, "Provincial Reconstruction Teams," based in each provincial capital, are responsible for the U.S. military's local development efforts. These teams have had no strategic impact on the insurgency, because they are too thin on the ground—the ratio of impoverished Afghan Pashtuns to provincial reconstruction teams is roughly a million to one. Few teams are able to visit every district in their province even once a month; it's no wonder that rural development has been marred by poor design and ineffective execution.

Local teams with on-site development personnel—"District Development Teams," if you will—could change all that, and also serve to support nonmilitary development projects. State Department and USAID personnel, along with medics, veterinarians, engineers, agricultural experts, hydrologists, and so on, could live on the local compounds and work in their districts daily, building trust and confidence.

Deploying relatively small units in numerous forward positions would undoubtedly put more troops in harm's way. But the Taliban have not demonstrated the ability to overrun international elements of this size, and the teams could be mutually reinforcing. (Air support would be critical.) Ultimately, we have to accept a certain amount of risk; you can't beat a rural insurgency without a rural security presence.

As long as the compounds are discreetly sited, house Afghan soldiers to provide the most visible security presence, and fly the Afghan flag, they need not exacerbate fears of foreign occupation. Instead, they would reinforce the country's most important, most neglected political units; strengthen the tribal elders; win local support; and reverse the slow slide into strategic failure.

THOMAS H. JOHNSON directs the Program for Culture and Conflict Studies at the Naval Postgraduate School at Monterey, California. M. CHRIS MASON is a senior fellow at the Center for Advanced Defense Studies, in Washington, D.C. He recently served in the U.S. Foreign Service on the Pakistan-Afghanistan border.

Afghanistan, Iraq, and U.S. Strategy in 2009

STEPHEN BIDDLE

A time traveler from 2007 would be shocked by the degree of consensus in today's defense debate. Just two years ago, a bitter partisan split over Iraq dominated American politics and fueled a major Republican defeat in midterm elections. Today, by contrast, the basic outlines of U.S. policy for both Iraq and Afghanistan are matters of substantial bipartisan consensus. Most Democrats, most Republicans, and the military all agree that there should be withdrawals from Iraq, reinforcements for Afghanistan, a buildup of indigenous Afghan security forces, an application of classical counterinsurgency (COIN) methods for U.S. forces in Afghanistan, and pressure on Islamabad to counter Taliban safe havens in northwest Pakistan. Likewise, most now agree that the Bush Administration's ambitions for modern, centralized democracy in Afghanistan were over-optimistic and will need to be scaled back at least for a long time; that negotiations with elements of the Taliban coalition could be useful in shrinking the opposition by inducing key components to stand down; and that progress in such negotiations will be limited until reinforcements turn the military tide. A number of official strategy reviews are ongoing, but the broad directions of the U.S. war effort are thus matters of widespread agreement already, and are unlikely to be challenged fundamentally by any of the reviews now underway.

For now, the debate is mostly over the details. And some of these details are very important. In particular, the *pace* of withdrawals from Iraq and buildups in Afghanistan is contested, and could strongly affect outcomes in either theater. There are also a number of key elements of the emerging consensus policy for Afghanistan that have been understudied and deserve closer scrutiny than they have yet received, including the sustainability of a larger Afghan security force; the integration of military and political strategies; tribal outreach; and the role of economic development assistance.

The biggest questions, however, lie on the horizon. A small but growing minority is calling for withdrawing U.S. troops from Afghanistan rather than reinforcing them. Comparisons between Afghanistan and Vietnam are becoming more common, as are references to quagmires, Russian defeats, or British failures. *Newsweek*'s February 9 cover is headlined "Obama's Vietnam."[1] If security trends in Afghanistan improve quickly, this nascent antiwar movement will remain small. But violence in Afghanistan is likely to get worse in the near term, not better. Indeed, a reinforced U.S. posture employing classical COIN techniques is likely to increase near-term casualties on both sides, much as it did in Iraq in 2007.

Classical COIN trades higher losses in the short run for stability and decreased violence in the longer run; where it works, this is a good bargain. But even when it works, it looks bad early. And this will promote a growing debate over the wisdom of the U.S. commitment to Afghanistan and thus a dispute over more fundamental issues than those in play today.

Given this, my testimony is intended to serve two purposes. I begin with the fundamental debate to come: is the war in Afghanistan worth waging? I argue that the antiwar position has merit, but that the case for reinforcement is stronger. I then turn to the largest of the questions now under active debate: how quickly should resources be transferred from Iraq to Afghanistan? Here I argue that slow is best—that gradual transfers make sense, but rapid ones risk more than they promise. And the most important near term improvement we could make in Afghanistan could well be a "political surge" with an emphasis on pressuring the Karzai government to reduce its corruption and reform its administration, but without requiring near-term troop counts that will be hard to provide without undermining the prospects for stability in Iraq. Success in Afghanistan is worth pursuing and will eventually require larger reinforcements, but in the near term it may be necessary to make do with smaller forces than we would like while working much harder to compel real political reform in Kabul.

I. Is the War in Afghanistan Worth Waging?

The first question—is the war in Afghanistan worth waging—rests on three sub-issues: what is at stake, what will it cost to pursue those stakes, and what is the likelihood that the pursuit will succeed?

The Stakes

The stakes in Afghanistan are high, but not unlimited. The United States has two primary national interests in this conflict: that Afghanistan not become a haven for terrorism against the United States, and that chaos in Afghanistan not destabilize its neighbors, especially Pakistan.

We invaded Afghanistan in the first place to destroy the al-Qaeda safe haven there, and its use in the 9-11 attacks clearly justified this. But al-Qaeda central is no longer based in Afghanistan, nor has it been since early 2002. Bin Laden and his core operation are, by all accounts, now based across the border in Pakistan's

Federally Administered Tribal Areas (FATA). The Taliban movement in Afghanistan is clearly linked with al-Qaeda and sympathetic to it, but there is little evidence of al-Qaeda infrastructure within Afghanistan today that could threaten the U.S. homeland in any direct way. If today's Afghan government collapsed, if it were replaced with a neo-Taliban regime, or if the Taliban were able to secure real political control over some major contiguous fraction of Afghan territory then perhaps al-Qaeda could re-establish a real haven there. But this risk is shared with a wide range of other weak states in many parts of the world, from Yemen to Somalia to Djibouti to Eritrea to Sudan to the Philippines to Uzbekistan or even parts of Southeast Asia, Latin America, or central, west, or North Africa, among other possibilities. And of course Iraq and Pakistan fit the description of weak states whose failure could provide havens for al-Qaeda. Many of these—and especially Iraq and Pakistan—offer bin Laden prospects superior in important ways to Afghanistan's. Iraq and Pakistan, for example, are richer and far better connected to the outside world than is primitive, land-locked Afghanistan with its minimal communications and transportation systems. Iraq is an Arab state in the very heart of the Middle East. Pakistan, of course, is a nuclear power. Afghanistan does enjoy a historical connection with al-Qaeda, familiarity to bin Laden, and proximity to his current base in the FATA, and it is important to deny al-Qaeda sanctuary on the Afghan side of the Durand Line. But its intrinsic importance is no greater than many other potential havens—and probably smaller than many. We clearly cannot afford to wage protracted warfare with multiple brigades of American ground forces simply to deny al-Qaeda potential safe havens; we would run out of brigades long before bin Laden ran out of prospective sanctuaries.

The more important U.S. interest in Afghanistan is indirect: to prevent Afghan chaos from destabilizing its Pakistani neighbor. With a population of 173 million (five times Afghanistan's), a GDP of over $160 billion (over ten times Afghanistan's) and an actual, existing, functional nuclear arsenal of perhaps 20–50 warheads, Pakistan is a much more dangerous prospective sanctuary for al-Qaeda, and one where the likelihood of government collapse enabling such a sanctuary may be in the same ballpark as Afghanistan, at least in the medium to long term.[2] Pakistan is already at war with internal Islamist insurgents allied to al-Qaeda, and by most measures that war is not going well. Should the Pakistani insurgency succeed in collapsing the state or toppling the government, the risk of nuclear weapons falling into al-Qaeda's hands would be grave indeed. In fact, given the difficulties terrorists face in acquiring usable nuclear weapons, Pakistani state collapse is by far the likeliest scenario for a nuclear-armed al-Qaeda.

Pakistani state collapse, moreover, is a danger over which the United States has limited influence. The United States is now so unpopular in Pakistan that we have no meaningful prospect of deploying major ground forces there to assist the government in counterinsurgency. U.S. air strikes can harass insurgents and terrorists within Pakistan, but the inevitable collateral damage arouses harsh public opposition that could itself threaten the weak government's stability. U.S. aid is easily—and routinely—diverted to purposes remote from countering Islamist insurgents, such as the maintenance of military counterweights to India, graft and patronage, or even support for Islamist groups seen by Pakistani authorities as potential allies against their Indian neighbor. U.S. assistance can—and should—be made conditional on progress in countering insurgents, but harsh conditionality can induce rejection of the terms, and the aid, by the Pakistanis, removing our leverage in the

process. The net result is a major threat over which we have very limited influence.

If we have few ways to make Pakistan any better, we should at least avoid making it any worse. With so little actual leverage, we cannot afford to make the problem any harder than it already is. And failure in Afghanistan would make the problem in Pakistan much harder.

The Taliban are a transnational Pashtun movement that is active on either side of the Durand Line and sympathetic to other Pakistani Islamist insurgents. Their presence within Pakistan is thus already an important threat to the regime in Islamabad. But if the Taliban regained control of the Afghan state, their ability to use a state's resources as a base to destabilize secular government in Pakistan would enable a major increase in the risk of state collapse there. Much has been made of the threat Pakistani base camps pose to Afghan government stability, but this danger works both ways: instability in Afghanistan poses a serious threat to secular civilian government in Pakistan. And this is the single greatest stake the United States has in Afghanistan: to prevent it from aggravating Pakistan's internal problems and magnifying the danger of an al-Qaeda nuclear sanctuary there.

These stakes are thus important. But they do not merit infinite cost to secure. Afghanistan is just one of many possible al-Qaeda sanctuaries. And Afghanistan's influence over Pakistan's future is important, but incomplete and indirect. A Taliban Afghanistan is a real possibility in the long run absent U.S. action, and makes Pakistani collapse more likely, but it does not guarantee it. Nor would success in Afghanistan guarantee success in Pakistan: there is a chance that we could struggle our way to stability in Afghanistan at great cost and sacrifice only to see Pakistan collapse anyway under the weight of its own errors and internal divisions.

The Cost

What will it cost to defeat the Taliban? No one really knows; war is an uncertain business. But it is very hard to succeed at COIN on the cheap. Current U.S. Army doctrine is very clear on this:

> [M]aintaining security in an unstable environment requires vast resources, whether host nation, U.S., or multinational. In contrast, a small number of highly motivated insurgents with simple weapons, good operations security, and even limited mobility can undermine security over a large area. Thus, successful COIN operations often require a high ratio of security forces to the protected population. For that reason, protracted COIN operations are hard to sustain. The effort requires a firm political will and substantial patience by the government, its people, and the countries providing support.[3]
>
> Insurgencies are protracted by nature. Thus, COIN operations always demand considerable expenditures of time and resources.[4]

In fact, the doctrinal norm for troop requirements in COIN is around one security provider per fifty civilians in the population to be secured.[5] Applied to the population of Afghanistan, this would imply a need for around 650,000 trained soldiers and police. Not all parts of Afghanistan are equally threatened; it is widely believed that the north and west of the country are much safer than the south and east. Even if one assumes that only half the country requires active counterinsurgency operations, however, this still implies a need for something around 300,000 counterinsurgents. Ideally most of these would be indigenous Afghans. But there is reason to doubt that the Afghan government will ever be able to afford the necessary number of troops; if any significant fraction of this total must be American then the resources needed will be very large.[6] And the commitment could be very long: successful counterinsurgency campaigns commonly last ten to fifteen years or more.[7]

At least initially, the casualties to be expected from such an effort would also be heavy. In Iraq, a force of 130,000–160,000 U.S. troops averaged over 90 fatalities per month during the most intense period of COIN operations in January to August of 2007. Depending on the troop strength ultimately deployed and the intensity of the fighting, it is not implausible to suppose that casualty rates in Afghanistan could reach comparable levels. And it may well take longer for those losses to reverse and decline in Afghanistan than in Iraq; it would be prudent to assume that fatality rates of perhaps 50–100 per month could persist for many months, if not years.[8]

The Odds of Success

In general, the historical record of great power success in COIN is not encouraging. The political scientists Jason Lyall of Princeton and Isaiah Wilson of West Point estimate that since 1975, the success rate of government counterinsurgents has been just 25 percent.[9] Given the costs of trying, this success rate offers a sobering context.

Moreover, the surge's recent success in reducing Iraqi violence does not imply that similar methods will necessarily yield similar results in Afghanistan. As many have noted, Afghanistan and Iraq are very different military, political, and economic environments.[10] The nature of the underlying conflict is also very different: Iraq had been an ethno-sectarian civil war of identity with secondary factional, tribal, or ideological elements; Afghanistan has been chiefly an ideological and factional war with secondary ethnic elements. Methods that work in identity wars do not necessarily make sense in ideological conflicts, and vice versa.[11] Perhaps most important, the surge, while *necessary* for success in Iraq, was not *sufficient* to bring this about. Its effects were due in large part to a powerful interaction between a new U.S. approach and a major change in Sunni alignment stemming from their defeat in Baghdad's sectarian warfare over the course of 2006. This realignment would have failed without the surge's protection, but without the realignment the surge would never have been enough to suffocate the insurgency on its own. Taken together, the surge and the Sunni realignment powerfully reinforced one another's effects. But the surge without the Sunnis' 2006 Baghdad defeat—which we did not cause—would probably not have worked.[12] The surge's dependence on the particulars of Iraq's 2007 strategic landscape thus counsels great caution in extrapolating from its success in 2007 in Iraq to Afghanistan in 2009 and beyond: the experience in Iraq does not prove that we have now discovered a universal key to unlocking counterinsurgency problems in all places and times. There are thus important grounds for caution and concern about the prognosis in Afghanistan.

Nor are current conditions in Afghanistan encouraging. Orthodox COIN theory puts host government legitimacy at the heart of success and failure, yet the Karzai government is widely seen as corrupt, inept, inefficient, and en route to losing the support of its population. Ultimate economic and political development prospects are constrained by Afghanistan's forbidding geography, tribal social structure, lack of infrastructure, and political history. The Taliban enjoy a cross-border sanctuary in the FATA that the

Pakistani government seems unwilling or unable to eliminate. Violence is up, perceptions of security are down, casualties are increasing, and the Taliban is widely believed to be increasing its freedom of movement and access to the population. And only some of these challenges are things we can affect directly: we can increase security by deploying more U.S. troops, we can bolster the economy to a degree with U.S. economic aid, and we can pressure Karzai to reform, but only the Afghans can create a legitimate government, and only the Pakistanis can shut down the safe havens in the FATA. We can influence these choices, and we must do so—to a much greater degree than we have so far. But we cannot guarantee reform ourselves, and to date neither ally seems ready to do what it takes.

But this does not make failure inevitable. The poor track record for COIN generally is due partly to the inherent difficulty of the undertaking, but most see poor strategic choices by many counterinsurgents as a major contributor to failure. Strategies and methods can be changed—it is possible to learn from experience. And the U.S. military has learned a great deal about COIN in recent years. The new Army/Marine counterinsurgency doctrine is the product of a nearly unprecedented degree of internal debate, external vetting, historical analysis, and direct recent combat experience.[13] None of this makes it a magic silver bullet for COIN success, and in important ways it makes underlying assumptions about the nature of counterinsurgency that made it an awkward fit for conditions in Iraq.[14] But those same assumptions make it a much stronger fit for Afghanistan, which is precisely the kind of war the manual was built around.

One of the doctrine's remaining shortcomings, moreover, is a problem the new administration seems likely to address. The new doctrine assumes a very close alignment of interests between the United States and its host government: the manual assumes that our role is to enable the host to realize its own best interest by making itself into a legitimate defender of all its citizens' wellbeing, and that the host will see it this way, too.[15] In many ways, the previous administration shared this view, offering assistance with few conditions or strings on the assumption that developing our allies' capacity for good governance was all that would be needed to realize better performance. In fact, though, many allies—notably including Hamid Karzai and Pervez Musharraf, have had much more complex motives that have led them to misdirect our aid and fall short of our hopes for their popular legitimacy. Some students of counterinsurgency have thus emphasized the need for conditionality in our assistance to reduce this problem of moral hazard: we should not assume that allies share all our interests, and we should impose conditions and combine carrots with sticks in order to push reluctant hosts toward behavior that could better realize our hopes for their broader legitimacy and thereby damp insurgencies.[16] The incoming administration has made it very clear that they intend to combine bigger carrots with real sticks in the form of prospective aid withdrawals should the recipients fail to adopt needed reforms. This is an important step forward in our ability to compete for hearts and minds with effective host governance.

The forces implementing that doctrine are also much improved over their ancestors in Vietnam, or even their immediate predecessors in Iraq in 2003–4. In fact, the U.S. military of 2009 has adapted into an unusually proficient counterinsurgency force. No large human organization is perfect, and there is important room for improvement. But relative to many great power counterinsurgents, the current U.S. military combines stronger doctrine with unusually extensive COIN combat experience, unusually systematic training, and resources for equipment and materiel that would dwarf most historical antecedents'.

Perhaps most important, we are blessed with deeply flawed enemies in Afghanistan. Afghans know the Taliban; they know what life was like under their rule. And polling has consistently suggested that few Afghans want to return to the medieval theocracy they endured before. Most Afghans want education for their daughters; they want access to media and ideas from abroad; they want freedom from thugs enforcing fundamentalism for all under the aegis of a Ministry for the Promotion of Virtue and the Prevention of Vice. Of course, these preferences are secondary to the need for security. And many are secondary to the desire for basic services such as courts free of corruption or police who enforce the laws without demanding bribes first. But because most Afghans oppose Taliban rule, we enjoy a strong presumption in favor of the government as long as that government can be made to provide at least basic services competently. The Taliban face an inherently uphill battle to secure compliance with their policies that a reasonably proficient government does not. And in a struggle for hearts and minds this is an important advantage.

The Taliban, moreover, are far from a unified opposition group. By contrast with the Viet Cong of 1964, for example, where a common ideology bound the leadership together and linked it to its fighters, the neo-Taliban of 2009 are a much looser, much more heterogeneous, much more divided coalition of often fractious and very independent actors. There is a hard core of committed Islamist ideologues, centered on Mullah Omar and based in Quetta. But by all accounts much of the Taliban's actual combat strength is provided by an array of warlords and other factions with often much more secular motivations, who side with the Taliban for reasons of profit, prestige, or convenience, and who may or may not follow orders from the Quetta Shura leadership. We often lament the challenges to unity of effort that flow from a divided NATO command structure, but the Taliban face difficulties on this score at least as severe as ours and potentially much worse: no NATO member is going to change sides and fight for the Taliban, but the Taliban need to be constantly alert lest one or more of their component factions leave the alliance for the government side. And this makes it very difficult for the Taliban to mount large-scale, coordinated offensives of the kind that would be needed to conquer a defended city, for example—such efforts would be very hard for any one faction or any one commander to accomplish without closely-coordinated assistance from others, yet such coordination can be very hard to achieve in such a decentralized, factionalized leadership structure.

The Taliban also face major constraints in extending their influence beyond their ethnic base in southern and eastern Afghanistan. The Taliban is an explicitly Pashtun movement. Yet Pashtuns make up less than 45 percent of Afghanistan's population overall, and constitute only a tiny fraction of the population outside the south and east. Afghanistan is not primarily an ethno-sectarian war of identity, as Iraq has been—most Taliban are Pashtuns, but most Pashtuns are not Taliban (in fact the government is itself run by Pashtuns such as Hamid Karzai). Afghanistan is a war fought over the Taliban's ideology for governing, not the hope for a Pashtun government. But whereas the government has members from many ethnic groups and a presumptive claim to the loyalty of all citizens, the Taliban has a much more exclusivist identity and is radically unpopular and unwelcome outside its regional ethnic base. This in turn will make it hard for them to conquer the north and west of the country, and acts as a limiter on their expansion in the near term. (It is worth noting that even in their first rule, the Taliban never completely secured the north—it was the unconquered "Northern Alliance's" hold over contiguous territory in that part of Afghanistan that provided allies, a base, and a jump-off point for the American Special Forces who teamed with them to topple the Taliban in 2001.)

This combination of a proficient U.S. military and a Taliban enemy with important weaknesses and vulnerabilities gives us an important *possibility* for successful counterinsurgency. This is obviously not a guarantee. There are major obstacles in Afghanistan, and even if there weren't, social science cannot offer that kind of certainty. If anyone thinks the new doctrine is an infallible cookbook for COIN success then they are mistaken. But neither is defeat in Afghanistan inevitable. Great powers do not always fail in COIN; the U.S. is an unusually experienced counterinsurgent force today; the Taliban have serious problems of their own; and astute strategic choices can make an important difference.

Assessment

The stakes, costs, and odds here make Afghanistan a closer call on the merits than some would assume. Reasonable people could argue that a combination of an uncertain prospect of victory with high costs and a limited ability to secure the real stake—a stable Pakistan—make COIN in Afghanistan too unpromising to expend the lives and dollars needed. Ultimately any such calculation is a value judgment: analysis can clarify the costs and the benefits, but rarely can the analytical merits predetermine whether the expected risk to human life is worth the chance of securing a stake.

But in making that value judgment it is important to keep in mind the gravity of the ultimate stake in Afghanistan. A nuclear al-Qaeda is a truly cataclysmic prospect. And Pakistani state collapse is a perhaps uniquely dangerous pathway to this. COIN in Afghanistan is indeed an indirect and imperfect means of preventing this. If we had better levers to mitigate this risk, then an expensive, difficult, protracted Afghan COIN campaign might be less necessary: we could compensate for the perils of cross-border destabilization from a Taliban Afghanistan in some other way. But there are very few other ways. War in Afghanistan is an unattractive option, but so is the alternative. Given this, counterinsurgency in Afghanistan, with all its warts and perils, may nevertheless be the strongest means at our disposal to affect the risk of Pakistani nuclear weapons falling into al-Qaeda hands.

II. How Quickly Should Resources Be Transferred from Iraq to Afghanistan?

To wage war effectively in Afghanistan will require troops and equipment now committed to Iraq. How quickly can they be shifted from the latter to the former?

There are several constraints here. Logistics, for example, is a potential limiter: the current basing and transportation infrastructure in Afghanistan cannot immediately accommodate a large increase in U.S. troops. Some months will be needed to build the facilities needed for a sustained deployment in such an austere, remote theater.

The most important constraint, however, is the competing demand for U.S. troops in Iraq. To resolve these demands requires answers to three key questions: how important are the relative interests at stake in the two theaters; how sensitive are outcomes in each theater to U.S. resource investments; and how volatile is the situation in each theater—how quickly could events turn for the worse or the better if resources were provided or withheld?

The Relative Importance of Iraq and Afghanistan

It is sometimes argued that Iraq, as a war of choice, is less central to U.S. interests than Afghanistan, where bin Laden organized the 9-11 attacks. This may well have been true in 2001 or 2003. But the situation is very different today. As noted previously, al-Qaeda central is now based in Pakistan, not Afghanistan, and the latter's influence on the former, while important, is indirect and incomplete. And our invasion of Iraq destabilized the country—and potentially the region—creating several major threats to U.S. interests in the process that did not exist to nearly the same degree prior to the invasion, but which now loom large for U.S. strategy.

In particular, the U.S. retains two primary interests in Iraq in 2009. The first is humanitarian. Having launched a war of choice in Iraq, we thus bear a heavy responsibility for the loss of innocent life that may follow from that decision. In Afghanistan, war was forced upon us by Osama bin Laden; in Iraq we may (or may not) have been justified in our choice to wage war in 2003, but we had a wider range of meaningful alternative options at our disposal than we did in 2001. And as such, our responsibility for using our resources in ways that reduce the conflict's humanitarian costs is greater than in Afghanistan. Of course we should always conduct operations in ways that limit collateral damage and the loss of innocent life, whatever the theater. In Iraq, however, there is an unusually strong normative case for expending resources and bearing burdens we might not in other places if by doing so we can limit the damage of a war for which we bear more than usual responsibility.

The second primary U.S. stake in Iraq is that the war not spread beyond Iraq's borders. Iraq by 2006 had become an unusually intense ethno-sectarian civil war. Such wars create many problems, but one of the most dangerous is contagion: they have a strong tendency to spread, drawing in their neighbors to an expanded conflict that can dramatically increase the war's damage and loss of life. Of the 142 civil wars fought between 1944 and 1999, for example, fully 48 saw major military interventions by neighbors.[17] This is always tragic, but for Iraq it could be disastrous: a war engulfing Iraq's neighbors could plunge one of the world's most important energy producing regions into chaos.

Today, Iraq is in the early stages of a negotiated settlement to its civil war in which the former Sunni insurgents and Shiite militias are observing ceasefires (and in which al-Qaeda in Iraq has been marginalized and restricted to a handful of remaining sanctuaries). The continuation of this settlement, and its maturation into real stability, is the best possible insurance against the danger of a wider war in the Persian Gulf. Such settlements, however, are notoriously fragile early on: of 23 such ceasefires between 1940 and 1992, 10 collapsed into renewed warfare within five years of the settlement.[18] Failure is not inevitable, but the fact of a ceasefire in most of Iraq today is no guarantee of enduring peace.

And if Iraq should return to violence, the risk of a re-ignited Iraqi conflict spreading may be greater than in most such wars. Each of Iraq's neighbors has vital interests in Iraq, and the threats to those interests posed by Iraqi civil warfare grow over time. Left to their own devices, civil wars such as Iraq's can take a decade

or more to burn themselves out. With some luck, Iraq's war could do this without spreading. But it is also distinctly possible that an increasingly virulent combination of refugee flows into neighboring states; the internal destabilization created by ill-housed, ill-fed, dispossessed and politically radicalized refugee populations; fears of regional domination by Iranian-supported Shiism; cross-border terrorism by Iraqi factions (especially the Kurds); and growing military capacity for intervention fueled by an ongoing regional arms race could eventually produce irresistible pressures for Syrian, Jordanian, Saudi, Turkish, or Iranian state entry into the war. And if one of these states intervened, the resulting change in the military balance within Iraq would increase the pressures on the others to send troops across the border as well. The result could be a region-wide version of the Iran-Iraq War sometime in the next decade, but with some of the combatants (especially Iran) having probable access to weapons of mass destruction by that time.

Of course nothing about Iraq is a certainty, and the probability of regionalization is not 1.0. But neither can it safely be excluded. If one considers the entire available empirical record of civil wars and outside interventions since 1944, controls for the unique features of the Iraqi case, and projects to possible restarted civil war durations of five to ten years, the best available estimates of the probability that the war spreads to two or more of Iraq's neighbors could be as high as 25 to 60 percent.[19] Averting such a gamble is perhaps the most important—and continuing—U.S. strategic interest in Iraq.

How Sensitive Are Outcomes to U.S. Resource Investments?

More U.S. resources for Afghanistan are *insufficient* to realize our primary interest there—the stability of Pakistan—but they may be *necessary* for this. Certainly a failed Afghanistan or a Taliban reconquest would make Pakistani stability much less likely. And to avert failure in Afghanistan will eventually require, *inter alia,* much more substantial U.S. investments there, including more troops. It may be possible to buy time through Afghan political reforms achieved via focused U.S. pressure on the Karzai government without a large near-term military reinforcement (see below). And near-term defeat in Afghanistan seems unlikely even without an immediate troop buildup (see below). But in the long run, the prognosis is poor without much larger security forces in Afghanistan, many of which will have to be American. Afghanistan could fail even with U.S. reinforcement, and more than just troops will be needed for a decent chance at success. But without additional U.S. resources, the Karzai government's ability to control its borders, control its territory, and prevent infiltration of Taliban and other Islamist fighters into Pakistan would be very limited, with potentially very dangerous consequences across the border.

Iraq, too, has important and continuing needs for U.S. troops. But those needs are very different in nature. Whereas U.S. troops' role in Afghanistan would be counterinsurgency warfighting, their role in Iraq is increasingly that of peacekeepers.

Negotiated civil war settlements such as Iraq's often fail, but where they do not, it is often due to the presence of outside peacekeepers. Ethno-sectarian identity wars aggravate deep seated inter-group fears and distrust; even when the shooting stops it can take years for rivals' expectations of one another to change and for retaliatory incentives to fade. Left to their own devices, spoiler violence can easily lead to escalatory spirals as groups who fear for their security at the hands of rivals take action themselves in self-defense. Indigenous government security forces can help, but they can also make matters worse where one group feels threatened by government forces under the control of their rivals—in Iraq, for example, many former Sunni insurgents remain deeply distrustful of Iraqi security forces under the command of a Shiite-led government. In such settings, outside peacekeepers reassure the parties that their rivals will not exploit them if they let their guard down or delay retaliation. Even if widely disliked themselves, outsiders are rarely seen as prospective genocide threats (as internal rivals often are); this enables outsiders to play a transitional stabilizing role that internal actors can find difficult to perform without stimulating fear of oppression.

In Iraq today, the only prospective peacekeeping force is the U.S. military. We may not be loved, but we are tolerated well enough to act as stabilizers where needed. And in fact, most of the activities of U.S. ground forces in Iraq today amount, in effect, to peacekeeping: enforcing ceasefire terms, damping escalatory spirals, reassuring wary former combatants that their willingness to stand down will not be exploited by their erstwhile enemies.

Peacekeeping of this kind can be labor intensive. In fact, the troop levels normally preferred for such missions are little different from those sought for COIN warfighting: about one peacekeeper per 50 civilians, or far more troops than we now have in Iraq. But such missions have sometimes been accomplished with much smaller forces. In Liberia, for example, 15,000 UN troops stabilized a ceasefire in a country of three and a half million; in Sierra Leone, 18,000 UN troops sufficed in a country of 6 million.[20] It would be a mistake to assume that such small forces can always succeed in a potentially very demanding mission, and more is always better. But it would also be a mistake to assume that only an impossibly large force will suffice.

The ideal duration of such missions can be long. But rarely are initial, relatively large, peacekeeping deployments maintained at that level for their entirety. As inter-group tensions and expectations of hostility recede, peacekeeping deployments can often be thinned gradually and progressively without reigniting violence. In the Balkans, for example, large early peacekeeping deployments were reduced slowly to levels of less than half their initial strength within four years of the ceasefires in Bosnia and Kosovo without a return to warfare.[21] This Balkan analogy would imply a safe peacekeeping drawdown trajectory for Iraq that would leave around 60,000 U.S. troops in the country by 2011.

A U.S. troop presence of 60,000 through 2011 would create obvious tension with the terms of the recent status of forces agreement negotiated with Iraq. Perhaps conditions in the country by 2011 will enable deeper drawdowns—or even the complete withdrawal of all U.S. forces as called for in the agreement—without a significant danger of renewed violence. And either way, Iraq is a sovereign nation; if they ask us to leave then we should and we must. But from the standpoint of stability alone, experience elsewhere suggests that a longer presence by a larger U.S. force than now foreseen in the status of forces agreement would offer useful insurance against a renewal of violence and the risk that this violence eventually crosses Iraq's borders.

As in COIN, there are no guarantees in peacekeeping—this is an insurance policy that sometimes fails. In Angola and Rwanda, for example, outside peacekeeping forces failed to prevent renewed warfare. Conversely, there is no certainty that even a precipitous U.S. withdrawal would spur a return to civil war. But on balance it seems reasonable to conclude that stability in Iraq remains sensitive to the presence of U.S. forces, and is likely to continue to be for at least several years to come.

How Volatile Are the Situations in Afghanistan and Iraq?

If both Afghanistan and Iraq are important and if both demand substantial U.S. deployments, then something important and valuable will have to be sacrificed; we do not have the forces to do everything we would like to do simultaneously. This places a premium on our assessment of the relative volatility of the respective situations: can we survive increased risk in the short term in one theater while meeting the other's demands, or is one situation or the other so close to failure that near term sacrifices would be fatal? Both theaters face some risk of near-term failure, but where is this danger greater?

The key issue here is not whether security trends are up or down in either theater. Everyone agrees that the trend today is up or steady in Iraq but down in Afghanistan. Rather, the real question is *how quickly could an uncertain situation reach a point of no return* if near-term troop levels were smaller than ideal, and how likely is this? In the longer term, an improving situation in Iraq should enable gradual shifts without great risk; the problem is the short run, where both Iraq and Afghanistan would ideally need the same troops, and the key issue is to assess the risk that shorting one theater or the other would create a problem from which we could not recover in the longer term.

Today, many would probably see Afghanistan as the greater risk of near-term failure. Some believe that the Afghan campaign is now teetering on the brink of defeat, whereas the situation in Iraq seems relatively stable in the near term. If so, then the safer course would be to fight the near-term fire in Afghanistan as soon as possible and take risks as necessary with the slower-moving situation in Iraq.

Imminent defeat cannot be ruled out in Afghanistan; certainly the war there is going badly and getting worse. But quick defeat is nevertheless unlikely in Afghanistan. By contrast, Iraq is more volatile than sometimes assumed. And whereas the U.S. could probably recover from some continuation of today's downward trends in Afghanistan, a turn for the worse in Iraq could well be unrecoverable at this point.

I base this assessment partly on the views of the theater command in Afghanistan, partly on the importance of political frustration for adverse near-term trends there, and partly on an analysis of the nature of ongoing security risks in Iraq.

As for the first of these points, in a recent visit to Afghanistan in November 2008, I posed this question—how quickly could the situation there reach a point of no return if reinforcements were smaller or slower than ideal—to the ISAF senior leadership and staff in Kabul. None believed that defeat was imminent or would result from a delay in the preferred reinforcements. All argued that success required larger forces (among other needs). But none saw defeat as a realistic outcome in the next year or two regardless. In fact, the most pessimistic assessment I could solicit was a projection of stalemate; some actually argued that improvement was possible without additional forces if ISAF strategy and policy coordination were reformed.

Their view was based largely on the perceived weakness of the Taliban opposition. Poor governance by the Karzai regime and insufficient troop levels had created an opportunity for the insurgency, and the Taliban had proved strong enough to exploit this opportunity to reduce security in the country. But the Taliban's unpopular ideology, inconsistent motives and interests, restrictive ethnic identity, and inability to coordinate efforts made them, in Gen. McKiernan's words, "less than the sum of their parts" and limited their ability to achieve theater success any time soon.[22]

Moreover, there is reason to suspect that the Karzai regime's poor civil governance may be so central to the recent downturn that a near term "political surge" (to borrow David Kilcullen's phrase) could buy valuable time even before larger-scale military reinforcements become available, reducing the sensitivity of outcomes there to U.S. troop counts per se for a time. In fact, political change may be the most urgent piece of the politico-military improvements needed—and either way it can be undertaken without the kind of near-term opportunity cost against the Iraq effort that troop increases create.

In objective terms, violence in Afghanistan, though increasing, is still very low by the standards of most such conflicts. In Iraq, for example, civilian deaths per hundred thousand members of the population had already reached 30 by 2004, just one year into the war; in Afghanistan, the death count for 2008 was under six per hundred thousand, or less than one-fifth as great.[23] Malaya is commonly cited as an example of an insurgency turned around by successful government strategy; one year into the Malayan Emergency, the civilian death toll had already reached nine per hundred thousand, a rate 50 percent higher than Afghanistan's today; two years later the Malayan insurgents killed 20 civilians per hundred thousand, or a rate three times Afghanistan's today.[24] Vietnam, of course, was hardly a COIN success, but it certainly featured a much higher death rate than Afghanistan's to date: the Viet Cong in 1966 inflicted about 180 civilian deaths per hundred thousand, or about 27 times the Taliban's current rate.[25] In fact, the overwhelming majority of Afghans, when surveyed, report feeling safe in their neighborhoods today. Parts of Afghanistan are very violent, but much of it is not.

Yet support for the government is plummeting, even in relatively peaceful areas, creating an important opening that the Taliban have been exploiting. The reason may well be that perceptions of violence elsewhere in the country are catalyzing frustration with incompetent and massively corrupt governance to create anger with the regime—and its foreign supporters—creating an opening for the Taliban, notwithstanding its limited intrinsic appeal and military shortcomings. Reducing the violence will be necessary to create real stability and defeat the insurgency, and this will require more troops. But in the near term, even sizeable reinforcements that do not reform Afghan governance are unlikely to reverse the government's loss of political support. And we can, in principle, be much more effective in compelling reform from the Karzai government than we have been heretofore even without massive near-term military reinforcement. This will require real political pressure on Karzai that combines promises of support and aid with threats to deny them in the absence of reform and demands that Karzai remove known offenders from his government. Nominal security conditions in the country are not yet so grave as to make such a program for better governance impossible in the absence of more troops—and more troops without such a program will do little to reduce public frustration with official corruption and incompetence.

This is not to say that a "political surge" in the absence of much larger military reinforcements can avert stalemate; real success in Afghanistan requires both governance reform and security

improvements, and the latter will be hard to provide without more troops. Stalemate, rather than success, is likely to be the best that can be accomplished pending major reinforcement. Nor would stalemate or unnecessarily slow progress be cost-free in Afghanistan. Either would increase the cost in lives and treasure needed for eventual success, and either one would increase the risk of failure in the longer term. It is sometimes said that insurgencies win simply by avoiding defeat—which is to say that stalemate favors the insurgent—and there is much truth to this. The worse the situation at the time of reinforcement, the harder it will be to turn the situation around when that day comes.

But costlier success or diminished long-term odds are not the same as near-term failure. The latter is, in the view of the theater command, beyond the Taliban's capacity to bring about, and it may be possible to lower the odds further with a political surge even before an eventual major troop buildup.

In Iraq, by contrast, we would have very little ability to rescue the situation if current trends reversed and violence returned. It is hard to imagine much public tolerance in the United States for a "second surge" in the event that the first one proved insufficient to keep Iraq stable. Nor is it easy to see this succeeding even if tried. The first surge was heavily dependent on several favorable preconditions for success—and especially the strategic effects of Sunni defeat at Shiite hands in the 2006 Battle of Baghdad and the ensuing growth of the Sunni Awakening movement.[26] If large scale violence returned after a major U.S. drawdown, this would imply that the Battle of Baghdad's effects had atrophied or been overtaken by events; the odds of a comparable piece of serendipity on this scale enabling a new surge to succeed in 2010 or 2011 would be long.

Potential stimuli for such a turn for the worse in Iraq are ubiquitous. Today's ceasefire rests in large part on a tremendously disaggregate series of around 200 bilateral agreements, mostly between Sunni Sons of Iraq (SOI) groups and the U.S. military. This creates a wide array of opportunities for individual SOI leaders to see what they can get away with in stretching the terms of their agreements, or for innocent errors to be misinterpreted as hostile acts, or for government crackdowns on miscreants to be interpreted by others as the beginning of a broader campaign of sectarian repression, or for an opportunistic government to exploit divisions among its opponents to try to crush partisan rivals by force. Any such event could give rise to violence which could become catalytic and create an escalatory spiral if not responded to promptly and even-handedly by a disinterested party. Iraq's provincial and national elections are opportunities for progress, but they are also potential flashpoints for violence if the losers fail to accept their defeat or if perceptions of vote-rigging or intimidation spread. Kirkuk poses a whole series of risks in the form of unresolved conflicts of interest between Kurds, Arabs, and Turkomen. The return of potentially millions of Iraqi refugees and internally displaced persons involves a tremendous risk of instability as mostly-Sunni dispossessed return to homes and properties now destroyed or occupied by mostly-Shiite squatters and find little or no government capacity to adjudicate their claims, make good their loss, or even house, feed, or care for them. "Crises of rising expectations" in which early progress in economic or political development create demands for faster improvement than immature governments can meet are common in recovering societies, and can easily lead to frustration even where there is progress in service delivery if that progress is too slow; service delivery in Iraq has never been very impressive, and could easily fall short of the expectations of an impatient public.

Some of these flashpoints, such as Kirkuk, could lead to open warfare at unpredictable times or places should Kurdish Pesh Merga militia, for example, clash with government forces seeking to enforce edicts rejected by Kurds. Many others, however, would be likelier to take a subtler turn in which alienated groups quietly reopen the door to bomb making cells and covert insurgents, enabling al-Qaeda in Iraq, for example, to return to parts of central and western Iraq from which it is now effectively banished, or enabling Jaish al Mahdi elements to operate once more under Shiite protection in the south. Even subtle, covert returns to violence, however, could quickly put Iraq back on a slippery—and steep—slope back to intense civil warfare as victims retaliate and fears return. Such a process is exactly how Iraq descended into intense civil war the first time around in 2004–06. The reestablishment of trust after civil warfare is a slow and fragile process; it is much easier to destroy than to restore once lost. If such a process is allowed to proceed very far unchecked it can place Iraq on a trajectory from which it would be very hard to recover, and this process could begin almost any time, and certainly very soon if U.S. forces were not in a position to respond while in its early stages.

Either Iraq or Afghanistan could thus clearly get worse in the absence of sufficient U.S. troops. But whereas we can probably recover from a degree of continued decline in Afghanistan, a failure to respond quickly to catalytic violence in Iraq could put the country on a trajectory from which recovery at this point would be very difficult. To an important degree, Iraq—though less violent than Afghanistan today—is thus probably more volatile.

Assessment

There are thus risks on all sides in shifting forces from Iraq to Afghanistan; no policy is without danger. On balance, however, the odds are that we can afford to wait in Afghanistan, whereas we may not be able to afford the consequences for U.S. interests if we withdraw too rapidly from Iraq.

How rapidly is too rapidly for Iraq, and how long must we wait for reinforcement in Afghanistan? Modest reductions in Iraq and reinforcements for Afghanistan are already ongoing, and can probably be tolerated without destabilizing effects for Iraq. Withdrawals much below the 10–12 brigade range in Iraq, however, should ideally await the aftermath of next year's national elections. As noted above, an analogy to the Balkans would suggest a safe withdrawal rate of something roughly on the order of 50 percent of the initial force over about four years from the time of ceasefire. Such a drawdown trajectory would make possible substantial reinforcements beyond the scale of those already announced for arrival in Afghanistan over the course of 2010 and 2011. Again, such plans are contingent on Iraqi approval for a slower withdrawal than the Status of Forces Agreement now foresees; this approval may not be forthcoming, in which case faster drawdowns will be required. But while this would be necessary under such conditions, it would not be conducive to stability. On balance, slower is thus better if it can be negotiated.

Notes

1. Note, though, that the subtitle reads "How to Salvage Afghanistan:" *Newsweek,* Vol. CLIII, No. 6. Note also, however, that the inside subtitle reads "Quagmire in the Making," without a question mark: p. 5.

2. On the size of the Pakistani nuclear arsenal, see Federation of American Scientists, Pakistan Nuclear Weapons, http://www.fas.org/nuke/guide/pakistan/nuke/ (accessed 7 February 2009). It is widely believed that Pakistan's nuclear weapons are stored in a disassembled condition, but that the components can be reassembled into working weapons quickly.

3. *The U.S. Army-Marine Corps Counterinsurgency Field Manual* (Chicago: University of Chicago Press, 2007), (republication of: Headquarters, Department of the Army, *FM 3–24: Counterinsurgency*), p. 4.

4. Ibid., p. 43.

5. Ibid., p. 23.

6. See Barnett Rubin and Ahmed Rashid, "From Great Game to Grand Bargain: Ending Chaos in Afghanistan and Pakistan," *Foreign Affairs,* Vol. 87, No. 6 (November/December 2008), pp. 30–44.

7. Seth Jones, *Counterinsurgency in Afghanistan,* (Washington, DC: RAND, 2008), p. 10.

8. The financial costs are also likely to be large. The Congressional Research Service estimates that the war in Afghanistan cost $34 billion in FY 2008, and projects that this figure will increase in coming years: Amy Belasco, *The Cost of Iraq, Afghanistan and other Global War on Terror Operations Since 9/11* (Washington, DC: Congressional Research Service, October 15, 2008), RL33110, pp. 6, 19.

9. Jason Lyall and Isaiah Wilson, "Rage Against the Machines: Explaining Outcomes in Counterinsurgency Wars," *International Organization,* Vol. 63, No. 1 (Winter 2009), pp. 67–106 at 69–71. For all counterinsurgencies since 1900, they find a government success rate of 40 percent; hence the odds have been getting worse over time. See also Ivan Arreguin-Toft, "How the Weak Win Wars: A Theory of Asymmetric Conflict," *International Security,* Vol. 26, No. 1, pp. 93–128, and Arreguin-Toft, *How the Weak Win Wars: A Theory of Asymmetric Conflict,* (New York: Cambridge University Press, 2005), which finds "strong actors" winning only 45 of 100 asymmetric conflicts between 1950 and 1998: p. 97 .

10. See, e.g., GEN David Petraeus, remarks at the U.S. Institute of Peace, January 8, 2009; reported by Armed Forces Press Service, January 9, http://www.defenselink.mil/News/newsarticle.aspx?id=52604. GEN David McKiernan, DoD News Briefing at the Pentagon, October 1, 2008, http://www.defenselink.mil/transcripts/transcript.aspx?transcriptid=4297.

11. See Stephen Biddle, "Seeing Baghdad, Thinking Saigon: The Perils of Refighting Vietnam in Iraq," *Foreign Affairs,* Vol. 85, No. 2 (March/April 2006), pp. 2–14.

12. For a more detailed analysis, see Stephen Biddle, "Iraq After the Surge," statement before the House Armed Services Committee, 110th Congress (2nd Session), January 23, 2008; also Linda Robinson, *Tell Me How This Ends: General Petraeus and the Search for a Way Out of Iraq,* PublicAffairs (New York: Perseus, 2008).

13. On the vetting and development process, see *U.S. Army-Marine Corps Counterinsurgency Field Manual,* pp. xlvii–xlviii.

14. In particular, the doctrine presumes an ideological struggle for the allegiance of an uncommitted public, rather than a highly mobilized ethno-sectarian war of identity, as Iraq has been: for details, see Jeffrey Isaac, editor, "The New U.S. Army/Marine Corps Counterinsurgency Field Manual as Political Science and Political Praxis," *Perspectives on Politics,* Vol. 6, No. 2 (June 2008), pp. 347–50, 349–50.

15. See, for example, *U.S. Army-Marine Corps Counterinsurgency Field Manual,* pp. 7–8, 25, 35, 37–39, 47 (e.g., paragraph 1-147: "Support the Host Nation").

16. For a more extensive discussion, see, esp., Daniel Byman, "Friends Like These: Counterinsurgency and the War on Terrorism," *International Security,* Vol. 31, No. 2 (Fall 2006), pp. 79–115.

17. Stephen Biddle, Jeffrey Friedman and Stephen Long, "Civil War Intervention and the Problem of Iraq," manuscript and supporting dataset. (Note that these data code as a "civil war" any internal conflict with at least 200 battle deaths; other coding rules with other criteria will imply other, often smaller, counts of wars but similar counts of interventions. Hence the intervention rate cited above is best regarded as lower bound.)

18. Barbara F. Walter, *Committing to Peace: The Successful Settlement of Civil Wars,* (Princeton: Princeton University Press, 2002).

19. Biddle, Friedman, and Long, "Civil War Intervention and the Problem of Iraq." The lower figure assumes five years of post-reignition civil warfare in Iraq; the higher figure assumes ten years. The results are derived from a probit analysis of 142 civil wars fought between 1944 and 1999; the computed probit coefficients were then used to perform a monte carlo simulation of potential interventions in Iraq given the specific values on the probit model's independent variables for Iraq and each of its neighbors. For a complete discussion of the method, data, and findings see ibid.

20. For Liberia, see the UNMIL website: http://www.un.org/Depts/dpko/missions/unmil/facts.html. For Sierra Leone, see the UNAMSIL website: http://www.un.org/Depts/dpko/missions/unamsil/facts.html

21. http://www.nato.int/sfor/docu/d981116a.htm

22. See Catherine Dale, *War in Afghanistan: Strategy, Military Operations, and Issues for Congress* (Washington, DC: Congressional Research Service, January 23, 2009), pp. 20–21, which reports on the same series of interviews.

23. Data from the Brookings Institute Iraq Index; civilian fatalities are for insurgent violence only and exclude estimated deaths from criminal activity: http://www.brookings.edu/saban/iraq-index.aspx

24. Data from Michael Clodfelter, *Warfare and Armed Conflicts: A Statistical Reference to Casualty and Other Figures, 1500–2000* (Jefferson, NC: McFarland & Company, 2002), p. 682.

25. Data from Ronald J. Cima, ed., *Vietnam: A Country Study* (Washington, DC: USGPO, 1987); and assuming a South Vietnamese population of 19 million in 1966.

26. See references in note 12 above.

Statement by Dr. **Stephen Biddle,** Senior Fellow for Defense Policy Council on Foreign Relations before the Committee on Armed Services, United States House of Representatives First Session, 111th Congress, February 12, 2009.

U.S. House of Representatives, February 12, 2009. Public Domain.

UNIT 9

International Organizations, International Law, and Global Governance

Unit Selections

Key Points to Consider

- Do you think the United States should work harder to make the United Nations a more effective body for achieving new international agreements? Why or why not?

- What is "minilateralism"? Do you agree or disagree that it is the best way to break the world's current deadlock on a number of increasingly important international issues? Why?

- Do you think the doctrine of the "responsibility to protect" (R2P) will prevent future genocides? Why or why not?

- Given the widespread use of such odious acts as rape as a weapon in international and civil conflicts, do you think that the rules of war codified in the Geneva conventions after World War II are adequate or is it time for new international rules or humanitarian conventions?

Student Website
www.mhhe.com/cls

Internet References

The Digital Library in International Conflict Management
http://www.usip.org/library/diglib.html

InterAction
http://www.interaction.org

IRIN
http://www.irinnews.org

International Court of Justice (ICJ)
http://www.icj-cij.org

International Criminal Court
http://www.icc-cpi.int/home.html&l=en

United Nations
http://untreaty.un.org

United Nations Home Page
http://www.un.org

Human Rights Web
http://www.hrweb.org

United Nations Peacekeeping Home Page
http://www.un.org/Depts/dpko/dpko

"A More Secure World: Our Shared Responsibility"
http://www.un.org/secureworld

Global Policy Forum
http://www.globalpolicy.org

Amnesty International
http://www.amnesty.org

International organizations consist of members who are sovereign states or other inter-government organizations, such as the European Union or the World Trade Organization. The most visible international organization throughout the post-World War II era has been the United Nations. Membership grew from the original 50 in 1945 to 185 in 1995. The United Nations, across a variety of fronts, achieved noteworthy results, such as the eradication of disease, immunization, provision of food and shelter to refugees and victims of natural disasters, and help to dozens of countries that have moved from colonial status to self-rule.

After the first Gulf War in the early 1990s, the United Nations guided enforcement of economic sanctions against Iraq, sent peacekeeping forces to former Yugoslavia and to Somalia, monitored an unprecedented number of elections and ceasefire agreements, and played an active peacekeeping role in almost every region of the world. However, the withdrawal of the UN mission in Somalia in the early 1990s, the near-collapse of the UN peacekeeping mission in Bosnia prior to the intervention of NATO-sponsored troops, and the delayed UN response in sending troops to monitor ceasefire agreements in East Timor and Sierra Leone in 1999, along with recent allegations of sexual abuse of local citizens and involvement in the illegal exploitation of natural resources levied against UN peacekeepers in the Democratic Republic of the Congo raise serious doubts about the ability of the organization to continue to be involved in peacekeeping worldwide.

Televised photos of UN peacekeeping forces standing by and doing nothing in the eastern province of the Democratic Republic of the Congo as thousands of civilians fled advancing rebel forces in 2008 further alienated viewing publics in the West. The fact that the United Nations helped negotiate a ceasefire that permitted civilians to return to their now-ruined villages received much less attention. Press stories usually fail to explain that UN peacekeeping forces typically operate under detailed mandates that permit them to observe and keep rival forces apart while not getting involved once fighting breaks out. Press stories rarely explain that these limited mandates are the only ones that will receive political support by member nations of the United Nations. However, these limited mandates will remain limited and a source of frustration and criticism of UN peacekeeping activities until such time that the member states of the United Nations reach a consensus on the need to amend the UN Charter or pass resolutions giving UN peacekeepers more authority.

The UN withdrawal from Iraq in 2003 after a bombing of the UN headquarters, subsequent statements by former Secretary General Kofi Annan that the U.S. military intervention in Iraq was a mistake, and the results of an investigation into an illegal kickback scheme in the UN-run Oil-for-Food program that implicated several senior UN officials, including the former Secretary General's son, greatly increased tensions between the United States and the United Nations. Some observers now call for the United Nations to scale back its current level of peacekeeping in order to focus more effectively on global problems that nobody else can or will tackle. Others worry that without U.S. backing, the United Nations will be unable to fulfill an ever-growing list of

© Comstock/PunchStock

requests in such diverse areas as military, weapons proliferation, economic, social, and the environment.

The policies of the Bush administration proved to be a difficult period for the United Nations. The Bush administration's emphasis on unilateral action and its doctrine of preventive war have posed a profound challenge to the United Nation's founding principle of collective security and threaten the organization's continued relevance. The war in Iraq brought these conflicts to a new height. Washington's rush to invade Iraq split the Security Council in ways that have still not healed. Yet the years since the Iraq invasion showed how much the United States still needs the United Nation's unparalleled ability to confer international legitimacy and its growing experience in nation building. Even after the UN presence left Iraq, the United States had to turn to the organization at the end of 2003 in an effort to build legitimacy and support for delaying elections in Iraq.

The United States once again looked to the United Nations to play an expanded role in Iraqi post-war reconstruction in plans that call for a gradual reduction in the number of U.S. personnel in Iraq. The policy reversal on the part of the Bush administration underscored the fact that the United Nations is a useful body. The Obama administration's emphasis on using multilateral diplomacy and institutions to solve international issues may further increase U.S. support for the battered international organization, especially if U.S. rhetoric is backed-up by renewed amounts of resources. One indication that the UN is likely to receive more U.S. support is the fact that one of the first acts of the Obama administration was to order the United Staes to pay back U.S. dues that had been withheld from the organization in previous years. These shifts in U.S. policies are a tacit recognition that the United Nations, despite all of its problems, remains an important actor in global areas to combat disease, poverty, and global crime. However, few observers doubt that the organization is in a crisis period and requires some major overhauls if it is to function effectively throughout the twenty-first century.

Among the recommendations made to the new UN Secretary General, Ban Ki-Moon, to make the organization run more efficiently is to chop deadwood and cut red tape within the organization and to accept that certain organs, such as the Human Rights Council, the Security Council, or the General Assembly may not be "fixable." Other analysts, including the editor of *Foreign Policy,* Moisés Naím, argue in "Minilateralism" that so many efforts to reach new international agreements within the United Nations and elsewhere have failed that it is time to focus on a strategy of "minilateralism." According to Naím, minilateralism is "the process of bringing to the table the smallest possible number of countries needed to have the largest possible impact on solving a particular problem, whether trade or AIDS." Naím believes this approach is the best way to break the world's untenable gridlock rather than continuing the current "multilateralism of wishful thinking."

The inability of the United Nations Security Council's permanent members to reach a consensus has delayed implementing resolutions that might stop the killing of innocent civilians in places such as Darfur, Sudan, or in the Democratic Republic of the Congo. One idea is described by Gareth Evans, President of the International Crisis Group, in "The Responsibility to Protect: Meeting the Challenges." Evans advocates creating a new international norm as one way to break the current deadlock in the Security Council over whether the UN should be given authority to intervene militarily in conflicts that have killed, or threaten to kill, thousands of innocent civilians. The idea was floated years ago by Canada's former Foreign Minister, Lloyd Axworthy. The idea is to use a new doctrine called "responsibility to protect" to impose upon the United Nations an obligation to shield people all over the world from genocide and ethnic cleansing. The new doctrine has been picking up support among American neoconservatives and evangelical Christians alike and is reflected in the wording of a recent UN Security Council that recognizes the right of the United Nations to intervene in a sovereign country if the national government fails to protect its own people. For the movement, Western diplomats are focused on trying to reach an agreement with the Sudanese government, the Arab League, Russia, and China on the terms for an expanded international peacekeeping force to enter Darfur. However, the new doctrine appears to lay the groundwork for future UN military interventions in civil conflicts, including ones that are objected to by the national government.

The lack of a global consensus about what the United Nations should do as violence continues in Darfur reflects a more basic disagreement among world elites about what security should entail and who should be responsible for guaranteeing global security. What should constitute universal human rights remains another core dispute in international relations and law. After the historic election in South Africa, the new government sponsored a Truth and Reconciliation Commission (TRC) that allowed victims to confront their oppressors directly. If accused individuals confessed, expressed remorse, and apologized to their victims, they were not prosecuted through the legal system for their crimes. South Africa's TRC became a model of one approach towards reconciliation that has been used by other war-torn societies. While most outside observers were impressed by the process, many South African victims were disappointed with the meager compensation sums that they received. The pros and cons of a TRC highlight how difficult it can be to structure formal processes for reconciliation after intense and violent conflicts.

Another approach for dealing with perpetrators of collective violence and crimes against humanity has been to establish special international tribunals. These special courts, established in Rwanda and Yugoslavia, have spent a vast amount of human and monetary resources and resulted in few convictions. Most of these courts have been established to deal with specific instances of crimes against humanities under the auspices of the International Criminal Court (ICC). The trial of the former Liberian President and war lord, Charles Taylor, was moved to The Hague in The Netherlands as there was concern that holding the trial in West Africa might contribute to additional instability and prove difficult to accomplish from a logistic and resource perspective. To date, none of the criminal tribunals set up in Rwanda, the former Yugoslavia, or Liberia, that were supposed to bring justice to oppressed peoples, have succeeded in directly advancing human rights or implementing the wishes of victims. All of these trials have been lengthy affairs costing billions of dollars. Many important countries, including the United States, continue to refuse to recognize the jurisdiction of the ICC due to sovereignty concerns and unwillingness to agree to allow U.S. military personnel to be liable for charges that would be tried under the ICC's jurisdiction. One or more of these reasons are why some have concluded that it would be better to abandon these special courts.

In contrast, others argue that such fledgling institutions as the ICC and new norms, such the Responsibility to Protect or 'R2P', should be supported as it will take decades to establish new effective international institutions and norms. Other international legal experts advocate rewriting or possibly even scrapping the Geneva Convention, written to prevent the same type of atrocities that occurred during World War II, from occurring again. However, some argued on the recent 60th anniversary of the Geneva Convention that the old rules may no longer apply.

Minilateralism

MOISÉS NAÍM

Never say never. Because of the global economic crisis, habits that seemed unalterable are suddenly being altered. Americans are now saving more and consuming less. Financial institutions are no longer betting the house on risky investments they do not understand. Wealthy oil-exporting countries are tightening their belts. At least some emerging markets long prone to financial accidents are behaving with uncharacteristic prudence. Everywhere, change is in the air.

Everywhere, that is, except in the way humanity responds to its most menacing threats. You know the list: climate change, nuclear proliferation, terrorism, pandemics, trade protectionism, and more. Not one can be solved, or even effectively contained, without more successful international collaboration. And that is not happening.

When was the last time you heard that a large number of countries agreed to a major international accord on a pressing issue? Not in more than a decade. The last successful multilateral trade agreement dates back to 1994, when 123 countries gathered to negotiate the creation of the World Trade Organization and agreed on a new set of rules for international trade. Since then, all other attempts to reach a global trade deal have crashed. The same is true with multilateral efforts to curb nuclear proliferation; the last significant international nonproliferation agreement was in 1995, when 185 countries agreed to extend an existing nonproliferation treaty. In the decade and a half since, multilateral initiatives have not only failed, but India, Pakistan, and North Korea have demonstrated their certain status as nuclear powers. On the environment, the Kyoto Protocol, a global deal aimed at reducing greenhouse gas emissions, has been ratified by 184 countries since it was adopted in 1997, but the United States, the world's second-largest air polluter after China, has not done so, and many of the signatories have missed their targets.

The most recent multilateral initiative successfully endorsed by a large number of countries was in 2000, when 192 nations signed the United Nations Millennium Declaration, an ambitious set of eight goals ranging from halving the world's extreme poverty to halting the spread of HIV/AIDS and providing universal primary education—all by 2015. Although some progress toward achieving these goals has been made—mostly thanks to Asia's spectacular economic performance—the failure of rich countries to fully fund these efforts, execution problems in poor countries, and the global economic downturn make the achievement of the goals by 2015 unlikely.

The pattern is clear: Since the early 1990s, the need for effective multicountry collaboration has soared, but at the same time multilateral talks have inevitably failed; deadlines have been missed; financial commitments and promises have not been honored; execution has stalled; and international collective action has fallen far short of what was offered and, more importantly, needed. These failures represent not only the perpetual lack of international consensus, but also a flawed obsession with multilateralism as the panacea for all the world's ills.

So what is to be done? To start, let's forget about trying to get the planet's nearly 200 countries to agree. We need to abandon that fool's errand in favor of a new idea: **minilateralism.**

By **minilateralism,** I mean a smarter, more targeted approach: We should bring to the table the smallest possible number of countries needed to have the largest possible impact on solving a particular problem. Think of this as **minilateralism's** magic number.

The magic number, of course, will vary greatly depending on the problem. Take trade, for example. The Group of Twenty (G-20), which includes both rich and poor countries from six continents, accounts for 85 percent of the world's economy. The members of the G-20 could reach a major trade deal among themselves and make it of even greater significance by allowing any other country to join if it wishes to do so. Presumably, many would. Same with climate change. There, too, the magic number is about 20: The world's 20 top polluters account for 75 percent of the planet's greenhouse gas emissions. The number for nuclear proliferation is 21—enough to include both recognized and de facto nuclear countries, and several other powers who care about them. African poverty? About a dozen, including all the major donor countries and the sub-Saharan countries most in need. As for HIV/AIDS, 19 countries account for nearly two thirds of the world's AIDS-related deaths.

Of course, countries not invited to the table will denounce this approach as undemocratic and exclusionary. But the magic number will break the world's untenable gridlock, and agreements reached by the small number of countries whose actions are needed to generate real solutions can provide the foundation on which more-inclusive deals can be subsequently built. Minilateral deals can and should be open to any other country willing to play by the rules agreed upon by the original group.

The defects of **minilateralism** pale in comparison with the stalemate that characterizes 21st century multilateralism. It has become far too dangerous to continue to rely on large-scale multilateral negotiations that stopped yielding results almost two decades ago. The **minilateralism** of magic numbers is not a magic solution. But it's a far better bet at this point than the multilateralism of wishful thinking.

We should bring to the table the smallest possible number of countries needed to have the largest possible impact on solving a particular problem, whether trade or AIDS. Think of this as **minilateralism's** magic number.

MOISÉS NAÍM is editor in chief of *Foreign Policy*.

The Responsibility to Protect
Meeting the Challenges

GARETH EVANS

L ast year, at the height of the Burma/Myanmar regime's bloody suppression of its protesting monks, a well-known Chinese professor from Shanghai was asked by an American newspaper for his reaction. His quoted reply, in two stark sentences, went to the core of the issue I have been asked to talk to you about this evening: *"China has used tanks to kill people on Tiananmen Square. It is Myanmar's sovereign right to kill their own people, too."*

For a great many people in the world, and certainly to Western ears, that is about as chilling and abhorrent a statement as it is possible to imagine, an apparent apologia not only for Tiananmen and the October Crackdown, but the killing fields of Cambodia, the genocide in Rwanda, the bloody massacre of Srebrenica, and the crimes against humanity continuing in Darfur. It seems to embrace the starkest possible interpretation of Westphalian principles—not only that what happens within state borders is nobody else's business, but that sovereignty is a license to kill. It not only challenges head-on those who would argue for the option of coercive external military intervention in at least some of these situations, but seems to ignore all the developments in international human rights law which have occurred since 1945—from the Universal Declaration and the Covenants, to the Genocide Convention and the Rome Statute establishing the International Criminal Court.

For many others, however, particularly in the global South, the Chinese professor's statement, while chilling in its directness and certainly less diplomatically expressed than it might have been, captures a sentiment which has great resonance in the developing world—and which has too often been ignored by enthusiastic human rights campaigners arguing for 'the right to intervene', by coercive military force if necessary, in internal situations where major rights violations were purportedly occurring. While 'the right to intervene' or 'the right of humanitarian intervention' might be seen in most of the global North as a noble and effective rallying cry—and was so seen through most of the 1990s—it had the capacity elsewhere to enrage, and continues to do so, not least among those new states emerging through the whole post World War II period, proud of their identity, conscious in many cases of their fragility, and all too vividly remembering the many occasions in the past when they had been on the receiving end of *missions civilisatrices* from the colonial and imperial powers.

There is a third way of reacting to the sentiment expressed in the Chinese professor's statement, and that is not to leap into either attack or defence but to treat it as a *challenge*—to find a solution to the problem of mass atrocity crimes which is neither an absolutist defence of all the worst manifestations of traditional sovereignty, nor an equally absolutist statement of the right to intervene coercively anywhere and any time when people seem to be suffering. At the 2000 Millennium General Assembly Kofi Annan, despairing at the lack of any kind of consensus on this issue throughout the previous decade, put the problem in the clearest of terms: *If humanitarian intervention is indeed an unacceptable assault on sovereignty, how should we respond to a Rwanda, to a Srebrenica—to gross and systematic violations of human rights that offend every precept of our common humanity?*

It was in response to this challenge that the concept of the responsibility to protect was born, in the 2001 report of that name by the Canadian-sponsored International Commission on Intervention and State Sovereignty which I had the privilege of co-chairing with the distinguished Algerian diplomat Mohamed Sahnoun. The core idea of the responsibility to protect (or "R2P" as we are all calling it for short in this age of acronymphomania—a condition not unfamiliar to military audiences!) is very simple. Turn the notion of "right to intervene" upside down. Talk not about the "right" of big states to do anything, but the *responsibility* of *all* states to protect their own people from atrocity crimes, and to help others to do so. Start with the traditional concept of sovereignty, and talk about the primary responsibility being that of individual states themselves, with the role of other states in the first instance being to assist them in that role. But don't stop there: make it absolutely clear that if states do not or cannot meet the responsibility to protect their own people, as a result either of ill-will or incapacity, it then falls to the wider international community to take the appropriate action.

Focus not on the notion of "intervention" but of *protection:* look at the whole issue from the perspective of the victims, the men being killed, the women being raped, the children dying of starvation; and look at the responsibility in question as being above all a responsibility to *prevent,* with the question of reaction—through diplomatic pressure, through sanctions, through international criminal prosecutions, and ultimately through military action—arising only if prevention has failed. And accept coercive military intervention only as an absolute last resort, after a number of clearly defined criteria have been met, and the approval of the Security Council has been obtained.

Well, as many blue-ribbon commissions and panels have discovered over the years, it is one thing to labour mightily and produce what looks like a major new contribution to some policy debate, but quite another to get any policymaker to take any notice of it. But the extraordinary thing is that governments *did* take notice of the R2P idea: within four years—after a series of further high-level reports and a great deal of diplomatic scrambling—it had won unanimous endorsement by the more than 150 heads of state and government meeting as the UN General Assembly at the 2005 World Summit.

The Summit Outcome Document was as explicit as it could have been: in a section headed '*Responsibility to protect populations from genocide, war crimes, ethnic cleansing and crimes against humanity*', there are two substantive paragraphs, the first focusing on the responsibility of sovereign states to protect their own peoples and of other states to assist them in doing so, and the second on the need to take collective action in the case of states 'manifestly failing to protect their populations', including through the Security Council under Chapter VII of the Charter. In just four years, a mere blink of an eye in the history of ideas, a phrase that nobody had heard of had become the central conceptual reference point, accepted as such by the General Assembly, sitting at head of state and government level, without a single dissenting voice.

But it was too early in 2005, and it remains too early now, to break out the champagne. Our Shanghai professor's statement, made two years after the Summit, is clear enough indication in itself that the notion that sovereignty has real limits is not exactly universally accepted. And there are plenty of signs, especially in the UN corridors in New York, where nothing is ever beyond argument, that much more work needs to be done to bed down the new norm. For whatever reason—embrace of the concept but concern about its misuse; ideological association of any intervention with neo-imperialism or neo-colonialism; or in some cases simply embarrassment about their own behaviour—there is an evident willingness by a number of states to deflate or undermine the new norm before it is fully consolidated and operational. The language of "buyers remorse" is in the air. There has been a falling away of overt commitment to the norm in sub-Saharan Africa (although in substance still remaining a significant theme in the doctrine of the AU and some of the sub-regional organizations), and some increased scepticism in the Arab-Islamic and Latin American worlds. And in Asia there was, frankly, never much enthusiasm to start with.

So for those of us who believe that, whatever the compelling attractions of traditional sovereignty, we cannot simply turn a blind eye to mass atrocity crimes, and that 2005 cannot be the high water mark from which the tides now recede, there is still a big job ahead. The immediate objective must be to get to the point where, when the next conscience-shocking case of large-scale killing, or ethnic cleansing, or other war crimes or crimes against humanity come along, as they are all too unhappily likely to, the immediate reflex response of the whole international community will be not to ask *whether* action is necessary, but rather *what* action is required, by whom, when, and where.

There have been some encouraging signs—in particular the swift and supportive diplomatic and political response to the crisis in Kenya early in 2008, when responsibility to protect language was much used—that this may be beginning to happen, but there are still three big challenges that need to be addressed if R2P is indeed to have complete reflex international acceptance in principle, and if it is to be given practical operational effect as new cases arise.

The first challenge is essentially *conceptual*, to ensure that the scope and limits of the responsibility to protect are fully and completely understood in a way that is clearly not the case now. In particular, it is to ensure that R2P is seen not as a Trojan horse for bad old imperial, colonial and militarist habits, but rather the best starting point the international community has, and is maybe ever likely to have, in preventing and responding to genocide and other mass atrocity crimes.

The second challenge is *institutional* preparedness, to build the kind of capacity within international institutions, governments, and regional organization that will ensure that, assuming that there is an understanding of the need to act—whether preventively or reactively, and whether through political and diplomatic, or economic, or legal or policing and military measures—there will be the physical capability to do so.

The third challenge, as always, is *political* preparedness, how to generate that indispensable ingredient of will: how to have in place the mechanisms and strategies necessary to generate an effective political response as new R2P situations arise.

The Conceptual Challenge

The conceptual challenge is to address a number of misunderstandings about the scope and limits of R2P—some of them cynically and deliberately fostered by those with other axes to grind, or interests to protect, but the majority the product of quite genuine misapprehension as to what R2P is all about. Let me focus for present purposes on just the two major ones.

The first is to think of R2P too narrowly and to think that it is 'just another name for humanitarian intervention'. This is absolutely not the case: they are very different concepts. The very core of the traditional meaning of "humanitarian intervention" is coercive military intervention for humanitarian purposes—nothing more or less. But "the responsibility to protect" is about much more than that. Above all, R2P is about taking effective *preventive* action, and at the earliest possible stage. It implies encouragement and support being given to those states struggling with situations that have not yet deteriorated to the point where genocide or other atrocity crimes are a reality, but where it is foreseeable that if effective preventive action is not taken, with or without outside support, they *could* so deteriorate. It recognizes the need to bring to bear every appropriate preventive response: be it political, diplomatic, legal, economic, or in the security sector but falling short of coercive action (e.g. a "preventive deployment" of troops, as in Macedonia in 1995). The responsibility to take preventive action is very much that of the sovereign state itself, quite apart from that of the international community. And when it comes to the international community, a very big part of *its* preventive response should be to help countries to help themselves. A good case study of what R2P means in its preventive dimension is *Burundi*, in Central Africa since 1994, where what could easily have become another Rwanda scale genocide has been staved off by a series of peacemaking, peacekeeping and peacebuilding initiatives by the African and wider international community.

Of course there will be situations when prevention fails, crises and conflicts do break out, and reaction becomes necessary. But reaction does not have to mean *military* reaction: it can involve political, diplomatic, economic and legal pressure, measures which can themselves each cross the spectrum from persuasive to intrusive, and from less coercive (e.g. economic incentives, offers of political mediation or legal arbitration) to more coercive (e.g. economic sanctions, political and diplomatic isolation, threats of referral to the International Criminal Court)—something which is true of military capability as well. Coercive military action is not excluded when it is the only possible way to stop large scale killing and other atrocity crimes, as nobody doubts was the case, for example, in Rwanda or Srebrenica. But it is a travesty of the R2P principle to say that it is about military force and nothing else. That's what 'humanitarian intervention' is about, but it's not R2P.

Even when a situation is very extreme, that still does not mean that coercive military force is necessarily the right course. Quite apart from the legal question of whether force is permitted under the UN Charter—which for nearly all purposes requires Security Council approval—there are a series of prudential criteria, or criteria of legitimacy, which should always have to be satisfied before it is exercised, and all the major reports on R2P leading up to the World Summit have spelled them out in similar terms.

The first of those criteria is certainly the seriousness of the threat: does it involve genocide or other large-scale killing, or ethnic cleansing or other serious violations of international humanitarian law, actual or imminently apprehended? Not ten years or more earlier, as was the case with Iraq at the time of the misguided invasion in 2003, but here and now.

But even if the threshold of seriousness is crossed in one or other of these ways—as was clearly not the case in Iraq in 2003—that still does not mean it is time, under the R2P doctrine, for the invasion to start. There are another four criteria of legitimacy, all more or less equally important, which also have to be satisfied if the case is to be made out for coercive, non-consensual military force to be deployed within another country's sovereign territory: the motivation or primary purpose of the proposed military action (whether it was primarily to halt or avert the threat in question, or had some other main objective); last resort (whether there were reasonably available peaceful alternatives); the proportionality of the response; and, not least, the balance of consequences (whether overall more good than harm would be done by a military invasion).

In the case of *Darfur*, a great deal of the debate has ignored these considerations, with the choice for the international community too often being characterized as one between the stark options of Doing Nothing and Sending in the Marines, without acknowledging the many way stations in between. There is no doubt that the "seriousness of threat" criterion has been satisfied, with since 2003, in this region of Sudan, more than 200,000 dying from outright violence or war-related disease and malnutrition, well over two million being displaced, peacekeeping efforts proving manifestly inadequate, peace negotiations going nowhere fast, humanitarian relief faltering, the conflict spilling over into neighbouring countries, and the overall situation remaining desolate. But the argument is very strong—and accepted by most governments, and relief organisations on the ground—that a non-consensual military intervention (even assuming that the troops could be found anywhere to sustain it) would almost certainly be disastrously counterproductive, in terms of its impact on current humanitarian relief operations and the very fragile north-south peace process.

Darfur still remains, on any view, an "R2P situation", and one moreover where the responsibility to react has shifted to the international community because of the manifest abdication of its own sovereign responsibility by Khartoum. The inability here to use coercive military measures does not mean that this is a case of "R2P failure": it just means that the international responsibility to

protect the people of Darfur against the incapacity or ill-will of the Sudan government has to take other forms, including the application of sustained diplomatic, economic and—as we are seeing now with the prosecution of Bashir—legal pressure to change the cost-benefit balance of the regime's calculations.

The other major conceptual misunderstanding about R2P is at the other end of the spectrum from those which take it that R2P is only about the application of military force. It's the idea that R2P is about every kind of situation in which humans are at risk. Of course one can argue, linguistically and as a matter of good public policy, that the international community has the responsibility to protect people from the ravages of HIV/AIDS worldwide; the proliferation of nuclear weapons and other weapons of mass destruction; the ready availability of small arms, and the use of landmines and cluster bombs; the impact of dramatic climate change, particularly on specific groups like the Inuit of the Arctic circle; and much more besides. But if one is looking for umbrella language to bring these issues and themes together, it is much more appropriate to use a concept like "human security" than to say these are proper applications of the new international norm of "the responsibility to protect".

It is not just a matter here of making the formal point that these cases are clearly not intended to be subsumed under the various descriptions of mass atrocity crimes that appear in the World Summit outcome document and the relevant lead-up reports. The argument is a more practical one—if R2P is to be about protecting everybody from everything, it will end up protecting nobody from anything. The whole point of embracing the new language of "the responsibility to protect" is that it is capable of generating an effective, consensual response in extreme, conscience-shocking cases, in a way that "right to intervene" language simply was not. We need to preserve the focus and bite of "R2P" as a rallying cry in the face of mass atrocities.

Clear thinking in this respect was very much put to the test in the context of Cyclone Nargis in Myanmar recently. French Foreign Minister Bernard Kouchner opened up a hornet's nest when he argued that the initial foot-dragging of the generals—with scores of thousands of lives being thought to be at risk as a result—was itself sufficient to trigger the R2P principle, and to actually justify a coercive intervention, at least in the form of the air dropping or barge landing of relief supplies. Many people, again mainly in the global South, feared that this was the thin edge of the wedge and that R2P would become an excuse for a whole new set of coercive intrusions.

So those of us who were anxious that the whole R2P principle was being put at risk had to scramble quickly to get the debate back on the rails. The way we did it was to go back to the basic core of the concept: R2P is about protecting peoples from mass atrocity crimes, not natural disasters or other ills man-made or otherwise. It was only if the regime's behaviour could reasonably be characterized as constituting a crime against humanity—because of evidence of deliberate intention to harm the surviving delta population, or perhaps because of reckless indifference as to whether they suffered or not—that the threshold application of R2P would be triggered, and even then the multiple prudential criteria would have to be satisfied. In the event, under immense pressure from ASEAN and other neighbours as well as the wider international community, the generals did start to cooperate sufficiently for the feared catastrophe to be avoided. But the case shows how important it is to maintain a clear head about what is, and what is not, an R2P situation if any kind of general consensus is to be maintained.

The Institutional Challenge

When it comes to meeting the institutional challenge of ensuring that R2P is effectively operational, there are a huge range of issues that need to be addressed. For a start, who is actually capable of doing what? There is a large cast of actors potentially available in the international community: the multiple entities that make up the UN system, other global and regional intergovernmental organizations (including the EU, AU and NATO), national governments, and nongovernmental organizations. But who among them can best do whatever job is required, by whatever means are needed—supportive, persuasive, or coercive? And in terms of process, what more needs to be done, in the crucial areas of diplomatic, civilian and military capability, to improve the effectiveness of the response to R2P situations, again across the whole spectrum from prevention to reaction to rebuilding? I have just written a book of some 350 pages, to be published next month, a large proportion of which is devoted to these issues, and I can't begin to spell out now in the time available what is required.

But it is perhaps worth saying to this audience that when it comes to *military* preparedness, and in particular preparedness not just to mount training or monitoring or showing-the-flag operations but to actually deal with those perpetrating or obviously about to perpetrate atrocity crimes—the situation faced for example by the Dutch peacekeepers in Srebrenica, and by UNAMID forces in Sudan and MONUC forces in the Eastern Congo almost every day—a great deal more needs to be done. Exercising this responsibility poses a number of very difficult problems for military planners because—as this audience will know much better than me—it is not the kind of role in which militaries have been traditionally engaged, where they have well-developed doctrine and for which they can draw on a large body of experience.

What is involved here is neither traditional war fighting (where the object is to defeat an enemy, not just to stop particular kinds of violence and intimidation) nor, at the other extreme, traditional peacekeeping (which assumes that there is a peace to keep and is concerned essentially with monitoring, supervision, and verification). The new task is partly what is now described as "peacekeeping plus" or "complex peacekeeping," where it is assumed from the outset that the mission, while primarily designed to hold together a ceasefire or peace settlement, is likely to run into trouble from spoilers of one kind or another; that military force is quite likely to have to be used at some stage, for civilian protection purposes as well as in self-defense; and where, accordingly, a Chapter VII rather than just Chapter VI mandate is required. New UN peacekeeping missions in recent years have been constructed almost routinely on this basis, but that does not mean that military planners and commanders are yet comfortable with running them.

And that is not the end of the R2P story: the other part of the task is that which may arise in a Rwanda-type case, where there is the sudden eruption of conscience-shocking crimes against humanity, beyond the capacity of any existing peacekeeping mission to deal with, demanding a rapid and forceful "fire brigade" response from a new or extended mission to quash the violence and protect those caught up in it. This is more than just "peacekeeping plus"—dealing with spoilers—but, again, it is not traditional war fighting either.

Together, these "peacekeeping plus" and "fire brigade" operations have been described as "coercive protection missions," which is as useful terminology as any to use in addressing what is needed to create the capability—essentially the same in both cases—to operate them effectively. But getting reasonably clear the overall concept of operations, as this language does, is only the beginning of the story. Operational effectiveness in practice depends on getting a number of other things right: *force configuration* (what kind of force structure, and quantities of personnel and equipment, do militaries have to have to be able to mount these kinds of operations, individually or collectively); *deployability* (how rapidly can the necessary forces get to whatever theater is involved); *preparation* (ensuring that doctrine and training are matched to these operations); *mandates and rules of engagement* (ensuring that they are appropriate for the particular mission proposed); and *military-civilian cooperation* (ensuring that structures and processes are in place to maximize the effectiveness of each). I know that systematic attention is being paid now to all these issues by a number of national forces, and increasingly by those multilateral actors capable of mounting military operations, but still not enough has been done. These problems are going to be around to haunt us for a long time yet to come.

The Political Challenge

The remaining challenge is the age-old one of mobilizing political will. Everything else can be in place, but without the will to make something happen by someone capable of making it happen, the institutional capability to deliver the right kind of response at the right time—whether at the preventive, reactive or rebuilding end of the spectrum—simply won't be there, and even if the capability is there, it will not be used. For almost any spread of options, inertia will have the numbers.

But what I have learned very clearly from four decades of trying to make things happen, nationally and internationally, is that there is no point in simply mourning the absence of political will: this should be the occasion not for lamentation, but mobilization by those both within and outside the decision-making system in question. To explain a failure as the result of lack of political will, or organizational will, is simply to restate the problem, not provide an explanation or any kind of strategy for change. Political will is not a missing ingredient, waiting in each case to be found if we only had the key to the right cupboard or lifted the right stone. It has to be painfully and laboriously constructed, case by case, context by context.

It means ensuring that there is knowledge of the problem; generating concern to do something about it by making the right arguments—not just moral arguments, but national interest arguments, financial arguments, and domestic political arguments; creating a sense of confidence that doing something will actually make a difference; having in place institutional processes capable of translating that knowledge, concern and confident belief into relevant action; and leadership—without which the ticking of all four other boxes will not matter: inertia will win, every time. The discouraging news is that achieving all these things, in both national and international decision-making, is very hard work indeed, and needs a strong measure of luck as well, particularly when it comes to leaders: whether in a situation of fragility and transition a society finds itself with a Mandela, a Milosevic or a Mugabe is not easy to plan. The better news is that at least the arguments and strategies are there, and that there are plenty of civil society actors and public sector actors around—I'm sure some in this room—with the competence, commitment and organizational capacity to advance them.

There is a lot more I could say on all these substantive issues, but let me finish on a more personal note. I suspect that for all of us for whom the idea of responsibility to protect really resonates, there will have been some personal experience which has touched us deeply. For many in Europe that will be bound to be scarifying family memories of the Holocaust or Bosnia; for others in Africa and Asia it may be a matter of knowing survivors from Cambodia or Rwanda or Darfur or any of the other mass atrocity scenes of more recent decades; for others still, perhaps—and I know this is true of many in the US—it will be the awful sense that they could have done more, in their past official lives, to generate the kind of international response that these situations required.

For me it was my visit to Cambodia in the late 1960s, just before the genocidal slaughter which killed two million of its people. I was a young Australian making my first trip to Europe, to take up a scholarship in Oxford, and I spent six months wending my way by plane and overland through a dozen countries in Asia, and a few more in Africa and the Middle East as well. And in every one of them I spent many hours and days on student campuses and in student hangouts, and in hard-class cross-country trains and ramshackle rural buses, getting to know in the process—usually fleetingly, but quite often enduringly, in friendships that have lasted to this day—scores of some of the liveliest and brightest people of that generation.

In the years that followed I have kept running into Indonesians, Singaporeans, Malaysians, Thais, Vietnamese, Indians, Pakistanis and others who I either met on the road on that trip, or who were there at the time and had a store of common experiences to exchange. But among all the countries in Asia I visited then, there is just one, Cambodia, from which I never again, in later years, saw *any* of those students whom I had met and befriended, or anyone exactly like them. Not one of those kids with whom I drank beer, ate noodles and careened up and down the dusty road from Phnom Penh to Siem Reap in shared taxis, scattering chickens and pigs and little children in villages all along the way.

The reason, I am sadly certain, is that every last one of them died a few years later under Pol Pot's murderous genocidal regime—either targeted for execution in the killing fields as a middle-class intellectual enemy of the state, or dying, as more than a million did, from starvation and disease following forced displacement to labour in the countryside. The knowledge, and the memory, of what must have happened to those young men and women haunts me to this day.

What this means is that my own attachment to the idea, and ideal, of the responsibility to protect is not just a matter of intellectual persuasion, but of very powerful emotional commitment. I know that will be the case for a great many of you too, as it is for people I meet in every walk of life in every part of the world.

You have a role, as senior military personnel, that may well put you, professionally as well as personally, closer to the cutting edge of confronting this problem than most others will ever have a chance to do. So let us work together, in all our different capacities, to ensure that, however many of the world's problems we are unable to solve in the years ahead, we at least make sure that when it comes to mass atrocity crimes we never again have to look back with anger, comprehension and shame after some new and terrible catastrophe, wondering how we could possibly have let it all happen again—as we've done so often in the past, after the Holocaust, after Cambodia, after Rwanda, after Srebrenica . . . Let's make sure that when it comes to making the responsibility to protect people from genocide and other mass atrocity crimes, we never again have to say "never again".

Lecture by **GARETH EVANS**, President of the International Crisis Group, to 10th Asia Pacific Programme for Senior Military Officers, S.Rajaratnam School of International Studies, Singapore, 5 August 2008.

UNIT 10

The International Economic System

Unit Selections

Key Points to Consider

- What are some of the ways the Chinese are seeking to rebalance their economy after the worldwide slowdown and declines in the values of their foreign exchange reserves?

- What are some future perils for the United States in maintaining the current trade relationship with China?

- Why are many analysts looking towards African, Asian, and Latin American countries to become the "engines of growth" that will pull the international economy out of its current slump? Explain why you do or do not agree with this assessment?

- To recover and grow economically, what must African countries do in the future?

- Do you agree with the "buy American" provisions included in the recent stimulus legislation even if there are negative ramifications internationally from implementing such provisions? Be sure you can provide a thoughtful rationale for your position.

Student Website

www.mhhe.com/cls

Internet References

The Earth Institute at Columbia University
http://www.earth.columbia.edu
Graphs Comparing Countries
http://humandevelopment.bu.edu/use_exsisting_index/start_comp_graph.cfm
International Monetary Fund
http://www.imf.org
Kiva
http://www.kiva.org/
Peace Park Foundation
http://www.peaceparks.org/
Transparency International
http://www.transparency.org/
World Bank
http://www.worldbank.org
World Mapper Project
http://www.sasi.group.shef.ac.uk/worldmapper
World Trade Organization
http://www.wto.org/

There had been signs of trouble in the West's strongest economies for several years. However, recent downward trends in Asia or Europe were usually short lived and out of sync with periods of economic slowdowns in the United States. These cycles helped to prevent a widespread global downturn. This compensatory mechanism failed during 2008 as it became apparent that the United States, Europe, and much of Asia, including key sectors in China and key emerging markets, were all starting to experience the worst economic downturn since the Great Depression of the 1930s at the same time. The majority of world citizens, who live in developing countries, never participated in the successful years. Instead, most people in the developing world had already seen their economic standard of living decline in the decades prior to the 2008 downturn.

The global slowdown appeared first as a series of interrelated economic crises in the financial, mortgage, and credit markets in the United States. Each of these crises soon were evident to some degree in many countries in Europe, Asia, and worldwide. The $700 billion dollar U.S. rescue package, that quickly grew to US$820 billion, passed during the closing days of the Bush administration and a series of additional stimulus measures passed by Barak Obama and the Democratic Party-controlled Congress after the 2008 election, may have averted catastrophic economic meltdown but failed to prevent a worsening economic slowdown in the United States or worldwide. Although the rate of decline appeared to have stopped, at least in the United States towards the end of 2009, it was also clear that the interrelated economic global crises had reversed significant amounts of progress made during more prosperous years.

Since 2008 presidents and prime ministers from major countries around the world have met in attempts to avoid a deepening worldwide recession and to restore confidence in the world markets. However, it proved difficult to agree on specific proposals. Key European allies of the United States pushed for broad new roles for international organizations, empowering them to monitor everything from the global derivatives trade to the way major banks are regulated across borders. But the former Bush administration signaled reluctance to go that far fearing that such proposals could potentially co-opt the independence of the U.S. financial system or compromising free markets. While being more receptive to listen to such proposals, the Obama administration has yet to agree to any of the new proposals designed to sharpen existing international regulatory tools or to create new international organizations. Representatives of China said they shared the call made by European leaders for new international coordination, but China, like the United States, was reluctant to cede national control or support the formation of new international organizations. As one senior Chinese official involved in the discussions noted, "It is important to have an agency which can coordinate the global market and policies of different countries . . . but China doesn't like the idea of having a global SEC since no organization should affect the sovereignty of countries."

The multiple international economic crises have served to underscore just how interdependent the economies of the United States and China have become. James Fallows explores the

© Imagestate Media (John Foxx)

growing interdependence between the United States and China in "The $1.4 Trillion Dollar Question." Here Fallows explains how "the Chinese are subsidizing the American way of life." However, the adverse impacts in China from the economic slowdown in the United States illustrates why Fallows asks whether "We are playing them for suckers—or are they playing us?" Joergen Oerstroem Moeller notes in "China to the Rescue: Growing out of the Financial Crisis," that collectively the United States, Europe, and Japan account for more than half and maybe even two-thirds of the global economy depending upon the calculating method. Thus, the Chinese suffered along with the West as their economies started to melt down. The first places in China to suffer were the export sectors specializing in consumer goods. More than half of all toy factories in China were forced to close immediately and millions of workers in manufacturing sectors lost their jobs. However, as Moeller goes on to describe, after an initial downturn, the growth of domestic demand in China is helping to recover lost jobs. Moeller concludes that to "rebalance the world economy we need to look to growth from countries like China instead of the US."

The growing importance of China in the international economy since the onset of the international slowdown has become apparent in several areas. The position of major economic powers such as the United States and China are the main reason why few measures came out of international summit meetings held since 2008. For example, the economic summit held on November 15, 2008 between the developed and developing countries had been billed as Bretton Woods II. The first Bretton Woods conference, held after World War II, had created the existing world order led by the World Bank and International Monetary Fund. However, there had been months of preparatory work prior to the first Bretton Woods conference. The conference led by the victors of World War II lasted three weeks. In contrast, proposals for new international institutions were presented with little or no preparatory work at an annual summit of world leaders. Thus, it is hardly surprising that the only agreement coming out of Bretton Woods II was a general agreement for a new committee of international experts who would review global conditions and regulatory measures and make non-binding recommendations. Many world leaders were willing to wait for a new round of talks until after President-elect Barak Obama came to power in January 2009. However it was clear to all attendees and observers of the meeting that neither the United States nor the G-8 had the capacity to solve the current economic crises without engaging a much larger set of leaders from emerging economies as well. After World War II, the United States was the sole world economic and political nation-state that had the resources and political clout necessary to shape the postwar economic era. This is not the case today even though most central bankers and elected leaders around the world looked to the United States initially to solve the current crisis. No country yet has a comprehensive strategy to protect one or all countries from the global economic slowdown. As the depth and breath of the economic problems became apparent at the end of 2008, it became clear that the financial system, financial regulation and coordination requires the cooperation and active participation of a broader and more unwieldy group, including emerging economies, many of them loaded with foreign exchange reserves, foreign debts and influence over global financial markets. World leaders and publics are just now beginning to learn that economic interdependence has a dark and uncertain downside.

Some observers are now worried about the fact that the Chinese are shifting their investment strategy worldwide to seek ownership in more strategic sectors of the economies in both the developed and developing world. In Western economies, this shifting investment strategy has led to growing concerns about the increased amounts of investment in key U.S. high tech industries by national sovereign funds. China's vast foreign exchange reserves have been increasing despite the global slowdown. During the first six month of 2009 the reserve amount jumped another $318 billion, a sum almost equal to the gross domestic product of Argentina! Since the onset of the global economic crisis, China had aggressively been trying to diversify assets that up to now have been overwhelmingly investments in the U.S. dollar. The plunge in the value of the dollar and other U.S. assets meant that China was one of the biggest losers.

With foreign reserves totaling $2,270 billion, even after recent loses are subtracted, there is a vigorous debate occurring inside China about when and how to convert foreign currency reserves from U.S. dollars and for more demand that the dollar be replaced as the global reserve currency. A more feasible idea that is gaining popularity in China that can be implemented relatively quickly is for China to start investing more of the reserves into the BRIC nations, i.e. Brazil, Russia, India, China, as well as other developing countries. This strategy involves more than the current rate of Chinese investments in foreign oil and other natural resources. The goal would be to help stimulate new development and trade between China and the developing world that would approximate a "Marshall plan" in the amounts of money lent to developing countries in Africa, Asia, and Latin America. If successful, such an approach would create new international demand for Chinese goods and a fundamental shift in the interests of many nation-states worldwide as most projects assume future economic growth and prosperity will require countries in the developing world to become important future "engines of economic growth."

Such a scenario assumes that countries in the developing world will be able to learn the correct lessons from the current economic downturn and overcome decade-old problems tied to political instability, poor governance, endemic corruption, growing economic inequality, and increased rates of poverty and unemployment. As Jeffry Herbst et al. discuss in "Africa and the Global Economic Crisis: Threats, Opportunities, and Responses," African states will only be able to recover and grow from the recent world slowdown if regimes can achieve and sustain macroeconomic stability and promoting. Whether such trends are possible for Africa and the rest of the developing world remains an unanswered but important question.

In the short run a more serious type of threat to international economic recovery may be a new round of protectionist measures being imposed through national protectionist trade and investment measures in response to domestic pressures to do more to protect the welfare of nation-states' citizens. A wave of protectionist measures worldwide could quickly erode progress made throughout the post-World War II era to liberalize the movement of goods, people, and money across borders. In "Trade Wars Brewing in Economic Malaise: Outrage in Canada as U.S. Firms Sever Ties to Obey Stimulus Rules," Anthony Faiola and Lori Montgomery describe how one such protectionist measure, the new "buy American" provisions in the U.S. stimulus bill, is hitting Canadian manufacturers doing business with U.S. state and local governments. Some Canadian businesses worry that they may have to shift jobs to the United States to meet "Made-in-the-USA" requirements. While the impulse behind such measures are understandable in light of the continuing hard economic times, if such provisions spread worldwide, they could trigger an era much like the one the world witnessed prior to the outbreak of World War II.

The $1.4 Trillion Question

The Chinese are subsidizing the American way of life. Are we playing them for suckers—or are they playing us?

JAMES FALLOWS

Stephen Schwarzman may think he has image problems in America. He is the co-founder and CEO of the Blackstone Group, and he threw himself a $3 million party for his 60th birthday last spring, shortly before making many hundreds of millions of dollars in his company's IPO and finding clever ways to avoid paying taxes. That's nothing compared with the way he looks in China. Here, he and his company are surprisingly well known, thanks to blogs, newspapers, and talk-show references. In America, Schwarzman's perceived offense is greed—a sin we readily forgive and forget. In China, the suspicion is that he has somehow hoodwinked ordinary Chinese people out of their hard-earned cash.

Last June, China's Blackstone investment was hailed in the American press as a sign of canny sophistication. It seemed just the kind of thing the U.S. government had in mind when it hammered China to use its new wealth as a "responsible stakeholder" among nations. By putting $3 billion of China's national savings into the initial public offering of America's best-known private-equity firm, the Chinese government allied itself with a big-time Western firm without raising political fears by trying to buy operating control (it bought only 8 percent of Blackstone's shares, and nonvoting shares at that). The contrast with the Japanese and Saudis, who in their nouveau-riche phase roused irritation and envy with their showy purchases of Western brand names and landmark properties, was plain.

Six months later, it didn't look so canny, at least not financially. China's Blackstone holdings lost, on paper, about $1 billion, during a time when the composite index of the Shanghai Stock Exchange was soaring. At two different universities where I've spoken recently, students have pointed out that Schwarzman was a major Republican donor. A student at Fudan University knew a detail I didn't: that in 2007 President Bush attended a Republican National Committee fund-raiser at Schwarzman's apartment in Manhattan (think what he would have made of the fact that Schwarzman, who was one year behind Bush at Yale, had been a fellow member of Skull and Bones). Wasn't the whole scheme a way to take money from the Chinese people and give it to the president's crony?

The Blackstone case is titillating in its personal detail, but it is also an unusually clear and personalized symptom of a deeper, less publicized, and potentially much more destructive tension in U.S.–China relations. It's not just Stephen Schwarzman's company that the *laobaixing,* the ordinary Chinese masses, have been subsidizing. It's everyone in the United States.

Through the quarter-century in which China has been opening to world trade, Chinese leaders have deliberately held down living standards for their own people and propped them up in the United States. This is the real meaning of the vast trade surplus—$1.4 trillion and counting, going up by about $1 billion per day—that the Chinese government has mostly parked in U.S. Treasury notes. In effect, every person in the (rich) United States has over the past 10 years or so borrowed about $4,000 from someone in the (poor) People's Republic of China. Like so many imbalances in economics, this one can't go on indefinitely, and therefore won't. But the way it ends—suddenly versus gradually, for predictable reasons versus during a panic—will make an enormous difference to the U.S. and Chinese economies over the next few years, to say nothing of bystanders in Europe and elsewhere.

Any economist will say that Americans have been living better than they should—which is by definition the case when a nation's total consumption is greater than its total production, as America's now is. Economists will also point out that, despite the glitter of China's big cities and the rise of its billionaire class, China's people have been living far worse than they could. That's what it means when a nation consumes only half of what it produces, as China does.

Neither government likes to draw attention to this arrangement, because it has been so convenient on both sides. For China, it has helped the regime guide development in the way it would like—and keep the domestic economy's growth rate from crossing the thin line that separates "unbelievably fast" from "uncontrollably inflationary." For America, it has meant cheaper iPods, lower interest rates, reduced mortgage payments, a lighter tax burden. But because of political tensions in both countries, and because of the huge and growing size of the imbalance, the arrangement now shows signs of cracking apart.

In an article two and a half years ago ("Countdown to a Meltdown," July/August 2005), I described an imagined future in which a real-estate crash and shakiness in the U.S. credit markets led to panic by Chinese and other foreign investors, with unpleasant effects for years to come. The real world has recently had inklings of similar concerns. In the past six months, relative nobodies in China's establishment were able to cause brief panics in the foreign-exchange markets merely by hinting that China might stop supplying so much money to the United States. In August, an economic researcher named He Fan, who works at the Chinese Academy of Social Sciences and did part of his doctoral research at Harvard, suggested in an op-ed piece in *China Daily* that if the U.S. dollar kept collapsing in value, China might move some of its holdings into stronger currencies. This was presented not as a threat but as a statement of the obvious, like saying that during a market panic, lots of people sell. The column quickly provoked alarmist stories in Europe and America suggesting that China was considering the "nuclear option"—unloading its dollars.

A few months later, a veteran Communist Party politician named Cheng Siwei suggested essentially the same thing He Fan had. Cheng, in his mid-70s, was trained as a chemical engineer and has no official role in setting Chinese economic policy. But within hours of his speech, a flurry of trading forced the dollar to what was then its lowest level against the euro and other currencies. The headline in the *South China Morning Post* the next day was: "Officials' Words Shrivel U.S. Dollar." Expressing amazement at the markets' response, Carl Weinberg, chief economist at the High Frequency Economics advisory group, said, "This would be kind of like Congressman Charlie Rangel giving a speech telling the Fed to hike or cut interest rates." (Cheng, like Rangel, is known for colorful comments—but he is less powerful, since Rangel after all chairs the House Ways and Means Committee.) In the following weeks, phrases like "run on the dollar" and "collapse of confidence" showed up more and more frequently in financial newsletters. The nervousness only increased when someone who does have influence, Chinese Premier Wen Jiabao, said last November, "We are worried about how to preserve the value" of China's dollar holdings.

When the dollar is strong, the following (good) things happen: the price of food, fuel, imports, manufactured goods, and just about everything else (vacations in Europe!) goes down. The value of the stock market, real estate, and just about all other American assets goes up. Interest rates go down—for mortgage loans, credit-card debt, and commercial borrowing. Tax rates can be lower, since foreign lenders hold down the cost of financing the national debt. The only problem is that American-made goods become more expensive for foreigners, so the country's exports are hurt.

When the dollar is weak, the following (bad) things happen: the price of food, fuel, imports, and so on (no more vacations in Europe) goes up. The value of the stock market, real estate, and just about all other American assets goes down. Interest rates are higher. Tax rates can be higher, to cover the increased cost of financing the national debt. The only benefit is that American-made goods become cheaper for foreigners, which helps create new jobs and can raise the value of export-oriented American firms (winemakers in California, producers of medical devices in New England).

The dollar's value has been high for many years—unnaturally high, in large part because of the implicit bargain with the Chinese. Living standards in China, while rising rapidly, have by the same logic been unnaturally low. To understand why this situation probably can't go on, and what might replace it—via a dollar crash or some other event—let's consider how this curious balance of power arose and how it works.

Why a Poor Country Has So Much Money

By 1996, China amassed its first $100 billion in foreign assets, mainly held in U.S. dollars. (China considers these holdings a state secret, so all numbers come from analyses by outside experts.) By 2001, that sum doubled to about $200 billion, according to Edwin Truman of the Peterson Institute for International Economics in Washington. Since then, it has increased more than sixfold, by well over a trillion dollars, and China's foreign reserves are now the largest in the world. (In second place is Japan, whose economy is, at official exchange rates, nearly twice as large as China's but which has only two-thirds the foreign assets; the next-largest after that are the United Arab Emirates and Russia.) China's U.S. dollar assets probably account for about 70 percent of its foreign holdings, according to the latest analyses by Brad Setser, a former Treasury Department economist now with the Council on Foreign Relations; the rest are mainly in euros, plus some yen. Most of China's U.S. investments are in conservative, low-yield instruments like Treasury notes and federal-agency bonds, rather than showier Blackstone-style bets. Because notes and bonds backed by the U.S. government are considered the safest investments in the world, they pay lower interest than corporate bonds, and for the past two years their annual interest payments of 4 to 5 percent have barely matched the 5-to-6-percent decline in the U.S. dollar's value versus the RMB.

Americans sometimes debate (though not often) whether in principle it is good to rely so heavily on money controlled by a foreign government. The debate has never been more relevant, because America has never before been so deeply in debt to one country. Meanwhile, the Chinese are having a debate of their own—about whether the deal makes sense for them. Certainly China's officials are aware that their stock purchases prop up 401(k) values, their money-market holdings keep down American interest rates, and their bond purchases do the same thing—plus allow our government to spend money without raising taxes.

"From a distance, this, to say the least, is strange," Lawrence Summers, the former treasury secretary and president of Harvard, told me last year in Shanghai. He was referring to the oddity that a country with so many of its own needs still unmet would let "this $1 trillion go to a mature, old, rich place from a young, dynamic place."

> "From a distance, this, to say the least, is strange," said Lawrence Summers—that a country with so many of its own needs still unmet would let "this $1 trillion go to a mature, old, rich place."

It's more than strange. Some Chinese people are rich, but China as a whole is unbelievably short on many of the things that qualify countries as fully developed. Shanghai has about the same climate as Washington, D.C.—and its public schools have no heating. (Go to a classroom when it's cold, and you'll see 40 children, all in their winter jackets, their breath forming clouds in the air.) Beijing is more like Boston. On winter nights, thousands of people mass along the curbsides of major thoroughfares, enduring long waits and fighting their way onto hopelessly overcrowded public buses that then spend hours stuck on jammed roads. And these are the showcase cities! In rural Gansu province, I have seen schools where 18 junior-high-school girls share a single dormitory room, sleeping shoulder to shoulder, sardine-style.

Better schools, more-abundant parks, better health care, cleaner air and water, better sewers in the cities—you name it, and if it isn't in some way connected to the factory-export economy, China hasn't got it, or not enough. This is true at the personal level, too. The average cash income for workers in a big factory is about $160 per month. On the farm, it's a small fraction of that. Most people in China feel they are moving up, but from a very low starting point.

So why is China shipping its money to America? An economist would describe the oddity by saying that China has by far the highest national savings in the world. This sounds admirable, but when taken to an extreme—as in China—it indicates an economy out of sync with the rest of the world, and one that is deliberately keeping its own people's living standards lower than they could be. For comparison, India's savings rate is about 25 percent, which in effect means that India's people consume 75 percent of what they collectively produce. (Reminder from Ec 101: The savings rate is the net share of national output either exported or saved and invested for consumption in the future. Effectively, it's what your own people produce but don't use.) For Korea and Japan, the savings rate is typically from the high 20s to the mid-30s. Recently, America's has at times been below zero, which means that it consumes, via imports, more than it makes.

China's savings rate is a staggering 50 percent, which is probably unprecedented in any country in peacetime. This doesn't mean that the average family is saving half of its earnings—though the personal savings rate in China is also very high. Much of China's national income is "saved" almost invisibly and kept in the form of foreign assets. Until now, most Chinese have willingly put up with this, because the economy has been growing so fast that even a suppressed level of consumption makes most people richer year by year.

But saying that China has a high savings rate describes the situation without explaining it. Why should the Communist Party of China countenance a policy that takes so much wealth from the world's poor, in their own country, and gives it to the United States? To add to the mystery, why should China be content to put so many of its holdings into dollars, knowing that the dollar is virtually guaranteed to keep losing value against the RMB? And how long can its people tolerate being denied so much of their earnings, when they and their country need so much? The Chinese government did not explicitly set out to tighten the belt on its population while offering cheap money to American homeowners. But the fact that it does results directly from explicit choices it *has* made—two in particular. Both arise from crucial controls the government maintains over an economy that in many other ways has become wide open. The situation may be easiest to explain by following a U.S. dollar on its journey from a customer's hand in America to a factory in China and back again to the T-note auction in the United States.

The Voyage of a Dollar

Let's say you buy an Oral-B electric toothbrush for $30 at a CVS in the United States. I choose this example because I've seen a factory in China that probably made the toothbrush. Most of that $30 stays in America, with CVS, the distributors, and Oral-B itself. Eventually $3 or so—an average percentage for small consumer goods—makes its way back to southern China.

When the factory originally placed its bid for Oral-B's business, it stated the price in dollars: X million toothbrushes for Y dollars each. But the Chinese manufacturer can't use the dollars directly. It needs RMB—to pay the workers their 1,200-RMB ($160) monthly salary, to buy supplies from other factories in China, to pay its taxes. So it takes the dollars to the local commercial bank—let's say the Shenzhen Development Bank. After showing receipts or waybills to prove that it earned the dollars in genuine trade, not as speculative inflow, the factory trades them for RMB.

This is where the first controls kick in. In other major countries, the counterparts to the Shenzhen Development Bank can decide for themselves what to do with the dollars they take in. Trade them for euros or yen on the foreign-exchange market? Invest them directly in America? Issue dollar loans? Whatever they think will bring the highest return. But under China's "surrender requirements," Chinese banks can't do those things. They must treat the dollars, in effect, as contraband, and turn most or all of them (instructions vary from time to time) over to China's equivalent of the Federal Reserve Bank, the People's Bank of China, for RMB at whatever is the official rate of exchange.

With thousands of transactions per day, the dollars pile up like crazy at the PBOC. More precisely, by more than a billion dollars per day. They pile up even faster than the trade surplus with America would indicate, because customers in many other countries settle their accounts in dollars, too.

The PBOC must do something with that money, and current Chinese doctrine allows it only one option: to give the dollars to another arm of the central government, the State Administration for Foreign Exchange. It is then SAFE's job to figure out where to park the dollars for the best return: so much in U.S. stocks, so much shifted to euros, and the great majority left in the boring safety of U.S. Treasury notes.

And thus our dollar comes back home. Spent at CVS, passed to Oral-B, paid to the factory in southern China, traded for RMB at the Shenzhen bank, "surrendered" to the PBOC, passed to SAFE for investment, and then bid at auction for Treasury notes, it is ready to be reinjected into the U.S. money supply and spent again—ideally on Chinese-made goods.

Spent at CVS, passed to Oral-B, paid to the factory, "surrendered" to the People's Bank of China, then bid at auction for Treasury notes, our dollar is reinjected into the U.S. money supply and spent again.

At no point did an ordinary Chinese person decide to send so much money to America. In fact, at no point was most of this money at his or her disposal at all. These are in effect enforced savings, which are the result of the two huge and fundamental choices made by the central government.

One is to dictate the RMB's value relative to other currencies, rather than allow it to be set by forces of supply and demand, as are the values of the dollar, euro, pound, etc. The obvious reason for doing this is to keep Chinese-made products cheap, so Chinese factories will stay busy. This is what Americans have in mind when they complain that the Chinese government is rigging the world currency markets. And there are numerous less obvious reasons. The very act of managing a currency's value may be a more important distorting factor than the exact rate at which it is set. As for the rate—the subject of much U.S. lecturing—given the huge difference in living standards between China and the United States, even a big rise in the RMB's value would leave China with a price advantage over manufacturers elsewhere. (If the RMB doubled against the dollar, a factory worker might go from earning $160 per month to $320—not enough to send many jobs back to America, though enough to hurt China's export economy.) Once a government decides to thwart the market-driven exchange rate of its currency, it must control countless other aspects of its financial system, through instruments like surrender requirements and the equally ominous-sounding "sterilization bonds" (a way of keeping foreign-currency swaps from creating inflation, as they otherwise could).

These and similar tools are the way China's government imposes an unbelievably high savings rate on its people. The result, while very complicated, is to keep the buying power earned through China's exports out of the hands of Chinese consumers as a whole. Individual Chinese people have certainly gotten their hands on a lot of buying power, notably the billionaire entrepreneurs who have attracted the world's attention (see "Mr. Zhang Builds His Dream Town," March 2007). But when it comes to amassing international reserves, what matters is that China as a whole spends so little of what it earns, even as some Chinese people spend a lot.

The other major decision is not to use more money to address China's needs directly—by building schools and agricultural research labs, cleaning up toxic waste, what have you. Both decisions stem from the central government's vision of what is necessary to keep China on its unprecedented path of growth. The government doesn't want to let the market set the value of the RMB, because it thinks that would disrupt the constant growth and the course it has carefully and expensively set for the factory-export economy. In the short run, it worries that the RMB's value against the dollar and the euro would soar, pricing some factories in "expensive" places such as Shanghai out of business. In the long run, it views an unstable currency as a nuisance in itself, since currency fluctuation makes everything about business with the outside world more complicated. Companies have a harder time predicting overseas revenues, negotiating contracts, luring foreign investors, or predicting the costs of fuel, component parts, and other imported goods.

And the government doesn't want to increase domestic spending dramatically, because it fears that improving average living conditions could paradoxically intensify the rich–poor tensions that are China's major social problem. The country is already covered with bulldozers, wrecking balls, and construction cranes, all to keep the manufacturing machine steaming ahead. Trying to build anything more at the moment—sewage-treatment plants, for a start, which would mean a better life for its own people, or smokestack scrubbers and related "clean" technology, which would start to address the world pollution for which China is increasingly held responsible—would likely just drive prices up, intensifying inflation and thus reducing the already minimal purchasing power of most workers. Food prices have been rising so fast that they have led to riots. In November, a large Carrefour grocery in Chongqing offered a limited-time sale of vegetable oil, at 20 percent (11 RMB, or $1.48) off the normal price per bottle. Three people were killed and 31 injured in a stampede toward the shelves.

This is the bargain China has made—rather, the one its leaders have imposed on its people. They'll keep creating new factory jobs, and thus reduce China's own social tensions and create opportunities for its rural poor. The Chinese will live better year by year, though not as well as they could. And they'll be protected from the risk of potentially catastrophic hyperinflation, which might undo what the nation's decades of growth have built. In exchange, the government will hold much of the nation's wealth in paper assets in the United States, thereby preventing a run on the dollar, shoring up relations between China and America, and sluicing enough cash back into Americans' hands to let the spending go on.

What the Chinese Hope Will Happen

The Chinese public is beginning to be aware that its government is sitting on a lot of money—money not being spent to help China directly, money not doing so well in Blackstone-style foreign investments, money invested in the ever-falling U.S. dollar. Chinese bloggers and press commentators have begun making a connection between the billions of dollars the country is sending away and the domestic needs the country has not addressed. There is more and more pressure to show that the return on foreign investments is worth China's sacrifice—and more and more potential backlash against bets that don't pay off. (While the Chinese government need not stand for popular election, it generally tries to reduce sources of popular discontent when it can.) The public is beginning to behave like the demanding client of an investment adviser: it wants better returns, with fewer risks.

This is the challenge facing Lou Jiwei and Gao Xiqing, who will play a larger role in the U.S. economy than Americans are accustomed to from foreigners. Lou, a longtime Communist Party official in his late 50s, is the chairman of the new China Investment Corporation, which is supposed to find creative ways to increase returns on at least $200 billion of China's foreign assets. He is influential within the party but has little international experience. Thus the financial world's attention has turned to Gao Xiqing, who is the CIC's general manager.

Twenty years ago, after graduating from Duke Law School, Gao was the first Chinese citizen to pass the New York State Bar Exam. He returned to China in 1988, after several years as an associate at the New York law firm Mudge, Rose (Richard Nixon's old firm) to teach securities law and help develop China's newly established stock markets. By local standards, he is hip. At an economics conference in Beijing in December, other Chinese speakers wore boxy dark suits. Gao, looking fit in his mid-50s, wore a tweed jacket and black turtleneck, an Ironman-style multifunction sports watch on his wrist.

Under Lou and Gao, the CIC started with a bang with Blackstone—the wrong kind of bang. Now, many people suggest, it may be chastened enough to take a more careful approach. Indeed, that was the message it sent late last year, with news that its next round of investments would be in China's own banks, to shore up some with credit problems. And it looks to be studying aggressive but careful ways to manage huge sums. About the time the CIC was making the Blackstone deal, its leadership and staff undertook a crash course in modern financial markets. They hired the international consulting firm McKinsey to prepare confidential reports about the way they should organize themselves and the investment principles they should apply. They hired Booz Allen Hamilton to prepare similar reports, so they could compare the two. Yet another consulting firm, Towers Perrin, provided advice, especially about staffing and pay. The CIC leaders commissioned studies of other large state-run investment funds—in Norway, Singapore, the Gulf States, Alaska—to see which approaches worked and which didn't. They were fascinated by the way America's richest universities managed their endowments, and ordered multiple copies of *Pioneering Portfolio Management*, by David Swensen, who as Yale's chief investment officer has guided its endowment to sustained and rapid growth. Last summer, teams from the CIC made long study visits to Yale and Duke universities, among others.

Gao Xiqing and other CIC officials have avoided discussing their plans publicly. "If you tell people ahead of time what you're going to do—well, you just can't operate that way in a market system," he said at his Beijing appearance. "What I can say is, we'll play by the international rules, and we'll be responsible investors." Gao emphasized several times how much the CIC had to learn: "We're the new kids on the block. Because of media attention, there is huge pressure on us—we're already under water now." The words "under water" were in natural-sounding English, and clearly referred to Blackstone.

Others familiar with the CIC say that its officials are coming to appreciate the unusual problems they will face. For instance: any investment group needs to be responsible to outside supervisors, and the trick for the CIC will be to make itself accountable to Communist Party leadership without becoming a mere conduit for favored investment choices by party bosses. How can it attract the best talent? Does it want to staff up quickly, to match its quickly mounting assets, by bidding for financial managers on the world market—where many of the candidates are high-priced, not fluent in Chinese, and reluctant to move to Beijing? Or can it afford to take the time to home-grow its own staff?

While the CIC is figuring out its own future, outsiders are trying to figure out the CIC—and also SAFE, which will continue handling many of China's assets. As far as anyone can tell, the starting point for both is risk avoidance. No more Blackstones. No more CNOOC-Unocals. (In 2005, the Chinese state oil firm CNOOC attempted to buy U.S.–based Unocal. It withdrew the offer in the face of intense political opposition to the deal in America.) One person involved with the CIC said that its officials had seen recent Lou Dobbs broadcasts criticizing "Communist China" and were "shellshocked" about the political resentment their investments might encounter in the United States. For all these reasons the Chinese leadership, as another person put it, "has a strong preference to follow someone else's lead, not in an imitative way" but as an unobtrusive minority partner wherever possible. It will follow the lead of others for now, that is, while the CIC takes its first steps as a gigantic international financial investor.

The latest analyses by Brad Setser suggest that despite all the talk about abandoning the dollar, China is still putting about as large a share of its money into dollars as ever, somewhere between 65 and 70 percent of its foreign earnings. "Politically, the last thing they want is to signal a loss of faith in the dollar," Andy Rothman, of the financial firm CLSA, told me; that would lead to a surge in the RMB, which would hurt Chinese exporters, not to mention the damage it would cause to China's vast existing dollar assets.

The problem is that these and other foreign observers must guess at China's aims, rather than knowing for sure. As Rothman put it, "The opaqueness about intentions and goals is always the issue." The mini-panics last year took hold precisely because no one could be sure that SAFE was not about to change course.

It is no exaggeration to say that the stability of the U.S. and Chinese economies over the next few years depends on how today's tensions are resolved.

The uncertainty arises in part from the limited track record of China's new financial leadership. As one American financier pointed out to me: "The man in charge of the whole thing"—Lou Jiwei—"has never bought a share of stock, never bought a car, never bought a house." Another foreign financier said, after meeting some CIC staffers, "By Chinese terms, these are very sophisticated people." But, he went on to say, in a professional sense none of them had lived through the financial crises of the last generation: the U.S. market crash of 1987, the "Asian flu" of the late 1990s, the collapse of the Internet bubble soon afterward. The Chinese economy was affected by all these upheavals, but the likes of Gao Xiqing were not fully exposed to their lessons, sheltered as they were within Chinese institutions.

Foreign observers also suggest that, even after exposure to the Lou Dobbs clips, the Chinese financial leadership may not yet fully grasp how suspicious other countries are likely to be of China's financial intentions, for reasons both fair and unfair. The unfair reason is all-purpose nervousness about any new rising power. "They need to understand, and they don't, that everything they do will be seen as political," a financier with extensive experience in both China and America told me. "Whatever they buy, whatever they say, whatever they do will be seen as China Inc."

The fair reason for concern is, again, the transparency problem. Twice in the past year, China has in nonfinancial ways demonstrated the ripples that a nontransparent policy creates. Last January, its military intentionally shot down one of its own satellites, filling orbital paths with debris. The exercise greatly alarmed the U.S. military, because of what seemed to be an implied threat to America's crucial space sensors. For several days, the Chinese government said nothing at all about the test, and nearly a year later, foreign analysts still debate whether it was a deliberate provocation, the result of a misunderstanding, or a freelance effort by the military. In November, China denied a U.S. Navy aircraft carrier, the *Kitty Hawk,* routine permission to dock in Hong Kong for Thanksgiving, even though many Navy families had gone there for a reunion. In each case, the most ominous aspect is that outsiders could not really be sure what the Chinese leadership had in mind. Were these deliberate taunts or shows of strength? The results of factional feuding within the leadership? Simple miscalculations? In the absence of clear official explanations no one really knew, and many assumed the worst.

So it could be with finance, unless China becomes as transparent as it is rich. Chinese officials say they will move in that direction, but they're in no hurry. Last fall, Edwin Truman prepared a good-governance scorecard for dozens of "sovereign wealth" funds—government-run investment funds like SAFE and the CIC. He compared funds from Singapore, Korea, Norway, and elsewhere, ranking them on governing structure, openness, and similar qualities. China's funds ended up in the lower third of his list— better-run than Iran's, Sudan's, or Algeria's, but worse than Mexico's, Russia's, or Kuwait's. China received no points in the "governance" category and half a point out of a possible 12 for "transparency and accountability."

Foreigners (ordinary Chinese too, for that matter) can't be sure about the mixture of political and strictly economic motives behind future investment decisions the Chinese might make. When China's president, Hu Jintao, visited Seattle two years ago, he announced a large purchase of Boeing aircraft. When France's new president, Nicolas Sarkozy, visited China late last year, Hu announced an even larger purchase of Airbuses. Every Chinese order for an airplane is a political as well as commercial decision. Brad Setser says that the Chinese government probably believed that it would get "credit" for the Blackstone purchase in whatever negotiations came up next with the United States, in the same way it would get credit for choosing Boeing. This is another twist to the Kremlinology of trying to discern China's investment strategy.

Where the money goes, other kinds of power follow. Just ask Mikhail Gorbachev, as he reflects on the role bankruptcy played in bringing down the Soviet empire. While Japan's great wealth has not yet made it a major diplomatic actor, and China has so far shied from, rather than seized, opportunities to influence events outside its immediate realm, time and money could change that. China's military is too weak to challenge the U.S. directly even in the Taiwan Straits, let alone anyplace else. That, too, could change.

A Balance of Terror

Let's take these fears about a rich, strong China to their logical extreme. The U.S. and Chinese governments are always disagreeing—about trade, foreign policy, the environment. Someday the disagreement could be severe. Taiwan, Tibet, North Korea, Iran—the possibilities are many, though Taiwan always heads the list. Perhaps a crackdown within China. Perhaps another accident, like the U.S. bombing of China's embassy in Belgrade nine years ago, which everyone in China still believes was intentional and which no prudent American ever mentions here.

Whatever the provocation, China would consider its levers and weapons and find one stronger than all the rest—one no other country in the world can wield. Without China's billion dollars a day, the United States could not keep its economy stable or spare the dollar from collapse.

Would the Chinese use that weapon? The reasonable answer is no, because they would wound themselves grievously, too. Their years of national savings are held in the same dollars that would be ruined; in a panic, they'd get only a small share out before the value fell. Besides, their factories depend on customers with dollars to spend.

But that "reassuring" answer is actually frightening. Lawrence Summers calls today's arrangement "the balance of financial terror," and says that it is flawed in the same way that the "mutually assured destruction" of the Cold War era was. That doctrine held that neither the United States nor the Soviet Union would dare use its nuclear weapons against the other, since it would be destroyed in return. With allowances for hyperbole, something similar applies to the dollar standoff. China can't afford to stop feeding dollars to Americans, because China's own dollar holdings would be devastated if it did. As long as that logic holds, the system works. As soon as it doesn't, we have a big problem.

What might poke a giant hole in that logic? Not necessarily a titanic struggle over the future of Taiwan. A simple mistake, for one thing. Another speech by Cheng Siwei—perhaps in response to a provocation by Lou Dobbs. A rumor that the oil economies are moving out of dollars for good, setting their prices in euros. Leaked suggestions that the Chinese government is hoping to buy Intel, leading to angry denunciations on the Capitol floor, leading to news that the Chinese will sit out the next Treasury auction. As many world tragedies have been caused by miscalculation as by malice.

Or pent-up political tensions, on all sides. China's lopsided growth—ahead in exports, behind in schooling, the environment, and everything else—makes the country socially less stable as it grows richer. Meanwhile, its expansion disrupts industries and provokes tensions in the rest of the world. The billions of dollars China pumps into the United States each week strangely seem to make it harder rather than easier for Americans to face their own structural problems. One day, something snaps. Suppose the CIC makes another bad bet—not another Blackstone but another World-Com, with billions of dollars of Chinese people's assets irretrievably wiped out. They will need someone to blame, and Americans, for their part, are already primed to blame China back.

So, the shock comes. Does it inevitably cause a cataclysm? No one can know until it's too late. The important question to ask about the U.S.–China relationship, the economist Eswar Prasad, of Cornell, recently wrote in a paper about financial imbalances, is whether it has "enough flexibility to withstand and recover from large shocks, either internal or external." He suggested that the contained tensions were so great that the answer could be no.

Today's American system values upheaval; it's been a while since we've seen too much of it. But Americans who lived through the Depression knew the pain real disruption can bring. Today's Chinese, looking back on their country's last century, know, too. With a lack of tragic imagination, Americans have drifted into an arrangement that is comfortable while it lasts, and could last for a while more. But not much longer.

Years ago, the Chinese might have averted today's pressures by choosing a slower and more balanced approach to growth. If they had it to do over again, I suspect they would in fact choose just the same path—they have gained so much, including the assets they can use to do what they have left undone, whenever the government chooses to spend them. The same is not true, I suspect, for the United States, which might have chosen a very different path: less reliance on China's subsidies, more reliance on paying as we go. But it's a little late for those thoughts now. What's left is to prepare for what we find at the end of the path we have taken.

JAMES FALLOWS is an *Atlantic* national correspondent, his blog is at jamesfallowstheatlantic.com.

From *The Atlantic*, January/February, 2008, pp. 36–48. Copyright © 2008 by James Fallows. Reprinted by permission of the author.

China to the Rescue
Growing out of the Financial Crisis

China has the wherewithal to lead the global economy out of its doldrums.

JOERGEN OERSTROEM MOELLER

While there is an emerging consensus on what ails the world economy there is no agreement on the treatment. Instead of a global economic policy a variety of national ones are being cooked up to satisfy national tastes that often contradict each other. The time has come—it is actually overdue—to recognize that stimulating global demand, bringing it into line with global supply, is the only cure.

The diagnosis reveals that global demand is too low, resulting in excess production capacity, exercising downward pressure on investment, wages, and property prices. The prescription calls for a rebalancing of demand and supply. Excess supply over investment in the 'fat' years, combined with an inventory build up, aggravate the policy dilemma. Experience tells us that cutting excess supply is an agonizing process that easily undermines confidence in a recovery, harming long-term growth prospects.

Individual countries may try to remedy excess production capacity by exporting more goods, but this shifts the calamity from one country to another doing no good for the global economy. If policy makers are allowed to walk down this path, protectionism will throw a spanner in the works of recovery as countries race to retaliate against each other.

The time has come—it is actually overdue—to recognize that stimulating global demand, bringing it into line with global supply, is the only cure.

But first we have to do away with the illusion that global growth will return to five percent. Growth will likely land one, maybe two, percentage points lower and stay there for a while, as the world waits to see how a rebalanced and restructured global economy will fare.

Taken together the United States, Europe, and Japan account for more than half and may be even two-thirds of the global economy depending upon the calculating method. Europe is trying hard to reform its economy, but results are still disappointing. Japan is facing a low-trend growth, if growth at all, due to demographics and the inability to restructure.

And we are unlikely to see private consumption drive U.S. economic growth as it has done for many years. The paradigm has changed. The halving of the oil price from summer 2008 to summer 2009 should have led to higher private consumption, but it didn't. A number of factors—the stock market, bankruptcies, and bailing out of GM to mention a few—depressed the willingness to spend and it is not clear to which extent better data will renew consumer confidence.

We are unlikely to see private consumption drive U.S. economic growth as it has done for many years.

Personal saving as a percentage of disposable income has rocketed from zero in April 2008 to nearly seven percent in May 2009; the highest figure in more than six years. Demographics too are turning against the United States. Economics tells us that private consumption for an individual peaks around 45–50 years of age and the baby boomers have passed that mark. There is no basis, then, to expect private consumption in the United States to rise or even correspond to the level around and prior to 2007. And without private consumption a recovery is unthinkable.

This leads to the conclusion that increasing demand can only be found outside the traditional heavyweights. The newcomers are China, India, and Southeast Asia plus a number of other countries around the globe. But as only China—and partly India—is playing in the big league, examining that country should prove instructive.

And it looks pretty good.

But the first step is to repudiate the thesis that China's domestic demand is still weak, signaled by the persistent balance of payments surplus. If domestic demand were rising as share of GDP, imports would pull the balance of payments towards a smaller surplus, runs the argument. But it is falling. The World Bank predicts China's surplus will fall to 8.3 percent of GDP in

2010 and 7.2 percent in 2011 from the 11 percent in 2007. The argument also overlooks the dramatic fall in commodity, food and energy prices: if the economy were unchanged, imports would have gone down, boosting the surplus further (they account for 28.8 percent of total import). Persistent domestic demand, holding up much better than exports and by doing so limiting the fall in imports, seems to be the best explanation for a falling, not rising surplus. Of course, the reported stockpiling of commodities by China's large state-owned corporations could have played a role too.

Household spending together with government programs should prevent a fall in China's GDP growth below the six-to-eight percent bracket.

Secondly, the composition of China's imports suggests domestic consumption is changing. Parsing the data, when one separates imports used to produce exports primarily for the United States from imports destined for domestic demand an interesting dynamic emerges. Imports for production of exports fell much sharper than imports for domestic demand. The fact that this trend has persisted over almost two years—since mid-2007—implies China's economy is being restructured.

Thirdly, recent figures suggest that real household spending is nine percent higher than a year ago, resulting in a hike in private consumption's share of total demand. Retail sales are rising even more—15 percent year on year—though this includes government purchases. On this basis it is plausible to assume that household spending together with government programs should prevent a fall in China's GDP growth below the six-to-eight percent bracket.

The world cannot expect the United States to lead the way out of recession and rebalance the global economy.

The room to maneuver for stimulatory measures is still available for China. But this is not the case for the United States and Japan, where public budget deficits have reached the breaking point with further measures likely to undermine whatever confidence in the economies are left. The United States is running a deficit estimated at 13.2 percent of GDP and Japan looks forward to as much as 11 percent according to the pessimists.

In the end, the world cannot expect the United States. to lead the way out of recession and rebalance the global economy. On July 10, Larry Summers, Director of the U.S. President's National Economic Council said to *Financial Times,* "I don't think the worst is over" and added "The global imbalances have to add up to zero and so, if the United States is going to be less the consumer importer of last resort, then other countries are going to need to be in different positions as well." To rebalance the world economy we need to look to growth from countries like China instead of the United States

Moreover, as the rising savings rate in the United States is likely to slow down the recovery, it will be easier to reduce balance of payments imbalances that have harassed the world for so long. Indeed U.S. exports rose and imports fell in May resulting in the lowest trade deficit for nearly nine years. If this trend persists, and basic economic figures suggest it will, U.S. borrowing will fall, inducing global capital to flow into productive investment rather than U.S. treasury bonds. (Of course, mounting healthcare cost, additional stimulus and greater welfare benefits could alter the situation.)

A reallocation of capital to healthier economies would make the goods and services market work in tandem with the capital market. This would not only benefit the global economy, harmed by the financial crisis, but also help weak economies overcome their imbalances. Most important of all: it would achieve a rebalancing without cutting global demand thus avoiding a global slump. But the United States must pay a price. China would begin to lead the global economy replacing the United States—a bitter pill, indeed.

Joergen Oerstroem Moeller is Visiting Senior Research Fellow, Institute of Southeast Asian Studies, Singapore and Adjunct Professor at Singapore Management University and the Copenhagen Business School.

Africa and the Global Economic Crisis

Threats, Opportunities, and Responses

Jeffrey Herbst et al.

Three magazine covers of February 2009 sum up the uncertain nature of the global economy in the wake of the current economic crisis: *Time* asks 'How Can We Get Out of This Mess?'; *Newsweek* states 'We Are All Socialists Now'; and *The Economist* contemplates 'The Return of Economic Nationalism'. It is therefore absolutely critical for Africa to draw the correct lessons from the current economic downturn and to respond in a manner that sustains the recent economic gains that the continent has experienced and positions African countries for further growth.

The global economy has entered into a very deep crisis, perhaps its most important slowdown since the 1930s, that today affects all economic activities and all places.

Critically, the priorities of African leaders should not change, despite the turbulence of the international economy. On the contrary, efforts to achieve goals associated with macroeconomic stability and the promotion of competitiveness should be accelerated. With growth and competitiveness as both national and continental priorities, resources can be mobilised, appropriate policies formulated and novel solutions brought to bear. When other priorities hold sway, growth is stymied. Only where a country has a sufficiently strong domestic coalition for growth is it likely that growth-oriented public policy will be pursued with vigour and determination.

The Global Economy

To understand Africa's prospects, it is first important to review the dramatic global events of the last year. The global recession, resulting from the excesses of the financial sector, spoils a period of record growth worldwide. In the early years of this millennium we were able to say, for the first time in history, that two-thirds of the planet's inhabitants lived either in a high-income or a high-growth economy. Technological and policy changes created new opportunities in the rich world, and most of the planet seemed to be able to participate in their benefits. A number of developing countries, especially in Asia, but also in Eastern Europe and Latin America, were pursuing a path of economic reform that unleashed their potential; the failure that most of Africa displayed in joining this trend seemed to be a specific problem of the continent, and hopefully a temporary one.

This good news emerged largely from three entwined changes that accelerated after the fall of the Berlin Wall and the collapse of Soviet communism at the end of 1989.

Firstly, the relatively protected economic environment that had existed for 40 years since the end of the Second World War moved rapidly towards greater integration of national and regional economies, in part sparked by the simultaneous application of digital technologies to communication flows. These comprise the policy and technological phenomena we understand today by the term 'globalisation'. The cross-border global exchange of goods and services and gross domestic product doubled between 1990 and 2007, and foreign direct investment increased nearly threefold annually, creating employment and income opportunities worldwide and allowing the participants to reap the many gains from trade. Gradually, also, the world's national financial sectors integrated into one.

Secondly, half the world's population, including the citizens of India, China, Vietnam and the Russian Federation, along with some of the Soviet Union's former client states, became participants in the global market economy and shared in its fruits. The most salient case is the massive change enjoyed by China. Twenty million rural Chinese have moved to the cities annually over this period, where they are three times as productive. This has resulted in a manufacturing and consumer boom. Export markets are ground zero of this change. In 1989 some 300 million workers in the world were involved in export activities; today, there are more than 800 million. In 1980 China's exports were less than $20 billion; in 2007 they exceeded $1 trillion.

Thirdly, there was a massive increase in the world's labour supply, exerting downward pressure on wages and upward pressure on productivity. In essence, countries were able to import deflation. Nations that were able to join the process, develop an appropriately productive business climate, put their trade logistics in order, adapt technologies, or place skills or scarce materials in the global market, reaped benefits. This distinguished them, more than ever before, from those that failed to improve their economic conditions and solely offered unskilled labour.

These changes, largely beneficial to the world, did not require, but were temporarily facilitated by, the consumer boom in the developed world and the ensuing credit surge and massive financial flows that were the seeds of our current problems.

Africa benefitted significantly from the developments discussed above. On average, although there are important differences among the four dozen African countries, economic growth began again across the continent in the mid-1990s, as nations reaped the rewards of the difficult economic decisions that leaders had made to structurally reform their economies. Significant progress was made in revaluing exchange rates, improving economic governance and increasing transparency. As a result, Africa was well situated to take advantage of the commodity boom that began after 2000. Indeed, growth across the continent had, until the international economy began to slide in 2008, averaged a healthy 5 per cent across Africa and the continent was no longer the slowest growing of the world's major regions. Africa had reaped significant rewards from opening to the international economy.

With hindsight, while the global economy grew, profound weaknesses were building up in the ever more rapidly expanding financial sector, driven by unprecedentedly low interest rates and the rapid expansion of credit. The meltdown started through the bursting of the housing bubble that certain regions of the United States nourished, and in which the banking sector was deeply involved. Mortgage lending had become so profitable, and was so unregulated, that banks and brokers began lending to borrowers under conditions that expanded the risk and the moral hazard involved. Such high-risk loans were then repackaged—'sliced and diced'—and became part of the holdings of banks throughout the world. As one set of banking assets lost value, the trust in and value of others eroded. Gradually, the dominoes kept tumbling, exposing all the excesses in risk with which the under-regulated American banking system indulged itself since the deregulation of the mid-1990s.

As banks and financial institutions kept reporting record losses and the real situation in their books became public, they lost access to funding and stopped granting credit.

Underfinanced, scared and having suffered some losses, the real economy of consumers and non-financial producers had to slow down and eventually cut their purchases,

investments, production and jobs, and a vicious cycle plunged the American economy into deep recession. Why did the crisis not stay a purely American one? This was because of the extent to which financial institutions in the rest of the world had financed the American credit boom and now were affected by the collapse of those assets; and the extent to which American consumer spending had driven expanding production globally.

Currently, what started off as a localised crisis in the U.S. mortgage market has expanded into a global liquidity and financial crisis. So, what is the likely environment that countries and businesses will have to operate in, and how might this affect Africa?

Some Impacts on Africa

For Africa, there are factors that both lessen and worsen this crisis.

In some respects, Africa is largely shielded from the immediate crisis because its financial systems, rudimentary and parochial, are not integrated with the global financial system. African economies have historically, with few exceptions (South Africa is one), progressed or struggled quite independently of the health and efficacy of their financial markets. For example, in many (though not all) African countries, interest rate levels—and levels of credit provision—are of little consequence for economic activity, because the penetration of the banking system is limited, and so reliance on credit is low to begin with. Further, sub-Saharan banks generally have minimal balance sheet exposure to foreign banks and securities, and therefore the type of balance sheet contagion now seen in Europe is unlikely to occur. Looking at the longer term, to the extent that it matters, African financial sector growth is far more reliant on local factors—inflation; economic health; and the long hard road of building sound domestic institutions and achieving a regulatory 'sweet spot' balancing supervision and market flexibility—than the health of global institutions.

Of course, this picture of a real economy floating free from a tiny financial sector is not wholly true. In Kenya and Nigeria, at least, a bank crisis would do real harm. In most other African countries, the very lack of development of financial intermediaries places a long-term brake on growth; yet, directly or indirectly, we all are borrowers from the very Western banks that are now illiquid and overly cautious. Also, South Africa's growth of the last decade has in large part been based on domestic credit extension that will not be sustainable under virtually any post-crisis scenario. Its vulnerability to portfolio flows to finance its balance of payments deficit threatens high inflation and a decline in the value of its currency—although in the long term this may not be a bad thing for its businesses and their competitiveness. Also, to the extent that large

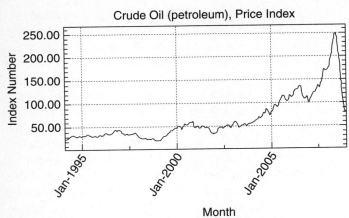

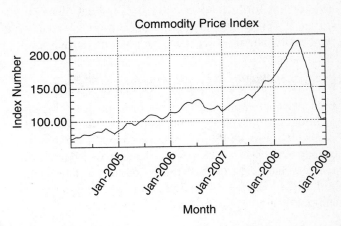

Figure 1   Crude oil and commodity price indices: 1995–2009[3].

corporations rely on roll-over funding from international capital markets, the impact could be quick and painful, even calamitous.

But although comparatively shielded from the immediate consequences of the global financial crisis, African economies can be greatly affected by the crisis if any of six effects turn out to be both large (which they already are) and persistent (which they look likely to be). These are:

1. commodity prices settling at sharply lower levels;

2. a shutdown of private sector international funding for long-term projects. The Institute of International Finance predicts, for example, that investment flows to developing countries may reduce by over 80 per cent from 2007 levels to $165 billion in 2009. Equally, many private companies in emerging markets will probably be unable to refinance their debt.[1] For example, there is $100 billion of maturing debt for private companies in Brazil, Mexico, India and others in the first half of 2009;

3. a sharp fall in official support for Africa, both bilateral and multilateral (as occurred during the emerging markets crisis of 1997/98);

4. a sustained fall in demand, not only for commodities, but for other products that African nations sell on the international market, which would endanger the sustainability of the export growth that we observe in a few countries, which was one of the few long-term drivers of economic prosperity observable in the last few years;

5. a reduction in tourism and other service sector trade and flows. The conservative expectation is that global tourism to developing country destinations will fall by 20 per cent during 2009, although the current

experience in select African countries suggests a greater downturn; and

6. a reduction in liquidity globally, placing downward pressure on African stock markets and currency values. Already, during 2009, African bourses are, on average, significantly down on their year-on-year values. Measured in dollar terms, most of the region's significant stock exchanges had already recorded negative returns during 2008: Egypt (−6.1 per cent), Nigeria (−54.2 per cent), Mauritius (−50.2 per cent), Kenya (−47.2 per cent) and South Africa (−45 per cent). Ghana, growing by 20.2 percent, was a welcome exception.[2]

Overall, for Africa, the most important possible short- to medium-term development is in the deflating of commodity prices. If the 'deleveraging' of assets persists worldwide, then everything that everyone owns will be less valuable. This would include commodities in the ground. This will be exacerbated by a recession in China—and there are already indications that China is, rhetoric apart, scaling back on its African interests. Oil is down nearly 300 per cent from its 2008 peak, and other commodities, from platinum to diamonds and copper to steel, have similarly collapsed. Like other developing regions, Africa should not expect much—in spite of the rhetoric—in the way of help from donors and other multilateral agencies. Even if the money is forthcoming, the history of the International Monetary Fund, for example, in managing such crises is less than spectacular. Even though the global economy has prompted the crisis in many African states, the trajectory of recovery is predominantly up to what African states do themselves.

Of course, there are positive impacts, not least the effect on the balance of payments of fuel- and food-importing nations. But for the above reasons, the global financial crisis *will* affect Africa—and, on balance, more negatively and profoundly than most realise, or are willing to accept.

Possible African Responses

As Africa contemplates a less generous world of rising prices, with more people likely to fall into rather than be lifted out of poverty, how might its leaders respond? Like their peers in the rest of the world, African leaders will have to manage fast-changing and challenging conditions. Those who do best will succeed at balancing short- and long-term needs, and political pressures and policy imperatives.

- **Short-term (<12 months): Stability and empathy:** Leaders will have to manage the economic and political fall-out from (initially) sharply lower natural resources, trade and tax revenues, accompanied by smaller aid transfers carrying greater conditionality. Given rudimentary domestic capital markets, most African leaders will have less scope than Western nations to buttress domestic demand through stimulus programmes. This means that businesses—not least those with the state as principal customer—may well be under financial pressure. Governments may have to provide some legal protection to firms. Many households, particularly those producing cash crops, will face sharp falls in income, and may need assistance, including possibly food aid. Donor funds ought to fund such support, together with other income support through, for example, public works programmes. Donor programmes need to be aimed at domestic expenditure with a large pro-poor income impact.

  African nations will also have to retain hard-won policy gains against temporary pressures. Unlike Western countries, where the greatest monetary policy risk is arguably deflation, African countries faced with large budget demands in the face of dwindling revenues may choose to increase money supply and accept higher inflation. The impact of *overly* loose monetary policies could be a sharp increase in domestic inflation, perpetuated by a falling currency. The resulting social, political and economic challenges would be large, and may stay with a country for a long time. Other sound policies also need to be protected: trade reforms should not be reversed for small countries, and key health, education and infrastructure programmes and expenditures need to be maintained. African leaders will need to build coalitions to support a small number of such clear priorities.

- **Mid-term (<24 months): Avoid learning the wrong lessons from the crisis:** Many international commentators are eager to use the current crisis to

justify that nations should push away from market-minded economic reform, trade promotion, foreign direct investment attraction and the other elements associated with globalisation that acted as growth drivers in so many countries. They are prone to interpret this crisis as the final collapse of the market system or of international trade, and to instead promote the idea that developing nations should go back to the past. This is an incorrect interpretation of what happened, and, indeed, the wrong advice. All the economies in the world are suffering the crisis, and there is no sign that those that pursued reform more effectively are suffering more. What has failed is a particular way of exercising financial regulation, not the overall mechanism of international trade. And while much needs to change in the now moribund British and American banking and financial systems, including massive state intervention and restrictive re-regulation, there is no evidence yet that small developing nations should shy away from market democracies, good governance, international trade and institution building.

- **Longer term (<36 months): Build 'growth coalitions' for competitiveness:** Major long-term trends have been driving capital to developing markets. The sources of growth in Africa, and indeed the developing countries in Asia and Latin America, have a sound basis and will reassert themselves. Critically, therefore, the long-term priorities of African leaders should not change, despite the turbulence of the international economy. On the contrary, goals associated with macroeconomic stability and the promotion of competitiveness should be accelerated. With growth and competitiveness as both a national and continental priority, resources can be mobilised, appropriate policies written and novel solutions brought to bear. When other priorities hold sway, growth is stymied. Only where a country has a sufficiently strong domestic coalition for growth is it likely that growth-oriented public policy will be pursued with vigour and determination.

In summary, Africa's relative isolation from the global economy will shield it from some aspects of the current global economic meltdown. However, the downturn in commodity prices and possibly in aid flows will stress certain countries, especially given the expectation of a slow U-shaped decline and recovery with a long period of stagnation to come. Moreover, the policy measures that stimulate domestic consumption available to some in Asia, for example, and in Europe and the United States are not available to most African countries.

In positioning themselves to take advantage of the next phase of growth, African countries would do well to put in place policy measures that support innovation, reject failure and reduce costs to the economy. To do so, African governments will have to cut excessive expenditure (such as foreign air travel and other largesse) while focusing on long-term investments, including in infrastructure and training. They should aim to assist the emergence of financial institutions, because, without reliable banks and efficient credit markets, Africa will remain poverty-stricken, at the mercy of the costly finance provided by weak institutions and narrow networks. Finally, Africa countries will have to keep the improvement of the enablers of competitiveness—including tax regimes, productivity and essential services—central to the national agenda.

Notes

1. *The Economist,* 29 January 2009 at www.economist.com/ finance/displaystory.cfm?story_id=13035552.

2. *Business Daily,* 13 January 2009 at http://www.bdafrica.com/ index.php?option=com_content&task=view&id=12238& Itemid=5813.

3. At http://www.indexmundi.com.

Professor **JEFFREY HERBST** is provost of Miami University; **DR. GREG MILLS** heads the Johannesburg-based Brenthurst Foundation; **STEPHAN MALHERBE** directs Genesis Analytics; and Professor **ALBERTO TREJOS** is at INCAE Business School in Costa Rica.

Trade Wars Brewing in Economic Malaise

Outrage in Canada as U.S. Firms Sever Ties to Obey Stimulus Rules

Anthony Faiola and Lori Montgomery

I s this what the first trade war of the global economic crisis looks like?

Ordered by Congress to "buy American" when spending money from the $787 billion stimulus package, the town of Peru, Ind., stunned its Canadian supplier by rejecting sewage pumps made outside of Toronto. After a Navy official spotted Canadian pipe fittings in a construction project at Camp Pendleton, Calif., they were hauled out of the ground and replaced with American versions. In recent weeks, other Canadian manufacturers doing business with U.S. state and local governments say they have been besieged with requests to sign affidavits pledging that they will only supply materials made in the USA.

Outrage spread in Canada, with the *Toronto Star* last week bemoaning "a plague of protectionist measures in the U.S." and Canadian companies openly fretting about having to shift jobs to the United States to meet made-in-the-USA requirements. This week, the Canadians fired back. A number of Ontario towns, with a collective population of nearly 500,000, retaliated with measures effectively barring U.S. companies from their municipal contracts—the first shot in a larger campaign that could shut U.S. companies out of billions of dollars worth of Canadian projects.

This is not your father's trade war, a tit-for-tat over champagne or cheese. With countries worldwide desperately trying to keep and create jobs in the midst of a global recession, the spat between the United States and its normally friendly northern neighbor underscores what is emerging as the biggest threat to open commerce during the economic crisis.

Rather than merely raising taxes on imported goods—acts that are subject to international treaties—nations including the United States are finding creative ways to engage in protectionism through domestic policy decisions that are largely not governed by international law. Unlike a classic trade war, there is little chance of containment through, for example, arbitration at the World Trade Organization in Geneva. Additionally, such moves are more likely to have unintended consequences or even backfire on the stated desire to create domestic jobs.

Buy American

Take, for instance, Duferco Farrell Corp., a Swiss-Russian partnership that took over a previously bankrupt U.S. steel plant near Pittsburgh in the 1990s and employed 600 people there.

The new buy American provisions, the company said, are being so broadly interpreted that Duferco Farrell is on the verge of shutting down. Part of an increasingly global supply chain that seeks efficiencies by spreading production among multiple nations, it manufactures coils at its Pennsylvania plant using imported steel slabs that are generally not sold commercially in the United States. The partially foreign production process means the company's coils do not fit the current definition of made in the USA—a designation that the stimulus law requires for thousands of public works projects across the nation.

In recent weeks, its largest client—a steel pipemaker located one mile down the road—notified Duferco Farrell that it would be canceling orders. Instead, the client is buying from companies with 100 percent U.S. production to meet the new stimulus regulations. Duferco has had to furlough 80 percent of its workforce.

"You need to tell me how inhibiting business between two companies located one mile apart is going to save American jobs," said Bob Miller, Duferco Farrell's executive vice president. "I've got 600 United Steel Workers out there who are going to lose their jobs because of this. And you tell me this is good for America?"

The United States is not alone in throwing up domestic policies assailed by critics as protectionist. Britain and the Netherlands, for instance, are forcing banks receiving taxpayer bailouts to jump-start lending at home at the expense of overseas clients. French President Nicolas Sarkozy initially insisted that his nation's automakers move manufacturing jobs home in exchange for a government bailout, but backed down after outrage surged among his peers in the European Union, of which France is a central member.

But the number of measures, both proposed and enacted, from the Obama administration and Congress in recent months has raised an alarm among foreign governments, pundits and news media outlets. The buy American provisions in the stimulus package, signed into law in February, were just the beginning. Last week, Obama unveiled a series of proposals aimed at increasing taxes by nearly $200 billion over the next decade on U.S. companies doing business abroad. At a White House event, Obama said the measures were designed to "close corporate loopholes" that permit companies to "pay lower taxes if you create a job in Bangalore, India, than if you create one in Buffalo, N.Y."

Keeping Jobs at Home

A slew of legislative proposals is also aimed at keeping jobs at home. In recent weeks, the House attached additional buy American provisions to a $14 billion clean-water fund that provides loans to local communities and a $6 billion program to finance environmentally friendly school construction projects.

Other pending measures would require the federal government to buy 100,000 U.S.-made plug-in hybrid cars, mandate that the president's airplanes be made in the country by a U.S. company, and force several federal agencies, including the Pentagon and Department of Transportation, to use only domestic iron and steel.

Last month, Senate Majority Whip Richard J. Durbin (D-Ill.) introduced a measure with Sen. Charles E. Grassley (R-Iowa) to tighten rules governing the H-1B visa program for guest workers. Among its provisions: Companies seeking to import specialized workers from abroad first must make a good-faith effort to recruit U.S. citizens.

"The H-1B program was never meant to replace qualified American workers. It was meant to complement them because of a shortage of workers in specialized fields," Grassley said. "In tough economic times like we're seeing, it's even more important that we do everything possible to see that Americans are given every consideration when applying for jobs."

Buy American provisions are not new. Federal transportation projects have been required to use domestic iron and steel since 1982, and some defense contracts are limited to U.S. bidders. But the stimulus package marks the first time a buy American mandate has been broadly applied to projects across an array of federal agencies.

No one appears to be more concerned than America's largest trading partner—Canada.

Initial concern north of the border over the buy American provisions died down after a clause, supported by the administration, was inserted in the bill clearly stating that the measure would not supersede existing U.S. trade obligations. During his Feb. 19 trip to Ottawa, Obama additionally pledged to avoid protectionism.

Creeping Protectionism

As passed, the act keeps that pledge, White House spokeswoman Jennifer Psaki said. "The president is committed to creating jobs in America and committed to global engagement with our trading partners and does not see any contradiction between those two goals," she said.

But in recent weeks as federal authorities drafted broad guidelines for implementing the law and hundreds of states and towns have begun preparing for stimulus-related projects, Canadian companies have been surprised to discover that while some federal contracts are still open to Canadian materials and equipment because of trade treaties, most of those issued by state and local governments are not.

The Government Accountability Office estimates that state or local officials will administer about $280 billion in stimulus spending, including about $50 billion for transportation projects. But federal authorities have determined that construction projects even partially funded with stimulus dollars must also buy American, dramatically increasing the universe of affected contracts.

As a result, John Hayward, president of Hayward Gordon, a Canadian manufacturer of pumps used in water works projects, says U.S. towns, including Peru, Ind., have told him that they can no longer buy his Canadian-made products.

"We're not China. We're not even Mexico. We have the same relative cost of labor as you do," he said. "If we have a better price, you should buy from us. That's what competition is supposed to be about."

To stay in business, Hayward is considering moving some manufacturing operations to the United States, potentially creating jobs here. That, Peru Mayor Jim Walker notes, is what the stimulus was supposed to be about.

"You're trying to get America turned around, trying to put Americans back to work," Walker said. "And if American taxpayers are paying for this, well then, Americans deserve the benefits."

UNIT 11

Globalizing Issues

Unit Selections

Key Points to Consider

- What will be the most important global challenges facing the world in the future?

- Do you believe that the world is a better place today than it was 10 . . . 15 . . . 20 years ago?

- Who wins and who loses in a future world characterized by climate change?

- Do you think a cap-and-trade system will be adequate for forestalling global warming? Why or why not?

- Will climate change and dwindling natural resources cause more violent political conflicts in the future?

Student Website

www.mhhe.com/cls

Internet References

Center for Naval Analysis "National Security and the Threat of Climate Change"
http://youtube.com/watch?v=RCfRGN0YlwQ

The UN Millennium Project
http://www.unmillenniumproject.org/

The 11th Hour Action.com
http://www.11thhouraction.com/

CIA Report of the National Intelligence Council's 2020 Project
http://www.cia.gov/nic/NIC_globaltrend2020.html

Commonwealth Forum on Globalization and Health
http://www.ukglobalhealth.org

Commission on Global Governance
http://www.sovereignty.net/p/gov/gganalysis.htm

Global Footprint Network
http://footprints@footprintnetwork.org

Global Trends 2005 Project
http://www.csis.org/gt2005/sumreport.html

Greenpeace International
http://www.greenpeace.org/international/

HIV/AIDS
http://www.unaids.org

RealClimate
http://www.realclimate.org/

At the beginning of the twenty-first century, there was a noticeable increase in efforts to predict important changes and to understand new patterns of relationships shaping international relations. For more than a decade, the United Nations sponsored Millennium Project has been assessing the future state of the world by tracking changes in a set of 15 Global Challenges identified and updated by over 2,000 futurists, business planners, scholars, and policy advisers. They provide a framework to assess global and local prospects, and make up an interdependent system: an improvement in one challenge makes it easier to address others; deterioration in one makes it more difficult. The 2009 State Of The Future Millennium Report summarized in, "The Seven Terrors of the World," involved 2700 experts from 30 countries. This recent report warned "that the world is facing a series of interlinked crises which threaten billions of people and could cause the collapse of civilization." The bleakest warning is on the danger of the climate chaos being caused by pollution, 15 wars, and the fact that three billion people will be without access to adequate water by 2025. Some of these predictions are eerily similar to those of another global prediction project undertaking by the Global Footprint Network. In a 2009 report, this organization, sponsored by several government aid agencies, warned that if current population and consumption trends continue several dozen nation-states will exceed their "biocapacity" within the next twenty years. The report goes on to predict that a number of countries, including Senegal, Kenya, and Tanzania, are set to reach their threshold of biocapacity in less than five years!

One threat to human security that most health experts agree is extremely likely to cause a global pandemic in the future is the bird flu. Since the appearance of a genetically mutated form of bird flu in Turkey at the beginning of 2006 there has been renewed concerns about the prospect of a global flu pandemic. Many experts believe that time is running out to prepare for the next pandemic and that a future bird flu pandemic is the most serious security threat facing the world because nothing else could inflict more death and disruption worldwide. Given the continued spread of HIV/AIDS, including the reoccurrence of increasing infection rates in countries such as Uganda and Thailand, who had previously managed to reduce their HIV/AIDS infection rate, and the heavy toll that the disease has already taken in large parts of the world, the threat of another global pandemic must be taken seriously. The difficulties that the United States and other Western countries had during 2009 producing and distributing enough H1N1 flu vaccine, despite a great deal of advance warning may foreshadow what can be expected in future infectious epidemics or pandemics.

During the fall of 2009, before the Copenhagen summit on climate control, there were several signs that the conference would fail to achieve it's target goals in terms of reducing greenhouse causing emissions. The most serious threat to implementing these goals is the fact that while most developed countries now support the targets agreed to at earlier UN conferences in terms of reducing global warming gases, few nation-states in the developed world are willing to pay to allow developing countries to continue their efforts to become economically developed nation-states, In "The Low-Carbon Diet," Joel Kurtzman argues

© MIXA/Getty Images

that "the free market has eliminated environmental hazards in the past . . . and can solve the problem of climate change today." According to Kurtzman, a cap-and-trade system—not a carbon tax or government initiatives to spur technological innovation—offers the best hope for reducing pollution and encouraging green growth. Time will probably be needed to determine if a free-trade or mixed public/private cap-and-trade system is feasible and comprehensive enough to help forestall global warming.

In the meantime, the majority of the world's population will continue to be poor and live in regions of the world that will be hit hard by the effects of climate change and rising sea levels. Yet most of the governments in the developing world lack the human and resource capacities needed to manage future catastrophes. These conditions are one set of reasons why many futurists are now predicting that state collapse, civil war, and mass migration will be inevitable in a warming world. While military superiority may aid Americans in struggles over vital resources, it will not be able to protect Americans against the ravages of global climate change. The recent rise of piracy off the East Coast of Africa may be a preview of one type of violent behavior that is likely to increase in the future. Increasingly complex emergencies after major hurricanes and other more virulent weather disturbances is another type of international phenomena that is likely to command more attention and resources in the future.

To date, much less agreement has been reached on the extent that global warming and dwindling natural resources are likely to combine to increase violent conflicts over land, water, and energy. However, the evidence is becoming much clearer that certain root causes of violent political conflicts such as environmental degradation and resource scarcities create the preconditions that facilitate future violence among groups. Many analysts now are warning that global climate change and dwindling natural resources are combining to increase the likelihood of violent conflict over land, water, and energy. The inadequate capacity of poor and unstable countries to cope with the effects of climate change is likely to result in state collapse, civil war, and mass migration. While military superiority may aid Americans in struggles over vital resources, it cannot protect us against the ravages of global climate change.

The Seven Terrors of the World

The world is facing a series of interlinked crises which threatens billions of people and could cause the collapse of civilisation, according to an international report out this week.

Climate pollution, food shortages, diseases, wars, disasters, crime and the recession are all conspiring to ravage the globe and threaten the future of humanity, it warns. Democracy, human rights and press freedom are also suffering.

The report, called 2009 State of the Future, has been compiled by the Millennium Project, an international think-tank based in Washington, DC, and involved 2700 experts from 30 countries.

"Half the world appears vulnerable to social instability and violence," the report says. "This is due to rising unemployment and decreasing food, water and energy supplies, coupled with the disruptions caused by global warming and mass migrations."

The project has been backed by organisations including United Nations agencies, the Rockefeller Foundation, private companies and governments. It provides "invaluable insights into the future for the United Nations, its member states, and civil society," according to the UN Secretary-General, Ban Ki-moon.

The report's bleakest warning is on the dangers of the climate chaos being caused by pollution. It also highlights the 15 wars taking place in the world. It further predicts there could be three billion people without access to adequate water by 2025.

The people in the world are at risk of several endemic problems "about half diseases," it says. These include HIV/AIDS, swine flu, drug-resistant superbugs and a string of new infections.

The global income from the proceeds of international crime is reckoned to be around $3 trillion.

"Democracy and freedom have declined for the third year in a row, and press freedoms declined for the seventh year in a row," the report says. The global recession was caused by "too many greedy and deceitful decisions," it argues, but there were now some signs that humanity was growing out of its "selfish, self-centred adolescence."

1: Environment

The most serious danger is the pollution that is affecting the climate, the report says. Every day the world's oceans absorb 30 million tonnes of carbon dioxide, increasing their acidity.

The number of dead zones—areas like La Jolla off the coast of San Diego, which have too little oxygen to support life—has doubled every decade since the 1960s.

The oceans are warming about 50% faster than the Intergovernmental Panel on Climate Change reported in 2007, while the amount of ice flowing out of Greenland last summer was nearly three times more than the previous year. Summer ice in the Arctic could disappear by 2030, the report warns.

"Over 36 million hectares of primary forest are lost every year," it says. "Human consumption is 30% larger than nature's capacity to regenerate, and demand on the planet has more than doubled over the past 45 years."

The strains these changes will put on the world include floods, droughts and storms.

"This important report puts climate change up there with the major economic, social and political challenges that the human race faces," said Dr. Richard Dixon, director of WWF Scotland. "Whether you are worried about food security, the threat of war or mass migration, climate change is going to make things worse."

The Millennium Project report argues that combating climate change requires a 10-year programme by the United States and China equivalent to the Apollo moon mission launched in 1961.

Other environmental problems are highlighted, including toxic waste dumping. About 70% of the world's 50 million tonnes of annual electronic waste is dumped in developing countries in Asia and Africa, much of it illegally.

A quarter of all fish stocks are over-harvested, the report says, and 80% cannot withstand increased fishing.

2: Food and Water

A global food crisis may be "inevitable," the report warns, because of an obscure fungus called Ug99 which causes stem rust on plants. It is threatening to wipe out more than 80% of the world's wheat crops, and it could take up to 12 years to develop resistant strains of wheat.

Food prices rose by 52% between 2007 and 2008, while the cost of fertiliser has nearly doubled in the past year. Meanwhile, 30%–40% of food production is lost in many poor countries because of a lack of adequate storage facilities.

Nearly a billion people are undernourished and hungry, while 700 million face water scarcity—this could hit three billion by 2025, the report warns. The world's population is expected to grow from the current 6.8 billion to 9.2 billion by 2050—and could reach 11 billion.

"Christian Aid's partners in developing countries are already reporting that water is hard to find," said Claire Aston, acting head of Christian Aid Scotland. "The idea that three billion people will be in this position as a result of climate change by 2030 is a frightening prospect."

Water shortages are also being worsened by the growing global consumption of meat. The report predicts demand for meat may rise by 50% by 2025 and double by 2050.

3: Disease

About 17 million people—nine million of them young children—are killed by infectious diseases every year, according to the report.

Half of the world's population is at risk from endemic diseases, with TB, malaria and HIV/AIDS together causing more than 300 million illnesses and five million deaths a year.

The number of people living with HIV/Aids is estimated at between 30 million and 36 million, two-thirds in sub-Saharan Africa.

The dangers from other diseases seem to be getting worse, too. Over the past 40 years, 39 infectious diseases have been discovered, and in the last five years more than 1100 epidemics have been verified. There are up to 20 new strains of "superbugs," such as MRSA, that are difficult to counter, while three-quarters of emerging pathogens have the ability to jump species.

Old diseases such as cholera, yellow fever, plague, dengue fever, haemorrhagic fever and diphtheria are re-emerging, not to mention new strains, like the H1N1 swine flu virus.

"Massive urbanisation, increased encroachment on animal territory, and concentrated livestock production could trigger new pandemics," the report cautions.

"Climate change is altering insect and disease patterns. Other problems may come from synthetic biology laboratories."

4: Wars and Disasters

More than two billion people have been affected by the world's 35 wars and 2500 natural disasters over the last nine years, the report says. By mid-2009, there were 15 conflicts raging around the globe—one more than in 2008. Four wars were taking place in Africa, four in Asia, four in the Middle East, two in the Americas and one, against terrorism, internationally.

"A pending unknown is whether Iran and North Korea will trigger a nuclear arms race," the report says. "Another more distant spectre, but possibly even a greater threat, is that of single individuals acting alone to create and deploy weapons of mass destruction."

The Iraq war has left behind an environmental catastrophe of 25 million land mines, hazardous waste, polluted water and depleted uranium contamination. "It will take centuries to restore the natural environment of Iraq," said the country's environment minister, Nermeen Othman.

The number and intensity of natural disasters is increasing, the report says. In 2008 there were a total of 354 disasters with an estimated 214 million victims, 80% of them in Asia.

Increasing climate chaos could exacerbate the damage wrought by natural disasters and see the number of people suffering grow to 375 million a year by 2015 and 660 million by 2030. Economic losses could reach $340 billion a year.

"The world has moved from a global threat once called the Cold War, to what now should be considered the warming war," said Afelee Pita, the UN ambassador from Tuvalu, a small, low-lying island in the Pacific Ocean.

The report also reveals the world recently escaped a potentially planet-ending event.

"In March 2009 an asteroid missed Earth by 77,000 kilometres," it says. "If it had hit Earth, it would have wiped out all life on 800 square kilometres. No-one knew it was coming."

5: Crime

Organised crime is very big business, according to the Millennium Project report, with an income of $3 trillion a year. That's twice as much as all the world's military budgets combined. This includes more than $1 trillion paid in bribes to corrupt officials, and maybe another $1 trillion from cybercrime thefts. Counterfeiting and piracy could bring in at least $300bn, the global drug trade $321bn, human trafficking $44bn and illegal weapons sales $10bn.

"Governments can be understood as a series of decision points, with some people in those points vulnerable to very large bribes," the report says. "Decisions could be bought and sold like heroin, making democracy an illusion."

Shockingly, there are reckoned to be between 14 million and 27 million people still being held in slavery, the vast majority of them in Asia. This is more than at the peak of the African slave trade.

The report argues that the world is beginning to wake up to the "enormity of the threat of transnational organised crime." The UN Office on Drugs and Crime has called on all states to develop a coherent strategy, but efforts are still piecemeal.

The 2009 G8 meeting of justice and home affairs ministers explored anti-crime strategies, and in June the United States launched the International Organised Crime Intelligence and Operations Centre.

"Meanwhile, transnational organised crime continues to expand in the absence of a comprehensive, integrated global counter-strategy," observes the report.

6: Human Rights

Freedom and democracy are waning, the report reveals. They have declined for the third year in a row, with press freedoms worsening for the seventh year in a row.

In 2008, democracy declined in 34 countries, and only improved in 14. Just 17% of the world's population lives in 70 countries with a free press, while 42% lives in 64 countries with no free press.

According to the Economist Intelligence Unit, 14.4% of humanity enjoys full democracy, while 35% live under authoritarian regimes. "Democratic forces will have to work harder to make sure that the short-term reversals do not stop the longer-term trend of democratisation," the report says.

Women account for more than 40% of the world's workforce but earn less than 25% of the wages and own only 1% of the assets, it found.

"Many countries still have laws and cultures that deny women basic human rights," the report states. "Gender equity is essential for the development of a healthy society and is one of the most effective ways to address all the other global challenges."

The human rights organisation Amnesty International warns that the recession is having a "devastating impact" on the world's poor, driving more and more people into poverty, unemployment and homelessness.

"The recession is also leading to repression of people who are desperate," said Amnesty's Scottish programme director, John Watson. "It is creating new tensions between governments and vulnerable people."

7: Science and Technology

The Millennium Report warns that, due to the staggering rate of technological advances, politicians and the public need a "global collective intelligence system" to track the effects of such rapid changes. Contingency plans need to be prepared by governments in case the speed of development has a "highly negative impact" on the human race.

Although advances in science and technology are increasing the chances of major breakthroughs in medicine, computing and biotechnology, these breakthroughs come with a health warning as we are unsure what the flipside may be. Some experts speculate that civilisation is heading for a "singularity," the report says. This would mean that "technological change is so fast and significant that we today are incapable of conceiving what life might be like beyond the year 2025."

The electronics company IBM has promised a computer capable of performing 20,000 trillion calculations per second by 2011—just like Hal, above, from *2001: A Space Odyssey*—roughly equivalent to the speed of the human brain.

On the upside, the boom in power generated by wind turbines and other renewable sources has been unprecedented. For the first time in 2008 the majority of the increase in electricity production in the United States and the European Union came from renewable sources.

"Mobile phones, the internet, international trade, language translation and jet planes are giving birth to an interdependent humanity that can create and implement global strategies to improve the prospects for humanity."

The Low-Carbon Diet

How the market can curb climate change.

JOEL KURTZMAN

The global economic crisis has battered the free market's reputation, but the market nevertheless remains a powerful tool both for allocating capital and for effecting social change. Nowhere is this truer than with the challenge of confronting and reversing climate change. Of all the market-based tools available for addressing this problem, the most potent are cap-and-trade systems for greenhouse gas emissions.

In their most basic form, cap-and-trade systems work by making it expensive to emit greenhouse gases. As a result, the owners of an emissions source are motivated to replace it with something less damaging to the environment. If they are unable to, the trading provisions allow them to purchase permits to continue emitting until they are ready to invest in new technology. Over time, as the amount of carbon allowed into the atmosphere is reduced, the price of a permit is expected to increase.

In existing cap-and-trade mechanisms, such as the European Union's Greenhouse Gas Emission Trading Scheme, governments cap the total amount of emissions allowed, and the amount of emissions permitted declines over time. Organizations such as utilities, factories, cement plants, municipalities, steel mills, and waste sites are given or sold permits that allow them to emit a certain portion of the relevant region's total greenhouse gases. If an organization emits less than its allotment, it can sell the unused permits to entities that plan on exceeding their limits. Under cap-and-trade systems, companies can trade permits with one another through brokers or in organized local or global markets.

The American Clean Energy and Security Act of 2009, the 1,201-page bill introduced by Henry Waxman (D-Calif.) and Edward Markey (D-Mass.) and passed by the U.S. House of Representatives on June 28, is an ambitious attempt by Congress to play catch-up after having failed to approve the Kyoto Protocol—which was ratified by 183 parties, including all the developed countries except the United States, in 1998. The bill adds further amendments to the Clean Air Act of 1970 and grants new authority to the Environmental Protection Agency (EPA), the Commodity Futures Trading Commission, and the Federal Energy Regulatory Commission, the last being the nation's main energy and electricity regulator. The bill also creates a registry of greenhouse gas emissions and systematizes what are now mostly haphazard efforts to offset emissions, such as planting trees, transforming animal waste into methane gas for energy use, and capturing methane as it escapes from landfills.

Most important, the bill seeks to reduce greenhouse gas emissions over time by creating carbon markets. The goal is to gradually reduce U.S. greenhouse gas emissions to 17 percent of 2005 levels by 2050, beginning with a modest three percent reduction by 2012. The bill would require reductions in emissions from most stationary sources of greenhouse gases, including power plants, producers and importers of industrial gas and fuel, and many other sources of carbon dioxide, such as steel mills and cement plants. It would also raise mileage standards and lower permissible emission levels for vehicles. Crucially, the bill puts its faith in the market and its ability to lower the cost of reducing emissions through the trading of permits. Although it seems revolutionary, this is not a new idea. For decades, markets have been used successfully as mechanisms for curbing different types of pollution.

Acid Test

The conceptual framework for cap-and-trade systems was laid out in the 1960s and 1970s by two economists, Ellison Burton and William Sanjour, who worked for the U.S. National Air Pollution Control Administration, which was eventually folded into the EPA. Beginning in 1967, they sought to develop decentralized programs to limit emissions of sulfur dioxide—a pollutant emanating from the smokestacks of coal-fired power plants that caused acid rain—and to limit them in the most inexpensive and efficient way possible.

Burton and Sanjour built computer models to simulate how market forces could be used to coordinate abatement activities by using penalties and—more important—incentives and rewards. From their perspective, the penalties and incentives had to be large enough to persuade emitters of sulfur dioxide to invest in changing their practices. Burton and Sanjour realized that the complexity of the problem was beyond the ability of any command-and-control model to solve because sulfur dioxide was emitted from tens of thousand of sources operated by thousands of different utility companies doing business under dozens of regulatory jurisdictions across the United States. Their approach proved to be remarkably successful.

Then, in the 1980s, the cap-and-trade model was employed successfully to eliminate the use of leaded gasoline in cars across the United States. When lead, a performance additive for internal-combustion engines, was found to cause neurological and cognitive disabilities in children, the EPA introduced a trading program to accelerate the phasing out of leaded fuels. The system the EPA deployed in 1982 put an overall cap on the production of leaded fuels but allowed refiners to buy or sell permits among themselves to produce those fuels, as long as they did not exceed the overall cap. At the time, the program was criticized as callous by some environmentalists, who believed it ignored the health risks to children and would allow corporations to profit even though leaded fuels were continuing to cause illness.

But the success of the program soon silenced its critics. It allowed refiners that had invested in new processes and plants for making unleaded fuel to sell their unused permits to refiners that had yet to make the change. As a result, capital flowed from leaded gasoline makers to unleaded refiners, acting as a tax on one and an incentive for the other. From a market-design perspective, the program created what economists call "strong positive feedback loops." By 1987, a mere five years after the program began, nearly all leaded gasoline had been eliminated in the United States, and other countries were copying the program. The lead-abatement program turned out to be cheaper and more efficient than anyone had predicted.

A similar approach was used to confront an even larger environmental problem: acid rain. By the 1980s, acid rain—the problem Burton and Sanjour had first studied—was causing enormous harm to the environment and seemed intractable. Sulfur dioxide and nitrogen oxide released into the atmosphere from coal-burning power plants and other factories was combining with water vapor to form acid rain, mist, and snow. This acidic precipitation fell into lakes and streams, killing fish, algae, and other forms of aquatic life. It also damaged crops, stripped the paint off cars, scarred archaeological landmarks, and was even implicated in certain types of cancer.

In 1979, the United Nations passed the Convention on Long-Range Transboundary Air Pollution, which marked the beginning of an international effort to reduce emissions of sulfur and nitrogen oxides. But it was not until the U.S. Congress passed the Clean Air Act Amendments of 1990 that the United States saw any meaningful reduction. The amendments enabled the EPA to place a national cap on emissions of sulfur and nitrogen oxides while allowing polluters to trade permits among themselves. Using 1980 emissions levels as the baseline, the program aimed to cut emissions of sulfur dioxide in half by 2010. In 2007, three years ahead of schedule, the agency's cap-and-trade program achieved its reduction targets. The cost to emitters, which the Congressional Budget Office had estimated would be $6 billion a year, came instead to about $1.1–$1.8 billion a year, largely because the program enabled emitters to choose their own solutions to the problem, rather than relying on a narrow range of mandated technologies and approaches. Thanks to this program, acid rain is no longer a first-order environmental challenge. And it can serve as an instructive model for policymakers seeking to combat climate change by creating a carbon market.

Capping Carbon

Although leaded fuels and acid rain were big issues in their day, they are small-scale problems compared to climate change. At its worst, acid rain harmed marine habitats and cropland, primarily in North America and Europe. But climate change affects the entire planet.

Climate change is not just an environmental problem; it is a humanitarian and health problem with multiple dimensions. Scientists warn that sea levels will rise, rainfall patterns will be altered, storm patterns will change, and the locations of deserts, cropland, and forests will shift. As a result, famine and disease could spread, leading to increases in migration from environmentally devastated countries to Europe and the United States.

But there is another issue that makes tackling climate change more difficult than removing lead from fuels or stopping acid rain: emissions of greenhouse gases are a byproduct of economic growth.

Leaded fuel was the key to only a single industry, and the processes leading to acid rain were central to just one or two sectors of the economy. Unlike these pollutants, emissions of carbon dioxide are fundamental to almost every aspect of the global economy. Leaded gasoline had a relatively cheap substitute (unleaded gas), and emissions of sulfur and nitrogen oxides have relatively straightforward technological fixes. By contrast, the fossil fuels that produce greenhouse gases are not so easy to replace.

To add to the complications, today's emerging economies—Brazil, China, India, and Russia, among others—are following the same carbon-intensive path to prosperity first taken by Europe and the United States over a century ago. Coal, oil, natural gas, and wood—all of which contribute to carbon dioxide emissions—remain the world's predominant sources of energy. Despite recent investments in alternative fuels, solar, wind, hydroelectric, geothermal, and nuclear power still only account for a small share of the world's energy supply. Moreover, trillions of dollars have been invested in finding, developing, refining, transporting, marketing, selling, and using fossil fuels. A large portion of these costs will be difficult, if not impossible, to recover if fossil fuels are phased out. For example, pipelines and storage facilities designed to transport oil and gasoline cannot be used for ethanol because of ethanol's corrosive effects; oil production facilities will not be needed at today's scale if next-generation cars are fueled by biofuels and natural gas or powered by electricity; and many coal-fired power plants will become obsolete once solar and wind energy become dominant. In short, changing the way the world produces energy in order to avoid the worst perils of climate change will be costly and complicated.

Rarely do industries—even those that pollute the most—willingly go out of business. Furthermore, until venture capitalists and other investors are certain that the economy is really transforming itself and that governments are committed to the transformation, few companies will gain access to sufficient capital to make the kind of large-scale investments necessary to change the terms of the world's energy-emissions equation. The transition from leaded to unleaded fuels cost refineries millions of dollars, and adding sulfur dioxide scrubbers to utilities' power plants cost them tens of millions, but a medium-sized solar- or wind-turbine installation could cost hundreds of millions, if not billions. And to complete the transition to new energy-production technologies, thousands of installations will be needed, along with infrastructure investments in projects such as enhancing the electricity-distribution grid. For policymakers, this presents a particular set of challenges. Weaning the global economy from carbon dependency and building an energy-efficient future will not be easy.

No Taxation without Mitigation

Cap-and-trade markets for greenhouse gases, such as the Chicago Climate Exchange (CCX), already exist in the United States, and a number of large companies and institutions have already joined the exchange to trade the right to emit carbon. These include Safeway; the Ford Motor Company; several universities; some smaller municipalities, such as Oakland and Berkeley, California; and several state and county governments. Although membership is voluntary, each entity signs a legally binding contract that requires it to reduce its emissions. In a few cases, companies have already made money as a result of their abatement processes, whereas others have had to pay in. Those that have profited joined the exchange because they knew that organizations that exceeded their contractually bound emissions targets would have to buy credits from those emitting less than their limit; polluters have participated in order to show their green credentials and to respond to consumer demand for cleaner energy.

In Europe, where adherence to the Kyoto Protocol is mandatory, the Greenhouse Gas Emission Trading Scheme has been operating since 2005 and allows the trading of emissions from stationary sources, such as electric utilities. The program is expected to trade permits for about 3.8 billion tons of carbon in 2009, according to Point Carbon, an independent research firm. The exchange covers approximately 10,500 sites, which emit about 40 percent of the region's greenhouse gases. Australia also has a market for carbon dioxide, and others are being formed in Canada and New Zealand. California, too, is likely to adopt a cap-and-trade system as a result of its own legislation, although a federal program could eventually take its place.

In 2008, the Milken Institute helped the Chinese city of Tianjin develop a plan for a greenhouse gas trading system linked to the CCX. A Chinese system using the CCX's trading technology could form the basis of a truly global market for greenhouse gases, with standardized contracts, auditing methods, and goals. Indeed, other cities in China are also interested in developing markets for carbon, and traders there and elsewhere have shown interest in investing in those markets. If China and the United States, the world's two largest emitters of greenhouse gases, joined with Europe and the world's other major emitters to form a global market for carbon, it is conceivable that carbon could become one of the world's most traded products. Such a globally linked carbon market could transfer billions of dollars a year to quickly fund new emissions-abatement projects. Tianjin's agreement with the CCX represents an early first step and a hopeful sign that China and the United States could join forces to address the problem of climate change.

Despite these promising examples, critics of cap-and-trade systems argue that imposing taxes on fossil fuels and on emissions of greenhouse gases, such as carbon dioxide, methane, ozone, and chlorofluorocarbons, is the better policy because it is simpler to enact, more difficult to corrupt, and easier to enforce. Although it is true, for example, that raising the price of cigarettes through higher taxes has helped curb smoking, increased taxation only addresses one side of the issue—restricting one type of behavior but not promoting another.

Of course, proponents of taxes argue that by making something more expensive, taxes will force enterprising individuals or organizations to seek alternatives. Although this might be true, taxes produce change in a slow, measured, and bureaucratic way. This occurs because taxation must be phased in and administered by the government; moreover, tax policy is always at the mercy of shifting political winds. When it comes to climate change, however, speed and certainty are important.

Cap-and-trade systems accelerate the process of emissions reduction by using incentives. Combining incentives with penalties helped rapidly remove lead from gasoline and reduce acid rain. It is doubtful that taxes alone would have been able to achieve these results, because no individual actor or organization would have received any tangible reward for changing its behavior.

Furthermore, because taxes raise prices, and because emissions of carbon touch almost all aspects of the economy, taxes would increase costs for a broad spectrum of industries, potentially slowing down the economy. With market-based mechanisms, however, capital is transferred directly from one organization to another: one part of the economy is penalized, but another is rewarded. Whereas taxes tend to act as a brake on the economy, cap-and-trade programs simply slow old sectors of the economy while jump-starting growth in new ones. As that happens, the promise of green industries and green jobs starts to become a reality.

Cap-and-trade programs function as a carrot and a stick. They add costs and difficulties to environmentally damaging processes, such as producing leaded gasoline or emitting sulfur and nitrogen oxides, and by allowing the trading of pollution permits, they transform those costs into incentives that reward emitters for changing their behavior. Fees charged for producing the wrong kind of gasoline went toward helping others produce the right kind. Money paid by slow-to-change producers of acid rain offset some of the costs of installing sulfur dioxide scrubbers in the smokestacks of utilities willing to change. In each of these successful examples, individual operators had to decide where to invest money. No government agency determined which smokestacks were to be fitted with scrubbers, which were to be replaced, and which were to be torn down. The government ran the programs and set the rules, but individual firms made the investments.

Similarly, using cap-and-trade systems as a policy tool for addressing climate change would allow a country's tens of thousands of carbon emitters to decide for themselves how to meet their region's overall emissions goals. It would also enable the emitters themselves to select which technologies to employ to reduce pollution, freeing the government from the responsibility of choosing winners and losers.

Under the cap-and-trade system approved by the U.S. House, most of the emissions permits—about 85 percent—would be allocated freely at first, and the remainder would be auctioned off. U.S. policymakers must be careful not to repeat the errors of those in Europe, where emissions credits were initially given out too freely because regulators overestimated the region's total emissions of carbon. This caused the price of permits to collapse to near zero soon after the program went into effect, in 2005. Over time, however, the price of carbon recovered, and it now hovers around $13 per ton. As prices increased, European emissions declined. And although some of Europe's reductions were the result of the global economic slowdown, the cap-and-trade system was responsible for a substantial portion of the cuts.

For the United States, the key to making a cap-and-trade system work lies in correctly estimating the number of permits that need to be issued and then allowing emitters to trade them like any other commodity. Once this is accomplished, significant amounts of capital from private sources would likely be invested in efforts to fight climate change.

By making pollution-abatement programs profitable for investors, the system would create financial incentives for investing in clean energy. Rather than financing climate-change measures itself, the government would simply set the rules and let the market take over.

The Forest for the Trees

Besides creating a framework for selling and trading permits, the House bill includes provisions for offsets. Offsets are activities undertaken, directly or indirectly, by an emitter to counteract the environmental damage caused by releasing greenhouse gases. The Clean Energy and Security Act recognizes that although countries have borders, the world's atmosphere does not. As a result, one ton of carbon released by an oil refinery in New Jersey, for example, could be offset by a reforestation program in the Brazilian Amazon—so long as it conformed to the rules laid out in the legislation and was subject to random audits. Offsets include programs that replace conventional energy with renewable sources, such as hydroelectric, wind, or solar power. They also include programs that turn animal waste into fuel.

Offsets are another way for companies and governments to counterbalance their emissions. One program involves emitters paying to plant trees or even entire forests, depending on the amount of carbon that needs to be offset. Because climate change is a global issue, tree planting can take place wherever it will do the most good, such as in the tropics, where some trees can grow very quickly and remove carbon from the atmosphere at an annual rate of about one-third of a ton per tree—significantly faster than trees planted in temperate climates. Offsets must involve new projects, not projects already under way, and their impact on the environment must be verified. Most of the world's carbon exchanges—as well as some brokers and nonprofit organizations—already trade or sell offsets.

In some cases, offsets accomplish multiple goals. For example, animal waste, which is a major problem for the world's dairies, poultry farms, and cattle ranges, is often simply left on the ground or raked into uncovered lagoons. But as it decomposes, animal waste emits methane gas, which is about 20 times as damaging to the environment as carbon dioxide. Methane emissions from animal waste are a global problem, and uncovered waste is also a threat to public health. Offsets purchased by U.S. and European emitters of carbon dioxide have transferred capital to nonprofit organizations that have reduced methane emissions from animal waste in remote villages in Africa and India by using simple measures to trap the methane. Some of these programs have used captured methane to generate power and run farm equipment and are now being used on a larger scale in Europe and the United States. By cleaning up the waste, these programs have made conditions more sanitary for rural workers and farm dwellers. Some dairies in the United States and elsewhere have begun highlighting their animal-waste practices as part of their marketing. In addition, health regulations in certain countries make converting animal waste into energy more profitable than paying to dispose of it. Although some of these programs would no doubt be carried out based on their own merits, cap-and-trade systems serve as accelerators for programs that make sense but would not otherwise be top priorities.

Market Magic

Climate change comes at a time when a number of technologies, such as wind power, geothermal energy, and certain types of solar energy, have matured to the point where they can produce abundant supplies of clean energy—albeit not as cheaply as traditional energy sources, such as coal. The missing ingredient for combating climate change is access to capital—a problem that cap-and-trade systems address head-on. Until permits are traded and the price of carbon is set, price uncertainty will cloud the market. Over time, however, as the number of permits falls at regular intervals, the price of carbon will likely rise. The cost for emitters will increase in inverse proportion to that for organizations investing in abatement. As industries and investors begin to see carbon winners and carbon losers emerge, behaviors will begin to change.

Even though the government will have a role in allocating some of the capital collected from the sale of permits, market forces will allow businesses to select those technologies that work best for them. If the income received by the government from the initial sale of permits is allocated to offset programs rather than being used to subsidize specific technologies, the market can work without creating the type of distortions that arise when policymakers attempt to choose winners and losers themselves.

Cap-and-trade systems do not need a lot of moving parts: they can be reduced to six basic elements. First, cap-and-trade systems need firmly set long-term emissions caps that place an unambiguous limit on the amount of carbon dioxide permitted to be released into the atmosphere over the long haul.

Second, permits must be allocated to emitters. Ideally, the initial permits should be free, so that the proceeds from trading go directly from major emitters to those cleaning up their acts, something that the oversight and auditing provisions of the American Clean Energy and Security Act of 2009 will ensure. The next best option is for the government to auction permits; as long as the government allocates the correct number of permits, based on the overall capped amount of emissions, the market will set a price. Because the costs of cleaning up the atmosphere and changing the way humans produce energy are so large, it is imperative that all proceeds from cap-and-trade systems be invested in programs that reduce pollution or in related offset programs. If emitters do not invest that money to curb emissions, they will find themselves penalized as carbon prices increase and their emissions costs rise accordingly.

Third, cap-and-trade programs should include offset provisions that provide emitters with alternative ways of removing carbon from the atmosphere. If a government auctions or sells permits, the revenue should be used to finance offsets, such as forestation projects, to avoid distorting the market by favoring one technology or initiative over another. Given the size of the emissions problem, there will be no shortage of offset programs from which to choose.

Fourth, emitters should be allowed to "bank" their permits so they can use them in the future. They should also be allowed to borrow permits against more expensive future allocations. Fifth, all emissions activities must be professionally audited to ensure that a ton of carbon really is a ton of carbon. Accounting firms, consultants, and nonprofit organizations can perform the audit function. They can do it through random checks, just as financial audits of large firms are conducted, or through technological means, such as by using permanently installed technology to monitor emissions. And finally, regulators and others must refrain from setting a minimum or maximum price for emissions and must allow the market to set its own.

It has been projected, based on EPA estimates of the future value of carbon, that the value of emissions permits as proposed in the House energy bill will be roughly $60 billion a year in 2012 and will increase to $113 billion in 2025. If sums this large were transferred annually from polluters to those undertaking alternative-energy, conservation, and emissions-abatement programs, these cash flows could help transform the economy into one that is more environmentally benign.

The market is a powerful force for allocating capital and creating wealth. And at a time when climate change threatens the globe, it can also be a powerful force for social change. With so much at stake for the environment, cap-and-trade legislation cannot wait.

JOEL KURTZMAN is a Senior Fellow at the Milken Institute and Executive Director of its SAVE program on alternative energy, climate change, and energy security. He is a co-author of *Global Edge: Using the Opacity Index to Manage the Risks of Cross-Border Business.*

Test-Your-Knowledge Form

We encourage you to photocopy and use this page as a tool to assess how the articles in *Annual Editions* expand on the information in your textbook. By reflecting on the articles you will gain enhanced text information. You can also access this useful form on a product's book support website at *http://www.mhhe.com/cls*.

NAME: DATE:

_____

TITLE AND NUMBER OF ARTICLE:

_____

BRIEFLY STATE THE MAIN IDEA OF THIS ARTICLE:

_____

LIST THREE IMPORTANT FACTS THAT THE AUTHOR USES TO SUPPORT THE MAIN IDEA:

_____

WHAT INFORMATION OR IDEAS DISCUSSED IN THIS ARTICLE ARE ALSO DISCUSSED IN YOUR TEXTBOOK OR OTHER READINGS THAT YOU HAVE DONE? LIST THE TEXTBOOK CHAPTERS AND PAGE NUMBERS:

_____

LIST ANY EXAMPLES OF BIAS OR FAULTY REASONING THAT YOU FOUND IN THE ARTICLE:

_____

LIST ANY NEW TERMS/CONCEPTS THAT WERE DISCUSSED IN THE ARTICLE, AND WRITE A SHORT DEFINITION:

We Want Your Advice

ANNUAL EDITIONS revisions depend on two major opinion sources: one is our Advisory Board, listed in the front of this volume, which works with us in scanning the thousands of articles published in the public press each year; the other is you—the person actually using the book. Please help us and the users of the next edition by completing the prepaid article rating form on this page and returning it to us. Thank you for your help!

ANNUAL EDITIONS: World Politics 10/11

ARTICLE RATING FORM

Here is an opportunity for you to have direct input into the next revision of this volume.
We would like you to rate each of the articles listed below, using the following scale:

1. **Excellent: should definitely be retained**
2. **Above average: should probably be retained**
3. **Below average: should probably be deleted**
4. **Poor: should definitely be deleted**

Your ratings will play a vital part in the next revision.
Please mail this prepaid form to us as soon as possible.
Thanks for your help!

RATING	ARTICLE	RATING	ARTICLE
	1. The Age of Nonpolarity: What Will Follow U.S. Dominance?		18. Somali Piracy: A Nasty Problem, a Web of Responses
	2. America's Edge: Power in the Networked Century		19. We Can't Afford to Ignore Myanmar
	3. The China-U.S. Relationship Goes Global		20. Not Your Father's Latin America
	4. India's Path to Greatness		21. Factors Affecting Stability in Northern Iraq
	5. The Russian-Georgian War: Implications for the Middle East		22. The Most Dangerous Place in the World
	6. Europe and Russia: Up from the Abyss?		23. Reading Twitter in Tehran?: Why the Real Revolution Is on the Streets—and Offline
	7. Israeli Military Calculations towards Iran		24. Al-Qa`ida's Pakistan Strategy
	8. The Long Road from Prague		25. Al-Qaeda at 20 Dead or Alive?
	9. The Terrorist Threat to Pakistan's Nuclear Weapons		26. Three Pillars of Counterinsurgency
	10. Evolving Bioweapon Threats Require New Countermeasures		27. All Counterinsurgency Is Local
	11. Obama's Foreign Policy: The End of the Beginning		28. Afghanistan, Iraq, and U.S. Strategy in 2009
	12. In Search of Sustainable Security: Linking National Security, Human Security, and Collective Security to Protect America and Our World		29. Minilateralism
			30. The Responsibility to Protect: Meeting the Challenges
	13. The Petraeus Doctrine		31. The $1.4 Trillion Question
	14. No Time for a Time-Out in Europe		32. China to the Rescue: Growing out of the Financial Crisis
	15. The Unbalanced Triangle: What Chinese-Russian Relations Mean for the United States		33. Africa and the Global Economic Crisis: Threats, Opportunities, and Responses
	16. Lifting the Bamboo Curtain		34. Trade Wars Brewing in Economic Malaise: Outrage in Canada as U.S. Firms Sever Ties to Obey Stimulus Rules
	17. Obama's Vietnam		35. The Seven Terrors of the World
			36. The Low-Carbon Diet

BUSINESS REPLY MAIL
FIRST CLASS MAIL PERMIT NO. 551 DUBUQUE IA

POSTAGE WILL BE PAID BY ADDRESSEE

McGraw-Hill Contemporary Learning Series
501 BELL STREET
DUBUQUE, IA 52001

ABOUT YOU

Name   Date

Are you a teacher? ☐ A student? ☐
Your school's name

Department

Address   City   State   Zip

School telephone #

YOUR COMMENTS ARE IMPORTANT TO US!

Please fill in the following information:
For which course did you use this book?

Did you use a text with this ANNUAL EDITION? ☐ yes ☐ no
What was the title of the text?

What are your general reactions to the Annual Editions concept?

Have you read any pertinent articles recently that you think should be included in the next edition? Explain.

Are there any articles that you feel should be replaced in the next edition? Why?

Are there any World Wide Websites that you feel should be included in the next edition? Please annotate.

May we contact you for editorial input? ☐ yes ☐ no
May we quote your comments? ☐ yes ☐ no